A GEOGRAPHICAL INTRODUCTION TO HISTORY

A GEOGRAPHICAL INTRODUCTION TO HISTORY

LUCIEN FEBVRE

Published by

FacsiMile Publisher
12 Pragati Market
Ashok Vihar, Ph-2
Delhi - 110052, India
Phone: 011-47034999
Email: www.facsimilepublishers.com
info@facsimilepublishers.com

Distribution Network
gyanbooks.com
India, USA, Canada, UK, Australia

ISBN: 978-93-6896-343-1 (PB)
First Published, 1922

2nd Impression 2025

Printed at: Gyan Press, Delhi.

A GEOGRAPHICAL INTRODUCTION TO HISTORY
Author: LUCIEN FEBVRE

The History of Civilization

A Geographical Introduction to History

A Geographical Introduction to History

By

LUCIEN FEBVRE

Professor at the University of Strasbourg

In Collaboration with

LIONEL BATAILLON

LONDON

KEGAN PAUL, TRENCH, TRUBNER & CO., LTD.

NEW YORK ALFRED A. KNOPF

1925

Translated by

E. G. MOUNTFORD and J. H. PAXTON

FOREWORD

THE EFFECT OF ENVIRONMENT ON MAN AND MAN'S EXPLOITATION OF THE EARTH

MAN comes before us on the stage of evolution as the flower of that urge of being which constitutes life itself. He has appeared to us as the logical agent, the creator of tools *and* words, *endowed with a surprising initiative which, as the centuries roll on, is constantly increasing his power, sometimes slowly, sometimes by brilliant inventions.*

What, then, is the rôle which has been played by the two factors, environment and race, both contingent no doubt, but both of wide compass? How far have they affected the progress of technique and thought? How much are we to retain of those philosophies of history, of those universal histories, which made of environment and race, or both, the arbiters of human evolution? [1] *The volumes of M. Febvre and M. Eug. Pittard* [2] *in this series—the first of which we have here—are designed to narrow this problem within the closest limits possible.*

*

* *

The problem of the influence of environment is not within the domain of a geographer pure and simple. The purely "geographical geographer" does not trouble himself about history, or is even disposed to absorb it in geography. The treatment of this complex problem needs a geographical historian, or a historical geographer, who is also more or less of a sociologist. The present volume will undoubtedly prove that an historian who has a wide and, at the same time, a profound conception of his work, who seeks to disentangle all the threads, external and internal, of human conduct, who, whilst specializing his studies, refuses to neglect anything which will contribute to their effectiveness—that such an historian, and there are very few such, is

[1] *See* La Synthèse en Histoire, *p. 77 ff.*

[2] *M. Eug. Pittard has kindly consented to undertake the task of the late M. Deniker, who was to have treated the subject.*

especially fitted to take up the important and delicate question of the relations between man and his natural environment.[1]

The great merit of Lucien Febvre, as will be seen, is that he submits to a merciless criticism all those vague ideas, disputable "laws", and ponderous pontifical pronouncements that are sometimes advanced without due reflection. The scientific spirit which animates him is up in arms against the pseudo-science which deals in theories of excessive simplicity and impoverishes the living reality. Before generalizing, it is necessary to particularize. The "problem of the environment" breaks up into an infinity of special problems which Lucien Febvre brings into clear relief. His book is undoubtedly rich in positive statement, and also in hypothesis—stated as such; but what he has aimed at especially is to show just how *the part played in History by the geographer's "Earth" can be determined. He relies, as we do, on the collaboration of other writers in this series for the utilization of his critical work, and the examination and completion of his suggestions.*

Thus the orientation of his ideas is in perfect agreement with the aims of the undertaking as a whole, since it seeks, not only to set out the actual result of historical labours, but to ask questions, to inspire students of goodwill to produce good studies, and to set before them an example of genuine synthetic work, consisting in analysis with the ideal of synthesis ever in view. Synthetic work is work within an ordered plan and not a premature presentment of unproven theories.

*

* *

Lucien Febvre has set definite limits to his subject out of regard for scientific accuracy. He does not deny the direct action of the environment on the physical and psychical nature of man; but he holds no brief for it, and leaves the subject severely alone.

In the primeval ages, especially, its action on every living creature was of capital importance. "It is undeniable," said Edmond Perrier, "that drought, humidity, a stronger or weaker wind-action, heat, light, and even electricity can modify either temporarily or permanently the individual characters of living beings, be they animals or plants. The nature of the food consumed

[1] *For many years Lucien Febvre has been dealing in the* Revue de Synthèse historique *with questions of human geography. See particularly vol. xiv, p.* 92; *xvi, pp.* 45, 217; *xvii, p.* 358; *xviii, pp.* 242, 269; *xix, pp.* 43, 99; *xxxv, p.* 97. *In this article he has also replied to various criticisms.*

and its superabundance or scarcity have a still greater influence. If we cannot yet afford to claim as much for the use or disuse of every organ, at least, it cannot be denied that exercise does expand the muscles and create new habits.[1] *Certain acquired characters—we are not concerned here to discuss the mechanism of heredity—are obviously transmitted by heredity. And, among those characters which life acquires from environment, there are some that are beneficial and that constitute the adaptation of the living being.*

The importance of this action of the external environment becomes more apparent when we come to consider the re-adaptations which follow, in the internal environment, from the stimulations received from without. Edmond Perrier, who, in the explanation of life, apportioned their proper shares to the various causes which theorists have often used in an exclusive manner, has insisted on these " powerful internal causes " of modification.

The elements which make up a living individual are at the same time independent and associated. Each cell contributes its part to the constitution of the common fund in which all share, and into which it pours all that is not required for its own needs, and all the results of its activity . . . Through the medium of this environment, the elements united in the same organism, which they are ceaselessly altering and which is affected by all the modifications experienced by them, whether due to the action of the external environment or not . . . thus react on one another, however far apart. An organism, therefore, bears within itself constant causes of modifications, which give it a plasticity sufficient to allow its continual adaptation to the environment in which it lives.[2]

Thus the formative influence of the environment, even where it is most incontestable, does not take effect without a rearrangement of the organism ; and we cannot over-estimate the importance of the " inter-actions of the complex organism-environment ".[3] *We shall have to return to this relation shortly and we shall see, from the part played by the internal environment, that the history of life is one of* active *adaptation.*

[1] *Perrier,* The Earth before History, *p.* 88 ; *cf. p.* 194.

[2] *Ibid., p.* 326.

[3] *E. Rabaud, " L'Adaptation et l'évolution," iii, in the* Revue Philosophique, *January–February*, 1922, *p.* 94.

It is no less true that environment explains race. Race, in theory, is a product of environment. But it is, as has been said,[1] *an* ante-historic *product; and M. Febvre, who is concerned with history—and with modern history by preference—had not to deal with this problem. We will content ourselves with remarking here that environment has assuredly impressed its mark on physical and psychical man, and that the force and persistence of that initial imprint still need investigation. For the rest, we would refer the reader to M. Pittard's volume.*

Another problem, however, now presents itself: up to what point in the historic period itself does the direct action of the environment continue to make itself felt? Since the influence of climate is exercised directly and visibly on the vegetable and animal worlds,[2] *are there any physical and psychical characteristics which a certain kind of habitat tends to impress, we do not say inevitably impresses, on its human occupiers? Stature, for instance, or pigmentation or anatomical structure of the groups into which the races are divided, their moral energy and intellectual aptitudes . . . what relation do all these bear to the conditions of the environment, to climate, soil, and food-supply? These delicate and complex questions pertain on the one side to anthropology and the medical sciences, on the other to collective ethology. They "may have their interest for the geographer, but are not within his province."*[3] *He must be well on his guard against accepting, as "scientific facts", very elementary theories of adaptation which competent scholars are in process of amplifying or altering.*

In the explanation of ethnic character especially, or the ways in which genius manifests itself, abuse has been made of "influences" which may be tempting to invoke and only too fatally easy to make do duty as explanations. There is nothing absurd in the contention that the mere contemplation of a landscape may contribute to the orientation of thought and the inspiration of art. It certainly would seem that the Parthenon could only have been born on the soil, and under the sky, of Attica. But for the establishment of relations of this kind the literary historian has ample scope. Men carry with them in their national or racial migrations, or in their individual wanderings, the mental imprint of their native landscape; and the elements of their

[1] *See* La Synthèse en Histoire, *p.* 78.
[2] *p.* 120.
[3] *pp.* 97–114.

psychical life are also infinitely numerous. The fact that the same region in the course of centuries may have supported populations of the most diverse kinds, and may have produced artists of almost opposite temperaments, is one very good reason for abstaining from hasty deductions. Probabilities must give place to the results of methodical research, and such research, which would contribute much that is useful to historical synthesis, is clearly not imposed on human geography.

* * *

What, then, is the correct attitude, in human geography, for anyone undertaking a limited and definite task? It can only consist, as L. Febvre shows, in studying the relations between the land and Life, *that is between the natural environment and the* activities *of its occupants.*

I have spoken, in my Synthèse en Histoire, *of the rôle played by environment from a strictly* eventual *point of view, if we may use the term in a particularly narrow sense. There are physical events which provoke human events.*[1] *Such physical happenings on the earth were of decisive importance above all in prehistoric times, and have had lasting consequences for humanity. But for many a long day now the importance of physical events such as earthquakes, inundations, and anomalies of temperature, has been less decisive though by no means negligible. The forms and the permanent resources of an environment are a factor of quite another type, of which the precise effect on the evolution of humanity has to be determined.*[2]

Now, it is through the medium of vegetable life more than anything that the land influences human life. To those empty and abstract frames, which an entirely theoretical geography looks on as predestined to hold States and to govern their history, L. Febvre opposes the " living covering " and the divers potentialities of the soil. He shows us that history, ever growing richer as it expands, is continually setting new problems to geography on the data of the environment, and on their utilization by man. It is the whole life of men, not only their political life ; it is the whole of their

[1] *See on this point De Morgan,* Prehistoric Man, *p.* 19, *in this series, and Cornejo,* Sociologie générale, *vol. i, p.* 286.

[2] *It must be observed that the manner of life intervenes in the formation of the collective character and that in this way an indirect action of the environment is added to a certain extent to the direct ethologic action.*

institutions, and, above all, but not exclusively, their economic organization which are in close relations with their environment.[1]

"Relations," that is, in the fullest sense of the word—reciprocal relations. It is not enough to distinguish, as do the geographers—whose labours have marked an advance—a static from a dynamic human geography, that is to say, the study of the action of environment on man, from that of man on environment. Human geography must be considered as a study of the continuous relations between two associated elements. Such an attempt conforms with the general orientation of natural science; our conception of the universe is modified as we devote ourselves more and more to really clearing up the relations between the different elements which are the rich substance of that reality, and criticizing or restricting the use of abstract notions of purely rational frames—such as absolute space and time.

Human beings are an element of the "landscape", an element whose activity is incorporated in it, a modifying agent of the environment which "humanizes" it. "Men, whatever they are doing, never get absolutely free from the grip of their environment,"[2] but they are never purely and simply acted on by it. A reproach was lately levelled at the authors of an interesting "geography of history" that they did not keep to the promise of their title. "Geographical determinism," it was said, "has [according to this book] the striking peculiarity that the same causes do not always produce the same effects. The authors are always striving to demonstrate the non-existence of the problem which they are proposing to solve. In fact, if there is no previsible or determinable action of the natural frame, it would seem that historical geography must disappear: there is nothing but plain history. And this is certainly the prevailing impression, despite some statements to the contrary, which have, however, a less general significance."[3] Lucien Febvre's merit is that he is fully conscious of all this in his treatment of the subject. "Some human geography is perhaps nothing but history revivified at its sources, rejuvenated in its methods, and happily revolutionized in its subjects."[4]

[1] *pp.* 82–87.
[2] *p.* 315.
[3] Revue de Métaphysique et de Morale, *October–December*, 1921, *suppt. p.* 12, *an account of* La Géographie de l'Histoire, *a work by J. Brunhes and C. Vallaux.*
[4] *p.* 352.

He has found striking formulæ in which to state the question precisely. Against the geographical determinism *of Ratzel he sets the* possibilism *of Vidal de la Blache.*[1] *"There is no rigid and uniform influence of four or five great geographical fatalities weighing on historical individualities."*[2] *The true and only geographical problem is that of the utilization of possibilities.*[3] *"There are no necessities, but everywhere possibilities."*[4] *The natural data are much more the* material *than the cause of human development. The "essential cause" "is less nature, with its resources and its obstacles, than man himself and his own nature."*

There are distinct zones which are distributed symmetrically on each side of the Equator, great climato-botanic frames, unequally rich in possibilities, unequally favourable to the different human races, and unequally fitted for human development; but the impossibility is never absolute—even for the races least "adapted" to them—and all probabilities are often found to be upset by the persistent and supple will of man. The "determinist" thesis has it that these frames constitute "a group of forces which act directly on man with sovereign and decisive power", and which govern "every manifestation of his activity from the simplest to the most important and most complicated."[5] *What really happens in all these frames, especially in those which are richest in possibilities, is that these possibilities are awakened one after the other, then lie dormant, to reawaken suddenly according to the nature and initiative of the occupier. "These possibilities of action do not constitute any sort of connected system; they do not represent in each region an inseparable whole; if they are graspable, they are not grasped by men all at once, with the same force, and at the same time."*[6] *The same regions, through the changes in value of their elements, have the most varied destinies. And it is human activity which "governs the game".*

There are no doubt among human groups similarities—or, at least, analogies—of life which are the result of the exploitation

[1] *p.* 20. *We would rather say to* necessitarism. *Determinism must be clearly distinguished from necessity.* Determinism *is* natural causality. *Among the causes which, in nature,* determine *phenomena, some are* contingent. *Among these contingent causes some are of a geographical order. The problem is to find out whether there are* geographical necessities, *whether natural facts can act as necessary causes on a humanity which is "purely receptive".*

[2] *pp.* 89–90.

[3] *p.* 349.

[4] *p.* 236.

[5] *p.* 171.

[6] *p.* 174.

of similar possibilities. But there is nothing fixed or rigid about them. We must avoid confusing once more necessity with possibility.

Thus, man needs bases, *from which he can start his attempts to utilize natural resources and remodel nature: mountains, plains, plateaux, valleys, sea-shores, islands, oases. But by an ingenious analysis, in which he gives proof of astonishingly complete documentation and a remarkable dialectical subtlety, Lucien Febvre shows that we should be misled if we sought absolute characteristics in these terrestrial forms. There is no "necessary and unique idea" of plateau, plain, mountain, with an inevitable and uniform action on man. There are geographical individualities of which we can at most classify the different possibilities for determining possible types of human adaptation.*[1] *And if we consider the smallest geographical units the most elementary and the most "natural", such as the valleys, islands, and oases, here, again, there are only "actions and reactions", the variable and complex play of possibilities. "If we were to look for a necessity, a 'law of the islands', which was imposed on man and on human societies, we should find only variety and difference."*[2] *The island, although it might seem one, is not an absolute unit. Isolation, like distance, is only relative and entirely a matter of standpoint. Navigation is not bound by the nature of the coast, and the most perfect morphological type involves no certain effects.*

Looking on them from an economic point of view, people are apt to consider certain forms of existence, or types of life *as dependent on certain environments. By their over-simple classification of* hunters, fishers, nomad cultivators, and sedentary agriculturists *economists have impoverished the rich texture of life. Types of life are very complex and varied in actual societies. If fixed conditions—the forest, the water, the desert, the valley before the cultivation of the plains—contribute to their first formation, they afterwards constitute an acquired possession interposed between nature and man; they are enriched by all sorts of foreign practices, and they end by modifying the environment more than they show its action. Even in the inferior stages of human evolution they have not the rigour and constancy which are commonly imputed to them, and the hierarchy which is usually established among them admits of many restrictions.*

[1] *pp.* 194, 202.
[2] *p.* 223.

Thus economic life, which is more closely bound up with the natural environment, can in a great measure be detached from it, and for still stronger reasons the political and demographical development of societies, the organization of States—with their frontiers, their routes, their towns and their capitals—depend but very little on it, and depend on it ever less and less. All this doubtless results as a rule from geographical possibilities; but all this, as expressing the life of societies, is in perpetual flux. It is from within, chiefly, that the evolution of political geography is to be explained. There are geographical nuclei *of cities and states whose destiny has been favoured by circumstances. Frontiers and caravan routes, the importance of the ports and marches—linked up as they are with that of the routes—the fate of cities and the birth of capitals constitute an integral portion of history, that is to say of chance and of will. And will, supported with ever increasing success by industry and science, " outwits nature." Long ago Michelet, speaking of Flanders, said " It has been created, so to speak, in defiance of nature;* it is a product of human labour ".[1]

L. Febvre does not treat directly the problem of finding out whether the grip of natural conditions on man is steadily weakening. Is that question an " idle " one, as he says? In any case, it is a complex one, and one part of it belongs to human geography. Its solution is, to a large extent, bound up with the study of race. Indirectly, and as far as it behoves him to do so, he answers it when he shows that " man, banished from geography as the patient, *reappears civilized in the forefront of it to-day as the controlling* agent."[2] *" We are dealing with man's work, man's calculations, man's movement, the perpetual ebb and flow of humanity; man—not the soil or the climate—is ever in the forefront."*[3]

In these close and constant relations between nature and man, it is man who always plays the more initiative part. He exploits nature to more and more purpose, and in exploiting it, or in order to exploit it, he interferes with it. He makes it serve his ends. What influences him is, after all, an internal force, and one that we know: his interests.

Lucien Febvre in his careful and scholarly book, is equally distrustful of mechanism and finalism.[4] *No one, indeed, would*

[1] Histoire de France, *v, p.* 320. *See Blanchard,* La Flandre, *p.* 520.
[2] *p.* 357.
[3] *p.* 283.
[4] *On finalism, see pp.* 55, 105, 120.

admit, as an explanation of the evolution of life, that it was either modelled from without by mechanical action, or directed by the "influence" of an environment "providentially prearranged". As to its inner finality, it is evidently only necessary to recognize where that incontestably lies: in the reflective thought of the conscious being.

Still, before and underlying conscious thought in life in all its degrees there is something which is neither mechanism nor finality, but from which finality proceeds, and that is logic.

L. Febvre would agree with me in stressing the idea of chance in history. But a clear distinction must be drawn between pure chance and historical hazards. Chance is only of interest to the historian in relation to logic according as it conforms or is contrary to human interest.

It is on interest—which, as L. Febvre points out, is visible in the conscious initiative of civilized man [1]*—on interest which is bound up with the logical principle,*[2] *on the desire to be, and to be to the utmost, that the whole evolution of life as well as of humanity rests. Not only does the living being* retain *what is useful to it, but there is every reason to believe that of its own will it provokes, by tentative experiment that gradually becomes assurance, modifications that will be of use to it. "Animals," says Perrier, "have been active agents in their own transformation."* [3] *The effect of the competitive struggle for existence—which, moreover, expresses the will to live—has been exaggerated. It is more especially against the unfavourable conditions of their environment that animals have had to struggle for life; the organism has successfully defended itself against them, it became "the artisan of its new organization and, so to speak, recreated itself by continuous effort".*[4] *We must not forget that "even in the case of what are called pre-adaptations the animal can derive advantage from the new characters it has acquired only by using its muscles and its nervous system differently from its previous habit; it acts on itself so as to make the most adequate use of these various features of its organization. Adaptation to the environment, which commenced, in this case, without the animal's will, ends under the action of that will . . ."* [5] *Even from the*

[1] *p.* 357.
[2] *See* La Synthèse en Histoire, *p.* 155.
[3] *Perrier, op. cit., p.* 144; *cf. p.* 192.
[4] *Ibid., p.* 190.
[5] *Ibid., p.* 132.

biological point of view, and still more from the psychical, there is an internal environment where a special causality holds sway. Thanks to logical causality, humanity escapes more and more from blind determinism, from the mechanical causality of the exterior environment.[1]

The present volume then falls harmoniously into line with its predecessors—with that of Edmond Perrier, who demonstrates the progress of life, and its triumphant growth to autonomy in the human form, and with those of Jacques de Morgan and of J. Vendryes, who set forth the emancipating results of those marvellous inventions, technique and language.

L. Febvre is no doubt specially preoccupied with the higher problems of human geography, those which are raised by the more civilized societies. But he defines rigorously the field of the true *historic geographer, or the retrospective human geographer who ventures into prehistory : " The relations between human societies of bygone times at different epochs in the various countries of the world, and the geographical environment* so *far as we are able to reconstruct it."*[2] *And his book is full of suggestions—which will be of use to our collaborators—on the initial limits and the changing possibilities of environments in their relations with human initiative. We realize, when reading him, that the great primitive migrations, and the spread of humanity over the world, are not simply the results of the physical transformations of the earth or of change of climate. We shall have to insist elsewhere*[3] *on the fact that migrations, like the process of thrusting national roots into the soil of the area occupied, tend to man's taking full possession of that environment into which he finds himself thrown, like Crusoe on to his island, while waiting for the day when he shall endeavour, in the fullness of time, to take possession of the very space in which his world revolves.*

Thus our work—a purely scientific one—is transformed in a quite objective way into a kind of epic, a "Légende des Siècles". Man is the hero—the great cause, *let us call him—who becomes more and more the master of nature, and would be still more so did he utilize better the resources he has created, and had he a less vacillating idea of " civilization ".*

* * *

[1] *See Déchelette,* Manuel d'archéologie préhistorique, *referred to by Brunhes and Vallaux in op. cit., p.* 28.

[2] *p.* 364.

[3] *Vol. v of " L'Évolution de l'Humanité ".*

Humanity escapes from its natural environment by the action of internal activity or logic ; the Idea*—the idea which men make for themselves of their environment, the idea which impels them to alter it—plays a part the importance of which cannot be exaggerated. It escapes also through the action of the social environment.*

And here we touch on a question which hitherto we have purposely avoided. We have spoken of the relations of the natural environment with "man", with "humanity". For Lucien Febvre, geography has no dealings with man, but with associations *or* societies *of human beings.*

After having described the early strife between geographers and sociologists in methodological discussions, and after having defended the geographical spirit against the criticisms and pretensions of sociology, he retains what is best in the ideas of the sociologists and underlines the importance of the social factor in the study of life in general and so much the more in that of humanity.

We may grant him that geography *has, in fact, only to consider systems of forces and vegetable, animal, and human associations. "Man" is a vague theoretical abstraction, "Humanity" is too vast, "State" is only one aspect of society. The relations of the earth and man only become patent to us in collective modes of life, and through the reaction of groups on environment. From the point of view of human geography, Febvre is right. But from the point of view of historical synthesis, there are some reservations to be made and definitions to be observed. It must not be imagined that, because the geographer is concerned with groupings only, society—as pure sociologists are disposed to argue or to think—furnishes the key to history. And it is, moreover, important to limit the idea of society, to define the social factor—*qua *social.*

L. Febvre, with Eduard Meyer, places out of court the theory according to which the family was the germ from which, by successive additions, States arose : The man plus the woman plus their children = the family. One family plus another family plus other families = the tribe. One tribe plus other tribes = a people. Groups of peoples united = a great nation. All these formations built up on the same plan take their rise from a series of successive propagations.[1] *This, says Lucien Febvre, is to build the edifice upside-down. And, in fact, the* juridical

[1] *p.* 314 ; *cf. pp.* 45, 149–50.

organization of the family seems to result rather from the existence of a larger grouping and a certain political *organization.*

But what is "primitive society"? What kinds of groupings does one glimpse across the distance of ages? Febvre encounters at the very threshold of history "vast societies spread out and covering extensive areas with the same civilization".[1] *States, taking the word in a very wide sense, he calls them with Eduard Meyer; nations, he says, with Jullian and Meillet. We believe that if these views prove acceptable and useful to human geography, they should, for historic synthesis, be examined at closer range in the volumes on* Race *and* From Tribe to Empire *included in the series.*

It is very necessary to distinguish between civilized states and social states. A "community of civilization" does not necessarily imply political unity nor even a well-defined social organization. What pre-history shows us, and, we may say, pre-philology also. are groups of similar men *rather than* associations of men. *Race, imitation—imitation of both manners and customs—and logic here play the main part. Primitive inventions, apart from the fact that they logically made their appearance in different places, are communicated and spread abroad the more easily in proportion to their immediate utility and to their power of satisfying essential needs and responding to vital interests. If humanity itself did not present identical features, at least there were vast masses of human beings with similar characteristics, for the very reason that men were less apt no doubt to take advantage of the possibilities of their particular environment; and nature moreover showed fewer differences.*[2]

The development of the social nucleus and the exploitation of the land are certainly bound up together. The history of that exploitation is the history, not of nations primarily, or of vast societies, but of human groups *(there is no objection to this term, which Febvre often uses) made homogeneous by similarities either hereditary or imitative, and by identical fundamental needs in their relations with the natural environment. In these* groups *with a diffused sociality nuclei of social crystallization are in some degree produced; more restricted* societies *are formed which really* organize *themselves, whose institutions in a large measure tend towards, and work for, the improvement of the*

[1] *p.* 157*: cf. pp.* 161–2.
[2] *See p.* 159.

means of existence. In virtue of this tendency, these societies— stricto sensu—*form, in their turn, by association still larger societies.*[1] *But struggle for life here plays its part as well as union. The egoism of societies displays itself in proportion to their increase in strength and numbers, and imperialism under various forms is one indirect way in which the land is exploited.*

These indications, intentionally little stressed, safeguard the rôle of the individual—even his rôle as a social agent—and allow the relations of the individual and the society, in the exploitation of terrestrial environment, to be determined accurately.

Febvre shows with great precision that society interposes practices, beliefs, and rules of life between nature and man; that man's utilization of possibilities and his exploitation of his environment are thereby hampered, so as, for example, to render his food singularly monotonous. "Nowhere is food eaten by savages without care in the choice.[2] *There are prohibitions, restrictions, taboos on all sides."* [3] *But this social constraint was, no doubt, not exercised at first in its full rigour. There was great homogeneity in primitive human groups, but there were necessarily differences (age and sex) and individual contingencies, however slight. In small societies the organization was not rigid enough at the beginning to stifle initiative. It is thanks to differentiation, to the individual alone, that life has been ameliorated and that society itself has been organized. It is the individual who is the agent of logic.*[4]

L. Febvre, who defends the "geographical spirit" against the sociologists, cannot be suspected of betraying the historical spirit in their favour. He has too vivid an idea of reality not to allow their share to individuals. He knows the "supple and tenacious" action of "those living things endowed with initiative called men, whether isolated or in groups." [5] *He knows well that the*

[1] *In very early times, no doubt, "it was necessary for men to form associations strong enough to defend themselves against attack, and to ensure their possession of the territories where their herds would not suffer on lands soon exhausted, and where different soils would supply pasturage at all seasons." Gsell,* Histoire ancienne de l'Afrique du Nord, *vol. i, p.* 241.

[2] *With certain reservations, to be stated more precisely elsewhere, on the presen food of primitive men and savages.*

[3] *p.* 166.

[4] *On this point see our "Foreword" to the volumes by de Morgan and Vendryes.*

[5] *p.* 87; *cf. p.* 63 *and p.* 277*—what is said of Mahomet.*

"deliberate activity", the "creative intelligence", and the "will-power exerted in the contest with the obscure forces of the environment and striving to utilize them and adapt them to its needs", which gave birth to States, belong to individuals[1]*; society does not think. He marks the difference which exists between the ethnic and human environment of societies, and the societies themselves. On all these points his book abounds in illuminating truths.*[2] *We need not dispute over words, we need only remember the care with which he wisely lays emphasis on the rôle of the "group" in human geography when he says, with regard to food, clothing, and various means of existence: "It is neither natural nor personal, this factor, but social and collective; not the man, we repeat, never the man, but human societies and organized groups."*[3]

We shall have to fall back on the social element, and to insist on the fact that society sometimes intensifies, sometimes paralyses the action of the individual, but that its constraining power, which varies with the times, is not at its maximum either at the origin or at the decisive epochs of a progressing civilization.

*

* *

We see what a world of ideas this book raises around the central problem. The book is at once objective and personal. It is interesting, and excites our sympathy the more by the enthusiasm which Febvre shows for the masters who were the source and inspiration of his ideas. Vidal, Rauh, Michelet—he who with his "marvellous sense of realities" "foresaw everything and divined everything . . ."[4] *It is a book in which there burns the fire of Michelet himself, his vibrating interest, his intuitive discernment of the complexities of life, while it shows solid knowledge, a critical mind, and a scrupulousness about detail which are sometimes wanting in the master-historian of the nineteenth century.*

It is lastly a book which has been rendered singularly meritorious by the circumstances in which it has been written. It is ten years ago since Lucien Febvre, alarmed and yet attracted by the difficulties of the task, took on himself the burden of treating the subject at our suggestion. Though interrupted by the war, in

[1] *p.* 337.
[2] *See especially p.* 337.
[3] *p.* 165.
[4] *pp.* 11, 55.

which he played his part fully and in person, and subsequently hindered by the active share which he has taken in the organization of the University of Strasbourg, he never withdrew his promise nor lost sight of his task; and now, after a great effort of perseverance, he has attained his goal at the date arranged. We owe him, in all justice—and the scientific public with us—special gratitude.

HENRI BERR.

AUTHOR'S NOTE.—*It is perhaps not altogether out of place to inform the reader that the entire plan of this book was conceived in* 1912–13—*over ten years ago. The work should have appeared early in* 1915, *and when the war broke out the chapters corresponding to the Introduction and to Part I were already completed.*

Taken up again in the Autumn of 1919, *after an interruption of five whole years, the manuscript had to be remodelled throughout. The references were revised and brought up to date, and the whole plan was modified in order to take account as far as possible of recent research. The scruples to which this reference to the date of conception of the book is due will, however, not be misunderstood.*

In addition grateful acknowledgment must be made to M. Bataillon for furnishing the author with notes and valuable suggestions, especially for the second and third parts, and for Chapter II of Part IV.

CONTENTS

CONCLUSION

MAPS

A GEOGRAPHICAL INTRODUCTION TO HISTORY

INTRODUCTORY: THE PROBLEM OF GEOGRAPHICAL INFLUENCES

THERE are two problems, we do not say great problems, for that would imply the existence of fixed data and preliminary certainties which are lacking in this case, but two vast and confused collections of ill-defined questions by which everyone who is interested in history is at once confronted. Two words, two labels rather, are sufficient to mark them. We call them commonly the "Problem of Race" and the "Problem of Environment", and it is of the second of these that we wish to state the terms. But how are we to begin? How should we conceive a general geographical introduction to the various special volumes of an elaborate enterprise of scientific synthesis? Let us attempt to set it out clearly, for this is no superfluous precaution.

We are proposing to consider, in one small book of four hundred pages, the vast question of the relation of the land to human societies and of human societies to the land. We propose to increase our difficulties by transposing the problem into terms of time, and by asking ourselves what conditions are imposed on history—imposed in advance—by the habitable earth, the οἰκουμένη of Humboldt, the *œcumene* of Ratzel, in its different portions and varying states. If it were a case of trying to arrive at positive results, of stating definite conclusions, and dogmatically formulating laws, would not the attempt be fantastic, not to say contrary to reason? Ought we not to emphasize at the outset that there cannot be, and ought not to be, a question here of anything but setting our feet upon the right road—of a critical and thoughtful examination of the problem itself, in fine?

I

History and Traditional Position of the Problem

We should certainly not be treading on virgin soil if we took things otherwise. Precedents and precursors are not wanting.

The problem is centuries old. Need we recall the work of Hippocrates *On Airs, Waters, and Places*,[1] and the contrast which this contemporary of Socrates draws between the inhabitants of hilly countries, beaten by rain and wind—people of lofty stature, gentle but at the same time brave—and the inhabitants of the light, open, dry lands with sharp climatic changes—a lean, sinewy race, blond rather than dark, and of a masterful and intractable nature? Hippocrates is the ancestor or rather the patriarch; and after him what a succession! First come the company of the ancients[2]: Plato in Book V of his *Laws*; Aristotle in Books IV and VII of his *Politics*; Galen, who as physician follows the lead of Hippocrates; Polybius; and Ptolemy, the author of the *De Judiciis Astrologicis* dear to Bodin; and all the Latin philosophers, moralists, scientists, or poets like Lucretius in Book VI of his *De Natura Rerum*. Then come all the moderns who seized at first on the ideas of the ancients and developed, enriched, and enlarged their uncertain and dogmatic conclusions in the light of wider experience. There is Bodin, in his *République*, endeavouring in the powerful and remarkable first chapter of Book V—to which we shall return later[3]—to mark out on the surface of the earth the great frames in which human societies were inserted: frigid, temperate and torrid zones with their subdivisions; Eastern and Western lands; plains, mountains, valleys; barren lands or lands of promise; places exposed to winds, or protected from them. There was no rigidity, moreover, nothing tyrannical in the action of these fundamental geographical conditions on men. Bodin had a clear idea of the insufficiency and arbitrariness of a rigorous geographical determinism.[4] Not only was he careful to make allowance for the exercise of human and divine will, but he had reasoning power, and knew that, in the same country, the same people may experience various vicissitudes, and may pass—the physical conditions never altering—through alternate periods of power and feebleness, of growth and decadence: he thus demonstrates experimentally "how largely food, laws, and customs have the power to change nature".[5] Later on, he again remarks very clearly (and this,

[1] Littré, Paris, 1840, Vol. II, 90.
[2] Cf. Heiberg, **XXXV.**
[3] Bk. II, Chap. I.
[4] Chauviré, **XXXVII,** p. 349 ff.
[5] Bodin, **XXXVI,** V, 1, p. 485.

be it understood, after having noted the action of locality and climate): "We will also say how much discipline can change the natural laws of men, *whilst rejecting the opinion of Polybius and Galen, who held that the country and the nature of the localities necessarily affect their customs.*" [1] This shows the wisdom and prudence of the old pioneer, who was proof against the intoxication to which so many others have since succumbed.

A century and a half later—we quote the more important writers only—and we have, thirty years before Montesquieu, the Abbé Dubos, the ingenious and rhetorical author of the *Réflexions critiques sur la Poésie et la Peinture* (1719). Bodin, the constructor, like Plato and Aristotle of old, of a Republic, had considered, especially, the influence of physical environment on the political life of men. The Abbé Dubos, for his part, attacked a problem, more limited, but at the same time immeasurably more complicated and subtle. In reality it is the problem of genius which he propounds—of genius which undoubtedly depends to a certain extent on moral birth; but "physical birth always turns the scale against moral birth".[2] This he demonstrates by studying "the effect of air on the human body" as it is manifested in the character of nations—and again by passing in review the climates more specially suited to the sciences and arts. Brunetière was certainly right when, in his study of the evolution of criticism, he drew the attention of the learned world once again [3] to the work of this somewhat compromising predecessor of certain modern "scientific" historians of literature and the arts. But Dubos is, in every way, plainly a retrogression towards the old Bodin. He is one link of the chain, but it is too large for its weight.

The work of Montesquieu is of a quite different character, and we shall have occasion to examine it in detail.[4] In the first place, the Abbé Dubos was concerned with climate only. Montesquieu, like Bodin, considers locality as well; and if he consecrates four books of his *Esprit des lois* (XIV–XVII) to the study of "laws in general", then of the laws "of civil

[1] Bodin, **XXXVI,** Bk. V, I, p. 464.
[2] Braunschvig, **XXXIX,** Chap. III, *passim.*
[3] Brunetière, **LI,** p. 144.
[4] Part II, Chap. I.

slavery, menial service, and the service of the state" in their relations to climate, he shows also in Book XVIII "how the nature of the country influences those laws". In the second place it is not a literary problem which has to be solved; it is (like Bodin's) a judicial and political problem, of wider extent, but infinitely less ambitious in its formulation. Lastly (and this calls for some remark) it is with a sort of restrained scientific faith, which can, however, be perceived as deeply active and vibrant, that Montesquieu—the Montesquieu who, in 1716, founded a prize for anatomy at the Academy of Science of Bordeaux, who worked seriously at the problem of aviation, and busied himself by turns between 1717 and 1723 with medicine, physics, and natural history [1]—approaches the great problem of physical environment as a whole, and solves it in the light of a rigid determinism. But how full of illusions is such a treatment!

*
* *

Many of our contemporaries hunt, with a rather naïve enthusiasm, for passages in ancient or modern authors from which to deduce some sort of definite notion of an influence of geographical conditions on men and their societies. Between Bodin and Dubos they set out on their quest—and return with hands full.

There is Corneille, in *Cinna* (Act II, scene II):

> "I dare to say, my lord, that to all climates
> All kinds of states are not alike adapted."

There is Malebranche, in the *Recherche de la Vérité*, in the chapter entitled "That the air we breathe causes some change in the mind also".[2] Not to go so far afield, we have Boileau in the *Art poétique* (Canto III, v. 114)—

> "Climate will oft produce humours diverse."

And still more distant, La Bruyère,[3] and the *Entretiens d'Ariste et d'Eugène* [4] of P. Bonhours, the *Digression sur les anciens et les modernes* of Fontenelle,[5] and the *Lettre à l'Académie* of Fénelon.[6] These and other literary quotations

[1] Dedieu, *Montesquieu*, Paris, 1913, pp. 6-9.
[2] Bk. II, Part I, Chap. III.
[3] *Caractères*, Ch. II, "Du Cœur," Rebellian, p. 120.
[4] Fourth conversation.
[5] Works, de la Haye, 1726, Vol. II, p. 126.
[6] Chap. IV.

are piously collected, as if they bore witness to intuitions of genius or to learned reminiscences; one might say, to a succession of flashes which illumined the night. Their number, even their feebleness and their small amount of originality, ought in reality to lead to other conclusions and observations. If we were more interested in the source of the common, current, popular ideas of the men of long ago, we might turn our thoughts, perhaps with some profit, to those almanacs which both spread and transmitted so many ideas of bygone centuries. To commence with the ancestor of them all, the venerable *Calendrier des Bergers*, "There are shepherds who say that man himself is a little world, by reason of the similarity he bears to the great world"; [1] there is nothing particularly modern or original in the idea. Still less is there anything scientific. But the opinions of the authors quoted above on "climate" and its influence are essentially of the same class of inspiration and come from the same source. They take us back to very ancient notions, largely of a magical origin and order. For generations which have all believed, with a blind and whole-hearted faith, in the influence of the stars on human life, physical and moral, as well as destiny—for generations which knew what part of the body was "governed" by a certain sign of the Zodiac (no book of hours, no almanac or calendar was formerly without its "anatomical man"; see the marvel of illumination in the *Heures de Chantilly*, and the coarse wood-cut in the *Calendrier des Bergers*; [2] the idea was the same, and we know from what distant sources it was derived),[3] for generations, moreover, who unhesitatingly calculated the psychological influence of Mercury or Saturn or Mars, there was nothing astonishing in the confused idea that the climate or the climates, themselves governed this or that portion of the human soul; or that, as Victor Cousin says in his distractingly poetical style,[4] they determined of necessity the nature of man in each

[1] Nisard (Ch.), *Histoire des livres populaires ou de la littérature de colportage*, Paris, d'Amyot, 1854, Vol. I, p. 125.

[2] Ibid., Vol. I, p. 139 ff.

[3] Cumont (Fr.), in the *Revue archéologique*, 1916, "L'homme astrologique des Très-Riches Heures."

[4] Brunetière, LI, p. 202.

country, the rôle which that country should play at every epoch, in short " the idea which it is destined to represent ".

There is no question here of hypothesis. A cursory glance at Bodin's headings and fundamental chapters is sufficient to prove the point. There is an agreement between geographical considerations, as we should say, but as Bodin did not say, since even the idea of modern geography was not born in his time, and the old astrological conceptions which lived in the depths of all minds in the sixteenth century.

He separates the temperate zone from the frigid and the torrid zones ; he distributes the human groupings into these three zones, and notes the influence on those groupings of the physical and especially of the climatic conditions which are precisely what constitute those zones ; but when he has done that, he hastens to add : " whoever considers the nature of the planets will find, it seems to me, that their position accords with the three regions I have named, giving the most distant planet, that is Saturn, to the Southern region, Jupiter to the middle one, and Mars to the northern . . . "—and thus started, he distributes his planets and deduces their influences (just like the anonymous compiler of the *Calendrier des Bergers* whom we have just quoted) and establishes the suitability of the whole to the human body, that " image of the body of the universe " : this he does with assurance for more than a large folio page.[1] Dreams, it may be admitted—chimeras for which the age was responsible ; but from among them we should pick out carefully Bodin's own ideas, and his scientific, or at least reasonable, observations.[2] And is that possible ? Is there really such a gulf between the two kinds of statement ? As far as Bodin himself is concerned, are not his astrological " dreams " directly responsible for a certain number of his " scientific " reflections, or what claim to be such ? But above all, and in a more general way, is not this influence of climate, for him, a fact of the same order, and does it not work in the same fashion as the obscure, mysterious, and in part secret influence of the stars and of the Zodiac ?

* * *

[1] Bodin, **XXXVI**, pp. 480–1.

[2] Chauviré, **XXXVII**, p. 349.

This observation does not seem to us superfluous. We do not know whether it has ever been thus put. When people attribute to the verses of Corneille or Boileau, which we quoted above, some unknown latent quality of scientific anticipation, they are making a mistake. For we are only in the presence of a reminiscence of some ancient author or (what comes, however, to the same thing) of some immemorial popular idea. But the important thing is that, in addition, a Bodin and two centuries afterwards a Montesquieu, though both had remarkably vigorous minds which set them far above the common level, and though the second had the benefit of two centuries of scientific research to raise him above the first (or at least to facilitate his efforts and modernize his treatment), were both at bottom bound by tradition. Bodin is personally more than half entangled in it. But Montesquieu, who would no doubt be astonished and much offended if he were accused of reviving it, nevertheless relies on it because he accepts the problem in quite the traditional manner, just as his predecessors have stated it. He may modernize the terms, but since he fails to analyse the idea of "influence" he is caught within the wheels of time, and they hold him.

The work of Buffon furnishes a very clear proof of this. Montesquieu was an amateur in scientific research, and, to a certain extent, a believer in science. Buffon was a scientific man—a practical scientist. Let us mark the difference. The Abbé Dubos is continually resuscitated, and his attempt to free himself from exaggerations and time-honoured inaccuracies is commented on [1]: " I distrust physical explanations," he writes, " because of the imperfection of that science in which it is nearly always necessary to guess ; but the facts which I state are certain " : a fine show of wisdom, which only disguises ancient and traditional commonplaces under a scientific mask. But Buffon is never quoted ; he, however, is in no need of resuscitation, for he is ever alive.

Buffon's idea is quite the modern one. There is no longer any question of " influences " more or less occult and mysterious, if not in their effect, at least in their method. Buffon's man is no creature of putty to be shaped by nature.

[1] Braunschvig, **XXXIX**, Chap. III.

He is a doer. He is literally one of the forces of nature. "For some thirty centuries[1] the power of man has been joined to that of nature and has extended over the greater part of the earth. By his intelligence the animals have been tamed, subjugated, broken in, and reduced to perpetual obedience. By his labours marshes have been drained, rivers embanked and provided with locks, forests cleared, moorlands cultivated . . . The entire face of the earth bears to-day the imprint of man's power which, although subordinate to that of nature, has often done more than she, or, at least, has so marvellously seconded her that it is by our aid that she has developed to her full extent." And undoubtedly there is here no question of man's independence of natural conditions. In a sense he is more subject to them than any other living being by the very reason of his ubiquity. Is he not the only living being who lives anywhere and everywhere that life is possible? "He is the only living being whose nature is strong enough, wide enough, flexible enough to be able to subsist and multiply, and to adapt himself to all the climates of the earth. . . . Most animals, far from being able to multiply everywhere, are bounded by and confined to certain climates, and even to particular countries; animals are, in many respects, productions of the earth; man is in every way the work of Heaven."[2] Leaving out the heaven (Buffon himself would not object), the modern idea, the idea of man as a natural agent, the idea which Vidal de la Blache has well stated in his articles on *Genres de vie*,[3] is in Buffon and not in Montesquieu—in Buffon who somewhere tries ingeniously to show how man can affect climate (and it matters little that the example was badly chosen). It is the idea that we are concerned with. That Buffon is not as a rule quoted when the "Church Fathers" of the theory of "environment" are searched, is to be understood, after all. He is without its bounds. He marks the starting-point of another idea than theirs—the complete antithesis of their idea. The earth, fashioned, altered, adapted, humanized by man, without doubt reacts in turn on him. But it is he who first exerts on it his power of adaptation and transformation.

[1] Buffon, **XLII**, p. 87.
[2] Ibid.
[3] Vidal de la Blache, **XCVI**.

We have lingered, and not without reason, over these distant precursors. There is nothing more essential in the study of any scientific question than to consider the manner in which the first investigators stated the terms of the problem before them, and seldom do we fail to find therein the deep-seated reason for many delays and difficulties. However, we do not intend to write a complete history of the problem of geographical influences. An entire book would be required for that, and one not very easy to write. For it would be necessary to face simultaneously in three main directions. The first, scientific. In the genesis of modern geography the part which has been played by naturalists and travellers, from Humboldt to Richtofen and Ratzel, is well known. The second, political in the wide sense of the word: here we should meet with all the intellectual progeny, all the direct descendants and moral heirs of a Montesquieu. The third and last, historical. For at the time when no geography, in the present sense of the word, was yet in existence, it was the historians who found themselves forced by the very progress of their special studies to propound a series of questions, we will not say geographical, but containing elements of a geographical order.

But whilst an Augustin Thierry, in the ruck of so many others, was still reducing the whole history of France to a long conflict between two rival races [1]; whilst he was showing at the beginnings of his country " two races of men, two societies which had nothing in common but religion, united by force, and face to face in one political grouping "; [2] whilst it seemed to him that " in spite of the lapse of time ", he felt " something of the barbarian conquest " still weighing upon him; a Jules Michelet, freeing himself by a vigorous effort from all this puerile ethical metaphysics, tried to lay the foundations of history on a " really sound basis ", the soil which bore and nourished it. Whilst geography had no place with Guizot or Thierry, he proclaimed energetically at the beginning of his celebrated *Tableau de la France* that history is, in the first place, all geographical: and reviewing his whole work in his fine *Préface* of 1869: " Without a geographical basis," he declares, " the people, the makers of history, seem

[1] Jullian, **LXXIV**, p. 8.
[2] *Essai sur l'histoire du Tiers État*, 1853, Chap. I, p. 14.

to be walking on air, as in those Chinese pictures where the ground is wanting. The soil too must not be looked on only as the scene of action. Its influence appears in a hundred ways, such as food, climate, etc. As the nest, so is the bird. As the country, so are the men."

By such striking formulæ, at once flexible and rich in precise thought, Michelet cleared himself, as Camille Jullian has well shown,[1] from the feeble and at the same time forced idea of his predecessor, Victor Cousin. That philosopher, allowing himself to be carried away by a frank and poetical determinism, exclaims in his *Introduction à l'Histoire de la Philosophie* :[2] " Yes, gentlemen, give me the map of a country, its configuration, its climate, its waters, its winds, and all its physical geography ; give me its natural productions, its flora, its zoology, and I pledge myself to tell you, a priori, what the man of that country will be, and what part that country will play in history, not by accident, but of necessity ; not at one epoch, but in all epochs ; and, moreover, the idea which it is destined to represent ! " We think inevitably of that other contemporary of the father of eclecticism[3] who himself also shouted, " Give me ! " What he wanted in order to remake the world was a " bladder inflated with its own vitality . . ." We think also irreverently of that judicial remark of Bodin that " all the great orators, poets, buffoons, charlatans, and others who allure the hearts of men by talk and fair words " are nearly all inhabitants of temperate climes. In fact, in spite of his boldness of statement and his imperturbable confidence, as much in his own genius as in the efficacy of laws, Cousin retained the notion that history was really a drama. And so it was fitting that a writer should, in the first place, be thoroughly acquainted with the theatre of the drama. A scenic and decorative idea, but a poor one and as artless as his times. We see how Michelet was able to enrich it and also to bring out its finer shades. His feeling for modern science and its needs was quite different from that of Victor Cousin. The only misfortune was that, when he wrote his brilliant *Tableau* in 1833, and even later in 1869

[1] Jullian, **LXXIV**, p. 10.
[2] Quoted by Brunetière, **LI**, p. 203.
[3] Raspail.

at the time of the *Préface de l'histoire de France*, geography did not yet exist.

Michelet understood that the soil is not, for human societies, a simple immovable stage, an inert plank of a theatre. He saw in the past of peoples a whole play of subtle, multiple and complex geographical influences. He perceived, he foresaw, he anticipated, in this as in everything else. His marvellous sense of realities and his faculty of divination guided him. He certainly would by no means have cried with an ill-inspired Ratzel,[1] "Always the same, and always situated at the same point in space, the soil serves as a fixed support for the human and changing aspirations of men," which is essentially the idea of Victor Cousin. Nor would he have added, by way of developing this puerile theory, and pushing it to extremes: "When they happen to forget this support, it makes them feel its power and reminds them by serious warnings that the whole life of the State has its roots in the soil. It governs the destinies of peoples with a blind brutality. A people should live on the soil which fate has given it; it should die there and submit to the law." No, Michelet gave no place in the development of human societies to such direct action, stamped, as the other says, with blind brutality. And, after all, could we have expected him, unaided, to advance much further, and to add yet more to his remarkable intuitions?

In fact, after the example of their master, every historian when composing, as was the custom, the history of a nation, Greek, Roman, or French, put at the beginning of his book a geographical sketch, more or less carefully arranged. In his *Histoire de la République romaine*, his earliest work which he commenced in 1828 (it appeared in 1831), Michelet, in the first chapter, described the appearance of modern Rome and Latium, then in the second chapter, sketching a picture of Italy, of the Apennines "with their severe landscapes cut out with a chisel," and of all that brilliant Southern world, he discovered something "exquisite and refined, but dry as aromatic herbs". Following him, Victor Duruy, to take a single example, placed a geographical description of Italy at the beginning of his vast *Histoire des Romains*[2]—of which it has been said that

[1] Ratzel, **LXXXVI.**

[2] The first two volumes appeared in 1843 and 1844; cf. Jullian, **XLV**, pp. 79 and 462.

it would not be conceivable but for the *Histoire Romaine* and the essays of Michelet on the Cæsars [1]—and later commenced his *Histoire de la Grèce* [2] with an account of the land and climate of Greece. So, too, did Ernest Curtius in his celebrated work,[3] for the movement was, of course, not limited to France; but we have no intention here of giving a history of these attempts. Though desultory and unsystematic, they are yet praiseworthy and full of interest. But when that kind of propitiatory homage had been once paid by all historians to the mysterious powers of earth and water—the more reverenced because they were only known from afar—all was said. It was no longer a question of land or climate. Things went on as if these complex influences, which were recognized and the action of which was foreseen, had never varied in power or method during the course of a people's history. It was as though England, for instance, a country without a navy up to the sixteenth century (though it had long before been a land of sailors), and a country without manufactures until the end of the eighteenth century, had none the less been from its origin down to our own times the wonderful island of iron and coal, isolated in the midst of the ocean, whose virtues and praises are so often sung.

In his *Préface* of 1869 Michelet asked: "does the race remain the same, uninfluenced by changing customs?" But neither he, nor any of his disciples, thought of replacing "race" by "land". Being historians, and not geographers, they thought as historians even of geographical things. Natural forces and human forces seemed to them to exercise an identical action on history. In nature, in fine—in the geographical frames which they delighted to describe in glowing terms—they depicted men as passive, as always enduring but never acting. "For the future, we know from the study of the land in Italy," concludes Victor Duruy, after having outlined his *Tableau d'Italie*, "that a population, placed in territorial and climatic conditions which vary in each district, will never be subjected to any of those physical influences whose invariable action produces uniform civilizations unreceptive of external influences." [4] And elsewhere, some

[1] Hauser, *Grande Revue*, 25th October, 1913, p. 649.
[2] First ed., Paris, 1862, Chap. I.
[3] At the beginning of his *History of Greece*.
[4] Duruy, *Histoire des Romains*, Vol. I, 1879, p. xxvii.

pages further back: "Geography never explains more than a part of history, but its explanation is a good one, men do the rest. According to the wisdom or folly of their conduct, they turn the work of nature to good or evil."[1] The idea is expressed in somewhat limited and hesitating terms, and these considerations of wisdom and folly have a very far-away sound. Duruy, however, was nothing more than a good historical student, diligent and conscientious, but without genius. But Taine, with his infinitely more vigorous intellect—Taine, whose influence in other fields is admittedly as great as that of Michelet on historians—what has he done beyond take up and utilize, as a rigid system, the current ideas to which everyone then subscribed?

His design is larger in appearance, and his point of view more free and extensive. He impartially divides up the concomitant influences of race, environment and time. In reality he builds only on the ordinary ideas and works, sometimes rather undecidedly, with nothing but the old materials. His conception of environment, for instance, is very complex. To Taine that word stands, not for the physical environment only, but for everything that environs a human being: climate, land, institutions, also religion and government—whatever constitutes "the material, moral, and intellectual atmosphere in which a man lives and moves". The influence of Taine on his contemporaries was strong and lasting. It was not exercised, like Michelet's, on historians especially. It ended rather in the creation of a sort of literary type which its votaries, very often students of politics or morals, have cultivated with more or less success. They all proclaim, with increasing insistence and fullness, that direct influences are exercised by the geographical environment, by the earth, by nature, by soil, and by climate on man, considered simply as man, or as a member of varied political societies. Such theories are the more easily accepted when we consider the vogue of evolutionary ideas in the second half of the nineteenth century and the diffusion in popular and non-specialist circles of the hypotheses of Darwin, which had the effect also of introducing those of Lamarck to the uninitiated.

These two naturalists had both given much reflection to the great problem of the "adaptation" of living beings to

[1] Ibid., p. 1.

the environments in which they are placed and must live. Their theories are without doubt profoundly different on many points,[1] but this is not the place, nor are we qualified to explain how or in what: they agreed, however, with one another in admitting that the adaptation of an animal was a consequence of the fact that that animal lived in a certain environment or behaved in a certain manner. Thereafter it mattered little that Darwin ascribed to natural selection what Lamarck attributed to need: nor did the authors of whom we are speaking trouble about the question. It was enough for them, or so, at least, they thought, to be able to establish a bond between the work of the naturalists, tending to interpret the relations between living beings and their environment, and their special work as historians, moralists, or economists, tending to define the relations of man with nature. What they knew in general of the opinion of savants reassured them about the solidity of their work and conferred on them, in their own and their readers' opinion, a little of the assured prestige enjoyed by the naturalists. The disputes which the Darwinians and the Lamarckians continued to carry on under their eyes, they summed up in their own way by saying that "Science" established the strict dependence of beings on their environments and that the birds and insects, for example, which lived on islands adapted themselves to insularity by losing their wings entirely, like the entomological population of Kerguelen Land; or by suffering atrophy to the extent of losing the power of flight like the great majority of the beetles of Madeira or the rails in Mauritius and New Zealand.[2] It was a logical conclusion from this (the facts being incontestable) that environment had a power of transformation which would not stop at insects or any animals whatever, but would be exercised on human beings, first of all physically, then morally. Yet the passage from animal to man and then from physical to moral might seem bold. But did not "Science" here again authorize it? And had not Darwin himself inaugurated the evolutionist ethics which Spencer was to develop and formulate as a system —to try to show how from the point of view of the moral

[1] On all this, cf. Cuénot, **LII**, p. 10 ff.

[2] Ibid., p. 173 ff.

consciousness, it was possible to pass from animal to man by the easy intermediary of the social instinct?

The more daring writers, however, needed no such justification, nor was the use of great scientific hypotheses like the evolutionism of Darwin, for entirely literary ends, and after a good thirty years' interval, the sort of thing to frighten people. Did not Brunetière, with complete candour, once make a theory of this practice [1] in certain admittedly very suggestive sentences in his book of 1890, *L'Évolution de la Critique*: "But if it is always well to distrust novelties and to wait . . . until they have, in the words of Malebranche, a beard on their chin, we may be certain that after the twenty-five or thirty years which have now elapsed the doctrine of evolution must have had something in it which justified its success . . . And since we know what profit natural history in general, history, and philosophy have already derived from it, I should wish to examine whether literary history and criticism cannot utilize it in their turn."

Thus, in perfect safety, a number of books made their appearance, some of them devoted to the study of a man, others to that of a people, or a school of art or a philosophic system, which complacently and ingeniously expanded the idea of environment. Some took to it, perhaps, as their real object; here is an example, if one is needed. A well-meaning popularizer,[2] with a very confident belief in his own capacity, shuts himself up in his own closet to reflect, as so many others had done, on the whole history of nations, and to discover the principle, the bond, and the explanation. By the side of M. de Tourville's *Nomenclature des faits sociaux* (we are dealing with an adept in *social science*), we imagine him putting on the table (presumably in order to support and at times excite the springs of his imagination) several good historical dictionaries, two or three recognized textbooks, and the *Géographie universelle* of Élisée Reclus, that Providence so often unacknowledged . . . Then, starting with a brilliant idea, an ingenious hypothesis worthy of romantic fiction, he sets himself with a kind of mechanical fury to extract from it universal consequences and we have in twice five hundred pages *Comment la route crée le type social* by Edmond Demolins.

[1] Brunetière, **LII**, *Leçon d'ouverture*, p. 2.
[2] Champault, **XVIII**, 1913, p. 60.

Let us turn over the pages, and open the book at hazard, or rather the first of the two books (I, *Les routes de l'Antiquité*, Paris, n.d.), which the author has devoted to setting out his theory of ways of communication as the natural alembic of civilizations, and here is, for example (p. 249), the glorious origin of the Chinese people. " The problem which presents itself is this : to find a route capable of training a people for agriculture, industry, and commerce, but for agriculture, industry, and commerce on a small scale only and in an intensive fashion . . . Such a route exists : it is that of Tibet ! " A simple fragment ; but does it not allow us to judge of this Apocalypse revealed to the Elect ?

What all these books, which we may call the literary progeny of Taine, offer to our curiosity, are syllogistic deductions or purely literary dissertations, whatever protests their authors may make against that description. Some of them are judicious, some are laughable, some are the work of conscientious scholars, and others are only improvizations. But all have a common fault, an old, sometimes a very old fault. On the one hand we have the natural Environment ; or again the Earth ; or, if it be decomposed (and what an effort of analysis !) the ground and the climate ; sometimes the climate alone—not so much because of any particular theory as of the old tradition. On the other hand, we have Man, physical and moral, individual and social, " natural " and " political ". Binding together these two groups of obscure forces, connecting with the physical world " that other world which is man ", is a network of influences which the author weaves more or less closely according to his knowledge or his ingenuity. Influence : " a kind of material discharge which ancient physics supposed to proceed from heaven or the stars and to act on men and things." Thus Littré himself, though quite impartial in the debate, also carries us back once more to the astrologies. But have we ever really got away from them ? Shall we, and all those whose work, unequal, but quite unsound throughout, we have just mentioned, ever get away from them ?

We will not insist on it. Let historians, men of letters, and philosophers forge if they please a chain of causality between the body of phenomena which they are studying and two or three complexes of geographical facts chosen without analysis or discretion. Let them by all means make the "powers of the soil" and the "forces of the climate" act on the "genius of peoples" and the "history of nations" as their fancy dictates. But they may adventure alone. Their work seems to us sterile—if not dangerous. They have taken the problem of environment ready set from an old-time tradition. They have not tried to rejuvenate its setting. They stick to that geographical influence, at once powerful and obscure, multiform and complex, which is exerted, they tell us, both on man physical and moral and on man social and political—on the colour of his skin, the shape of his body, the strength of his organism, his psychic qualities and defects, his judicial, economic and religious institutions—even the productions of his mind, the creations of art and genius. They state it as a fact. But they do not prove it.

Are we then to say that geography, which is commonly supposed to explain so many things, explains nothing? We must not jump at such a conclusion. How is geography concerned in the matter up to the present?

II

Human Geography and its Critics

Geography must be sought where there is no doubt about finding it—among the geographers. Anyone nowadays who wants instruction on the relations between the land and history—I mean conscientiously and with guarantees—must apply to them first. He should and he can. The old geographer, whose only care was to describe, enumerate, and make inventories, is no more. For physical geography, based on the physical and natural sciences—geology, climatology, botany, zoology—has disentangled itself from them little by little, made sure of its methods, defined its own object clearly, and become conscious of its individuality. This was due to the pioneer efforts of Alexander von Humboldt, the author of the *Kosmos*, and of Karl Ritter, whose *Die allgemeine vergleichende Erdkunde*, translated in 1836 by Buret and Desor, became in French the *Géographie générale comparée*, or the study of the earth in its relations with nature and with the history of man. Meanwhile, a new geography was slowly arising through the personal and professional activity of one

Friedrich Ratzel, a zoologist and traveller, who developed into a zealous and profound geographer.[1] It owed to Ratzel its baptismal name, anthropogeography: human geography, as we should say more readily in our language, which dislikes long composite words.

In the two volumes of the *Anthropogeographie*, the standard work of German geography, published in 1882 and 1891, in the celebrated collection of geographical manuals published by Engelhorn at Stuttgart, the whole life of men, all their multiple activities, human groups, and human societies are studied methodically, rationally, and collectively in relation to their geographical environment. In the *Politische Geographie*, which appeared later in one volume, it is more especially the life of political societies, of States, which is considered in its relations to the soil, that terrestrial substratum "always the same and always situated at the same point in space" which—as Ratzel once wrote in the *Année sociologique*—serves as a fixed foundation for the moods and changing aspirations of men, and governs the destinies of peoples with a blind brutality.

However, alongside this, a geographical school was being developed in France, around, not a naturalist like Ratzel, but an historian. Paul Vidal de la Blache,[2] who after 1872 began to direct his attention to geography, first studied the works of Humboldt and Ritter, then travelled all over Europe, slowly ripened his ideas on human geography, tested them by comparison with the books of Ratzel, whose weaknesses his critical sense soon detected, and at last became the undisputed master of a group of disciples who throng the French universities and Lycées. He produced no great dogmatic treatise like the *Anthropogeographie* or the *Politische Geographie*, but a series of articles,[3] at once practical and critical, in a rather precise style, with sudden illuminations like flashes of divination and understanding—and with what power of suggestion and even of inspiration all through! It is a unique book,[4] with a character of its own, a masterpiece, but devoid of all dogmatism and quite inimitable—the rich collection of the *Annales de*

[1] Brunhes, **LXVI**, pp. 41–9 (Bibliographical references).
[2] Born in 1845, died in 1918.
[3] Bibliography, Nos. **XXIX** to **XXXIII** and **XCV** to **XCVII**.
[4] *Tableau de la France* (**CCXXXII**).

géographie (since 1891). A mind, moreover, which enlarged its influence by teaching at the École Normale Supérieure (1877–98) and then at the Sorbonne: a mind bent on free research, on alert and vigorous investigation—the mind of one who would arouse enthusiasms rather than repeat catechisms.

The original work of the French geographical school founded by Vidal de la Blache, its particular contribution to science, consists of a series of regional monographs of various types, which allow individual temperaments full licence of expression and statement, but which are marked by common aims: the *Plaine picarde* by Albert Demangeon, *Flandre* by Raoul Blanchard, *Basse-Bretagne* by Camille Vallaux, *Les Paysans de la Normandie orientale* by Jules Sion, and *Les Pyrénées Méditerranéennes* by Maximilian Sorre[1]—so many accurate, methodical, exhaustive monographs, so many attempts to account, by the aid of geography, for the characteristic traits of a district, of a geographical region of France. These no longer breathe the old prophetic spirit which survives only in so many of the amateur works to which we have just referred. Rather do we find the caution and circumspection of workers trained in critical methods and in the utilization of the data supplied by the natural sciences; and the necessity is recognized of not juggling rashly with obscure and grandiose ideas such as the earth, or the climate, or man—but of devoting themselves to patient and unambitious analyses. Thus by the labours in Germany of the disciples and the opponents of Ratzel,[2] as well as by the work in France of the pupils of Vidal de la Blache, there was gradually established a real science of the relations of man with nature—his present relations, and his relations in the past. It was a young science, but vigorous, full of sap and growth, inspiring devotion, and arousing enthusiasm and sometimes exciting in new converts somewhat premature hopes and intemperate zeal. We can hardly help smiling when we learn from an admirer, overcome by emotion at his discovery, that "geography comprehends all the sciences, opens all vistas, embraces all human knowledge"[3]—their enumeration follows;

[1] Cf. Bibliography, Nos. **CCXVII** ff.

[2] Cf., for example, Wagner (H.) in *Zeitschrift der Gesellsch. f. Erdkunde zu Berlin*, **XXXVI**, 1891; and Penck, **LXXXII.**

[3] Albert Favre, "Les enseignements de la guerre" (*Grande Revue*, September, 1917, p. 439).

we finally reach the conclusion, too grandiose for us to resist the temptation to quote: "We place the University of France on the summit of a pyramid, with the word *geography*, towards which all human knowledge tends, full in evidence!" But this in itself is a force: it is not every study that provokes such crises of delirious worship; and only active torrents, the streams that carve out their beds, deposit such high-water marks of foam on their banks. It is a fact that a science has been established to study the relations between man and his environment. It has its methods, its doctrines, its schools; its chairs, too, and its periodicals, and its manuals for teaching; its results also which give their testimony. In Universities everywhere, or nearly everywhere, human geography has won the freedom of the city. It can estimate with pride its influence on the period, detail its conquests, enumerate its victories.[1] Now, to our great advantage, we are at the end of our trouble and anxiety. Unable to trust ourselves to the impressionism of the "essayists" of yesterday, we have found our guides, our true guides. Let us trust in them to resolve the problem of the earth and history. Their science, young but tested, will lead us to the goal without stumbling . . . Perhaps. But we remember what we said above: the work is one of finding our direction and of critical reflection. There is no question of anything else at present. But of this there should be no lack.

* * *

We will not enter at once, however, into theoretical details. We will not ask whether there are not really any cracks in the geographical edifice, and whether it is possible to follow at the same time, and with the same sense of security, the "determinists" after the manner of Ratzel, and what we may perhaps call the "possibilists" after the pattern of Vidal. The question is too large to be dealt with in an Introduction; we shall have to study it at greater length. For the present we will consider appearances only. When we try to judge contemporary geographical work (we speak only of that of the anthropogeographers) one word in particular suggests itself—

[1] Brunhes, **LXVI**, Chap. X, "L'Esprit géographique."

ambition. It is not we who make the charge. The young human geography has rivals—and critics. Nothing is more natural. Young sciences which become conscious of their own individuality and vindicate their right to a free and independent existence never grow on a soil which is free and void of obstacles. Intoxicated, moreover, with their first discoveries and astonished at their first successes, they are often wanting in prudence and sometimes in restraint. They cannot control themselves, restrain their ideas of conquest or calm the fever of their growth. Hence disputes with the seniors who are in office, or with the juniors, who are themselves also on the ladder. Hence always, and as if of necessity, the old accusation of ambition. Human geography has not escaped it.

The voice of the seniors is heard, harsh and arrogant; and everyone can recall the grumbling protests of the geologists, ill-content to see the physical geographers revolt from their jealous tutelage, and consoling themselves by repeating that in France the *Leçons de géographie physique* by Lapparent were the work of a geologist and that Davis in the United States began as one of them. They are feeble recriminations, like the accusation of parasitism so often made, which Vidal de la Blache felt obliged to confute again in 1913[1]: "In the complexity of the phenomena which intersect in nature there should not be one way only of arriving at a study of the facts. It is a good thing to consider them from different angles. And if geography takes into account certain data which bear another brand, there is nothing in that appropriation which can be taxed as unscientific." The truth of this is evident. Vidal de la Blache might also have added the remark of a skilled biologist, J. Costantin, who, when considering the relations between geography and biology, says that very often "it is on the borderlands of a science that new problems are encountered, and that unexpected and interesting solutions are found."[2]

We may put aside the quarrels of young rivals and their attempts at annexation. There is nothing in them peculiar to geography. When considering the human sciences we all

[1] Vidal, **XXXIII**, pp. 289–90.

[2] Costantin, **XI**, 1898, p. 193. Cf. also Douxami, "La géographie physique et la géologie" (*Revue Encyclop.*, 1897).

know what difficulties the complexity of their relations creates for logicians anxious about the strict arrangement of methods and limits. There are ethnography and anthropology; nobody is ignorant of the long disputes, not yet quite settled, which set them at loggerheads. In Germany, how many articles, dissertations, large volumes sometimes, have been written to separate clearly, by consideration of facts or principles, those too indefinite studies, with many names, uncertain meanings, and often baffling contiguity: *Volkskunde, Voelkerkunde, Ethnologie, Voelkerpsychologie, Voelkerwissenschaft?*

It is with Sociology that Anthropogeography, or Human Geography, is bound to clash.

* * *

Sociology is itself also a young science, active and of vigorous growth. It has its turbulencies and its ambitions. Moreover, many of its professors exhibit a quite peculiar liking for definitions of words and ideas, the delimitation of domains and influences, and a beautiful logical order. It is true notably of that little group of scholars whom Émile Durkheim [1] had been able to collect round him before the tragic events of 1914–19 intervened to break it up almost entirely. From 1896–7 these workers were connected with the critical and at the same time constructive work of *L'Année sociologique*, a valuable miscellany full of ideas and suggestions, and one which has exercised a more or less direct but always fruitful influence on a whole generation.

Strong in their arguments and full of reliance on the firm armour of classifications, which became every day more complicated or, we might say, more precise, the disciples of the master, the sociologists of the *Année*, did not abstain from vigorous attacks and disparaging criticisms, nor from commenting on error or confusion which they thought they could detect in others. Historians are certainly well aware of this; and those who are not need only glance at the numbers of the *Revue de Synthèse historique* about the years 1902 and 1903, which saw, among others, the controversies of F. Simiand and P. Mantoux.[2] Human geography could not and should

[1] 1858–1917.
[2] Bibliography, **XXIV** and **XXVII.**

not expect to escape the criticism of a school so powerfully organized and so full of ardour and confidence in the future.

It was not that the hostility of the sociologists was in the least due to foregone conclusions or prejudice. On the contrary, from the very start, the work of Ratzel held their attention closely. More than that: immediately after the publication by the German geographer in 1897 of the *Politische Geographie*, *L'Année Sociologique* published some interesting papers on the Land, Society, and the State, in which the Leipzig professor himself summed up his most characteristic theories.

Let us note, moreover, in passing, that such a summary, being altogether abstract, theoretical, not to say arid and destitute of the numerous examples and the abundance of records which give their chief value to the works of Ratzel, was not the best means of allowing the non-geographical readers of the *Année* to form a fair and exact idea of the aim, methods, and character of the new science. But in the same volume, by a remarkable coincidence, Durkheim himself (p. 550 ff.) gave an account of the two crowded and bulky volumes of the *Anthropogeographie*. And though he expounded its fundamental theories, though he saw in the work of the German geographer a new and sincere effort, full of promise—he yet made his reservations, in a series of concise paragraphs, from his point of view as a sociologist, and raised objections which demanded further consideration. Since that first encounter, in fact, not only Durkheim himself, but others of his fellow-workers, notably F. Simiand, M. Mauss, and M. Halbwachs, have at different times returned to the question in the *Année*, and always in much the same spirit. Whoever wishes to study the subject has only to refer to the accounts inserted under the head of Social Morphology in the sixth section of the successive volumes of the series. Above all, he should consult the detailed article which M. Marcel Mauss, in collaboration with a well-known Americanist, M. Beuchat, devoted in the *Année* of 1904–5 to the "Seasonal variations in Eskimo societies". The sub-title defines precisely the idea of the authors: "A study of social morphology," M. Mauss calls it. It consists of an illustration and of a demonstration—we might easily say of a manifesto, if the word was in the least suitable to the tone of the article. So the interest of sociologists in Anthropogeography is not merely passive, but tends rather to oppose than to accept it. Their objections need close examination, but not for the mere idle pleasure of raising a great theoretical debate, one of those burning doctrinal controversies which delight the philosopher and infuriate the specialist, who is compelled to defend himself and his most cherished ideas. For the sociologists do not content themselves with attack. They construct, and on their own ground. They propose to substitute for the anthropogeography of Ratzel a science, better defined, they say, and more strictly delimited—a sociological science, the aim of which they make clear, and to which they give, in advance, the name Social morphology. This attitude determines our own. A choice has to be made. We dismissed above, in a few words, those brilliant but ill-arranged essays of which so many ingenious minds have been guilty. And if, to us, the action of nature on societies derives its power precisely from the fact that it is not exercised in the same way as the action of men; if we believe, with Vidal de la Blache, that it is "an imperceptible and complex interference, the results of which slowly accumulate—a gradual and continuous process which even owes its power to that continuity," what use could we have for all the superficial relationships and deceptive analogies which have for so long been a burden to us? There is, as we said, no method or scientific arrangement about them.

But here we have first one guide offered us, and soon afterwards a second. The young science of human geography offers us its attested facts; social morphology, a wise and considered assistance. In which are we to trust? We must first listen to both sides, and examine the criticisms which the science of sociology boldly brings against its predecessor. And even if these criticisms do not induce us to leave the geographical road; if they do not shake our belief in the legitimate existence or in the efficiency of human geography as a real and autonomous science, will they not help us to a better statement of the great problem, or rather of the numerous series of complex problems which we are attempting to deal with?

Criticism of method, and criticism of results also, that is the way we must follow. Collections of samples abound; we need not uselessly increase their number. It is possible that in some subjects questions of dogma may be put aside, or not even examined at all. But here, with several rival sciences in an indeterminate state, the question of method is not on the threshold, it is at the very heart of the subject.

Let us have geography, and geographical method; but only if it commends itself to us after long and serious examination—after an exhaustive effort to determine the guiding principles carefully and surely.

III

The Plan and Objects of the Book: The Geographical Spirit

We shall not, however, confine our efforts to this first object only, since that would be inadequate. Indeed, the consideration which we shall give to the objections brought by the sociologists against the theory and practice of geographers will enlighten us beforehand as to the nature of the questions which they are proposing to study. But this indirect approach, this kind of reconnoitring from the outside, useful and instructive though it may be, will not excuse us from entering in and examining the arrangements in detail. It will at least have rendered us a great service if it prevents us from yielding to the attraction of the "general picture" and of the "short but complete summary".

We might indeed be able to start from those great geographical unities, those great natural regions which we are accustomed to recognize in the universe—to examine them one after the other, to enumerate their fundamental characteristics, and to consider in a way their relations with the history of the peoples who have succeeded one another in those regions. This would be historical and topographical progress of apparent simplicity. But what practical good could we expect from it? Would it not imply, in the first place, an intimate and personal acquaintance with all parts of the world and with the individual histories of all nations? To reconstruct unaided, and in a more profoundly geographical spirit, the work which the collaborators of the *Weltgeschichte* of Helmholtz have failed to bring at any rate to any useful end—that would be a chimerical project. Where is the man, historian or geographer, who would risk such an attempt to-day and not know beforehand that it was doomed to failure? On what useful monographs, on what preparatory research, could he rely? Books there are certainly, such as *American History and its Geographic Conditions*,[1] by Miss E. C. Semple, which claim to explain all history by geography. But can the critical mind be disarmed by these attempts because of their manifest good faith? We think not, and the aspirant who would attempt such a venture would find himself condemned to collecting here and there odd elements of a miscellany of historico-geographic anas; like those naturalists of whom the Genevese Horace-Benedict de Saussure, the "discoverer" of Mont Blanc, complained, "who walked, or rather crept, with their eyes fixed on the ground, picking up little bits here and there, without looking at the general view." "They resemble," he added, "an antiquary who should scratch the soil of Rome in the middle of the Pantheon or the Colosseum to look for bits of coloured glass."[2] Wise and modest antiquaries: they at least did not claim to reconstruct an entire Pantheon or Colosseum of coloured glass.

It will, in fact, be the business of the different co-workers in this series to take account in their special studies of those geographical factors which enter only partly, but as an essential part, into what Taine called in one word Environment. There are none who would be better qualified for that task than the specialists themselves on each branch of history—provided always that they are well acquainted with the parallel efforts of geographers and of the principles established after critical study by their special researches. Otherwise it would be necessary to place this book at the end, and not at the beginning, of the series.

But no sooner has that idea been disposed of than another suggests itself—not to be tied down to the various countries or to their various histories any longer, but to separate by comparison and abstraction the part played in human history by a certain number of factors which are specially marked as geographical: distance, area, position, etc.; to illustrate that part by examples borrowed from all regions and all histories in turn; to compose, in this way, a book of generalities the conclusions of which would be universally applicable. It is an attractive plan, but one of equal difficulty.

[1] Boston and New York, 1903.

[2] *Voyages dans les Alpes*, Neuchâtel, Vol. I, 1780, p. 111.

In the first place, such books exist. And if they are of unequal value, some of them realize the ideal of a good book—and of a useful book. Why summarize once more the *Anthropogeographie* or the *Politische Geographie* of Ratzel? To what purpose re-write the two compact little volumes of Camille Vallaux, *Le Sol et l'État*, or *La Mer*, or the huge work, crammed with unequal matter, of Miss Semple, who wrote in 1911 her *Influences of Geographic Environment?*

Let us get to the root of the matter. All the personal mastery of a Ratzel, all his profound and extensive knowledge of the world, all his historical and above all ethnographical learning, cannot take the place of a good century of careful and methodical research. And it is, to our mind, precisely the great fault of such enterprises that they hide the difficulty and delude us as to the depth of our ignorance; that they create in our minds, always naturally slothful and ready to be satisfied by a general formula, the illusion that the reality has been fully grasped in abstractions, however rich they may be and however much they may mirror the many-sidedness of life. We have been supplied with a sort of formal catechism and are too apt afterwards to relax our thought or attention. Structures such as those of Ratzel, permeated as they are by ideas and considerations not all of which are strictly scientific (as has been only too clearly demonstrated by events since 1914 which have proved that the *megalostatism* of the German master was not merely a point of view), such structures bear witness to the powers of a gifted architect.[1] But under their shade an army of disciples and followers sleep in idleness—people of whom Rauh[2] has said that "they are always more intransigent than their master, because they only partly understand him, and are afraid they will deny his meaning if they deny a single word". Their need for precision can only be satisfied by a formula. We must beware of falling into this attitude of routine and mechanical conservatism.

* * *

We know in reality little or nothing as yet of the influence of geographical environment on human societies. And for

[1] Brunhes and Vallaux, **LXVIII**, p. 324 ff.
[2] Rauh, **XXV**, p. 29.

a very good reason: the geography which will explain that influence has scarcely been born and established. Has it a method? Yes and no, for it has several—especially that geography which people are more and more agreed in recognizing as a "human" geography. It has several methods, between which careful observers hesitate. Its only defect is that of youth. Sociology and many other allied sciences have similar doubts. But the setting and elucidation of the problems we are considering is the concern of geography. It at least attempts them, and later we shall have to record its attempts and to defend them against rivals. The scientific position, then, of the problem of the "environment"—we do not say its solution—depends essentially on the arrangement and manner of application of a universally accepted geographical method.

But if there is still any hesitation or dispute among geographers about the method, we have now what already constitutes a kind of geographical mind or attitude. We have now, in the special labours undertaken by geographers, and in their numerous efforts of thought and comparison, distinctive ways of looking at things, in default of a definite method. This is a fact the importance of which, in our opinion, should not be underrated. Some little time ago Frédéric Rauh, in his striking book on *La Méthode de la psychologie des sentiments*, threw a clear light on the primordial rôle of the scientific spirit "which manifests itself in different ways, precisely because in its pursuit of different objects it is always the same".[1] And in place of the "crude and sterile knowledge" which is alone likely to be attained by those who "want to know too much" he advocates everything which may open up to us "wide and fruitful approximations, suggestions ever renewed with life". There is great danger, he insisted, in these matters "of discouraging and interfering with discovery. Discovery, which depends on contact with the complex reality, is of more value than proof which follows slowly after it".[2] In any case it is the appearance of such a geographical spirit, this detachment of a special geographical attitude, which will enable us to carry out our task.

We must free ourselves from any pre-determined historical or topographical order, and from any systematic or pre-

[1] Rauh, **XXV**, p. 25. [2] Ibid., p. 23.

conceived design of forcing certain general data to fit in with reality, or of making certain abstract characteristics true for all history and all countries ; and we must endeavour to define as clearly as possible the proper attitude for geographers and historians to adopt towards the delicate questions of influence, after making a determined effort to classify these questions and show their scientific place in the near future. But all this will evidently only mark a brief moment in a continuous scientific evolution. It may also suggest the true means of combating and destroying certain false ideas, of giving precision to certain vague ones, and of hastening on the hour when brilliant generalizations, ingenious theories, and subtle literary comparisons will finally give place to truly scientific work. The spirit is already manifest. We must assist it, to the best of our power, to find and establish itself. To it and to its manifestations we must devote ourselves ; not to the compilation of an empty catalogue of illusory results. A critique ?—the effort would be wasted. A positive theory ? —the attempt would be culpable. With a science in the making, we must look to its promises and its aspirations.

* * *

It is unnecessary to repeat here that such anticipations are one of the objects, if not the chief object, of the various volumes in this series. But we may add a personal word.

It is an historian, with the aid of another historian, who is about to try, as an historian, to determine the relations between the earth and history ; and an historian devoted by taste and conviction to the study not of those so-called primitive or archaic societies which a certain illusion and a no less certain want of evidence make us prone to consider as " simple " and closely dependent on " nature ", but of those very societies of modern times which there is a tendency sometimes to characterize as almost completely withdrawn from physical influences and geographical conditions. This is due to no mere chance, and still less to a childish desire of the author to disguise himself for a time as a geographer for the sake of seeing how it suited him. The plan was, on the contrary, well considered and, I may add, the necessity for it almost evident.

The delicate point, it may be supposed, is not that as regards the relations of geography and history the latter has at least as much to say as the former in a matter of common interest: that is a purely verbal controversy. But on such a subject at the present day, the book of a geographer would be almost inevitably, and by the force of circumstances, a picture. Whether it is better or worse is a matter of small importance, but it would be a picture: a grouping of trivial but seductive facts which seem to prove the traditional geographical contentions. The fact is that geography believes that it possesses a method. It looks on itself as a science. By virtue of that law which Rauh [1] formulated in the thoughtful essay which we quoted above, when he said that a young science at first naturally models itself on an already established neighbouring science, human geography, the younger sister of physical geography, renovated by the study and the influence of the natural sciences, still retains some marks of its first origin, and occasionally that of a strict determinism which it cannot easily shake off by its own efforts. Or rather, some of its votaries succeed completely in doing so, others with less success: whilst others again feel no need for the liberation.

With history it is not so. She does not yet entirely believe in her position as a science.[2] In other words, she does not seem to be a scientific figure in her own eyes. On this she is hardly to be congratulated. Still, this inferiority has certain advantages.

The historian is not hampered by a doctrinal subservience either to a collection of historical theories with a pseudo-scientific appearance which would curb his freedom of individual judgment or to a body of preconceived theories, the outcome of antique regulations, on the working of which his own work would at times be modelled. In other words, where the geographer would no doubt see a picture, or a sketch, there is nothing to prevent the historian from making a free critical study. It is of this critical study that we propose to sketch the main lines.

There will be no dogmatic rigidity, as we have made evident; the plan will be elastic, and the conclusions will not be hard

[1] Cf. Rauh, **XXV**, p. 13 ff.
[2] Cf. Berr, **XXI**, Parts II and III.

and fast. To bring out a point of view is neither to recreate it nor to reconstruct it logically. It is rather to take it in its most combative form, when in violent conflict with those in disagreement with it: and in this we have the aid of the sociologists. It is also to follow all its steps and manifestations without churlish pedantry, and with a critical sympathy which awaits what the future may have in store.

PART I

HOW THE PROBLEM SHOULD BE STATED

THE QUESTION OF METHOD

OF all the workers whom the *Année Sociologique* brought together, Émile Durkheim was the first, as we have said, who brought his critical reflection to bear on modern geography and its recent attempts at co-operation in the rational study of man. After him—with sometimes a slight difference of form—pupils and successors have manifested the same spirit. The starting-point which all adopt is very clear.

The typical and acknowledged representative of the " human geographers " is F. Ratzel. Now Ratzel in the *Anthropogeographie,* his most comprehensive work and his masterpiece, sets out to study all the influences which the soil may exercise on social life in general. Such a design is chimerical.[1]

It is beyond the powers of a single man. That is obvious, and is no objection. But it is beyond the power of a single science. This needs to be stated, because it is not generally understood. For the multitude of problems which are thus set is really infinite. And, what is more serious—for after all when we have the principles established and the rules fixed, the solution of an infinite number of problems is only a matter of time and patience—these problems are heterogeneous. So absolutely heterogeneous that a wise division of labour is indispensable.

It is possible that the nature of the soil and the nature of the climate have an influence on the collective outlook of men, on the myths, the legends and the arts of different peoples. That has to be determined ; but is it not for *religious sociology*, or even for *aesthetic sociology*, to develop the study of such influences ?

[1] Durkheim, **XVII**, Vol. III, 1898–9, p. 356.

D

There is no a priori impossibility that the nature of soil and climate have an influence even on the character of nations, on their ways of thought, on their political, legal, or moral tendencies. But is it not for *collective ethology* to verify this in the course of the general inquiry which it is conducting into such tendencies, all the factors and conditions of which it aims to disentangle ?

It is more than probable that soil and climate influence the distribution of men on the surface of the globe, and facilitate or hinder their concentration or dispersion. It is for *demography* to undertake the study both of that concentration and of that dispersion.

One sees the objection that may be raised. It is claimed that a science has been formed in order to answer the question : " What are the influences which the geographical environment exercises on the different ways in which human societies manifest themselves ? " That is an immense question. It can be broken up into a multitude of secondary questions all of which belong to quite distinct sciences. How then could a single man, unskilled in each one of these sciences, be found, under the name of geographer, skilled in them all ? Geography regarded in this light is only an impudent interloper on ground reserved to economists and sociologists. All its conclusions belong to the domain of some special sociological science. It vanishes and ought to vanish *qua* distinct science. It can logically claim for itself only, so to speak, an " appendicular " existence. The sociologist alone (sociologist as a genus, demographer, ethologist, etc., as species) has the right to consider methodically and cautiously questions geographers have hitherto rashly claimed as their own . . . But do they not treat of them all ? Do not geographers study, in addition to the influence of environment on societies only, its influence on man in general ? The distinction is illusory if man is only an abstraction and if there exist for the geographer, as for the sociologist, only human societies and isolated human beings. Appendicular knowledge . . . At the most, we can conceive that from the accumulated results obtained by the labour of sociologists a new study will spring up, a sociological study, one of those which, taken as a whole, constitute " Sociology ". It will be *Social Morphology*. " It is known," writes M. Mauss, at the commencement of the interesting memoir already mentioned,[1] "that under this name we designate the science which studies the material foundations of societies with a view not only to describing, but also to explaining them—that is to say, the form which they assume when they are establishing themselves on the land, the number and density of their population, the manner in which it is distributed and the *ensemble* of the things which serve as a seat of collective life." Thus is reborn from its ashes, but under a different name, anthropogeography, previously sacrificed on the altar of confusionism. More modest, we are assured, better regulated in its aims, less rash in its methods, social morphology will occupy a favourable position. There is no risk that it will wander off into blind alleys or dissipate itself in futile endeavours, for the morphologist will follow in the wake of a science with a limited scope and well-defined aims. Its task will be precise and relatively easy. And nothing will be sacrificed with which human geography either deals, or would consider it useful to deal, or could reasonably wish to elucidate. M. Mauss assures us anew of this. Here is an example, and a very significant one. After having stated in another volume of the *Année sociologique* [2] that H. Schurtz, in his *Völkerkunde*,[3] understood by anthropogeography not so much the influence of geographical situation on man in general as "the study of the action of terrestrial phenomena on societies considered chiefly from the point of view of habit", M. Mauss, with the ardour of an heir-presumptive, rushes to the rescue of anthropogeographers thus reduced to a bare living. "If Schurtz had included in his definition," he writes, "as he might have done and as would have been logical, not only the study of the environment of peoples, of their movements and of their gradual attachment to the land and of the States (political geography), but also that of the movements of population, the formation of towns and in general the distribution of individuals over the surface of the globe—he would have arrived at the idea of social morphology which we are defending here."

Nothing could be clearer or more illuminating than such passages. They throw full light on the keenness and reality of

[1] Mauss, **CCXV,** p. 39.
[2] **XVII,** Vol. VIII, 1903–4, p. 167.
[3] Leipzig–Vienna, 1903.

the rivalry. To the objection that they are purely theoretical, we may rejoin that in matters of research the instrument, the method, and the spirit are surely of no little importance.

Human geography or social morphology, geographical method or sociological method; the choice must be made. There is no question here of a quarrel of schools, or, if I may be allowed the expression, of shop—but of fundamentals. Our first duty is to proceed to the examination of these.

CHAPTER I

Social Morphology or Human Geography

THE first accusation of sociologists against human geography is simple. It can be expressed in one word. It is that of ambition.

Nothing, geographers are told, is more restricted, and at the same time nothing is more ambitious, than their conceptions. Whether they are considering a group of men or a human society, they look at the soil on which the group or society in question actually rests. That terrestrial support, that underlying basis of societies, is not for them inert and powerless matter. It acts on the men whom it supports. It " influences " them physically and morally. It " explains " them as a whole and as individuals. It explains them, and it alone can explain them. It alone acts on them. It alone influences them. Here we have the usual exclusiveness and foregone conclusion; the professional bias of the specialist shows itself only too clearly.

The geographer starts from the soil, not from the society. It would doubtless not be claimed that the soil is the " cause " of the society. Ratzel contents himself with saying that it is " the only essential bond of cohesion of each people ".[1] But it is to the soil that his attention is chiefly directed. It is the geographical factor with which he is concerned, and whose action and efficacy he means to disengage and to exhibit. " Instead of studying the material which underlies societies in all its elements and under all its aspects," M. Mauss reproaches him,[2] " it is chiefly on the soil that he concentrates his attention. That is what is in the forefront of his research." Social morphology would be very different. It also would treat of what underlies societies, but only as one of the elements

[1] **LXXXIII,** Vol. I, pp. 1–2.
[2] Mauss, **XVII,** 1904–5, p. 42.

which aid in an understanding of the life and destinies of those societies. It would not begin by deifying, so to speak, that privileged element by attributing to it a sort of creative power—making it the begetter and the animator of forms of society. This study, since it bears on " the mass of individuals who compose the different groups, the manner in which they are disposed on the soil, the nature and form of every sort of thing that affects their collective relations ",[1] would take rank amongst those special sciences of which Sociology, in the eyes of MM. Durkheim and Fauconnet,[2] constitutes, so to speak, the " Corpus ". But what the sociologist, as opposed to the geographer, puts in the forefront of his treatment is not " the Earth " but " the Society ". In other words, the problem is not the same whether one is and proclaims oneself a geographer or a morphologist. And, therefore, M. Mauss is constrained to say[3]: " If to the word ' anthropogeography ' we prefer ' social morphology ' to designate the science which has been the result of this study, it is not due to a mere taste for neologism, but because this difference of label marks a difference in point of view." We agree. We would even go further and say: the difference is in reality such that social morphology and human geography cannot be substituted for one another. But a study of the two rival schools " in action " will demonstrate this better than any theoretical discussion.

I

The Objections of Social Morphology: Human Groups Without Geographical Roots

There is no human group, no human society, without a territorial basis. Such is the normal point from which geographers start in their speculations. But the formula is to a certain extent of doubtful accuracy. For there are many groups and many societies—particularly amongst

[1] Durkheim, **XVII**, 1899, p. 520, and Halbwachs, *La Classe ouvrière et les niveaux de vie*, p. 369, n. 1.
[2] " Sociologie et sciences sociales," in the *Revue Philosophique*, May, 1903.
[3] **XVII**, Vol. IX, 1904–5, p. 44.

those which sociologists sometimes prefer to study—over which the influence of the "geographical substratum", so dear to Ratzel, makes itself, after all, very little felt. In spite of a remarkable lack of geographical ideas, the various researches of German, English, and American ethnologists on the uncivilized societies of the New World and of the Pacific have already shown us that primitive men are not acquainted with strictly territorial methods of grouping only. Totemism in particular is at the root of a multitude of social formations without any apparent geographical roots.

We will take as an example, the Arunta, that people of Central Australia whose very complex organization has been brought to our knowledge in all its details by careful and serious writers—an organization so complex that we notice at times, as in other cases, very important differences between the observers. Let us refer to the most trustworthy works, and in particular to those of Spencer and Gillen, which are classic in sociology. These authors fully described in 1899, one after the other, the native tribes of Central Australia—and in 1904 those of the North of the same continent.[1] They are accurate observers and well supplied with facts, although, as M.J. Sion has pointed out,[2] they made the serious mistake of describing religious and social phenomena among peoples whose material life they have not studied. However, their labours call our attention to three kinds of distinct elementary groups amongst the Arunta, which overlap one another, and are interlaced in the most complicated manner. In the first place groups are met with which are properly territorial, distinguished from one another by place-names, and each possessing a slice of land of known and definite limits. But side by side with these are a certain number of those matrimonial classes which E. Durkheim has described in his memoir on *L'Organisation matrimoniale des sociétés australiennes*,[3] and there also are totemic groups which include natives, in this case, without any kind of localization or geographical distribution. It is not, moreover, the non-territorial groups which play the least important part in

[1] Bibliography, **CCXII** and **CCXIII.**
[2] *Revue de géographie annuelle*, Vol. I, 1906–7, p. 417.
[3] **XVII,** Vol. VIII, 1903–4, p. 121 ff.

the collective organization of the Arunta—quite the contrary. And Durkheim himself has often insisted (particularly in his interesting notice of Howitt's book dealing with the native tribes of South-East Australia) [1] on the extreme vagueness of the actual territorial organization of these Australian societies—at least in the eyes of contemporary white observers.

A similar state of things is found throughout the rest of the great Australian continent. The tribes are generally provided with two organizations, the one based on geographical divisions, the other dependent on the matrimonial regulations. The same holds good of the Solomon Islands, where the Germans have studied the system, and where totemic groupings, distinct from the villages and territorial groupings, which are sometimes composed of the bearers of different totems, are similarly intermixed; and also of a number of the wild tribes of Brazil,[2] who live in the forests and have never passed the stage of barbarism. It is curious, moreover, to see how the totemic principle fades in face of the territorial principle, represented in this case by the village community. But why multiply examples of facts now well established? [3]

We can look with indifference on the use that may be made of this against "geographical pretensions", but a few remarks may, perhaps, not be out of place.

Firstly, the passage is often made from the non-territorial to the territorial groupings. The former tend gradually to localize themselves geographically. Totemic organizations without a geographical basis are mentioned, but it is amongst peoples —such as the Pueblo Indians of Arizona and New Mexico— who have modelled the structure and construction of their houses and villages on a totemic organization, exceptionally preserved in a life which has become almost urban.[4] And even in Australia, in that part of it where a number of almost similar peoples live alongside the Arunta, the tribes dwelling nearer to the Gulf of Carpentaria do not present the same anomalies.[5] Their totemic groupings and territorial groupings are combined. Each locality has its own totem and one does

[1] **XVII**, Vol. IX, 1904–5, p. 358 ff.
[2] Beuchat, **CIC**, p. 253.
[3] Cf. **XVII**, Vol. III, 1898–9, pp. 340, 345; Vol. IX, 1904–5, p. 356, etc.
[4] **XVII**, Vol. VII, 1902–3, p. 649.
[5] Durkheim, **XVII**, Vol. VIII, 1903–4, p. 120.

not meet there bearers of different totems ; so the administrative chief of the locality is also the religious chief. There is, however, nothing surprising in this confusion. Durkheim gives the reason for it [1] when he notes that it exists where the totem is transmitted in the paternal line. Marriage, then, does not introduce in each generation totems of foreign origin and importation.

On the other hand, however, we cannot look on these non-territorial groupings as " in the air ", like those people in the Chinese paintings of whom Michelet speaks in a celebrated passage. It is impossible, says Durkheim,[2] in one passage where he is particularly considering the native tribes of South-East Australia—it is impossible that a social group should not be attached in some sort of way to the territory which it occupies and should not bear any mark of it at all. A careful analysis would reveal without much difficulty a geographical factor in the least " territorial " of associations—when the effect of climate had to be considered. There are, for instance, on the Pacific coast of North America, human societies with a double organization, like those of the Kwakiutls, which have been studied by the American scholar, F. Boas.[3] One of these is for the uninitiate and lay life, and is marked by a division of the men into families, classes, and tribes. The other is for the religious life, and is based on groups, each under the protection of a different divinity or spirit. But the lay organization holds during the summer only, and the religious organization during the winter ; and so geography would regain its rights, even if it were not already evident otherwise that the geographical consequences of the summer regime would not all disappear with the cold season. But, independently of these particular facts, the remark of Durkheim was one to follow up and examine carefully.

Ratzel, dominated both by his foregone conclusions as an anthropogeographer, and by pre-occupations of a political rather than a scientific order, which at times makes the later and less instructive of his great works, the *Politische Geographie,* resemble a sort of manual of German Imperialism, writes : " If the simplest types of State are unimaginable without a soil

[1] Ibid.
[2] **XVII,** Vol. IX, 1904–5, p. 360.
[3] **XVII,** Vol. III, 1898–9, p. 336.

which belongs to them, it should be the same with the simplest types of society; the conclusion is inevitable."[1] "Family, tribe, community are only possible on a soil, and their development can only be understood in relation to that soil." In the first place those groupings are not the only ones which represent the simplest types of society. There are others, which we have just mentioned, in the genesis, the development and the nature of which the soil plays undoubtedly a very limited part. But after all, of what exactly is it a question? "The simplest types of State are unimaginable without a soil *which belongs to them.*" The last four words are doubtless not put there by chance. "Family, tribe, community are only possible on a soil, and their development can only be understood in relation to that soil." Is there really more than a shade of difference between the second formula and the first? The difference might be expressed by saying that the first belongs to a social morphology and the second to human geography. But it is curious and rather piquant to see that Durkheim, when remarking that "it is impossible that a social group should not be attached in some sort of way to the territory which it occupies, and should not bear any mark of it at all", refers (although the word "occupy" is very equivocal) to the second conception—the same one which he criticizes elsewhere—whilst Ratzel, on the other hand, seems to tie himself to the first. But neither text is perfectly clear, and their very ambiguity shows how insufficient the work of analysis remains.

There was evidently ground for the distinction. There are the social formations on a territorial basis: those which appropriated more or less strictly a piece of land, reserved it for their own use, and considered it as their particular domain. That piece of land is in a way their projection on the soil; it is even their form in the strict sense of the word: what Mr. Bouglé plainly expresses when, in analysing in his turn the conception of social morphology in the *Année Sociologique* of 1900, he summarizes the ideas of Durkheim:—"the word 'form' is here used in its strict sense. It is a question of material forms, susceptible of graphical representations."[2]

[1] Ratzel, **LXXXVI.**
[2] **XVII,** 1900, p. 112. The whole development is useful as a precise statement of the sociologist's idea of morphology.

And the sociologist adds that these forms " constitute the true domain of social morphology ". Here we have something precise. There remain other social groups which have no special reserved domain, no territory of their own or definite boundary. The human beings who form them live on a soil, in a country, under a sky, common to all and the same for all. Resting on a terrestrial soil, in a certain way they share in it : they bear the mark of it, Durkheim says ; but their group, as a group, has no form graphically representable. There is no piece of land which is properly the " territory of the group ".

But when that has been said, have we got very far ? Has the distinction a real value ? Does it support the claims of the sociologists against the geographers ? We are the less inclined to think so because of those facts about transition which we spoke of above and which must be remembered. Of the Australian societies, on our knowledge of which all this debate depends, Durkheim remarks [1] that the organization doubtless commenced by being totemic and only became territorial afterwards. Or, more exactly, at the time when only the totemic organization existed, what there was of a territorial nature in the social organization was at first insignificant—at least if we are to believe in the sociologist's analysis ; it is not a question, we repeat, of simple data, easy to interpret. " What marked the limits of the society was not any material barrier, what determined its form was not the configuration of the ground. The tribe was essentially a collection, not of districts, but of clans, and what made the unity of the clan was the totem and the ideas of which it was the emblem." In the last analysis, what remains after all this discussion is this : that one of the most important objects of study for the sociologist—these groups which are not essentially territorial—offers after all little scope for geographers. May we say, however, that they offer more to them, in spite of everything, than to the morphologists ? In such a case the latter can only put in a declaration of bankruptcy : where there are no " forms " to study, morphology cannot claim a place. For geography, on the other hand, it is possible that the group, as a group, may escape

[1] **XVII,** Vol. IX, 1904–5, p. 360.

it. But there remain for it the ground on which the men live, the climate, the products, and all the conditions of existence which belong to places which men frequent and which they occupy as members of groups of other kinds—the territorial groups. We thus see, doubtless a little more plainly, the real difference between the two rival conceptions, morphology —and geography.

II

The Objections of Social Morphology: The Ambition of Geography

Other objections of the sociologists are better grounded and give more precision to the charge of ambition. One example will serve to prove this, and one that is the more typical because we shall take it from a writer who knew better where he was going. It was a cherished idea of Vidal de la Blache [1] that the cultivation of rice, by the abundance of nourishment which it produces in a small space, as well as by the perpetual care which it requires, exercises a profound influence on the societies of the Far East. A family of rice cultivators in Cambodia, he notes, can live, if strictly necessary, on two and a half acres of land; but on the other hand numerous and constant workers are necessary. What is the consequence? Vidal de la Blache, doubtless carried away by his surroundings, by his audience, and by the subject of his lecture—the geographical conditions of social facts—sketched it one day in the following manner at the École des Hautes Études sociales: "I must be careful not to generalize overmuch; but if, in these societies of the Far East which centre round China, a strongly constituted system of family and village is really the corner stone, we see the relation of cause and effect between the method of cultivation due to the geographical conditions and the only truly popular form of organization which we find there." [2] Whatever ingenuity there may be in the remark and however subtle

[1] Cf. also Woeikof, **CXXIV**, p. 228.
[2] Vidal, **XXXI**, p. 18 (the text goes back to 1902).

the analysis—there is manifestly loose thinking here as well as " ambition ". For there exist many other civilizations, characterized by other types of life, under other skies where a firmly constituted family life appears to be the true " corner-stone " of the society. And moreover, in such a matter, care should be taken to guard against the old prepossession that the social organization proceeds from low to high, by the progressive agglomeration of groups at first very simple and afterwards larger if not more complex: clans, villages, tribes, and nations. The family organization is not the first. In all climates and in all civilizations it has received its rules of government from without. It has received them not from geographical conditions but from the dominant higher power of the State, from the political society as a body.[1] The family organization being granted, there is nothing more probable than that the cultivation of rice in the countries of the Far East, where it predominates, has contributed to maintain that organization and to increase its power and influence. But we cannot go further and say with Durkheim—this time without reservation: " geographical influences are doubtless far from being negligible, but it does not appear that they have the kind of preponderance which is attributed to them . . . There is not one of the features constituting social life for which they can, as far as we know, account." And he adds: how, moreover, could this be possible " since the geographical conditions vary from place to place—and we find identical social types (except for irregularities in individuals) in the most different parts of the world ? "

One more example. We need not be afraid of multiplying them in a matter of this sort. The human habitation, the house, is one of the most remarkable features in these " humanized landscapes " which we have so constantly before us and which the geographer should study most carefully. In our Western countries it is such a familiar sight that we actually suffer by its prolonged absence. In such a wild and desolate solitude as the furthest points of Armorica on which a wild sea beats ceaselessly—a windmill, spreading its crossed wings on the stern and naked line of the horizon,

[1] See *infra*, in Part II, Chap. III.

gives us an undefinable feeling of confidence and peace: something of that emotion which Percival Landon experienced on his route to Lhasa when, on the lofty plateaux of Tibet, he chanced to see the stunted outline of a willow with green leaves. But can we say (as has been said) that this house, this abode of man, however well adapted by its aspect, by its arrangements, and by its materials to the soil that supports it, and the climate that suggests it, is a geographical fact? A human fact if you will—but that is not the same thing.

There is some geography in a wheat field, but a wheat field is not a geographical fact. At least, it is one for the geographer only. He has to consider "the house", but only what there is geographical about the house—and not everything about a house is geographical—and is it even the business of geography to account for the essential idea of that house?

It would certainly be very easy to set out here a string of quotations which would show that some geographers take but a faint interest in anything outside their own work, exhibiting a sort of frank youthful arrogance somewhat irritating to their neighbours, combined with a propensity to be satisfied with words and formulæ provided that they are trenchant and summary. How many there are who go carelessly about the world furnished with two or three large master keys, trying them on all the doors they come across: happy if only they can find one where the bolt moves, however badly. "The first need of man is water. When surface water is rare as in Beauce, or in the white and dusty Champagne, and in limestone countries generally, villages cluster densely round certain places where water is found or else stretch for several miles along a watercourse. When water is abundant and well distributed, as in the Ile de France, the Limousin, Brittany, Wales, etc., the dwellings are scattered"[1] . . . Two extracts from a large-scale map to illustrate the statement and we have a general law formulated, a fixed geographical law, whose application knows no limit. But it is clear that "if the water oozes into any small hole that is dug, the houses might be scattered over the country, and that this isolation

[1] Lespagnol, **LXXIX**, p. 523.

would be less easy for them in the opposite case."[1] They might . . . As a matter of fact, it is only a question of possibilities. Again, if the influence of the local physical environment is undeniable, does that mean that all others are excluded? May it not happen, for example, that sometimes even the structure of the village has been conceived on another soil, and in another climate, by a population of emigrants? May it not be that the newcomers have built and arranged their dwelling after the familiar type of their fatherland? May not this type have been modified (without altogether obliterating it)[2] if experience did not allow it to be kept unchanged? Take the case of the region of Caux: the population is scattered in the west and concentrated in the east: the physical conditions in the two districts are very nearly identical, and there is nothing to prevent the east from making ponds or the west from boring wells.[3] The Cauchois farm, so constant in type, is no doubt suitable to the needs of the locality. But other farms, built on a different plan, would satisfy these needs equally well.[4] These are the remarks of a geographer. They prove clearly that their author is not disposed to remain content with the big keys of which we spoke previously. They do not prove that there are not many who hurry along their own road and neglect the corrective faculty and the necessity for looking at things from a neighbour's point of view. In the case of the house there is a natural tendency to neglect, if not to deny, the racial influences which Meitzen formulated unchallenged,[5] though objections could easily have been raised—or those historic influences which are not necessarily all racial and the action of which must be considered when geographical analysis fails. Such unconscious or wilful ignorance of the force of tradition and the persistent action of social causes may well justify the sociologists in blaming geographers for faults that are only too common. The faults are those of a young and vigorous science which does not know how to limit its own domain and at the same time that of its neighbour.

[1] Sion, **CCXXIX**, p. 465.
[2] Ibid., p. 466.
[3] Ibid., p. 493.
[4] Ibid., p. 495.
[5] Bibliography, **CLXIII**; cf. also Brunhes, **LXVI**, pp. 760–70.

To sum up. We understand better now what the social morphologists mean when they denounce "that science with great ambitions which calls itself human geography".[1] The reproach of ambition, from their pens, implies two distinct grievances. Geographers wish to explain by geography, or at least claim as a subject of study, human societies from the least to the greatest, from the most rudimentary to the most complex; and one might think, to listen to them, that all social groups are amenable to their science, when, in reality, such is not the case, and all non-territorial groupings ought to escape from their clutches. In the second place, as far as concerns even those social groups which are undeniably amenable to their methods, they claim to explain too many manifestations by geography, and by geography only. Here they make the evident mistake of ignoring the science of sociology with its modest views and cautious methods, because it has a limited objective and one determined beforehand.

But on the first point we have given explanations. The complaints made against geography are not really valid. There are groupings of men in the origin of which the soil, simply as soil, pure soil, if we may say so, plays an insignificant part, since these groupings have no soil of their own, or, to be more exact, since they have not cut their particular piece out of the general material. But there are other geographical factors besides the "soil" which influence the life of societies. And from the grip of these, the men who compose the non-territorial groups in question—and who, moreover, belong equally to other groups which are on a territorial basis—do not escape. Do they really escape, however, from the grip of the soil? If not, social morphology cannot help us here, since it deliberately concerns itself only with forms. Must we choose? It is not easy to say. For there is no equivalence, it will be granted, between the two objects proposed for our choice.

And as to the second point: "When such a multiplicity of facts is passed in review," writes E. Durkheim à propos of Ratzel,[2] "with the sole object of finding out what part the geographical factor plays in their origin, its importance

[1] Simiand, **XVII,** Vol. XI, 1906–9, p. 723.
[2] **XVII,** Vol. III, 1898–9, p. 557.

is *necessarily* exaggerated just because the other factors which equally intervene in the production of the same phenomena are lost sight of." The remark shows sound judgment. But "necessarily" is undoubtedly a little harsh. That it fits Ratzel is very possible, but it certainly would not do to generalize it, or to suppose that it could be applied to all geographers. "Causes of all kinds cross and interfere with one another to produce the actual appearance of our old historic countries. The study of them is a delicate one. We find groups of causes and effects, but nothing which gives, on the whole, the impression of necessity. It is evident that at a certain moment things might have taken another course, and that this has depended on an accident of history. There can be no question of geographical determinism: yet geography is the key which cannot be dispensed with." And later, "in the explanation of these very complex facts which have been subject to varied circumstances of time and place, geographical analysis, as well as that of ethnic and historical influences, ought to have its share. The exclusive use of one method of interpretation would not satisfy a mind devoted to truth and not to a system." Where do we find a trace in these thoughtful words, or in the book which they introduce and recommend, of that "necessarily" foregone conclusion (Durkheim), or of that exclusivism of which M. Mauss speaks elsewhere? Yet they are the words of a geographer whose qualifications no one will deny—Vidal de la Blache.

III

Ratzel's Mistake: Why he does not cover the whole of Human Geography

We have here to deal with a mistake common amongst methodologists who are not specialists in the sciences they discuss. The most wary and careful do not escape it. They are obliged to inform themselves on the subject as briefly as possible, and therefore to confine themselves to one man and to one book. But to criticize and to pass judgment on the whole of a science which is in course of creation and is still feeling its way by taking a single book, pointing out its aims and its defects, and then generalizing from it, is a dangerous method of procedure. This, however, is what sociologists seem in a large measure to have done.

The book on which they have started certainly appears to be well chosen. Ratzel's *Anthropogeographie* is his chief work, but when M. Mauss, following Durkheim, calls its author the "founder" of anthropogeography, he exaggerates, although it is true that he is one of the founders. Still Ratzel and his disciples are not the only people who are concerned with human geography. The French school clearly recognizes the godfather of anthropogeography. When the *Annales de Géographie* were started, in 1891, one of the first numbers contained a detailed summary of the principal ideas and the favourite themes of the German geographer from the pen of L. Raveneau and under the title of *L'Élément humain dans la géographie*. When, later, the *Politische Geographie* appeared, Vidal de la Blache personally pointed out its interest, and took it for a text when writing, in his turn, *La Géographie politique*. Later still, M. G. Hückel summed up, still in the *Annales* and for the benefit of French readers, the main features of *La Géographie de la Circulation selon Frédéric Ratzel*.[1] However, notwithstanding these numerous evidences, it would be absolutely incorrect to suppose that all the very enterprising, curious, and interesting work of our geographers was dependent on Ratzel. Many of them, who would perhaps admit to a distant acquaintance with him, would yet be very surprised to hear this. What, in fact, interests them most of all is monographs on certain regions. Theoretical works, compendious books on the object, the aim, and the methods of human geography are very rare in France. We can only name the very suggestive, vivid and concise articles of Vidal de la Blache; Brunhes' great book, unequal in value and very loose in construction, but abounding in references; and lastly the two books of Camille Vallaux: *la Mer* and *le Sol et l'Etat*, two recent volumes (1908 and 1911) in the little *Encyclopédie scientifique Doin*,[2] which show plainly the influence of Ratzel, but not without reservations or criticism or qualification. These are all,

[1] Bibliography, Nos. **XCX** (Vidal) and **LXXI** (Hückel).

[2] The greater part of the ideas which they contain are to be found expressed in a new form in a recent work by C. Vallaux in collaboration with J. Brunhes (**LXVIII**).

and they are few. But they are enough for French geographers. Human geography is, in their opinion, too young, too new, and has still too far to travel, too much to learn and to attempt, to be able at present to attend to definitions or effective limitations. By seeking hastily to shut itself into a narrow sphere, would it not risk leaving the best and most genuine part of itself outside ? That is one point of view at any rate, and it may be added that in England, in the United States, in Italy, and elsewhere there are "human geographers" whose work and whose aims are in no way Ratzelian. In France, Ratzelianism was perhaps a prestige—which is not necessarily a reality.

Yet another thing : at the same time that Durkheim declared that the *Anthropogeographie* of the German master was an effort, no doubt chimerical, "to study all the influences which the soil can exercise on social life in general," Vidal de la Blache wrote in the *Annales de Geographie* : "To restore to geography the human element, the claims of which seem to have been forgotten, and to reconstitute the unity of geographical science on a basis of nature and of life : such is a summary of the plan of Ratzel's work." [1] The two opinions obviously differ. Can it be that one of them is mistaken ?

In fact, at the very time when Ratzel seemed chiefly preoccupied with determining the influence of geographical conditions on the destinies, and especially on the histories, of men, he was working with all the power of his infinitely varied knowledge to demonstrate in man one of the most powerful factors in geography : that is to say, in reality to found and create human geography. The work of the Leipzig professor is not one of those which can be expressed by a single formula. Durkheim saw this and noted it. In that critical account, to which we have so often referred,[2] he wrote : "There are in the *Anthropogeographie* three different kinds of questions. Firstly, Ratzel busies himself with establishing by the aid of maps—faithful in this to the teaching of Humboldt, who inspired the publication in 1836 of Berghaus's *Atlas physique*—the manner in which

[1] **XI,** Vol. XIII, 1904, p. 417.
[2] **XVII,** Vol. III, 1898–9, p. 550 ff.

men are distributed and grouped on the earth. Then he is at pains to explain the distribution and division which result from the perpetual movements, of all kinds and origins, which have succeeded one another in the course of history. Lastly, and only lastly, he pays attention to the various effects which their physical environment can produce on individuals, and through them on society in general." Now, " this last order of problems is very different from the other two : it occupies, moreover, only a small place in the book, and only the last two chapters are especially devoted to it ; for, as the author confesses, these questions only just border on anthropogeography." [1] We would add, for our own part, that this third part of the *Anthropogeographie*, which is dominated by prejudices of a personal nature, political or otherwise, is certainly not the most valuable. It is none the less true that the criticism of Durkheim really bears on this alone, or almost alone, and that, the reader's attention having been directed to it in advance by the sub-title of the first volume : Principles of the application of geography to history (*Grundzüge der Anwendung der Erdkunde auf die Geschichte*), it seems to have attracted and provoked the general charge of ambition which, through it, Durkheim has brought against all the young geography.

It would be a little outside the scope of our present subject to ask ourselves how Ratzel could openly and consciously lay himself open to these criticisms. A scholar as he is, well versed in the natural sciences, he has upheld more than anyone that great idea of terrestrial unity,[2] the conception of which by Bernard Varenius, in 1650, was enough to make us acclaim him to-day as the true founder of scientific geography.[3] As a geographer he has throughout his life striven, in every development of his work, to keep human geography in close contact and permanent solidarity with physical geography. Why did he so depart from his usual prudence, lose sight of the very principles of his research, and stretch out his hand to those ambitious people who would fain dream of a philosophy of geography, as others formerly

[1] Durkheim, ibid.
[2] Vidal de la Blache, **XXIX**, p. 129 ff.
[3] Gallois, *Journal des Savants*, 1906, pp. 148–62.

imagined a philosophy of history, or to those submissive people who reduce it to the rank of a humble servant,[1] the Cinderella of history, as it has been called, *historiarum ancilla*? If it is true, and it is, that in the first volume of the *Anthropogeographie* "the main idea undergoes many eclipses"[2]; if it is true that Ratzel's dialectic is not afraid of the most flagrant contradictions, can it all be explained by these weaknesses? We do not think so. Ratzel's mistake, in our opinion, lay in accepting too readily certain problems in the traditional form. This meant that he did not think of seriously revising their terms and enunciation. He and his disciples, and the geographers of other schools according as they deserve or justify the criticisms which we have quoted, are, perhaps, above all, only victims: the victims of circumstances of a chronological kind independent of their own will: to put it more plainly, the victims of History.

IV

Human Geography the Heir of History

Certainly, if there is to-day a human geography in the process of formation, it would be a strange thing to claim its paternity for the historians. For in its genesis, scientific men on the one hand, naturalists and travellers and politicians on the other, have played quite the most important part. It is none the less true that at a critical epoch, and by reason even of the absence of an organized geographical science, it was the historians, as we pointed out before, who had to take, and did take, those preliminary steps which determined its future.

In the time of Michelet, even in the time of Duruy, there were no geographers except some sedentary scholars, great amateur travellers around their libraries, who consciously practised what Bersot, according to Vidal de la Blache,[3] called "the difficult geography, that of the text-books".

[1] Raveneau, **XI**, Vol. I, 1891–2, p. 332.
[2] Ibid., p. 345.
[3] **XI**, 1905, p. 194.

As for the "easy" geography, it was reduced, in the end, to catalogues. It was a branch of knowledge, useful practically, but wanting in all substance and interest. There was nothing in the work of its professors—nor moreover in the memoirs of the successors of d'Anville—which could give the historians any precise idea of the aim, the method, or the exact bearing of a geographical science which was not mixed up with a description.

But on the other hand, when Michelet, in his preface of 1869, proclaimed the necessity of basing history in the first place on the soil [1] — what was history then ? What was it, we may ask, in spite of the efforts of Michelet to enlarge it, to enrich it, and to change the traditional idea of it ? To retrace the past of France was always to set out in a double picture the long struggle of the Kings, to establish from the point of view of domestic politics a rule of monarchical centralization and absolutism, and their long effort, from the point of view of foreign policy, to group the provinces, little by little, round the domain, and finally to fill the predestined frame with a land entirely French, that privileged compartment of Europe which was bounded by the "natural frontiers". The lengthy effort and struggle were all political in character, and history remained before all things a study of politics—and if Michelet, with his universal divination and foresight, is not to be suspected of having arbitrarily restricted the idea, if he desired, as he loved to say, the resurrection of the entire life of the past, of the soil, and the men, the people, and the chiefs, the events, the institutions, and the beliefs, if he felt it to be necessary that "the political history should be enlightened by the internal history, that of philosophy and religion, of laws and literature", here again he was able only to foresee, to divine, and to desire : for economic and social history are not improvised.[2]

Political history—political geography : the second, as nearly all the dictionaries of the middle of the century note, was "only a branch of the first", "and of statistics," it was sometimes added. The form of States, their area, the variations of that form and of that area by dismemberment

[1] See Introduction, p. 11.
[2] Jullian, **XLV**, p. 47.

or accretion—that was what the historian used to ask the geographer to represent to him and aid him to understand. He naturally started in all his researches from the political map of the world as it had been made by centuries of history and successive generations of men. His task was not to explain, but to justify. For a naive finalism controlled his researches, and a more or less conscious feeling that a sort of preliminary necessity imposed on States the form in which we see them.

Kingdoms and republics were thus inserted normally in the traditional framework of the five parts of the globe. Water-tight compartments, fixed and providentially made beforehand to receive them, and well provided with natural frontiers, actually did receive them. Let us, moreover, remark that the first attempts of the men who tried, at the beginning of the century, to institute under the name of comparative geography a more really scientific study, were not of a nature to change the ideas of the historians.

When Karl Ritter tried to compare geographical forms it was the continents, the ancient divisions of the world, those creations of ancient history, that he had in his mind.[1] He looked on them complacently as so many " terrestrial individualities ". And it was massive Africa, with its rudimentary civilizations, which he compared with Europe, sharply demarcated, precocious, and refined, an old theme so often repeated since ; the whole, as if Europe, Asia, Africa, and America, those " unities " unknown to our modern geologists, botanists, or zoologists, were in truth anything but collections of heterogeneous fragments, incongruous assemblages of pieces.

This question of the divisions seems to be purely a matter of form : it is in reality of the first importance. It touches, as has been well shown, on the very conception that anyone has of geography, and with regard to this subject it would be well to re-read a remarkable article by M. P. Vidal de la Blache on *Les divisions fondamentales du sol français* which appeared in 1888 in a scholastic review [2] and was reproduced

[1] Cf. Mehedinti (S.), *La géographie comparée d'après Ritter et Peschel*, **XI**, 1901, p. 7.
[2] *Bulletin littéraire*, Vol. II, 1888–9.

later, in the form of an Introduction, at the beginning of a manual of secondary education.[1] But in the time of Ritter, and even later, no one knew of it.

It was in vain that even from the end of the eighteenth century Guettard, Monnet, and Giraud-Soulavie already had glimpses of the great idea of the natural region : M. L. Gallois' book established it conclusively.[2] In vain, later on, Coquebert de Montbret and Omalius d'Halloy tried to divide up the lands " by combining the nature and quality of the soil with their geographical position ". In vain, even, de Caumont, Antoine Passy, Dufrénoy, and Elie de Beaumont,[3] these last in 1841 in their celebrated " *Explication de la carte géologique* ", proclaimed with a singular boldness and foresight for men so badly equipped the bond which joined physical geography with geography strictly so called, on the one hand, and that which joined geography with geology on the other ; and justified the absolute necessity for the geographer to take true natural regions as the object of his study: this was the talk of geologists, and the geographers of the time did not seem to hear. It seemed to all of them more simple to install themselves like hermit-crabs in the old shells of political and administrative history. After describing France in its provinces, they dissected it into its departments. And far from trying to bring into nature some more rational principle of division, they were haunted by the altogether political idea of a linear frontier and a strict line of demarcation. " We have supposed France divided into ten principal parts which are called *Régions*," wrote the geographical editor of the *Statistique générale et particulière de la France* [4] in his *Introduction*, at the very beginning of the century. " This method has seemed to us all the more advantageous in that it is independent of all the divisions which politicians or the administration could consider useful." [5] Very good ; but

[1] *La France, cours de géographie à l'usage de l'enseignement secondaire*, by P. Vidal de la Blache and P. Camena d'Almeida, Paris.

[2] *Régions naturelles et noms de pays, étude sur la région parisienne*, Paris, 1908. Cf. Febvre (L.) in *Revue de Synthèse historique*, Vol. XVIII, 1908, p. 269.

[3] On all these precursors, cf. L. Gallois, **XXXIV**, p. 21 ff.

[4] *Statistique générale et particulière de la France et de ses colonies, avec une nouvelle description . . . de cet Etat, par une Société de gens de lettres et de savants*, edited by P. E. Herbin, Paris, year xii (1805), 7 vols.

[5] Op. cit., Vol. V, p. 1. The quotation is from Herbin.

he adds also: "Each of these ten regions is composed of an almost equal number of departments."

But why go back so far? Have we not also seen the belated disciples of Buache themselves distributing departments as best they could in the Procustean bed of "river basins" rigorously encircled by the "lines of the water-sheds"[1]—those mountain caterpillars which on the maps cross the "marshes of the Pripet", or run cheerfully from one end of Europe to the other, "from Cape Vaigatz to Cape Tarifa"?

Historians or geographers manifested the same exclusive care for forms, in the external or graphical sense of the word—in the sense which Ingres gave to it at the same period in his æsthetic controversies with Delacroix—but neither history nor geography knew anything then of Delacroix.

The relations between the soil and history have been mentioned. The soil, so to speak, was the bare soil, the pure soil, independent of its living covering of animals, plants, trees, and human beings. It was the ground-soil, the supporting floor, the great rigid stuff out of which States carved their domains. The sole interest it possessed for students was the consideration of these carved-out domains.

V

Survivals of the Past: Old Problems and Old Prejudices

We may seem to have digressed from Ratzel and the disputes between social morphology and human geography, in fact, from the very object of this book, but it is not so in reality.

In truth, our ideas of history and our ideas of geography have been profoundly changed to-day. It is no longer the political, judicial, and constitutional armour only of the people of times gone by, nor their military or diplomatic vicissitudes which we set ourselves patiently to trace. It is their whole life, their whole material and moral civilization, the whole evolution of their sciences, arts, religions, industries, trade, divisions, and social groupings. The history of agri-

[1] With regard to the theory of river basins, which was at that time an advance, cf. L. Gallois, op. cit.

culture alone and of the rural classes in their efforts to adapt themselves to the soil, in their long but discontinuous labour of clearing, deforestation, draining, and settlement—how many problems does it not raise, the solutions of which depend in part on geographical studies ? The enlargement of history, the development of geography : let people consider the effects of this double revolution which we have here indicated, and it will be understood that the whole problem of the relations between the soil and history can no longer be set for us as for the men of 1830 or 1860.

This will be understood, but it has not been generally understood as quickly or fully as it should have been—such a creature of tradition is man !

When, after the gradual creation of a human geography and its organization as a science, the historians were able to think of seeking its assistance, its representatives, when directly consulted on questions apparently of a geographical order by men to whose authority they had often submitted, did not immediately recognize that they ran the risk, in deserting their own domain, of allowing themselves to be led as hostages or prisoners on to ground which they had not chosen, and which was not their own. Their error was excusable, but it was a grave one.

Indeed, there can be no science unless students have full initiative. A science is not created by simply replying to a set of questions formulated from without in the name and the strict interests of another science. To collaborate assiduously with another science through the *Intermédiaire des chercheurs et des curieux* and to reply conscientiously to the questions of others—that does not constitute a science. It is open to historians to ask themselves, in their own name and on their own responsibility, what part geographical conditions played in the development of a special race—themselves regarding these conditions in advance as being given once for all and as forming a sort of blockade with permanent and always similar effects : geographers ought not to limit their ambition to satisfying such curiosity expertly. But how can we pretend that they have not done so ?

We have already called attention to the confusion, formerly so general and withal so natural, between political divisions and divisions properly geographical. Yet only yesterday a geographer described as a framework to his study "of physical geography and native civilizations" (its subtitle)[1] the political or rather the administrative limits of a section of a French colony, without any thought of investigating what "natural regions" there might be to delimit and characterize in the vast territory which he was considering!

We called attention also to the "graphic" prejudice if we may so call it, of Ritter, when he compared contours without troubling at all about their genesis, and spoke of continents "as one would in ethnography speak of a negro, or in botany of a palm-tree".[2] But in our own days and every day—a geographer quite recently again emphatically denounced the proceeding[3]—we see comparisons made between countries as different as Italy and Korea. A lover of forms, with gratified eye, will follow, on a map of very small scale in a scholar's atlas, the contours of these two peninsulas; he looks at them, describes them as equally lengthy, running in the same direction, divided in the same way by a chain of mountains, and to perfect the parallel, he compares the position of the two political centres, Seoul and Rome. We called attention lastly to the idea of predestination. There are still many books in which France, England, Italy, Spain, are described as so many geographical units whose truly providential homogeneity is pointed out, whilst Lorraine, Burgundy, Franche-Comté, and Provence figure in their turn as natural regions, as frames fashioned from all eternity to contain provinces—as if these same countries, these basic unities, these very ancient terrestrial individualities designated often by immemorial names ought not all to be examined with the most minute critical attention.

So the old prejudices are perpetuated. So the problems which time rejuvenates continue to be set in the traditional forms. And here precisely lies the error of Ratzel, in so far as there is an error. The author of the *Anthropogeographie* has not freed himself altogether from a bastard tradition, or rather, after using the most useful and strictly geographical

[1] Machat (F.), *Guinée Française. Les Rivières du Sud et le Fouta-Dialon*, Paris thesis, 1906.
[2] Mehedinti, op. cit., p. 5.
[3] Vallaux, **XCIII**, pp. 26–7.

part of his work to deal it the most fatal blow, he has not seen fit to repudiate it altogether.

There are in the *Anthropogeographie*, said Durkheim, three distinct orders of questions, the third very different from the other two. This is true, and the very remark, the statement of that difference, should perhaps have led its author to further reflection. In a similar case Vidal de la Blache, when considering the place of man in geography, says : " It is a question of studying in him one of the powerful agents which are at work upon the modification of the surfaces : a strictly and purely geographical question." [1] And, we would add, one which Buffon previously saw clearly and propounded vigorously. It is quite another question " to determine what influence geographical conditions have exercised on their destinies, and especially on their history ", to seek, as Ratzel said, the principles of the application of geography to history. In some cases, the distinction is the same. The error of the Leipzig professor was in not having made his choice between the two questions—in having collected, examined, and put them both together on an equal footing in his book.

And not only, we fear, in the *Anthropogeographie*, but perhaps even in the *Politische Geographie*, does the difficulty arise. This is evidently not the place to repeat a criticism, often made—and rightly made—of the confused and at times contradictory ideas of Ratzel about the predominant part that is played in the life of political organizations by pure space, space considered by itself and independent of the geographical characteristics which we think are generally inseparable from it. A concise exposition of them will be found not only in the *Politische Geographie*, but in the work entitled *Raum und Zeit in Geographie und Geologie* (*Naturphilosophische Betrachtungen*, Leipzig, 1907). But if Ratzel was the author of that theory, so eminently vulnerable that he himself has elsewhere, in his own book, destroyed it, it was because a political idea obsessed him [2] ; it was because a traditional idea was imposed on him ; it was because, in surveying all the states scattered over the surface of the

[1] Vidal, **XXXIII**, p. 298.
[2] Cf. especially Vallaux, **XCIII**, Ch. V, p. 145 ff., and Brunhes and Vallaux, **LXVIII**, Ch. VII, p. 269 ff.

globe, he reduced their multiple, rich, and varied life to a single manifestation; to the desire, the hope, and the permanent greed for extension—a scientific term to designate simply the ambition to conquer—that essential sign, according to Ratzel, that infallible criterion of vitality and of greatness in States. But who does not recognize here, in spite of a learned and quite philosophic transformation, the old attitude which we have just remarked, the overwhelming and exclusive care for external shapes, boundaries geographically defined, "outlines"—obedience, in a word, to the suggestions of political and territorial history?

In reviewing a book by Arnold Guyot,[1] Ampère wrote: "M. Guyot has tried to explain history by geography." "This statement," Vidal de la Blache declares vigorously,[2] in quoting the words, "if it were well founded, would not be more reasonable than to leave out geography in the explanation of history." Nothing could be truer. Historical facts and geographical facts are for us to-day two different orders. It is impossible and absurd to attempt to intercalate members of the one series in the other—like so many links or interchangeable rings. There are two chains: they must remain separate, or else why distinguish them?

To grasp and reveal, at each instant of their duration, the complex relations of men, the actors in and the creators of history, with organic and inorganic nature, and with the many factors of their physical and biological environment, is the proper rôle of the geographer when he sets to work on human problems or researches; we intend to attempt to show this more fully. Such is his task. He could have others only by usurpation or capitulation. At the beginning and even in the middle of last century historians had no clear idea of this. Whence could they have obtained it? To geography, which existed only as a descriptive science, as a list of names, they set questions solely in the interests of their own work. Generally they answered these themselves as historians; the geographers of their time would not have answered them otherwise. But when geographers to-day, forgetting the advance due to their own efforts, still dally

[1] On Guyot, cf. Ratzel, **LXXXIII**, I, 2nd ed., p. 37.
[2] **XI**, 1905, p. 196, n. 1.

over similar problems always set in the traditional manner, and when some sociologists, while allowing certain "reasonable" restrictions and limitations, consider themselves as being fundamentally candidates for the geographer's entire heritage, it is no doubt easy to grasp both the cause and the difficulties of such a situation. And so we see plainly that the dispute on method, and even the history of the facts, have another value than that of mere curiosity.

VI

A Modest Human Geography

Our geography, in fact, no more follows that of the Bourbon Restoration than our history treads in the footsteps of Augustin Thierry. What is its task, and in what spirit is that conceived? How is it conceived by those of our geographers who do not willingly step into Ratzel's shoes, and who, having arrived by slow stages (not however without much groping, as we have had occasion to point out previously), at a firm conception of geography, of its aims, and of its methods, are not liable to metaphysical intoxication? A rapid indication of this, attacking the very fundamentals of the problem, will be the best means of clearing up the charge of "ambition" which we undertook to discuss.

"Geography," wrote Vidal de la Blache, the head of our French school of geography, in 1913—that is to say, towards the end of his life and at a time when he had fully elaborated his method—"geography, getting its inspiration, like its kindred sciences (N.B., 'like the other *natural* sciences'), from the idea of terrestrial unity, has for its special mission to find out how the physical and biological laws which govern the world are combined and modified in their application to different parts of the surface of the earth. It has for its special charge to study the changing expressions which, according to the locality, the appearance of the earth assumes." [1]

This definition would have charmed Alexander von Humboldt, the founder of botanical geography, and author of

[1] **XXXIII**, p. 291.

De distributione geographica plantarum secundum caeli temperiem et altitudinem montium,[1] who always gave so much attention in his travels and writings to the analysis of landscapes. We know well enough that Vidal de la Blache himself excelled in such analysis[2]: and also that he had made a long study of the works of Humboldt, as well as those of Ritter. A remarkable coincidence: we read, in an interesting and original thesis of the same date, this statement: "We willingly acknowledge that the whole of geography lies in the analysis of landscape"; and further on, "all the ideas of the bio-geographer are drawn from the contemplation of landscape."[3] The aphorisms are interesting, whatever reservations they may evoke; but do they not exclude from the domain of geography the whole mass of problems which are connected with man and human societies? By no means: the very geographer from whom we have just quoted two passages betraying the influence on his thought of a geo-botanist—Ch. Flahault—implicitly avows it: "the other means of knowledge," he declares, "the plundering of statistics, and the historical analysis of the evolution of human groups according to the documents of archives, serve only to give precision, to complete, and to rectify the ideas which we draw from the direct study of nature." The evolution of human groups according to documentary archives! But where do the archives come into the landscape? It is because man, by the same right as the tree,[4] and by better, fuller, and different rights, is one of the essential factors of the landscape.

Man is a geographical agent, and not the least. He everywhere contributes his share towards investing the physiognomy of the earth with those "changing expressions" which it is "the special charge" of geography to study. Through centuries and centuries, by his accumulated labour and the boldness and decision of his undertakings, he appears to us as one of the most powerful agents in the modification of terrestrial surfaces. There is no power which he does not

[1] Paris, 1817.
[2] A. Demangeon, "Vidal de la Blache," p. 8 (*Revue universitaire*, June, 1918).
[3] Sorre, **CCXXX**, p. 10.
[4] Ibid., p. 39.

utilize and direct at will; there is no country, it has been said, which does not bear the marks of his intervention. He acts on the soil as an individual. He acts on it still more collectively —by means of all his groups, from the least to the greatest, from the family groups to the political ones. And this action of man on his environment is the part which man plays in geography.

Vidal de la Blache, in the article previously quoted, insists that "Geography is the science of places, not of men".[1] Historical analyses of the evolution of human groups from documentary archives. . . . Yes, geography ought to obtain the aid of such analyses, and such documents; but what it ought to expect from them is not information as to the part played by the soil in that evolution, nor the influence which geographical conditions are able to exercise in the course of time on the destinies and even on the history of peoples; but assistance in determining what action the peoples, the groups, and the societies of men have been able to exercise, and, in fact, have exercised, on the environment. "To explain the geographical phenomena of which man has been the witness or the contriver, it is necessary to study their evolution in the past by the aid of documents." These are the words of Demangeon.[2] We see that he, too, does not abandon geographical ground in order to obtain his perspective.

"Geography," continues Vidal de la Blache, "is interested in the events of history in so far as they stimulate and reveal, in the countries where they occur, peculiar qualities and potential powers which without them would have remained latent." This definition, as anyone may see, is purely, strictly, egoistically geographical. And this time the point of view is perfectly clear. "Geography is the science of places, not of men." Here, in truth, we have the anchor of safety.

If we re-examine now the criticisms mentioned previously, do they still possess the same bearing? Evidently not.

We see what a danger there is to anyone who studies the action of geographical conditions on the structure of social

[1] Vidal, **XXXIII**, p. 298.
[2] "Les Recherches géographiques dans les Archives" (**XI**, 1907, p. 193 ff.). Cf. also *Les Sources de la géographie de la France aux Archives nationales*, Paris, 1905.

groups, of losing his way; we mean, of attributing a value of first-rate importance, not merely decisive, but unique, to these geographical conditions. He is not unlikely to see in them "the cause" of a certain social structure, of whose ubiquity he may be ignorant. But let us reverse the terms and ask ourselves, not what is the action of social groups on the geographical environment but, with much more precision and scruple—geography being the science of places—what features of a given "landscape", of a geographical ensemble directly grasped or historically reconstituted, are explained or can be explained by the continued action, positive or negative, of a certain group, or of a certain form of social organization. Let us, for instance, having established the unnatural extension in ancient times of certain crops to countries where their cultivation seemed to be impossible, connect that fact with the regimen of isolation, under which all human groups strive above all things to be self-supporting and not to buy anything from others. In that case, if we are prudent, we run no risk of error, or confusion, or improper generalization. We say "If we are prudent": it would have been better to say "If we are not exclusive". For the vine in Morvan,[1] so widespread in the Middle Ages that a commune of the canton of Toulon-sur-Arroux, Sanvignes (*Sine Vinea,* says a register of benefices of the fourteenth century, quoted by de Charmasse), took its name from a radical, absolute and almost unique incapacity of the soil to nourish that plant of hot climates—the vine, there, as in Normandy and Flanders,[2] was a result of the regimen of isolation; and, in this connexion, we may also note the influence exercised on that paradoxical culture by the practice of mixing with the wine, honey, cinnamon, and coriander, which turned it into hypocras and masked the native roughness of the most unsatisfactory vineyards.

* * *

In reality, if we wish to regard it from the point of view of man—but it must be understood that this is only one

[1] De Charmasse, *Cartulaire d'Autun*, I, 2, p. 74, and Levainville, **CCXXV**, p. 152.

[2] Sion, **CCXXIX**, p. 149; Musset, "Limite de la culture de la vigne dans l'Ouest de la France," XI, 1908, p. 268; Blanchard, **CCXVII**, pp. 37–8.

point of view among many others—what geography studies, and what it informs us about, is the environment in which human life is unfolded. In the first place it describes, then it analyses, then it tries to explain that life, by a continual attention to repercussions and interferences. It includes even man, through his works; works of destruction and of creation, personal works, and indirect works. It includes him in precisely the same degree as he acts on his environment wherever he sets his mark on it, and modifies it by adapting it to himself.

It does not say, and it ought not to say: "A man's house is explained by the soil." It states, and it ought to state, simply: "That house, a building sometimes humble, sometimes stately and complicated, at once novel and traditional in character, which as such escapes the clutch of the geographer, belongs nevertheless to the landscape, depends on the geographical environment, and is adapted to it by certain elements, certain arrangements, and certain secondary or fundamental characteristics, and by that and by that only it becomes amenable to my jurisdiction."

Similarly it does not say, and it should not say: "The growth, the extension, the evolution of this State is explained by the soil which it occupies, by certain advantages of position or of situation." No, for naturally enough the sociologists would come forward and say: "Who but a sociologist should know everything that concerns the material structure of groups and the manner in which their elements are distributed in space? And this is in fact the object of a special sociological science: social morphology."

The soil, not the State: to this geography must confine itself. And just as it can reach and lay hold of those immaterial things, institutions, through the medium of the objects which bring them to light, and which the ethnographer collects and classes in his museums, so it must do with human and political societies: it does not lay hold of them directly, but by the traces they mark on the surface of the earth, and by the imprint they leave there. It is, so to speak, their projection upon the soil.[1] What of the rest?

[1] The phrase is Simmel's: "Räumliche Projectionen socialer Formen" is the title of an article in the *Zeitschrift f. Social-Wissenschaft* of 1903, Vol. V, p. 287 ff.

As to the rest, all are at liberty to draw upon the labours of geographers in their general treatises or their regional monographs for the elements of their personal structures. The savant who proposes to explain in terms of soil and climate the formation of the instincts which he studies, and the features from which he synthesizes—as Boutmy, for example, explained the collective physiognomy of the English or the American people—is at liberty to borrow from geographical studies of England the facts and elements which he will combine after his own fashion, and for his own purposes. But it is collective ethology [1] that he is thus producing, not geography. He handles geographical ideas, no doubt, but he handles them as an ethologist and for ends which are not geographical.

Similarly, the sociologist who, "looking on societies as mere groups of men organized at fixed points of the earth," does not fall into the error "of considering them as if they were independent of their territorial base" is at liberty to inquire to what extent "the configuration of the soil, its mineral riches, its fauna, and its flora affect their organization".[2] He also will be handling geographical ideas, which he will take ready elaborated from the books of geographers; but he will handle them as a morphologist, and for ends which will not be geographical.

To put it another way: social morphology cannot hope to suppress human geography to its own profit, because the two studies have neither the same method, the same tendency, nor the same object.

[1] Berr, **XX**, 85 ff.
[2] Mauss, **CCXV**, p. 42.

CHAPTER II

THE QUESTION OF PRINCIPLE AND THE METHOD OF RESEARCH—HUMAN EVOLUTION, HISTORIC EVOLUTION

YOU have wisely thrown out ballast, we shall be told. It is plain that by taking things in this way, by reducing geographical pretensions to their lowest terms, by claiming for anthropogeographers merely a share, sometimes more, sometimes less, of collaboration in a work of general explanation, you escape that reproach of ambition which sociologists bring so vehemently against those whom they all confuse, either purposely or carelessly, with the impenitent Ratzelians.

Yes, we escape it—but only to expose ourselves to objections of another nature. There are two of these, more especially, which we must now state as clearly as possible, and discuss. One concerns the principle. There is, of course, nothing irremediable in the errors with which sociologists reproach geographers, who are taxed by them with ambition in every sense of the word. If the latter claim simply for geography—as they are doing more and more, and with good reason—a variable share in the explanation of facts infinitely complex, without deriving them from the mechanical action of a rigorous determinism, they will be free from the charge. But they will not create a science by so doing. This, it is plain, is a fundamental objection, and one which must be closely examined. The other, though merely a question of method, is not less serious: geographers, faced with inextricably involved and complex phenomena, study them as they are presented, alleging that the different series of which they are composed act and react and so among themselves explain one another. This is an error of method. The true line to follow would be to analyse the complexes minutely, to decompose them into their several elements, and to study these one by one in a definite manner, separating each one from all the others, and using a strictly comparative method. This could be done by social morphology. Geography confesses itself powerless to accomplish such a work.

Once more we repeat that to state and then discuss such grievances is not to indulge in a purely academic debate on methodology. It is to acquaint ourselves, in a specially vivid manner, with the very foundation of the question which concerns us.

I

The Objection of Principle: Is there a Science of Geography?

The chief complaint—which we may call the complaint of principle—has been stated with most trenchant vigour by Simiand, notably in a detailed critical account of a certain number of geographical works,[1] particularly the regional monographs of Demangeon on Picardy, of Blanchard on Flanders, of Vallaux, Vacher, and Sion on Lower Brittany, Berry, and the peasants of Eastern Normandy.[2] His argument is as follows; we give it in his own words:—"The whole essence of the geographical explanations which our authors try to give of the facts or economic institutions which they are considering, plainly consists, in brief, in reducing them to certain of their technical conditions (raw materials, tools, etc.), and in showing that these technical conditions conform to the physical conditions of the observed region, or closely depend upon them." But "the fact that there are sheep in a country does not suffice to explain the possession of a woollen industry". Similarly, "it does not follow that because there is a watercourse men will know how to utilize it, and desire to do so, nor that because there is arable land men will know how to till it, and desire to do so." Lastly, "our geographers themselves furnish us with typical examples which tell in exactly the opposite sense to the geographical thesis." Is one wanted? It is "Demangeon who tells us of an iron industry installing itself [*sic*] in a country where there is neither iron nor coal (*La Picardie et les régions voisines*,

[1] **XVII,** Vol. XI, 1906–9, p. 729 ff.
[2] Bibliography, Nos. **CCXXIV, CCXVII, CCXXXI, CCXXIX.**

pp. 286 ff.) and finds nothing to explain it but the amount of labour available, a state of things which is found in many other countries where no industry springs up, and which, moreover, remains a possible condition only, and not an explanation ". That last word should be borne in mind.

We imagine that Simiand does not attach any very great importance to his grievances against " our authors ", as he calls them. What he wishes to call attention to is this : that the economic fact does not necessarily result from the technical conditions, and does not depend " on the things themselves ", but " on the ideas of men about those things " ; these are first truths which have for a long time been taught to children in geography classes. And we can understand that sometimes geographers, in their adventurous folly, still seem to pay too little regard to the principles which they teach elsewhere. These slight failings may be regrettable, but they do not warrant the charge of an error in principle.

Then there is the reproach which Simiand levels, directly and by name, at Demangeon. Here, he says, is a geographer who proposes to " study in a definite geographical region the mutual relations of man and Nature ". After a careful, precise, and detailed study of the physical conditions of that region, he reviews first its agriculture, then its industries, with the object of finding out what they both may, or may not, owe to the geographical environment. He finds, firmly planted in one of the " districts " he examines, a metallurgical industry which plays a prominent part in the life of the men of that country ; as a geographer he asks himself whether there is not some geographical reason for the existence of that industry : he makes his inquiries in all good faith and scientific sincerity, without any preconceived ideas, and concludes that there is none.[1] A striking proof, it seems to us, that the geographer is not " necessarily " led, as Durkheim asserts, " to exaggerate the importance of the geographical factor." The result, moreover, is a most interesting one, scientifically speaking, although (or because) negative, since the inquiry conducted by a geographer results in showing that there is no place for geography to intervene in the explanation of a certain fact of an economic order—the fact is established

[1] Simiand, **XVII**, Vol. XI, p. 724.

(always supposing that the inquirer has not erred through ignorance or carelessness), and now the ground is left free for other scholars, each in the name of his own science and with his own methods. It is for them in their turn to take up the inquiry, for them to continue the research further, each one taking his share; they are merely warned that the geographers give it up. . . . What more simple, more natural, or more legitimate?

Why, therefore, these reproaches that are explained with such difficulty? For this reason, apparently: because the sociologist has constructed an ideal human geography for himself. It is against this that his criticisms are directed. They attack geography, not such as it is found in the hands of Demangeon, Vallaux, or Sion, but such as the sociologist chooses to conceive it. One word in the argument of Simiand, indeed, needs particular notice. "The example furnished by M. Demangeon," he says, "tells in exactly the opposite sense to the geographical thesis." The geographical thesis? What thesis?

Demangeon proves that the origin and development of iron-working in the Vimeu cannot be explained by the presence of iron or coal. He says so. What thesis then is it that the example discredits? It can only be a general one which might be formulated in these words: "There is no industry which is not essentially due to causes of a geographical order."

But should anyone chance to come across this statement—a pure hypothesis—in some badly written pamphlet, or some over-ambitious programme of human geography, what real value, what convincing power would it have? The valuable part of the labours of geographers is their work and its results, not what they themselves say nor what they think about it. But now that we have made this reservation, which is altogether a theoretical one, let us return to the argument: where is this thesis to be found? Whose is it? Is it to be found anywhere in the works of the author criticized? If so, in what page and what line?

To return to Demangeon—since it is he, really, who is in the dock—did he say at the beginning of his thesis: "I propose to show that geography alone explains and is sufficient to explain all the manifestations of the economic activity of men in the plain of Picardy?" If he did say so, the case need go no farther—though with the reservation we noted a few lines above. But he did not say so, any more than Vallaux, another of the geographers taken to task by the sociologist, began his book on *le Sol et l'Etat* with the heading: "the theory of a strict physical determinism, which would keep the life of States in the straight paths traced for them in advance by nature." On the contrary, he starts with this formal declaration: "There is no single political society within the limits of the *œcumene* whose evolution has been rigorously determined by the soil on which it lives and the surroundings among which it moves."[1] But it is not a question of a theoretical statement only; the whole book is written in a spirit of hostility to the exaggerations of Ratzelian determinism, and shows, moreover, a vigorous spirit of criticism and scientific impartiality.

What Simiand assumes, imagines, and attacks, has not been said by either Vallaux or Demangeon. Very well, then, they were wrong not to have said it!—that is what, as a good logician, the sociologist could and should have claimed. They are wrong because they claim to be composing a scientific work: because they write geographical books, and this geography, they say, is a science, an explanatory science, a search for causes. Still, if they limit themselves to declaring with Vidal de la Blache—whose clear statements we quoted above—that in the present aspect of our old historic countries, where causes of all orders cross and interfere with one another, we find "groups of causes and effects", but without any of them being subject to anything resembling a "total impression of necessity", if they claim for their particular method of investigation, that is for geographical analysis, simply "its share in the explanation of very complex facts", they are judged. For by that very modesty, by that moderation, they abandon the idea of an explanatory science in the full sense of the word. They will obtain "possible conditions" not "explanations". The words are Simiand's[2]: we think that by these alone we are justified in having quoted their

[1] Vallaux, **XCIII**, p. 18.
[2] Loc. cit., p. 720; for the force of the word "explanations" see Berr, **XX**, p. 50.

author as fully as we have done. Thus, behind this conflict in the last analysis, lies a certain strict, rigid, absolute conception of causality.

II

Geography makes no Claim to be a Science of Necessities

The question is too large to be formulated and discussed in a few lines, nor is that our intention, as may well be supposed. But it has been so often disputed amongst scholars and logicians,[1] and antagonistic views have so often been presented, maintained, and developed, that we may indicate in a few words which one we are here adopting.

"The same conditions have the same results." Causality may thus be defined very simply, and we might perhaps even find a definition still more concise. It brings to mind the very suggestive lecture by M. P. Langevin on The Evolution of Space and Time,[2] and the discussion which followed at the French Philosophical Society [3] on "Time, Space, and Causality in Modern Physics". But the elaboration of such ideas is a work which is not done on the spur of the moment, and which moreover we cannot think of undertaking here. "The same conditions have the same results." If that definition be accepted, the whole discussion rests on the single word "conditions". Not that the word is obscure, or that there is any doubt about its meaning. A determinant cause is the ensemble of the phenomenal conditions which determine a phenomenon. According to a saying of Laplace, which has often been repeated lately, "the universe to anyone who looked on it just as it is would only be a single great fact." From which it follows, they say,[4] "that every fact is, so to speak, embedded in that single reality," and that the determinant cause consists "in an indefinite number of conditions". There is no difficulty on that point. But can

[1] Cf. particularly Berr, **XX**, introduction to Part II; and also **XXI**, p. 42 ff.
[2] **XIX**, Vol. X, 1911.
[3] *Bulletin de la Société*, January, 1912.
[4] Berr, **XX**, p. 47.

the geographer really discover conditions which are simple and, so to speak, abstract? That is the true question.

The sociologist denies him that power. But he claims to possess it himself—he alone. And that because, unlike the geographer, he defines his aim: to disengage a function whose different states he will have to seek in time and space. So be it; but where will he get even a first idea of those functions?

Is he going to deduce it? But on what principle, on what pre-determined authoritative classification? (Like some diplomat in his office in London or Paris who lays down a colonial frontier with rule and compasses according to latitude and longitude!) Is he going to work it out, like the physicist, by experiment? But then he must make that experiment clear—or rather the innumerable preliminary experiments necessary before the scientific experiment can be launched. And first he must take matters as a complex whole, and specialists, before they start pulling out the threads one by one, unravelling the tangled skein, each according to his personal dexterity and ingenuity, must give up pulling out one here and one there, at their own sweet will; must give up their individual hesitations and tentatives, false moves and haphazard search. And then, when that is done, when, after that long toil and research with full experience and a full supply of facts, the different orders of factors have been isolated and determined to the supreme joy of the classifiers, it may easily happen that they must again be resolved in terms of each other, thrown into the common stock, and distributed in new systems: this is what happens, for example, in biology. So that, after all, there is always the same preliminary need for the sociologist or the geographer to devote himself to the same uncertain and troublesome labours if he wishes his work to be real and efficient. And by so devoting himself, he undoubtedly does scientific work, in the strict sense of the word.

Are we alone in thinking so? Can this protest against the narrowness of the idea of causality, which claims to be exclusively scientific, be drawn up against geography alone? In a recent book, full of these questions of method, and entirely devoted to the objections, criticisms, and deductions of the active sociological school of Durkheim, Henri Berr, at the close of his study of what he calls " the articulations of historic synthesis," says[1]: "We have shown that the work of the objective sociologists has the fault of being too exclusive, but that, considered as a methodical effort to prove conclusively 'that society is a factor, and an important factor, in history', it accomplishes a legitimate and necessary task. We may admit that different classes of workers take different points of view and devote themselves to the study of a certain class of causes, and that each directs the search for the part played by the different factors as far as possible in the direction he has especially chosen. We may admit it; but if the research is to have any real efficacy, although specialized, it must be made free from all prejudices, and must take account of the opposition of other factors. It must be prosecuted to the uttermost, without claiming more than its due."

In applying these reflections to geography and reproducing them as a conclusion to our own dispute, are we misled by a merely formal reconciliation? We know quite well that Berr was thinking chiefly of the organization of work and of the method of research. But may we not couple his remarks with those which we ourselves have previously made?

In reality, when we read carefully the most recent works of our qualified geographers, when we follow them in their researches, when we fully understand their methods and the spirit in which their work is done, and then, when we afterwards hear the often disconcerting criticisms of the *Année*, we can reckon, with full assurance, that a word like Durkheim's "necessarily" meant to him, not practical necessity, but a logical and theoretical necessity. And in the same way, if we wished to prolong the debate, very similar remarks might be made about Simiand's criticisms on the theory, so familiar to geographers, "that man acts on nature as much as nature acts on man." But why should we trouble to insist on it?

A great and profound misunderstanding separates geographers and sociologists. Whilst the former are striving more and more to avoid in their researches anything like systematic deduction, whilst they seek simply to analyse actual situations because these happen to interest them, without any preconceived ideas and foregone conclusions of theoretical

[1] **XX**, p. 227.

simplification, whilst all their efforts are directed to freeing themselves from the narrow idea of a strict and, so to speak, mechanical determinism, the latter, whatever they may do or say, do not manage to free themselves from some kind of "passivist" conception of the mutual actions and reactions of men and their environment. Are we wrong? Do we exaggerate? But, when Mauss, for instance, grants us that it is legitimate, useful, and scientific to study to what extent "the configuration of the soil, its material wealth, its fauna, and its flora affect the organization" of men, or when Durkheim, condescendingly enough, grants that if "*certain particularities* of economic life depend on the fauna and the flora, it is the economist who should be aware of it", what conception do they then express?

The language is, in fact, materialistic, and the conception is materialistic. We know quite well that they are not the only people to use it. They are in good company, as we have already said, with the greater part of the historians who are absorbed in these questions—and even, at times, with more or less qualified geographers. In Brunhes's *Géographie humaine* we read the following passage: "According as human groups are placed in certain geographical frameworks, they are obliged to grow certain crops; here palms, there rice, there wheat; here they are compelled to raise horses and mares, as in the grassy steppes of Central Asia; there animals of the bovine species, as in the mountains of Central Europe, or in the islands of Lake Chad, or on the shores of Lake Rudolph; elsewhere sheep, as on the lofty, dry plateau of Spain or Barbary."[1] A good application, obviously, of the eminently exceptionable theory of passive adaptation—if the expression "are compelled" does not in reality give the author away. But for anyone who follows the efforts of the great majority of his colleagues (and as a rule, his own as well) it is legitimate to speak by contrast of a kind of "geographical spiritualism"—in the sense in which "economic spiritualism" is used with reference to Karl Marx and Engels and their theory of value, and which is really Marxism.[2]

The initiative and mobility of man: these are what geographers to-day are striving to bring into prominence.

[1] **LXVI**, p. 58. [2] Rauh, **XXVI**, p. 71.

They are not striving to show us beings passive under the dominant influence of environment and controlled throughout their whole public and private histories or personal existence by a number of natural forces whose action is direct and whose effect is immediate. In the same way, they no longer regard the land and the soil as an assemblage of fixed frameworks, a number of closed compartments inside which distinct races retire, live, and fight each other. But, on the contrary, they regard the land and the soil as powerful agents in the fusion of races; for affinity alone takes no account of states, but of the real interests which result from the domain inhabited—in the same way, they think and know, according to the zoologist Jacobi, that "the dependence of beings in relation to their substratum—the terrestrial soil—is the cause of the great movements of those beings on the planet". This is true of animals—and human societies are animal societies: and nothing better or more surely destroys the old pernicious notion of beings "acted on" passively by physical environments.

Such is the argument, such the opposition. And we think that we have already accomplished a great deal in setting it out clearly for all to see.

III

The Question of Regional Monographs

There is, as we said above, a second complaint which sociologists readily lodge against geographers: this is a complaint as to method.

At the end of his long and interesting criticism of the regional monographs of the French school, Simiand concludes as follows[1]: "Let us imagine, on the contrary, that instead of attacking a problem which at present (and no doubt for a long time to come) is so insoluble"—the problem, that is, of the relations which exist between nature and man in a definite geographical region—"the same men . . . had set themselves to study, one the forms of the dwellings, another

[1] **XVII**, Vol. XI, 1906–9, p. 732.

the distribution of houses and groups of houses, another the localization of certain industries, etc., each one for the whole of France, or even, if necessary, of Western Europe, at the present time, and also, as would no doubt be necessary, in the past: is it not probable that they would have arrived at a perception and even a clear establishment of more conclusive relations, and would have penetrated more quickly and surely into the heart of such phenomena as the science of social morphology may legitimately undertake the task of explaining?" The suggestion is not a new one. Nor the dispute. The same Simiand had already, in 1903, delivered a vigorous attack, in the second of two articles in the *Revue de Synthèse* which made some stir at the time—(they had for their title: *Méthode historique et Science sociale*, and for their sub-title: *Étude critique d'après les ouvrages récents de M. Lacombe et de M. Seignobos*)—on a favourite idea of historians: what he called the social *Zusammenhang*. "The frame of the traditional historical work," he wrote, "is defended with more plausibility by recent methodologists, in the name of a principle which merits serious consideration. The different orders of facts which can be distinguished in the life of a society have not an entirely independent existence or evolution: they maintain among themselves certain relations of harmony or of reciprocal influence: they are bound together by a *Zusammenhang*, which is an essential element in their explanation." [1] This is what Hauser is translating in his own way, when he says that [2]: "In social life everything is bound together. At any moment whatever, amongst any people whatever, there exists a strict solidarity between the private, economic, judicial, religious, and political institutions, and the variations in these different characteristics are found associated with the social species as with the animal species." But, replies Simiand, "they tell us that it is history alone whose traditional method assures the recognition of that bond, and which thus furnishes the most exact picture of a given social life." An error, a profound error in the eyes of the sociologist, who immediately sets up the new comparative method in opposition to the traditional historical one.

[1] **XVII**, Vol. VI, 1903, p. 134 ff.
[2] Hauser, **XXIII**, p. 114.

"The conquest of the world, the advent to power of the *homines novi*, the modifications introduced into citizen ownership and the *patria potestas*, the formation of an urban plebs, the invasion of Italy by the arts of Greece and the Eastern religions, the degeneration of the old Latin manners, Scipio Æmilianus, Cato, the *Græculi*, the Bacchanalian court, Plautus and Ennius—all these together form an inseparable *complexus*, all these facts explain one another much better than the evolution of the Roman family is explained by that of the Jewish family, or the Chinese, or the Aztec." Thus the thesis of the historians, as formulated by Hauser.[1] But Simiand says that "to limit and confine a study to a single society in order to exhibit the social *Zusammenhang* is to condemn it in advance never to be established. Causal relation can only exist where there is regular connexion and if there is an identical repetition of the stated relation. The unique case *has no cause*, and is not scientifically explicable".[2] The two theses clash; but who does not sense in advance the opposition which Simiand sets up anew between his idea of analytical and comparative morphological studies and the watertight conceptions of the "regionalist geographers"?

There is something, to be sure, in Simiand's criticisms. But I am afraid that they are less applicable to the geographers than to the historians. In the first place, we are well aware of the ingeniously malicious explanation which he gives "of the affection of the methodological historians for this determination of the *Zusammenhang*, thus understood". If they think so much of it, it is, in his opinion, because this badly analysed idea allows them "to continue the traditional grouping of human facts according to regions, nations, and political unities", and shows in this way their continued need "of borrowing their fundamental frameworks from political history and making all the other orders of facts fit in with it, however badly".[3] But the remark certainly does not apply to those geographers who prove themselves scrupulously careful to respect the great principle: "geographical divisions must be purely geographical."[4]

In the second place it is evident, as has been said, "that if the author of a regional monograph has a too restricted

[1] Ibid., p. 414.
[2] **XVIII**, Vol. VI, 1903, p. 138.
[3] Op. cit., pp. 133–4.
[4] Vidal, **XXX**, p. 9.

horizon, abstains from all comparisons, and, in addition, embraces in his explanations too large a number of human facts he is liable to deceive himself about the relations which he claims to establish between certain geographical characteristics and certain social phenomena." [1] But this, after all, merely amounts to saying that a good geographer requires some intelligence and a certain geographical training, which, we imagine, is self-evident. For we should like to know which of the authors whom Simiand quotes and criticizes is the one who has never had any curiosity except about his own region—Picardy or Flanders, Eastern Normandy or Lower Brittany—and who is so new to his studies that he does not know, for instance, what the monographs of his predecessors have already established about the relations between the dwelling and the environment.

Lastly, we quite understand that the idea of Simiand is shared by some geographers—that it is expressed, for example, by the author of a treatise on irrigation [2] which, however, is not exactly a regional monograph. Brunhes writes in his manual of human geography [3]—inspired, moreover, by an article of Vidal de la Blache: "in my opinion, regional geography should crown and not initiate geographical research." [4] May we say, however, that neither this advice nor these authorities entirely convince us?

*

* *

Let us return now to the problem of the house. To study the forms of dwellings, or the distribution of houses and villages over the whole of France. . . . The task is indeed formidable: much more formidable even, and more chimerical, in spite of appearances, than that of reconstituting "the whole of a region", and trying "to grasp it all and explain it all at the same time". [5] This is a question of a practical order. The value of the chapters which regional geographers write on houses lies precisely in the fact that they are "chapters" of a whole: that their authors have acquired and show a perfect preliminary acquaintance with the region

[1] Berr, **XX**, p. 93.
[2] Brunhes, **CI.**
[3] Brunhes, **LXVI**, p. 615.
[4] Vidal, **XXXI.**
[5] Simiand, op. cit., 732.

and its various characteristics: that they have made a long and minute analysis of the extremely different elements which may be found and are found in the human house. But to entrust them with the task of studying the houses in all the regions of a territory like France—or even like Western Europe—is to condemn them to ignorance of any but the most obvious realities, and to make the work easy, commonplace, superficial, and paltry—a second-hand work which any man of medium intelligence could perform on the subject without any special training; or else to condemn them to a detailed, profound, and personal knowledge of each region, to a full and minute study, only a very small part of which would afterwards be of any use: a task evidently absurd and impossible.[1]

There is here then a problem of the rational organization of the labour. When we possess yet more good new regional monographs, then, and then only, by grouping and comparing them with the utmost care shall we be able to take up the general question, and to make a fresh and decided advance towards our end. To proceed in any other way would mean setting out on a kind of rapid excursion, fitted out with two or three simple and large ideas. It would mean passing over, in most cases, anything peculiar, individual, or irregular—that is to say, in short, all that is most interesting. It would almost inevitably mean a concession to that "mania for classification" which a geographer of great ability denounced not long ago. "A mania for classification"—let there be no mistake about it: the phrase is addressed to geographers only; and the example which Gautier gives is a strictly geographical one. It concerns the formation of the dunes in the Sahara, in reference to which the author points out the difficulty we always experience "in conceiving the complexity of a natural process".[2] "Because the dunes are formed by the wind, the wind must be made to explain everything, not only the exterior shape of the dunes, but even the formation of the sand which composes them."

[1] It is interesting to compare with the chapters on "the house" by various French regionalist geographers, the best contributions which are contained in the two volumes of the *Enquête sur les conditions de l'habitation en France* by the Committee of Historical and Scientific Works, an inquiry prefaced by a list of questions and an introduction by A. de Foville, **CLXIV** and **CLXIVa**.

[2] E. F. Gautier, "Etudes sahariennes," **XI**, 1907, p. 123.

Nothing could be truer. As soon as we seek the causes of a fact in physical geography, we see their number and their complexity. Take, for instance, the question of the extreme dryness of the Australian desert. It is not enough to adduce the scanty rainfall.[1] The most important factors are great heat and dry winds; allowance must also be made for the massive nature of the continent, the topographical and structural details, the absence of any interior relief, the existence of important mountains on the Eastern side only, the position of Australia in the track of the trade wind, and, when that trade wind is interrupted and replaced by rainy winds, of the slight force of those aerial currents, and the predominance of the dry South-East winds over the monsoons from the North-West, and a number of other phenomena. And could one expect that in human geography a single analytic and comparative formula, without any regional and synthetic basis, would suffice?

Emphatically, no: we need not here place the two methods face to face, and show how irreconcilable they are. Regional studies which excluded all comparison would be valueless, if they were really possible. But, as it has been well said, "it is no less true than it is legitimate and necessary to proceed with studies arising from geography—contingent, but of a geographical nature," and that, inversely, "by starting from social phenomena, we tend to push the geographical factor too much into the background."[2] For sociology is not considered as a mere contributory factor by a sociologist.

IV

The Complete Solidarity of Political and Human Geography

The fact is that political history, economic history, and social history are closely bound together. In the same way there can be no political and historical geography without social geography, nor social geography without economic geography, nor economic geography without physical

[1] The whole of this is from the study by Lespagnol, **CCVII.**
[2] Berr, **XX**, p. 93.

geography. They are a linked and indivisible series, and the best qualified geographers have ever recognized the fact clearly.

It was quite a long time ago—in 1898, shortly after the appearance of the *Politische Geographie*, the year that Durkheim made a close examination of the work of Ratzel—that Vidal de la Blache declared that for his part " the facts of political geography still remain much too vague, unless they are adapted to physical geography ".[1] And he added " We firmly believe, for our part, that nothing could be more definitely advantageous for political geography than the very remarkable development which is taking place under our eyes in the physical study of the globe. The relations between man and the environment in which he exercises his activity cannot fail to be more clearly revealed, as we come to make fewer blunders about the study of forms, climates, and the distribution of life ".

This was quite definite, and on this point his doctrine has never varied. Several years afterwards, in an article on the teaching of geography, Vidal de la Blache again wrote: " Human geography ought not to be treated as a sort of epilogue. If physical geography is its foundation, it in itself supports these economic facts, which are the rule of modern life. To the testimony that language and history bring to the knowledge of human societies, natural conditions and environment add their share."[2] And Gallois, also, in a book we have often quoted, says[3] " When we wish to explain human facts, we must always consider the possible influence of environment. But how are we to recognize that influence without a preliminary, independent study of physical environment? How are we to discriminate which is a human fact and which is a natural fact, if we commence by confusing in the same picture the work of men and natural conditions? Clarity has gained nothing by that kind of compromise."

May we be pardoned for insisting on this point, as it appears to us of primary importance. We know that sociologists do not accept such ideas—though they are, as we see, those of all qualified geographers—without certain reservations. But if they think they can repudiate these ideas, if they think they can cut the wasp into two sections with a pair of scissors—

[1] Vidal, **XCV**, p. 98. [2] Ibid., **XI**, 1905, p. 196.
[3] Gallois, **XXXIV**, p. 224.

" geographic " geography if we may so call it, on the one hand, and anthropogeography on the other—it is doubtless because they have been led to do so by the persistent errors and want of clear-sightedness of certain geographers, but it is also because they revert, purely and simply, to the old errors of the historians ; it is because they take the old standpoint of the latter, and re-state the problem in the same terms.

Social morphology is not and cannot be the equivalent of human geography. We certainly have no objection to its existence and its development. We consider it perfectly legitimate that sociologists should be interested, as historians were formerly, in the influence which geographical conditions may exercise on the development of societies. But that is only one part of the general problem which confronts us, one special way of looking at it, which can only lead to fragmentary conclusions, and which, above all, does not suffice in itself. For, let us note : if sociologists in their study of social morphology go much further, and obtain more precise and more interesting results, than the historians who follow Michelet or Taine, it is to the progress of geography that they owe it : human geography in strict solidarity with physical geography.

They are necessarily dependent on geographers—just as, in large measure, they need the aid of history.[1] For they are under no illusion, we imagine, that geography and geographical considerations are improvised. In their miscellany, *L'Année sociologique*, a geographer has said so in words which are rather fanciful, perhaps, but just. How many different kinds of knowledge are indispensable to anyone who wishes to show " to what extent man is the slave of the soil and the climate in order that we may then see to what extent he has freed himself ! " And Vacher gives the list [2] : " To have carefully examined the soil and its architecture . . . to know how the weather has sculptured the earth's surface in order to perceive which portions have specially attracted men, and in what directions they have been able to circulate . . . to inquire into atmospheric movements and the physiognomy of the seasons, on which agriculture depends "—all this falls to the lot of the anthropogeographer, and all of these are tasks

[1] Cf. Mantoux, **XXIV**, *passim*. [2] **XVII**, 1903–4, Vol. XIII, p. 613.

which require a long apprenticeship, a long initiation, the acquirement of a science—all tasks also which show the close bond between human and physical geography, and the direct dependence of the former upon the latter. To disguise that dependence would be to deny the legitimacy and the specific character of anthropogeography. To voice it is to render untenable the doctrine which would absorb it in social morphology.

But who is to prevent the morphologist from attaining all the knowledge just enumerated by Vacher? Nobody, without a doubt; but then he will be a geographer and not a sociologist—or will he be both? By privilege then, since sociologists have so often pointed out the incurable clumsiness of the historians who have ventured into their preserves (and we do not say that they were wrong).

V

The Legitimate Object of Research: The Relation of Environment to Society in its Historic Evolution

One last objection before leaving this question of method. The problem under consideration deals with the relations between History and the Soil. But it is doubtless already apparent that we have on several occasions substituted for that already sufficiently vast and comprehensive formula, one still more vast and comprehensive: we have spoken of the relations between environment and human society in its historic evolution.

Is this a personal idiosyncrasy, an attempt to amplify and complicate still further this complex and weighty problem? Or are we dealing with a certain confusion, doubly blameworthy when such delicate subjects are in question, that confounds the State with Society and social evolution with historical evolution, human geography as a whole with political and historical geography properly so called?

To repeat a distinction dear to Ratzel, we know that in reality the State is not Society. We know that though, in our Western European countries, the State seems often to take its rise from the development of society, and the political organization to result from the economic, demographic, and moral state of the country, it is otherwise with countries like British India,[1] where a political regime of foreign importation is imposed on an indigenous social state that has been cemented by time—an old regime of castes, juxtaposing family and professional groups, but powerless to unify them and co-ordinate them by common action; or even countries like Russia,[2] where the social organization seems almost entirely the work of a State which was chronologically antecedent to it. There the political structure has in a great measure determined the social structure.

But we know also that, as Ratzel has said,[3] "society is the medium through which the State becomes attached to the soil." From which it follows, he adds, that the relations of society with the soil affect the nature of the State at whatever phase of its development we consider it. And he quotes examples: "When economic activity is only slightly developed whereas the territory is wide and consequently easily alienated the result is a want of solidarity and stability in the constitution of the State. A thinly scattered population, which requires much space, produces a State of nomads whose distinctive characteristic is a strong military organization, necessary for the defence of such vast territory with such a small population."

The analysis is ingenious: but obviously it still provides that same formal and military conception whose insufficiency we have already shown—that same almost entire regard for organization alone, that same love of abstract ideas which, in the geography of communications, hid from Ratzel all the realities of trade and allowed him to see nothing but a mechanism.[4]

For our own part, we give another meaning and another content even to Ratzel's formula. We do not see in society a mere jack-in-the-box, the spring of which is now compressed and now extended in its box—the State. We have every

[1] Vidal, **CXVII.**
[2] Milioukoff, **CCXXVII.**
[3] Ratzel, **XXXVI.**
[4] Cf. Hückel, **LXXI,** p. 402: "Geographical and still more political expansion (according to Ratzel) have all the distinctive characteristics of a body in motion which expands and contracts alternately in regression and progression. The object of this movement is always the conquest of space with a view to the foundation of States, whether by nomad shepherds or by sedentary agriculturists."

intention of studying the social groups established on the soil and obtaining their living from it, both in themselves and for themselves.

We see these groups determined, to a great extent, by their economic needs: to our mind, it is these same needs in the first place, and the efforts of men to satisfy them, that explain the profound influence of geography on the evolution of human society.

We see the State itself born, as a rule, out of the exploitation of the soil. For us, close bonds between economic and political groups exist not only when, in our own day, a certain chartered company is gradually transformed into a colonial State, but just as truly at the other end of the chronological scale, when, for instance, we try with Camille Jullian [1] to grasp the profound reasons which have grouped certain tribes in districts utterly dissimilar into the political unity of a Gaulish nation. Convergence towards the same river, dependence on the same route, subordination to the same cross-roads, necessary barter between plain and mountain region: these nations, these peoples which comprised many tribes, first formed societies for barter, mutual protection, and material and moral solidarity. A people and region acted and reacted on one another. Between the men and the country which they held to be their own there was so much reciprocal adaptation that even to-day, as Camille Jullian shrewdly remarks, the aspect of the country along the main communications of France changes precisely where the boundaries of the Gaulish cities formerly lay. These cities were political unities, as we said before. But they were equally, or even primarily, economic unities.

*

*   *

Such ideas, we are well aware, may and do raise criticisms and objections.

For Camille Vallaux, interpreting and at the same time trying to rectify the ideas of Ratzel, "the bond between the Soil and the State exists above and outside all the economic resources which the soil can supply, because the soil is the necessary base for the activity of the social groups organized

[1] **CLXXII,** II, p. 30 ff.

with a view to common action, which we call States." [1] And we know how this geographer proposes to distinguish between the *political soil*, the field of action offered throughout the world to all forms of the activity of States, and the *economic soil*, containing its natural riches, whether exploited or not, from which each State draws its strength and ability to endure.

The distinction is ingenious and has its utility. It may put us on our guard against a certain idea of the State which is too grossly materialistic and an economic which is far too rudimentary. Still, we must guard against pushing it too far.

To illustrate his distinction, Camille Vallaux offers an example: that of the French Sahara. "No sensible man," he says, "can think, in spite of certain assertions to the contrary, that France has annexed the Sahara to its African territories for the sake either of utilizing the sand of the Erg and the stony tablelands of the Hamada, or of forming lines of communication between Algeria and the Sudan." [2] Evidently! But when the author concludes that this example "enables us to understand the value attributed, from the political point of view, to regions or ground whose economic value is nil", is he not going too far? Does he not slip into speaking, though evidently in error, as a man of business or as the governor of an Eastern country calculating the probable benefits and the possible yield of an occupation and exploitation of colonial territories, and not as a geographer?

In fact, the economic value of the Sahara is not "nil". It is a real one to those populations to whom the Sahara is the natural centre of action and of existence—to those Tuareg tribes which possess certain desert zones and communications with the wells and springs, and to those sedentary Ksourians of the Oases, whose economic relations with the nomads are now well known.

Such political organization and society as exist in the Sahara—outside the modern colonial boundaries, if you will —rest on an essentially economic basis. And who can suppose that if France has extended her hold over such a territory, it is not on account of these same societies which it enclosed, societies whose relations and connexions with the "economic

[1] **XCIII**, p. 38. [2] Ibid., p. 39.

soil" we have just pointed out? In a similar way, there is no room in Tibet for European colonization. The profit would be too small for the outlay. And yet in the lofty valleys to the south there have grown up, among the desolate solitudes of Central Asia, human oases with a civilization having its literary men and its artists, as well as its material resources and an agriculture and cattle industry quite sufficient to sustain it.[1] "Of no economic value." Here, again, the formula would be out of place; or rather it would only have a financial and mercantile meaning.

In fact, under slightly different forms, the same thing may always be remarked. Whoever studies States in their historic evolution should not concern himself with their external life only, with their growth and extension and—we might say, if the words were not so often too ambitious—with their foreign policy.

Their means of existence and natural growth; their economic hold on the soil they occupy; their internal structure and development: these are so many questions to be studied closely if we would measure the profound and manifold influence of geography on the evolution of those sovereign societies called States. The problem cannot thus be solved by broad comparisons, general analogies, and unproven assertions. Nothing has really been accomplished when, with no matter how many manuals of *Kulturgeschichte*,[2] and with their adaptations of the hoary remains of Ritter, it has been solemnly decreed (under pretext of the evolutionary laws of historical geography) that countries with an unindented coast—still the same persistent survival of the famous theory of littoral articulations[3]—and countries distant from the sea having an extreme climate, that is, presumably, such countries as the massive and torrid peninsula of Arabia, the centre and cradle of Islam, have no part in the history of civilization, whereas others (let us suppose again) such as Corsica and Korea . . .

It is not true that four or five great geographic influences

[1] Sion, **CXCVI,** p. 94.

[2] Cf. to quote one example, the *Handbuch der Kulturgeschichte* by Henne am Rhyn, Leipzig, 1900.

[3] There is a detailed criticism of this theory in Vallaux, **CCXXXVII,** p. 27 ff.; cf. also an article by M. Dubois, "Le rôle des articulations littorales," **XI,** 1892, p. 131 ff., and Part III, Chap. II.

weigh on historic bodies with a rigid and uniform influence; but at every instant and in all phases of their existence, through the exceedingly supple and persistent mediation of those living beings endowed with initiative, called men, isolated or in groups, there are constant, durable, manifold, and at times contradictory influences exercised by all those forces of soil, climate, vegetation—and many other forces besides—which constitute and compose a natural environment.

PART II

NATURAL LIMITS AND HUMAN SOCIETY

CHAPTER I

The Problem of Boundaries
Climate and Life

AS followers of a well-qualified master, we have frequently repeated that there is no problem in Geography more important than that of boundaries or dividing limits. In this, as in other matters, the manner in which the problem is set allows us largely to forecast the answer, and nothing is simpler than the traditional position of the question.

We make our start with a first abstraction : MAN, a malleable being, submissive to the action of his natural environment. And it is supposed that this environment (let us say, the EARTH) acts on him and transforms him by means of two powers, two sovereign forces : SOIL and CLIMATE. It is granted, certainly that, heredity forms one of the factors in human evolution, but all the others are derived from habitat. These exercise their power at the same time on individuals and communities, and are not only efficacious agents in somatic transformation, but are equally the determinants of political and moral ideas and realizations—the very basis of history.

I

The Traditional Idea of Climate : The Pioneers

Thus the problem still appeared a simple one to Montesquieu when he composed *L'Esprit des Lois*, as simple as it appeared long before to his predecessor, Jean Bodin, whose influence over him, however, we must not exaggerate.[1]

[1] For different theses on this point, cf. Flint (R.), *La Philosophie de l'histoire en France et en Allemagne*, p. 15 ff. ; Errera, " Un précurseur de Montesquieu, Jean Bodin " (*Ann. Arch. Belgique*, 1896) ; Fournol, *Bodin, prédécesseur de Montesquieu*, Paris, 1896, thèse de droit ; Dedieu, **XLI,** Chap. VII ; Chauviré, **XXXVII,** p. 348 ff. and p. 512 n.

If Montesquieu read at all carefully the *Six Livres de la République* of the Angevin politician; if consequently he read, enjoyed, and made great use of the rich and full first chapter of the fifth book, from which it follows "that there are nearly as many varieties in the nature of men as there are in that of countries, seeing that, in the same climates, it is found that the Eastern people are very different from the Western, and that in the same latitude and at the same distance from the Equator the Southern people are different from the Northern; and, what is more, that in the same climate, latitude, and longitude a difference is noticed between mountain regions and plains"[1]—he knew and followed other guides also, men with a spirit nearer to his own than Bodin ever was. A traveller, for instance, like Chardin, whose influence over the ideas of Montesquieu has been shown by Dupin; or the English doctor, Arbuthnot, author of an *Essay on the effects of air on the human body*, translated in 1742 by a Montpellier doctor, Boyer de Pédrandié: for there is no doubt, from the allusions made by Dedieu in his study on *les Sources anglaises de l'Esprit des Lois*, that he traced to that practitioner the ideas of a number of passages in Montesquieu's fourteenth, fifteenth, and seventeenth books.[2] But whatever may have been the sources of *L'Esprit des Lois*, its author none the less considers MAN only, isolated man, a particular individuality, a physical unit; there was nothing in that to shock a mind of the eighteenth century contemporary with Rousseau and his *Contrat Social*. Confronting him are SOIL and CLIMATE, two great forces, the gross power of which he considered, without analysing their mode of action in too much detail; no more thinking of studying them in their component parts than of uniting them in their effects.

Montesquieu, in Book XVIII of *L'Esprit des Lois*, studies the action of the soil on the judicial institutions of men, but very lightly and very briefly. His analysis does not go very far. What he understands by the soil, what interests him under that name is, as he often says, "the nature of the earth." But he does not introduce any precise geological or topological idea under cover of that expression. The science

[1] Bodin, **XXXVI**, p. 461 ff.
[2] Dedieu, **XLI**, Chap. VII, p. 212 ff.; also his *Montesquieu*, Paris, 1913, pp. 55, 75.

of his time scarcely permitted it. His idea is purely utilitarian and, moreover, very vague: the ground has only two qualities, it is good or bad. "The sterility of the ground in Attica established a popular government there, and the fertility of Lacedæmon an aristocratic one"[1]: such is a simple example of the deductions of Montesquieu.

In indicating briefly the consequences of sterility upon a country, they are certainly not in advance of those of Bodin: the greater ingenuity of the inhabitants, sobriety, the thronging of people to the towns: witness Athens of old, and Nuremberg in the sixteenth century "full of the most delightful artisans in the world" as also Limoges, Genoa, and Ghent: "for enemies do not want an unfertile country, and the inhabitants, living in safety, increase and are obliged to trade or work."[2] The superiority of analysis here and the "geographical spirit" appear to be on the side of Bodin, not of the President. If the latter at times introduces the idea of surface relief into his chapters—plain or mountain—it is merely to account for abundance or sterility; the fertile countries "are the plains where no man can dispute anything with one stronger", whilst in the mountain country "a man can keep what he has, and has little to keep".[3]

Similarly, if, in the same Book XVIII, the author frequently introduces the notion of different walks of life, if he speaks of hunting, fishing, cattle-rearing (these notions do not exist in any clear and distinct manner in the work of Bodin), it is to tack on these secondary modes of subsistence to cultivation and tillage. "Hunting and fishing," says Montesquieu in Chapter IX (*Du terrain de l'Amérique*), "supply men with abundance"; they thus complete the work of nature, which of herself produces many fruits on which man can subsist. There we have simple ideas, simple actions, and unsound generalizations.

As to climate, Montesquieu devotes to it more space and attention. It was an old tradition to attribute a large influence to it; the author of *L'Esprit des Lois* was, moreover, countenanced not only by his remote predecessors, Bodin

[1] Montesquieu, **XL,** I, XVIII, Chap. II.
[2] Bodin, **XXXVI,** p. 485.
[3] Montesquieu, **XL,** I, XVIII, Chap. II.

or even Hippocrates, who was just at that time experiencing a veritable rejuvenation, but also by a whole series of contemporary publications and studies, to which Dedieu[1] has very properly called our attention. So Montesquieu required not one, but four books (XIV–XVII), to establish first the relations of climate with laws in general, then with the laws of " civil slavery ", " domestic slavery ", and lastly " political servitude ". But here again the analysis remains rudimentary. This is not intended, of course, as a criticism, for Montesquieu could not outstrip the scientific movement of his epoch; but, in fact, through the whole course of the four books, climate has only one meaning, that of temperature; climates are hot, or cold, or temperate. Here we have already signs of a first distinction, a first outline of " natural boundaries "; but as yet how rough and superficial they are! For instance, in Book XVII, Chapter III, Montesquieu remarks: " Asia has properly no temperate zone, and places which have a very cold climate are contiguous to places with a very hot one. . . . In Europe, on the contrary, the temperate zone is of great extent, although it is situated in climates which differ very much among themselves. . . . But since the climate becomes colder insensibly as we go from south to north . . . it follows that each country is very nearly similar to its neighbour." And from this difference between the two continents Montesquieu draws a complete parallel. In the same way, further on, he says boldly (Ibid., Chap. VII): " Africa has a climate similar to that of the South of Asia, and it is in the same state of servitude." But what is it which characterizes the climate of Southern Asia in the eyes of Montesquieu? Nowadays we think at once of the rains, of the great regulating and nourishing phenomenon of the monsoons. As for Montesquieu, he still thinks only of " the heat ". Southern Asia is a very hot country; Africa, similarly, is a very hot country. His analysis goes no further.[2] It goes no further than that of Aristotle in Book VII of the *Politics*: " The inhabitants of cold regions are courageous,

[1] Dedieu, **XLI**, p. 205 ff.

[2] It should be noted that this reduction of the notion of " climate " to that of " temperature " may be understood when we consider that Montesquieu bases this part of his book largely on the work of a physician, Arbuthnot, who is studying the effect of heat and cold on the human body. Cf. the comparisons made by Dedieu, **XLI**, pp. 214–16.

and fought for liberty. The Asiatics are wanting in energy, so they are formed for despotism and slavery. . . ."

Why all these remarks on the old theories of Montesquieu? Why this retrospective voyage into the past? In the first place, when we wish to give an exact account of the modern position of a scientific problem, it is never useless to go back to its origin. In the second, is it mere curiosity? Has the state of mind which these eighteenth century writings reveal entirely disappeared, never to return? It must be confessed that it has not.

*

* *

Geographers of the school of Ratzel continue to regard the relations between men and environment very simply and very roughly, notwithstanding a marked affectation of prudence in method.

Miss Helen Churchill Semple, on the very threshold of her large and interesting manual of human geography, *The Influence of Geographic Environment*,[1] enunciates the revised and amended articles of the Ratzelian dogma, and lays down in her third paragraph the method to follow—to compare typical people of all races in all stages of civilization and in similar geographical situations. If there is a difference it is due to race. If there is agreement, it is due to environment. Thus we have two elements: the environment, too complex to be accurately defined; the man, too abstract, even if we study him within the limits of his race; the idea of race, moreover, remaining still to be determined. Were we wrong to remark on the persistence of a too elementary conception of these questions?

The weakness of their position is shown, too, by the attitude of the Ratzelians themselves. They affirm stoutly, for instance, the permanence of the action of geographical factors and environment, except in the case of some neutralizing intervention. Hence they conclude that islands, deserts, or steppes create economic, ethnic, and historic analogies; and some of them are pliant enough to identify the cases of England, Japan, Melanesia, New Zealand, and pre-historic Crete. Or again,

[1] Semple, **XC.**

they proclaim that the steppes and the deserts of the ancient continent have given birth to nomad tribes who invaded successively the rich countries bordering on their pasture lands: they then compare among themselves not only the nomad tribes of to-day, but those of all ages . . . and they lose, as they go on, their original criterion. To explain why, at an interval of some hundreds of years, Cossacks and Huns have both been induced to migrate, Miss Semple affirms that these migrations are connected with the nature of the air, which is dry and stimulating (a very vague factor), and with the difficulty of existence in a poor country—a new criterion which is not at all the same thing as environment, although it may depend on it.

In the same way, the whole evolution of Spanish history is retraced for us in terms of environment. Was it not geography, it is asked, which in the first place exposed that peninsular country to Saracen invasions, and moreover at a point where the expansion of Islam was increased by all the activities of the Islamized Berber countries? Doubtless, but what is there strictly geographical in that action? Again, we are told, the necessity of driving out the Moors brought about a sort of political crystallization of the Iberian state; it became a camp of Christian adventurers with its centre in the desert plateau of Castile. Granted; but what is there really geographical in that? It is added, it is true, not quite correctly, that there was neither commerce nor industry in Spain at that time, and that life was more intense in the plains and on the coast than in the interior; but is this action connected with the double criterion of man and environment? Then comes the war of 1492 and the fall of Granada. The old conditions are changed, we are told. Perhaps; but was the fall of Granada properly a geographical fact? In the second place, would it not be well to remember that Spain has been defined as a land bordering on the countries of Islam? But now, on the contrary, a new discovery has suddenly been made—it is essentially, we are now told, a country situated between the Mediterranean and the Atlantic, which, peopled by men of a warlike and adventurous nature, ought to have on that account a great maritime and colonial destiny. Then the final tragedy: the Spanish Empire collapses. The English and Dutch alliance is invoked, but no mention is made of the fact that, the two elements dear to Ratzel, race and environment, not having been sensibly modified, such a catastrophe (like all the revolutions which have preceded it) can scarcely be explained by " geography ".

Indeed, for historic facts of the kind quoted by Miss Semple, the application of the theory of Taine, who at least added to the action of environment and race that of " the time ",[1] would seem really much more satisfactory. We hasten to say that it would not really be so, but would only seem so. For it is, in fact, an impossible and puerile ambition to contemplate treating such complicated problems in the mass. In vain we may say that the environment should be looked at from a wide point of view, and that to account for present realities, consideration should be given both to the anterior and final habitat. Such complications are useless. We refuse to believe that much light can be thrown on the history of Austria by dividing that country up into an Adriatic part, a Danubian part and a non-Danubian part, and in considering for each of these regions the Latin influence, the Bavarian and German influence, and the Greek or Russian influence respectively—even if we add the consideration of the Turkish invasions and of the Hapsburg changes in foreign policy in correlation with the power of the Sultans or the Tsars. In a word: what problems are we to resolve when none is stated?

We see better now how impossible it is to study as a whole what has long been called " the relations between the earth and man ". It was thus that philosophers formerly aspired to solve " the problem of physical and moral relations ". It is necessary, if any useful advance is hoped for on the question, to substitute for " Man ", an abstract entity, " Human Societies ", then by another hardly less delicate analysis to examine closely the nature of " the Earth " and separate from one another the different elements which affect human life, in order to be able, passing on to synthesis, to recompose them and combine them rationally. In other words we must separate the question into its self-contained portions. These having been chosen on acceptable principles, their value must be studied so as to avoid any illusions or

[1] On the mutual relations of race and environment in the works of Taine, and especially on his wide idea of environment, cf. Lacombe, **XLVIII**, p. 14.

any ground for criticism of the kind we have just formulated. There is no question here, moreover, of losing sight of the unity of the physical world—that unity whose clear and lively perception remains the basis of all geography. But to divide the difficulties into as many parcels as is necessary for their better solution has not ceased, since the time of Descartes, to be a safe rule of scientific method.

Only, and we must state it emphatically, there is nothing simple in the operation. These bounds to be marked out must be as homogeneous as possible, and capable in reality of offering human activity an assemblage of conditions sufficiently similar. How are we actually to map them out so as to fulfil the many conditions, and according to what principles are we to determine their nature, number, and limits? Once chosen and defined, what value must we attribute to them? These are all very large and difficult questions. They bring into play our whole knowledge of the physical world, but they require, on the other hand, very clear and precise ideas about the activities of man in Nature. Let us simplify them as much as possible, and since there is no question of completeness, let us attack one of the influences which have been so long familiar in history. Let us analyse and decompose into its elements the old traditional notion of "Climate" as the generator of individual forces and social powers.

II

Climate and the Human Physical Organism

The notion of climate is evidently a much more complex one to our contemporaries, even the least well informed, than to Montesquieu, and *a fortiori* to Bodin. They usually know, and the boldest generalizers among them grant, that it no longer covers the secondary idea of temperature only. Through the influence of the renovators of physical geography they borrow their data correctly from astronomy, meteorology, and physics. They do not forget the part played by latitude or insolation, nor the influence of the ocean masses, the marine currents, prevailing winds, and altitude. But even when they see clearly that the old division of climates into hot, cold, and temperate, gives a clear idea neither of their general distribution nor of the general distribution of temperature; when, similarly, they try to combine in the notion of climate all those which we have just enumerated, or to unite with it the notion of geographical position or of altitude, are they therefore free from that vice which appeared so conspicuously in the obsolete work of Montesquieu? No, if they always confront isolated men with a physical force, or collection of forces, supposed to be acting directly and immediately on those men. For what is the use in that case of their erudition, so often unproductive, and their learned observations as to the climatic advantage conferred on the Western regions of the continents in the Northern hemisphere in comparison with the Eastern ones,[1] an advantage which does not, however, prevent the East from being frequently the seat of mighty civilizations? It is an abuse of methods that are barred, a display of false science[2]; an inability to set and *a fortiori* to solve any problem; but, at any rate, it does not omit to take into consideration first of all the primordial problem—the action of climate on man.

How then are we to look upon this action? We see at the first glance that it is a double one, and that we must examine at the same time its effects on the bodies and characters of men: on the body first—the physical organism.

It is an action which, from early times, has occupied the minds of scholars, who were inclined to consider that climatic agencies exercised a direct influence on human bodies analogous to that which they noticed on all living things, animal or vegetable. Under the influence of special "stimuli", we were told, physiological adaptations appeared. Darwin made it one of the elements in natural selection. Lamarck built upon it his doctrine of evolution. Philosophers like Herbert Spencer or Auguste Comte attributed considerable importance to it. In their train a whole Pleiad of anthropologists and doctors accumulated observations, remarks and detailed confirmations. For a long time general considerations were used, sometimes abused, on the tonicity of different climates. Heat debilitates, enervates, and makes the human organism languid. Cold renders it duller, slower,

[1] See, for instance, the work of Miss Semple, **XC**, Chap. XVII.

[2] In the chapter quoted from Miss Semple, what force have those dissertations on the topography of the Tundras and the phenomena of capture?

but also more robust and more concentrated: commonplaces have been developed a thousand times since Bodin, who stated them boldly, and have been refuted also a thousand times by the most elementary facts. The ambition of our scholars was to go further both in extent and depth.

But if we leave generalities altogether and continue with the analysis, are we not venturing out of the domain of geography? Yes, indeed, and entering on that of anthropology, or even at times of pathology.

Let us take one of the facts of this order which has from very early times occupied the attention of observers and provoked their comments. Is it true (as people have never been slow to point out) that there is an evident relation between climate, and especially temperature, on the one hand and the colour of the skin on the other? But is the setting and the attempt at solution of that very delicate question necessary to geography?

No doubt the geographers could aid the anthropologists to establish the fact that to-day, as things actually stand, the coloration of the skin has no apparent relation to climatic factors. They will confirm those easily observable facts, namely, that there are relatively fair people in the tropical zone, American Indians for example, and that there are races relatively dark in the Northern frigid zone, such as those which Bodin designates [1] as "swarthy from extreme cold", the Lapps and the Esquimaux. And if it is often difficult to fix a strict limit between colours—are the Fulahs and Abyssinians black or white?—they will hasten to fall back upon Emile Gautier's remark that the problem has at all times appeared difficult,[2] so much so that neither the ancient Greeks and Romans, nor in later times the Arabs of Algeria, have had a real word in their language for "negro", so difficult did it seem to them to fix a strict and inflexible line of demarcation in the familiar and continuous series of shades.

But when that is done, and when they have noted furthermore that the South American tribes who pass their lives in the shade of the forests are of a lighter colour than those who live in lands without perpetual shade, or reciprocally

[1] Bodin, **XXXVI**, p. 465 ff.

[2] Gautier, **CLXXXI**, pp. 131–2 ff.

that the tribes of tropical Africa who live on the coast of the Cameroons are darker than those who inhabit certain wooded mountains,[1] will it fall to these geographers, *as geographers*, to establish that climate and more especially luminosity seem to produce actually only slight and unstable variations in the colour of the human skin ? Will it fall to them to study the distribution of the pigment in man, and to connect the lighter colouring of the ventral side of the body with a stronger action of light ? Will it be their business to unravel the general causes which make the hair of different races dark or light, or which explain the variations in its length, manner of growth, and thickness, its marked regression in the tropical regions, its very obvious persistence in the cold ones ?

*

* *

And what of the whole problem of the human races—not only of their origin but of their different aptitudes, of their different habitats, of all that assemblage of facts which Zimmermann enumerated some time ago in his critical survey [2] of Brunhes's book ?

No doubt, as Zimmermann said, geography cannot but be interested in all these facts, since they imply considerations of distribution and localization which are unquestionably geographical—since, for example, at the present time there are no ubiquitous races, but all appear attached to a definite domain which constitutes the zone best suited for their development and expansion, and the zone of least resistance. Beyond 40° of North latitude bronchial diseases are fatal to negroes : this is a fact. Equally true is the fact that men accustomed to live between the isotherms of 40° to 70° find living difficult under the isotherm of 77°. The alternative heat and the humidity cause affections of the head, liver, and kidneys which produce general weakness, especially amongst those who use alcohol, and give rise to great mortality, besides arresting reproduction. But if geography can help to set the problem, if it provides at least one of the essential data, can it find the solution ? Certainly not, and the author whom we quote grants it for his part, for example, when he writes

[1] Semple, **XC**, Chap. II, *passim*.
[2] Semple, **XI**, Vol. XIX, 1910, p. 109.

of the Sahara, that very probably the key to the different reactions which the people of the Sahara manifest to the climatic conditions of their habitat " lies in the hereditary physiology and pathology of the races ". It is, he adds, a problem of medical geography.

This is evident, and there are many other problems. The more we know and study the world and men, the more problems of this order arise. For a long time the attempt was made to explain by the ocean currents [1] the distribution in the Southern seas of the two races, Melanesian and Polynesian, who share them. But another factor certainly intervenes: the unequal resistance of the " fair " and the " dark " to malaria. The most wretched conditions of existence have not prevented the Polynesians from colonizing certain islands exempt from that scourge, but islands where the vegetation supplied abundant resources, but which were unhealthy, were occupied by the Melanesians, who were more resistant, more capable of adapting themselves to a dangerous climate, and more capable of acquiring in time a remarkable immunity from the most dangerous fevers: here is another problem for medical geography.

But what can be more interesting to a geographer than the great dispute [2] which has been waged during recent years on the question of whether there is gradually growing up, in the anthropological sense of the word, and under influences which can be unquestionably traced directly or indirectly to the soil and the climate, an American race?

We know what extraordinary results have been reached by the Commission of Inquiry on that matter appointed by the Senate of the United States, under the direction of a well-known anthropologist, Boas: how the different types of emigrants, whatever their origin, rapidly blended into a common type: even the shape of the head, long or round, was changed and soon approached a uniform mean. This was due to the evident influence (at least, if we may believe the inquirers) of the environment, temperature, light,

[1] On this point, besides the old work of Quatrefages, **CCIX**, cf. Tilenius, in *Mitteil. der anthropol. Gesellsch. in Wien*, Vol. XXXVI, 1906 (*Verhandl.*), p. 122.

[2] There is an account of the thesis of Boas, without restrictions or reserves, by P. de Biermont in *Revue générale des Sciences*, 30th December, 1913.

and food. But it is not geographers who have to state the problem, because it is not geographers who can solve it.

Neither is it for them—taking another and different kind of instance—to enter into the question of the adaptation to extreme climates of Europeans from temperate countries, the Dutch, for instance, settled in the tropical Colonies belonging to the Netherlands.[1] Do they, or do they not, reveal any difference of physique when compared with their compatriots who have remained in Holland? Are the modifications noted important, or are they confined to some secondary variations—a certain softening of the tissues, a greater elasticity of the limbs, which would tend to allow those acclimatized to bend as flexibly as the people of the Far East? These questions appear to be very simple,[2] and in theory are easy of solution: but how much debate and controversy have they not occasioned!

However, we must not confine ourselves to climatic influences only, and leave out what pertains to the soil: a very opportune thought, as it will save us much repetition! Is it a fact that in limestone countries the bony part of animals is excessively developed, whereas it is restricted in countries where there is little lime? This is an old belief, which still persists. Has walking on the flat had such a very clear influence over the many characteristic physical peculiarities which are noticed in Flanders amongst cattle and horses, as well as amongst men, such as an exaggerated development of the pelvis, breadth of buttocks, distance between the thighs due to the size of the pelvis as well as to the atrophy of the adductors, prominence and flaccidity of the abdomen, breadth and flatness of the outspread foot? Some have claimed that this is observable, and it has been emphatically stated by Baroux and Sergeant, the authors of a curious book on "Flemish bovine, equine, and human breeds in relation to walking on the flat". And the so-called "haughty Flemish look", is it not the normal way in which men of a flat country carry their heads so that they can freely scrutinize the horizon

[1] Cf. the researches of Kohlbrugge, analysed in *L'Anthropologie*, **XVI**, 1911, p. 205.

[2] Miss Semple enumerates a whole series in her Chapter II (**XC**, pp. 33, 34, 35 especially).

without being absorbed, like the mountaineer, in the irregularities of the ground, which he must watch carefully ?

And similarly, passing on to other environments, is there not room for studying and pointing out such somatic modification, as is entailed by shipboard life among men whose environment condemns them to spend their lives on the water, such as the relative atrophy of the legs, the powerful development of the arms, noticed amongst the people of Barotse Land and of the Zambesi, amongst the natives of Tierra del Fuego and of the Aleutian islands,[1] or, still more definitely, amongst the Flemings,[2] in whom we find a certain projection of the right shoulder-blade and a certain fold of the skin under the right buttock, owing to the general handling of the boat-hook, which is used to move the little country boats along the canals and rivers ? And again, is it simply peninsularity or insularity—that insularity which is said to account for the diminutive size of Iceland, Shetland, Corsican, and Sardinian ponies, and to explain the dwindling in size of those imported into the Falkland Islands in 1764,[3] is it that insularity, the isolation of ages, the prolonged existence for generations far from the great routes of circulation and intercourse, with, as a corollary, consanguinity in marriages, which gives such a curious look to some of the Breton folk, and those physical features, for instance, amongst the Bigoudens of Pont l'Abbé, which are so like racial characteristics—the flattened face, short stature, and swarthy complexion ? [4] Or are we to look on those strange-looking men and women as descendants of foreign races—Uralo-Altaics established in furthest lands as the result of very ancient migrations ?

These are some of the questions, taken as examples from among many others, which are interesting to the geographer ; but they do not belong to his province. He may perhaps be able to assist in setting them correctly. He is not qualified to set them for himself. He must wait until they are solved ; not by him, but by others.

*

* *

[1] Paris, Tallandier, 1906.

[2] Semple, **XC**, Chap. II, p. 35.

[3] Baroux et Sergeant, op. cit.

[4] Vallaux, **CCXXXI**, pp. 63–4.

We insist strongly on this point, and not without reason. Generally, as is well known, and as we had occasion to remark previously, it is the fate of scientific theories to be adopted by men of literary culture precisely at the moment when, losing their value, they fall into discredit. At the precise moment when naturalists are rejecting the old finalist theory of "adaptation", it is not right that geographers should obstinately profess it more or less openly and cleave to it. We say only a word about the matter here, as we shall have to return to it later.

Adaptation, in the old literal sense of the word—the idea that any organism placed in a certain environment acquires, by the direct and mechanical action of that environment, characteristics which give it special advantages there and disadvantages elsewhere—this idea has had its day in the domain of science. It is not true of plants. It is not true of animals. It is vigorously combated by biologists versed in physical chemistry. And whilst combating it in 1911, by his suggestive theory of pre-adaptation,[1] Cuénot proposed to replace it in the first edition of his great work on *La Genèse des Espèces animales*.

Now it is incontestable that the problem of influences has been devised, in history, during recent years, by men who were feeling the great counter-blow, the influence of the great theories which have divided, between them, the last century: Lamarckism and Darwinism especially. The influence of the environment was Lamarck's share, the idea of adaptation that of Darwin. And this spell was doubtless more or less clear, and conscious. It was in no way imaginary.

Is such an influence legitimate? Is there any analogy between the problems set by naturalists and those which preoccupy anthropologists? There is, if we institute an analogical parallel between the life of individuals and that of human societies; but is such an analysis anything but a purely arbitrary and verbal affair? Furthermore, what if adaptation be only a name and the influence of the environment only a formula, if the best-informed naturalists are gradually abandoning their old point of view, permeated as it was with finalism, and adopting much more stern ideas and conceptions

[1] See in the 2nd edition (**LII**), p. 449 ff.; cf. also Cuénot, "Theorie de la Préadaptation," **XIX**, Vol. XVI, 1914, and Bohn, ibid., Vol. XVIII, 1915.

of a physico-chemical nature such as those put forward by Loeb ? [1] For the moment we will only state the question. It shows us how wary geographers ought to be when venturing on foreign ground ; as wary as sociologists—if not more so—or as social morphologists venturing on geographical ground. And it shows us another thing besides : the influence of climate on the different somatic characteristics of man, such as his height and colour, and the details of his anatomical structure, problems which would appear relatively simple, and are yet of the greatest uncertainty and very far from solution. What are we to think, then, of the infinitely more complex problems which we have now to examine rapidly ?

III

Climate, Human Character, and Actions

Just as there is said to be a direct and immediate action of climate on the physical nature of man, there is also said to be an action on his moral nature—on his character. The idea is not new. It is even very curious to find that, from the first, it has attracted the attention of inquirers more than the question of physical action, doubtless because it possessed some more subtle quality and offered more scope to ingenuity.

In fact, Bodin's colossal effort already treated of moral and psychological influences. We must not lose sight of his object : it was to show how the " form of the Republic " ought to accommodate itself to the " diversity in men " [2]—to their moral even more than their physical diversity ; and it was from this that he set out to teach " the means of knowing the nature of a people ", and how the people of temperate climes have more force than " those of the South " and less craft and more talent than " those of the North " [3] ; but that these last are remarkable for their brutal cruelties, like mad beasts, whilst the first, " like foxes, expend all their powers upon satiating their vengeance." For the rest, does one not know that the spirit of enterprise is " peculiar to the Northern peoples " ; that knowledge of Nature and sacred things, and

[1] Cf. for instance his book, *La Dynamique des Phénomènes de la Vie* (Fr. edition, Paris, 1908), lectures 7 and 8, on " Tropismes ".

[2] Bodin, **XXXVI**, p. 461.

[3] Ibid., p. 467.

the capacity for "separating the true from the false", are reserved to the Southerners [1]; and that the prudence necessary for command belongs to the people of temperate zones? Bodin does not stop here, as we might suppose. He goes so far even as to sketch the chart of judicial eloquence, as his latest biographer, Chauviré, expresses it: are not the great orators, "legislators, lawyers, historians, poets, buffoons, charlatans, and others who allure the hearts of men by talk and fine words," nearly all "from the temperate regions,[2] the discourse of reason being too mild for the rough Northern people, and too mundane for those of the South, who wish to be enlightened by some sign or by divine oracles which transcend human speech"?

These are dreams and fantasies, but after all not more illusory than those of the good Abbé Dubos, who claimed, at a considerably later date, however, to be able to solve the problem of genius by an examination of the organs and the quality of the blood, on the assumption that the blood itself depends on the air which the lungs breathe and on which the stomach is nourished.[3] How much more scientific is the sensible and cautious Fontenelle, who, in 1688, remarks simply, in the first pages of his *Digression sur les Anciens et les Modernes*,[4] that "different ideas are like plants or flowers, which do not grow equally well in all climates": and he adds that owing to the "linking together and reciprocal dependence existing between all parts of the material world, the climatic differences which affect plants ought to have some effect on brains also". A cautious remark, and one which has the reserved tone of an unverified hypothesis!

Indeed, excuses may be made for Bodin and all his successors, and for Montesquieu himself after the Abbé Dubos. If their ideas seem to us rather puerile, we must not forget that their thought was not always as unfettered as they themselves may have desired. A passage from the Abbé Dubos, which Braunschvig, his latest critic, quotes but does not criticize, is very typical in this respect [5]: "Why," asks the author of the *Réflexions*, "are the nations so different from one

[1] Ibid., p. 480.
[2] Ibid., p. 478.
[3] See above, in the Introduction.
[4] Selected works, Amsterdam edition, Vol. II, 1742, p. 126.
[5] Braunschvig, **XXXIX**, p. 45; Dubos, **XXXVIII**, II, Sect. XX, p. 264.

another in shape and stature, in desire and intellect, although they descend from a common ancestor?" By this last hypothesis, which no one at that time would have dared to dispute, research was directed in advance towards climate. But however that may be, what was wanting in all these more or less brilliant and ingenious theorists was an analysis of the real data of the problem.

What is meant by character? Does it embrace the entire psychological life of individuals? Bodin, with his usual boldness, directed his attack straight at the intellectual faculties,[1] and "as there are in man three principal parts of the soul, that is to say, the imagination or common sense, the reason, and the intellectual part", he deduced at great length, in consequence, that to each of the great climates of the world, hot, cold, and temperate, corresponded a special blossoming of one of these divisions of the soul. Montesquieu, for his part, when he declared that hot climates produce unchangeable civilizations,[2] was apparently concerned most with activity; he started, however, with the general idea that "the character of the mind and the passions of the heart are very different in different climates".[3] But Buckle confined himself to the domain of sensibility when he ascribed the development of imagination and superstition in India to the conditions of life in that country. Only, none of them are precise (and their successors imitate them in this prudent reserve) as to the question in hand! Is it individual or collective psychology?

It is difficult enough, in the case of individuals, to define the idea—none too clear in itself—of character, and ethology, which studies the subject, is still only in its infancy.[4] But what are we to say about that collective ethology which proposes to study "the character of a given historical group which is in any way distinct and tangible—peoples ancient and modern—and organized in political societies, linked to the soil, and constituting an individuality"?[5]

A French character, an English character, a German

[1] Bodin, **XXXVI**, Vol. V, 1, p. 480.
[2] Montesquieu, **XL**, Chap. XIV, IV.
[3] Ibid., Chap. XIV, 1.
[4] Berr, **XX**, p. 73; Febvre, "A propos d'une étude de psychologie historique," **XVIII**, Vol. XXVII, 3, 1913.
[5] Berr, **XX**, pp. 80–1.

character. . . . Have not these popular data been used—and abused—to a sufficient extent, and for interested purposes? Has not the invariable type of Frenchman, American, or German—even of the Latin or Anglo-Saxon—of all times and of all ages, been sufficiently reconstructed, more than ever by the aid of pseudo-historical erudition? And have not many admirable collective portraits been produced, based upon Geography? This verbiage is somewhat ridiculous when it is not also dangerous. Has the "French" character remained stabilized since the times of Cæsar and Vercingetorix? Do the remarks of Cicero and Cæsar on the Gauls hold good for Frenchmen to-day? And would their type be so little changed in the course of a history which has been singularly stirring, as all will allow, and terribly abundant in catastrophes and revolutions, that it could be gathered without any doubt by comparing documents contemporary with St. Louis, Louis XIV, the Terror, and lastly the third Republic—after as well as before the world war? The delusion is eternal, and the snare of words identical. Hence so many false ideas, the fruit of words insufficiently or inexactly defined, run through the whole course of history. In the same way, throughout the whole modern epoch, there circulates an indistinct and confused notion of the "bourgeoisie", that redoubtable scourge of all social history.

But, to keep to what specially concerns us at present, who does not see the illusion of figuring to oneself the past of a people "as a kind of river, whose current always flows in the same direction".[1] And, moreover, "so that it may be possible to discover the character of a people, it is necessary for that people to have a character,[2] that is to say that a certain combination of moral characteristics should be found among the thousands of men who compose that people, and that, on the other hand, this combination should not be found in any other people." Thus is the problem admirably stated by that forcible writer, Paul Lacombe, who seizes with a firm and courageous grip the subterfuges and seductive but vain guesses of Hippolyte Taine. And when he adds: "Whence have we drawn our idea of character? From observation of individuals. We have then applied that idea to a people

[1] Lacombe, **XLIX**, p. 11.
[2] Ibid., p. 10.

—which has no real individuality," perhaps he shows a rather excessive pessimism in place of his usually somewhat excessive optimism. Does he not, however, go to the root of the matter when he says[1]: "'The Frenchman' is no more real than 'man'. He is an abstraction, an extract, in the same way as man. . . . Taine's remark, which has been supposed unanswerable, has often been quoted: 'I see many men, I do not see "man".' To which it suffices to reply, 'I see many Frenchmen, I do not see *the* Frenchman.' Is it a less hazardous operation to make an abstraction of a Frenchman than of a man? And on the other hand, even if it succeeded, would the success of this operation be more fruitful, more useful, and more effective, than a just abstraction of man?"

We may say, in conclusion, that the analysis has not been made. "Ethology is not yet established, and will not be yet awhile." We are still in the lisping stage. Under these circumstances, to speak of the influence of geographical environment, or, more precisely, of climate, on the character of peoples is to try arbitrarily to explain the unknown.

*

* *

Granted, we shall be told. But while we are awaiting the analysis of this evidently complex and variable idea of character, are there not simple characteristics which are readily grasped, data which can be reckoned, brute facts of moral or criminal statistics which bear indisputable witness to the direct and immediate influence of climate on human actions? But where do such facts lead us, and how are they to be interpreted?

Here, for example, is a study in criminal statistics. It relates to sexual crimes in Italy: "Coefficienti biologichi e sociali dei reati sexuali."[2] The author, Signor Ficai, proves that these crimes are infinitely more numerous in the South than in the North of the country. There is an increase of 90 per cent, he tells us, as we go from Lombardy to Sicily. He concludes that the climate is responsible! Is it not evident from the statistics that sexual crimes depend on the temperature?

[1] Ibid., p. 41; cf. also pp. 47–9.
[2] In *Scientia positiva* of January, 1898; Discussion in **XVII**, Vol. II, 1898, p. 427.

But is this conclusion legitimate? Is there really a direct, obvious, and simple climatic influence? How much might be said on the subject! The author remarks that in Italy, which he has chosen as the subject of study, the number of sexual crimes is in direct relation to the physiological energy of the individuals, as evidenced by the birth-rate—which is, moreover, in direct proportion to the increase in number of crimes against the person. The counter-proof is striking. The number of sexual criminals is in inverse ratio to that of diseases and cases of degeneracy: and, in fact, there are infinitely more people in hospital and invalided from epilepsy, cretinism, goitre, and mental maladies in the North of Italy than in the South. But are physiological energy and a high birth-rate, and, inversely, degeneracy and mental diseases in this case, and always, due to climate? Crimes against morals and crimes against the person seem to obey the same law. Is this law, then, of a geographical order, so that we can speak of the law of climate? And if it is true that crimes against morals are more numerous where suicide is less frequent and popular education less advanced, are we to conclude that suicide and ignorance are, in their turn, the direct results of climate?

We must therefore distrust, in this case, simple solutions and evidence so strong that it cannot be disputed! Southern Italy, sexual crimes! Ficai says: it is the climate! But side by side with him, in the same year, or nearly so, Niceforo, for his part, replies: race and economic factors.[1] The same starting-point; the same statistical data, more general in the one case, more specialized in the other. 10,000 Sardinians necessitate 178 proceedings in the criminal courts, 10,000 Calabrians account for 124, 10,000 Sicilians for 100, 10,000 Campanians for 97, but 10,000 Lombards for 48 only. Called in as explanatory factors we have the Mediterranean race, so violent, so impulsive, so predisposed to homicide; also the capitalist regime and the *latifundia* deserts and the exploitation of the peasants of Sardinia and Sicily. . . . As if the Mediterranean race were anything but an assumption; as if, granted a Mediterranean race, we were authorized to think that "its temperament" would incite all the individuals

[1] We are here following the remarkable discussion in *L'Année Sociologique*, **XVII**, Vol. II, 1898, p. 414 ff.

who compose it, indifferently, to homicide, and that we need not trouble ourselves about the social and individual conditions of existence! As if, lastly, capitalism, which does not manifest itself there in any of its essential characteristics, which might lead to an increase of criminality, notably in the concentration in towns of a large working-class population, tied down to the special conditions of life proper to such populations—as if all these explanations really explain anything at all.

Climate, race, capitalism. Why not "civilization" simply. When we find that the Spain of to-day, excluding Catalonia, that Sardinia, Sicily, and to a certain extent Corsica, the Roman States, and Naples, have a very similar criminality, instead of supposing a mysterious and quite undemonstrable action of "climate"; instead of creating the fiction of a Mediterranean race doomed to moral inferiority, which, it would seem, was not always its apanage in the past—why not simply remember that all these countries, from the end of the Middle Ages up to the last revolutions of the nineteenth century, have been subject to the constraints of the same regime of mental oppression and juridico-political inertia, which we need not describe in detail? Hypothesis for hypothesis, this appears certainly more plausible than the others—and easier also to justify.

At heart, many geographers of to-day are aware of these difficulties. To avoid the inconveniences they cannot fail to see, they transpose them. They no longer speak of the simple and direct action of climate. For the idea of climate they are fain to substitute that of the "kind of life" which includes climate among its elements. But what does it all amount to? To a diptych of "hot countries" and "cold countries" like Miss Semple's?

Hot countries—the gay and smiling peasants of Andalusia lead an easy life: hence improvidence, hence gaiety, hence emotional and imaginative character—that of all the Mediterranean peoples and the Negroes. At the same time we find a taste for spending, facilities for an easy life on small means, low wages, a degraded proletariat, a levelling from below.

Cold countries—the rough and surly peasants of Asturias show the effect of lack of comfort; hence forethought—hence seriousness, hence a reflective and prudent character, that of all Northern Europeans. At the same time a sense of economy and of moderation, a voluntary home life with its even tenor and modest joys; high wages, wisely used by prudent workmen; the hierarchy of a strict capitalism.

And the picture may be enriched and enlarged by contrasting the seriousness of the Northern Chinese with the gaiety of the Southern: the relative gaiety of the Ukranians with the surliness of the Northern Russians, the genial spirit of the Southern Germans with the taste for active enterprise shown by the Baltic Saxons. It may even be noted that the Southern peoples, the Jews, for instance, conceive Hell as a place of fire, and the Northerners, such as the Esquimaux, as a frozen region.[1] It must be confessed, in truth, that all these little ingenuities do not take us very far. It is Bodin,[2] revised, corrected, and considerably enlarged; but it is never anything but Bodin.

Nevertheless, an inquiry into the idea of character is all to the good.

But what is it that we call climate? Let it not be said, above all, this time, that the inquiry has been made or is being made progressively, adducing the number of excellent manuals, French and others, on climatology and meteorology. What is of importance in this case is a detailed analysis of climates considered *with reference to man*. But who would dare to attempt that analysis at the present time?

There is a sensible difference between the scientific and the popular ideas of climate. This is a fact which Raoul Blanchard, to quote him only, has lately brought into prominence in his book on Flanders.[3] "The climate of that country," he says, "has not a good reputation. Strangers who come to live there never cease talking of the weariness with which Flemish air affects them. On the other hand, an examination of averages shows that the Flemish climate is satisfactory." This is a statement of the problem, and it is notable as relating to a country without violent differences of temperature, without any extremes of rainfall; a country temperate and moderate in every respect.

[1] Semple, **XC**, Chaps. II and XVII, *passim*.
[2] Bodin, **XXXVI**, Vol. V, 1, p. 486.
[3] Blanchard, **CCXVII**, p. 14.

Now there is no question about the number of attempts which have already been made, if not to solve, at least to state this problem correctly; but how many are there still left to make? The constituent elements of climate may perhaps be susceptible to numerical valuation. But their convergences, their coincidences, and their discordances, their meetings and their separations, their combinations and their dissociations, all those elements, in fact, which give to each climate its own character, its powers over life, its importance and value to man—these are surely not amenable to statistical treatment. A classification of climates as a whole still remains to be found—of climates in their relations to man—which shall be more complete and better adapted than that of Köppen. His, however, is based on plant life—a life which can "express very clearly, if it has been well chosen, the cumulative effects of different climatic phenomena".[1] But putting aside this study of the complete character of different climatic zones, what a number of new questions have to be decided in the study even of each zone—what a subtle and delicate appreciation of its repercussions on man is needed: the mechanical, physiological, and psychological repercussions of the different elements of a given climate!

The study of climates in their relation to the flora, that element of life which is relatively fixed, is still in its infancy. We are only just beginning to take note of distribution rather than of mass statistics. An analogous piece of work has to be done for man; but how much more difficult,[2] more lengthy, and more complicated will it be!

To sum up: the only ideas which used to attract the attention of inquirers bent on investigating the relations of man with his environment were those which bore on facts of anthropology, medicine, climatology, or ethology. What appears essential to us now was formerly ignored or neglected.[3]

[1] Brunhes, **LXVI**, p. 305. In place of "cumulative" we should prefer "concomitant".

[2] Cf. the insufficiency from the point of view of human geography of efforts like those of Herbertson, with his "Natural Regions of the World" (*Geogr. Teacher*, iii, 1905).

[3] Huntington's *Climate and Civilization* came under our notice too late to be utilized in this discussion. It is an interesting attempt at systematization (**LXXIII**).

IV

Climatic Action takes place through the Medium of the Vegetable Kingdom

There certainly is a climatic action on man, but it is not tangible, nor is it in the province of geography, which comes into relations with it only through the action of climate on the natural environment. In other words, the action of climate on the natural environment in which man lives must be known before we can understand the action of climate on man.

Now this action is exercised first on the form of the earth, on its modelling. The most powerful, effective, and constant agents of erosion—running water, glaciers, and wind—are all due more or less directly to climate. The only two powers which escape it are sea and fire. And this climatic action is the more powerful in that it is not confined to its own epoch. Whoever wishes to know all about the modellings of a region must consider, not only the part played by climate to-day, but also that of the climate of the past. Need we mention the vast scientific literature which, in our own days, scholars of the first rank have devoted to the great advance, or rather successive advances, of quaternary glaciation—in Europe, Asia, and America at the same time? It is not only "the causal problem" which has attracted the attention of these scientists, and the possibility, for instance, of finding a connexion between certain of these extensions and the disappearance of the lands which then united Europe to North America and prevented the warm Equatorial currents from entering and raising the temperature of the Arctic Ocean [1]; but it is "the problem of consequences" also, for these are certainly not negligible.

It is not a question of what we may call "local consequences" only, the formation of "sites" for example; the site of Chicago, the battlefields of Lake Garda, the site of Sion in Valais, and so many other examples which have been classic for ages, and which would fill books. But are not the con-

[1] Hypothesis of Krischtafowitsch (*Bull. Soc. belge Géol.*, **XXIV**, 1900, pp. 292–305).

ditions of life in immense countries like Canada,[1] Finland and the Baltic plateaux, still largely influenced by the disadvantages of a network of rivers combined with the special difficulties of a topography of glacial origin? Is it, on the other hand, a matter of no importance to anyone who wishes to understand the distribution of the economic zones in Russia and Western Siberia, that he should know how to discover their first rough outlines in the geography of the past?[2] The region of Czernoziom is the southern part of the plain and was already dry in the Miocene epoch. The forest and marshy region

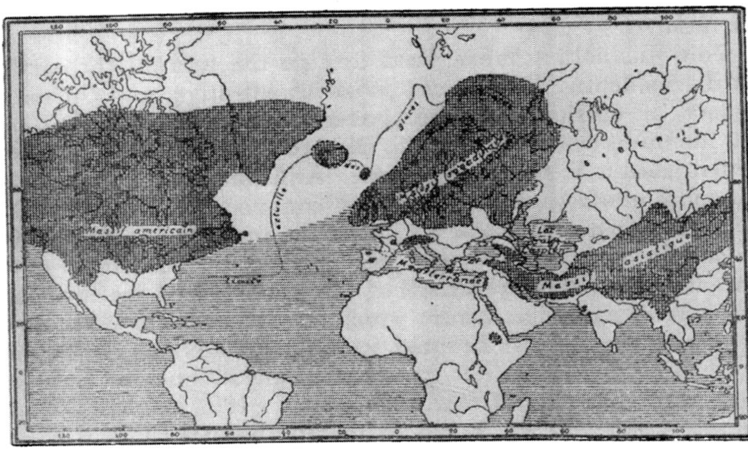

FIG. 1.—Maximum extension of Pleistocene glaciers (after De Morgan).

of the centre is a region of Pleistocene deposits. The frozen Tundra, with its mosses and its peat bogs, is a region of glacial formation. But it is equally important to know that the major portion of these areas was inhabited relatively late—and that just because the ice lasted so long. It was apparently the southern zone of the peaty steppe, the zone of Czernoziom, which was first peopled[3]; then Central Russia, the forest zone, but only towards the tenth century before our era. In the North the stone industry lasted, and the reindeer survived,

[1] Baulig, **XI**, 1908, p. 441.
[2] Raveneau, **XI**, 1898, p. 358.
[3] It is here a question of the prehistoric population. For the peopling of Russia in historic times, see Book III, Chap. I.

until an epoch little distant from our own era.[1] Even in the eighteenth century, Pallas, who wrote the *Description de toutes les nations de l'Empire de Russie* (1776), saw the Woguls in caves, living entirely by hunting and fishing, and breaking up bones in order to make a kind of soup from them. This is a good example of persistence well into the eighteenth century of the kind of life led by Mousterian man.[2]

But why concern ourselves with such far-off countries? Has not the influence of the extended quaternary glaciation

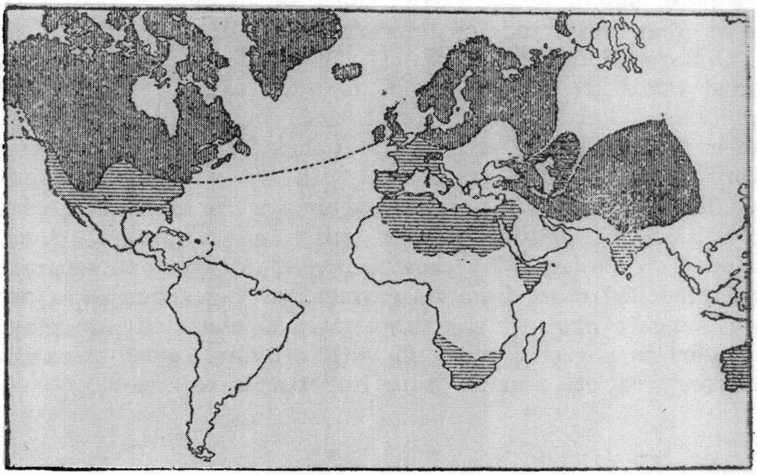

FIG. 2.—Ice and the expansion of palæolithic industry (Chellean and Acheulean type) (after De Morgan).

on the development of life in our regions of Western Europe been strikingly expounded? Vidal de la Blache, notably, has shown [3] admirably how the low and sunny region which extends diagonally from the Garonne to the South of Brittany, the earliest and most completely freed from the glaciers, was one of the first where primitive humanity began to flourish.[4] If he often speaks of the "precocity" of France, it is an idea he shares with the pre-historians: does not Sophus

[1] Zaborowski, **XI,** 1901, p. 143.
[2] De Morgan, **CLXXIV,** p. 121.
[3] Vidal, **CCXXXII,** p. 29.
[4] Vidal, **CCXXXII,** pp. 29–30.

Muller[1] describe those same countries, for the same reasons, as the chief centre of the most ancient culture? It is a matter of some importance, no doubt, to anyone who is studying the origins of human settlement, to know that "paleolithic Europe was not the Europe of to-day", but rather those regions spared by the ice[2]—and that all pre-historians agree that no human artefact or stone implement has been found in the deposits of the maximum glacial extension.

Thus climate, controlling erosion, has a powerful influence in the modelling of the earth; and that modelling in its turn is of great importance in determining the life of man.

One question arises here. If the forms which the surface crust takes are of importance to man, are they important *as forms*? Certainly not; or at least, considered in this way, their rôle is a very feeble one, and their influence on societies very small, even in connexion with the sites of towns or smaller settlements. For here again we are concerned with conditions of lighting, laying out, and insolation, which depend on climate. But how are we really going to separate the modelled crust from its garment of vegetation, how are we going to abstract the simple forms, where climate plays its part in covering them all with a living carpet of extraordinary variety and of prime importance to men?

*

* *

Plant life is the true intermediary between the inorganic world and the other. From the former it draws chemical elements which it decomposes in order to assimilate them, by means of its roots from the soil and its respiratory organs from the open air, so that it constitutes, as Vidal de la Blache has somewhere said, "a living manufactory of food." On this chiefly, and almost on this alone, depends the continuance or the disappearance of the animal population of a country, whether herbivorous or not. That is why it can be truly said that botanical geography is "the intermediate link" between physical and political geography.

Botanical geography takes climate into account before everything. Not that œcology, the science of "the local

[1] **CLXXVI**, p. 4.
[2] Ibid., p. 3.

environment" which Schimper, in his *Pflanzengeographie* has based so firmly on physiology, neglects to study other things besides climate, such as the action of the soil, according to its greater or less fertility, its permeability to air and water and its richness in chemical substances, obnoxious or beneficial to calcicole, calcifuge, or halophil plants. Not that it neglects even very precise considerations of surface relief, and the influence on the life of plants of a ground which is flat here and hilly there, sunny here and shaded there. But these are by no means all the effects of climate on the character of the soil, on its "edaphic" factors! Is it not a fact that the same soil, as Penck has noted, in different geographical environments—that is to say, when subject to different climatic influences—will be moss-covered or barren? Do not the plants themselves, to the experienced eye, seem to show by their outward appearance the essential characteristics of the climate—the more or less powerful and prolonged action of heat or cold, light or darkness, the wind which bends, or stunts, or withers them, and above all, drought or humidity?

For water is the great preponderating factor in any inquiry into vegetation: water suspended as vapour in the air, water circulating in the soil and bathing the roots. It was not without reason that Penck, in 1910, proposed to substitute for the old classifications of climates founded on temperature, a classification based essentially on the effects of water in and on the soil: snowy climates, moist climates, arid climates.[1] There is, in fact, a complete botanical physiognomy, to which physiology soon gives the key; the leaves of green hygrophil plants, spread out as if to offer full scope to evaporation; the leaves of xerophil plants, stunted, hard, pale, sometimes appearing to be covered with a thick varnish, sometimes transformed into thorns, instruments for absorption, a perpetual check upon transpiration. Experiment in this matter has lent valuable aid to observation.

We know how a temperate plant species transported to a cold mountain is seen rapidly to change its aspect, to grow stunted and cling to the soil, to thicken its tissues, and to strengthen them with protections against the cold—in short, to acquire the character of Polar plants, and become

[1] Zimmermann, **XI,** 1910, p. 87.

first of all biennial, then perennial: the successful experiments of Gaston Bonnier leave no doubt on this point.[1] And similarly, an annual plant of the temperate regions becomes, in hot climates, under the action of quite different œcological factors, a tree with perennial foliage—and the *Senecio vulgaris* which grows by our roadsides, weedy and humble, is called in tropical Africa *Senecio johnstoni*,[2] a tree three times the height of a man. . . . These are classic examples of the power of climate in the vegetable world: we do not add, of course—and clear proofs of the finalist theory of adaptation.[3]

But is this power exercised also on the animal world? There is no doubt that in the first place it is so. Broad or folded leaves; horizontal or vertical leaves like those of the eucalyptus; high, low, or creeping branches; thick, spongy, or thin tissues; these are so many effects of climate on plants. And the white coat of Polar animals, the grey or tawny livery of the beasts of the desert, the fine hair of the wool-less sheep of the Central Sahara, the thick down on the birds of Arctic lands—these are so many effects of the same climate on animals.[4] But how much deeper, more universal, and more important, is the action of the plant world on the animal world.

One thing was observed long ago. In a last analysis it is not the reindeer which on the border of the Arctic Circle supports the precarious life of the Hyperboreans, of the *Randvoelker* of the North, it is the lichen, the precarious but adequate food of the reindeer. And further still: considerations of food are not the only ones in question. Hahn, in his fine study of domestic animals and their relations to human economy[5]—a study which has for its sub-title "A Geographical Sketch"—has shown us what close bonds unite the animals which he is studying with agriculture, with methods of exploiting the soil, and with different forms of economic organization. But the free, wild animals, those that leap, burrow, climb trees with their sharp claws, the fleet-footed creatures of the steppes with slender and powerful

[1] Bonnier, *Le monde végétal*, Paris, 1907, p. 335 ff.
[2] Costantin, **CIV**, p. 194 ff.
[3] There is a non-finalist explanation in Bohn, **XIX**, 1915 (Vol. XVIII).
[4] See the collection of proven facts collected by Cuénot, **LII**, and the discussion of them from a non-finalist point of view.
[5] Hahn, **CXXVIII**; cf. Caullery, **CXXVI**.

limbs, are they not entirely adapted to certain forms of vegetation, to certain domains of the vegetable world? Here then, again, it is the action of climate which affects them—but always through the medium of the plant.

And in the same way it is the plant, too, which plays the chief part in the life of men, whether vegetarians or flesh-eaters. It supplies them directly or indirectly with the greater part of their food. But it supplies them also, very often, with the materials necessary for their buildings, their dwellings, the first elements of their tools and clothing. But why elaborate the list of examples? They simply confirm what we have established already: that if the action of climate on man is not direct, it is none the less important and constant.

And the conclusion to be drawn from all these facts is simple. The natural limits for which we are seeking must be marked out according to climate, considered as a means of controlling the distribution of vegetation.

The principle is established. These frames can only be climatico-botanical.

CHAPTER II

The Determination of Natural Areas and their Boundaries

I

Complexity of the Idea of Climate

IN the last chapter we used the term " climatico-botanical frames ", not climatic simply, or botanical; and this advisedly. Anyone who compares three maps of India—showing the rainfall, vegetation, and density of population—sees at once well-marked and striking relations between these three documents. In some parts there are regions of abundant rainfall, and therefore of rich cultivation and overflowing population; in others, regions of slight rainfall, poorer cultivation, and scanty population. The one thing depends upon the other.

These three maps, neither too schematic nor too simplified, but constructed from numerous well-chosen and safe data, explain each other even in detail; but they cannot possibly do so in all details or to the last detail. If, for example, the botanical map enables us to see why, since it shows in the *Regur* district, instead of rice, both cotton and dhurra (or *Cholum*), its especial plant, these regions of India, though equally well watered, are less populous than the region of the Ganges, it does not, on the other hand, explain why the Burmese coast, with its 118 inches of rain, has fewer inhabitants than Sind, which receives only 11 inches, or why the mountainous western part of Mysore supports fewer inhabitants than the Maidan [1] on the East. It is none the less true that this map—difficult to construct, and, when made, equally difficult to interpret—is essential to an understanding of the way in which climate affects man.

Why insist on this? Because when anyone studies the two simple, rough maps showing rainfall and d n sity of population, the impression is generally so strong, the similarities so

[1] For all this, cf. Vidal de la Blache, **CXCVII**, p. 360 ff.

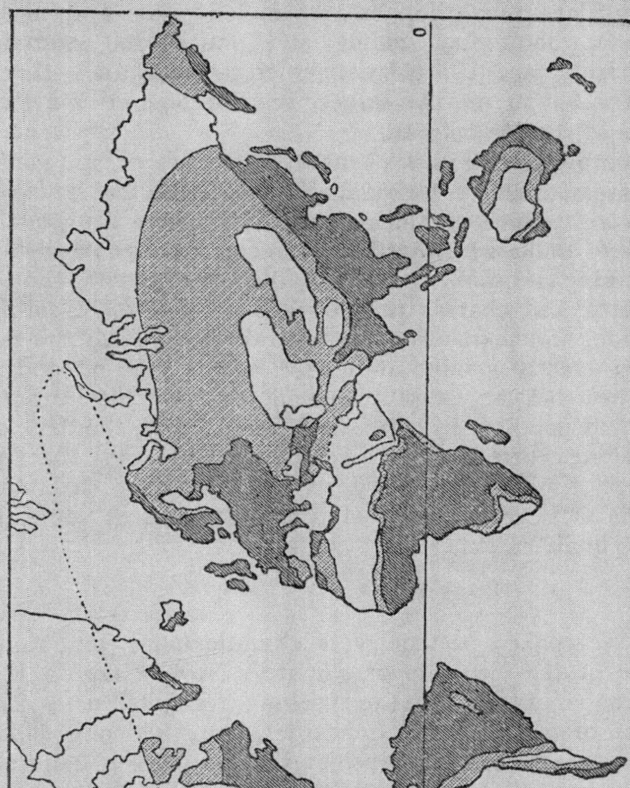

FIG. 3.—RAINFALL: SHOWING DESERT, DRY, AND HUMID REGIONS.
Dark areas: more than 20 in. per an.; *shaded areas*: between 10 and 20 in.; *white areas*: less than 10 in.
After Supan, *Verteilung d. mittl. jähr. Regenmenge auf d. Erdoberfläche.* (Hann, *Lehrb. d. Meteorol.*, 3rd ed., 1915.)

evident, that, without looking for the intermediate link, he is apt to assume that the two ends of the chain are directly connected—i.e. to make the population dependent on the rainfall. Here then the observer is led away and biassed towards a somewhat rough and much too summary determinism: and the old danger crops up again; the old error of believing in the direct, immediate, and inevitable influence of climate on man.

But comprehensive views, synthetic conclusions, and general relations can only be formulated safely when no doubts or illusions as to their signification or their value are possible. The case of India, which we have just considered, is one of the most striking and most carefully studied, but it is not the only one. Maps and charts, more or less schematic, of rainfall, cultivation, and population, in Australia give, with the same force, an exactly similar impression of the relation and the dependence between two phenomena of distinct orders—rainfall and population. And in a general way, the dark and light shadings correspond so much in maps [1] all over the world that their similarity is very remarkable. But deductions from this fact require for their proper treatment some preliminary qualifications.

*

* *

We have spoken previously of climatic maps, and rain is only one of the elements of climate. Now, what do these rainfall maps, of which we are speaking, really tell us? They are maps of mean annual quantities, from which it follows that they leave out of consideration any other factors of climate except rainfall, and the many different ways in which the distribution of the gross amount varies. But we are coming more and more to understand that in the study of the rainfall of a country the total amount of annual fall is not the only important consideration. For one thing, there are varieties of precipitation: rain and snow. The question is far from negligible. Woeikof has often insisted

[1] *La Géographie humaine*, by J. Brunhes (**CXVI**), renders the approximation very easy by superposing the two maps, drawn on the same scale, 1 in 90,000,000 (figs. 11 and 12, p. 89). Cf. ibid. the two charts, 118 and 119, *grands emblêmes climatiques* and *zones de transition* on the same scale, also superposed, but less clear. Compare also the maps in this book.

on its importance as far as Russia and Siberia are concerned. This is so great that the Russian peasants, in order to retain the snow on their fields from which the wind can easily drive it, make use of devices—cutting their stubble very long, for instance.[1] Woeikof also remarks that to the east of Lake Baikal, in the mountains of Khamar-Daban, the ground is not constantly frozen, whilst in the valleys and the plateaux of Transbaikalia, at a lower height above the sea-level, and more to the south, the water mills are stopped for five or six months,[2] the reason being that in October, whilst the valleys and plateaux see the sun, the vapours of Lake Baikal are condensed in abundant snow on the heights; this snow remains on the ground in the winter and protects it from the frost. Some degrees further south the snow becomes rain, and the protection no longer exists. But the rainfall charts give only the bare figures.

It is to be remarked also that the duration of the rainy season is an element of prime importance, as Passerat has shown very fully in his account of the Asiatic monsoons.[3] If two countries receive the same annual rainfall, it is not a matter of indifference whether this quantity falls in three months or spreads itself more or less equally over the whole year. In the one place there will be a short-lived luxuriance of vegetation, followed by a drought which destroys, or at least suspends, all plant life; in the other, a regular vegetation which will persist and develop throughout the whole year. But the maps of annual rainfall do not bring out such differences. They show a quite abstract and theoretic similarity between two fundamentally dissimilar countries—a mathematical similitude when the question is of a biological order. The example which Passerat gives is a striking one[4]: the tea plant is cultivated with equal success in Southern China, Japan, Annam, and Ceylon. These are four countries in which the annual rainfall differs very considerably, but which on the other hand resemble one another in the fact that the rainfall is spread over the whole year. The resemblance is more important than the difference.

[1] Woeikof, **XCVIII**, p. 196.
[2] Ibid., **CXCVIII.**
[3] Passerat, **XI**, 1906, p. 193 ff.
[4] Op. cit., p. 112.

So much for the nature and duration of precipitation, but the "time" is of equal importance.[1] Few examples of this are more striking than that of the great agricultural countries, the great producers of cereals, such as Russia. Bad harvests, here, are almost entirely the result of drought. This drought is due not to the abnormal scarcity of the total rainfall, but to its unequal distribution—to the insufficiency of moisture in the two months of August and September, which ruins the winter sowing, or of April and May, which spoils the spring sowing.[2] So, similarly, in India, which is situated rather on the outskirts than in the centre of the monsoon district, everything depends on the caprices and vicissitudes of the monsoon at its commencement in June, or at its end in October. On them, more than on the variations in the total rainfall, hangs the fate of the chief and most important *Kherif* harvest, which nourishes those overpeopled countries in which it has been said that a multitude of lives "hang only by a thread".[3] In such countries as India and Southern Russia, indeed, it is from overpopulation that the danger arises. Nor must we forget, when we class as desert or semi-desert all the countries which receive less than 20 inches of rain in the year, that these form altogether three-fifths of the land above sea-level. And they are not negligible countries, from the historical point of view, if it is true that it was precisely in the desert and semi-desert that the ancient civilizations both of the Old[4] and New World were born. In such countries the consideration of the time of the rainfall is of supreme importance.

There is no need to multiply examples. We might vary them, complicate them, and introduce other considerations. We might note the disturbing influence of early or late frosts; those which, for example, explain the precocity of harvests in certain countries which would be otherwise highly productive, such as, for example, Manitoba, where, since the winter is very long and delays the sowing of seed till June, the summer

[1] It is equally necessary to consider to a certain extent what might be called the chemistry of the rains. Cf. G. Capus, "La valeur économique des pluies tropicales," **XI**, 1914–15, Vol. XXIII–IV, pp. 109–26, on the richness in nitrogen of the heavy rains of the hot inter-tropical regions.

[2] Hitier, **CXVI**, p. 266.

[3] Vidal de la Blache, op. cit., pp. 363–4.

[4] Boule (M.), Report on a memoir by Mathew, "Climate and Evolution," in **XVI**, 1916, p. 498.

is too short, with the fear of frost before the harvest is ripe, for cereal cultivation.[1]

We have said all that is essential. One last and very striking illustration may be taken from a region close at hand. Let us consider only the gross amount of rainfall in Europe itself. One of the best watered countries it contains, and therefore, we might imagine, one of the most favourable to vegetation, is Herzogovina, where a town named Crkvice, at an altitude of 3,250 feet, has an annual rainfall of 175 inches, whilst that of Cattaro on the Dalmatian sea coast, is 150 inches—very little less. And it is not merely from these exceptional records, but from the general average of rainfall, that Herzogovina, the most sterile and arid country in modern Europe, is considered one of the best watered countries. What a paradox! But in truth, the combination of a climatic factor (violent and heavy rains), a geological factor (great surfaces of fissured limestone), and an agricultural factor (the absence of soil) with a factor which is essentially historic and human (deforestation, especially during the epoch of Venetian domination)[2] does away with the apparent contradiction. The analysis is still incomplete, especially as regards the climatic factor.

But what a warning is here for those who feel tempted to relate charts of rainfall to those showing population without studying the third map that shows the distribution of plant life in quantity and kind!

II

The Climatico-Botanical Areas in Regard to Humanity

Faced by such great difficulties, need we abandon all attempts at synthesis and leave matters in absolute uncertainty? By no means. It is possible, in spite of such difficulties, to recognize general limits and to mark out areas of the earth's surface which, viewed broadly, do actually present certain real and important analogies as regards the conditions of primordial existence.

First of all, there is a region between the Tropics that is

[1] **XI,** 1901, p. 279.
[2] Brunhes, **LXVII,** pp. 5–6.

differentiated fairly clearly. Here the sun's rays fall perpendicularly throughout the year, twice from the zenith at the Equator itself, and once at each of the Tropics: hence powerful insolation, which raises the temperature considerably, causes an expansion of the air column, and induces an upward movement of the air at the point where the sun passes in the zenith. This is called the Zone of Equatorial Calms. The ascending movement of the air naturally causes the heavy equatorial rains which last almost throughout the year, with, however, two well-marked paroxysms at the Equator itself. In proportion as we pass away from it towards the Tropics, the two paroxysms draw nearer together and leave room for a dry season. When we reach the Tropics they coincide, and we get clear-cut distinction between two alternate seasons, one fairly short, wet, and hot and the other long, dry, and somewhat cooler.

In spite of many variations which are easy and instructive to consider, this zone presents very remarkable common characteristics in both continents throughout its whole extent. In it the temperature is generally high and very constant [1]; the rainfall is abundant and spread nearly equally over the whole year [2]; all the conditions are exceptionally favourable to the development of an exuberant vegetation, dominated by immense trees which lift their heads to a height of more than 200 feet. It is also a land of mighty rivers, such as the Congo and the Amazon [3]; a land of virgin forests with their tall, dense vegetation, their innumerable lianas and epiphytic plants, which make a tangle of the undergrowth. Here are Humboldt's *Hylœa,* in the basin of the Amazon and the great Congo forest, slightly different in nature but of the same appearance; here, too, are the forests covering part of Australia, the Malay Archipelago, Ceylon, and Madagascar.

Outside this area conditions are different; over great spaces the combined action of rain and heat has transformed the

[1] Singapore, lat. 1° 15′ N., mean for the coldest month 87°, for the hottest month 91°; Cayenne, lat. 4° 56′ N., 85°, 89°; Colombo, lat. 6° 56′ N., 87°, 90°.

[2] Singapore, mean annual rainfall 91·7 in. in monthly proportions of: January 76, February 66, March 71, April 73, May 68, June 82, July 65, August 104, September 79, October 84, November 118, December 114 (according to Angot).

[3] Congo, mean outflow at the mouth, 1,000,000 cub. yds.; Amazon at high water, 1,500,000 cub. yds.

volcanic and archæan rocks into sterile laterite. Gradually, moreover, as we go further north or south from the Equator, we find the forest gives place to steppes, merging first into savannah which itself merges into steppe; this transformation is fully realized in the zone, or rather the two zones, which lie immediately to the north and to the south of that of the Equatorial calms—the zones of the Trade Winds.

*

* *

These open up quite different possibilities. We have mentioned how, the further we advance towards the Tropics, the two paroxysms of rain, which in the north and in the south of the Equatorial region correspond to the two passages of the sun in the zenith, gradually draw nearer to one another. Consequently, the year no longer consists of four alternate seasons, two of relative dryness and two of more persistent rain,[1] but of two seasons only, with very marked differences: a short rainy season and a long dry season.[2] There are equally marked differences in the temperature, for the increasing dryness increases the changes due to latitude.[3] The barometric conditions are similarly altered. The marked difference which exists between the general high barometric pressure in the tropical regions and the low pressure in the Equatorial calms gives rise to a system of constant winds [4]—the Trade Winds—which blow from the north and from the south towards the Equator, but are made to deviate from this course by the earth's rotation.

[1] For example, Bogota in Colombia, lat. 4° 35′ N., mean annual rainfall 63 in., of which 11 per cent falls in January and February, 25 per cent in April–May, 9 per cent in July–August, and 28 per cent in October–November.

[2] Bombay, for example, lat. 18° 54′ N., mean annual rainfall 73 in. The proportions for the seven months from November to May are 6, 1, 2, 1, 0, 0, 5; from June to October, 263, 342, 201, 146, and 33 (according to Angot).

[3] Hahn gives, **LVII**, Vol. II, I, p. 7:—

	Annual mean. degrees	Hottest month. degrees	Coldest month. degrees	Difference. degrees
At the Equator	25·9	26·2	25·5	0·7
In Lat. 10° N. .	26·4	26·7	25·7	1·0
In Lat. 20° . .	25·7	28·1	21·7	6·4
In Lat. 30° . .	20·3	27·3	14·6	12·7

[4] Cf. chart of annual isobars. Maximum of 766 in the Northern Hemisphere in the east of the Pacific, and to the west of the Azores; in the Southern Hemisphere (less continental) maximum of 766 in the south-east of the Pacific and of 764 in the south-east of the Atlantic and between Africa and Australia. At the Equator, equal pressures, or less than 760.

K

Here the extremes of temperature and the drought of one part of the year are continually worsening the conditions of vegetable life; the winds, as violent as they are regular, hinder the growth of the young trees; the botanical character of the country, also, changes. We pass first, by a series of intermediary stages, from the Equatorial forest to what is called the *Campos*, in Brazil, the *Llanos* round the Orinoco, in Venezuela and in Colombia, the *Veldt* or *Savannah* in Africa. The possibility of settlement or migration for man is here wonderfully increased. Wherever the rainy season is long enough to allow the soil to support a population, a serious settlement of the land is possible. This settlement is, moreover, often widely extended, for human groups can only exist on steppes when there is plenty of elbow room, permitting them to range far afield in search of their daily bread. The series of transitions, however, still continues to unroll. The region which extends beyond the Tropics, between 20° and 30° north or south latitude, is a fairly dry region of dry winds, and of maximum subtropical barometric pressure, and on the whole of very slight precipitation. These are unfavourable conditions; and if, in addition to them, the country is in the form of a basin, and the surrounding mountains condense whatever moisture might be brought by winds from the ocean, the rainfall of itself is clearly insufficient to support vegetation.[1] The herbage becomes scanty and impoverished and finally disappears, and we get desert, where, as a rule, only rare xerophil plants can grow. Favourable accidental conditions alone will now permit the formation of cultivatable districts, which are always artificial and precarious; man will be able to settle in the oases only. Such is the state of things in the Sahara, in the Libyan and Arabian deserts, in those of the Thar, Persia, Turkestan, Mexico, Colorado, and the Great Basin in the Northern hemisphere; and similarly in the Kalahari, and the deserts of South Madagascar, Australia, and Patagonia in the Southern hemisphere. Instability

[1] Continuation of the previous table according to Hahn :—

	Annual mean.		Hottest month.		Coldest month.	
	N. Hemi.	S. Hemi.	N. Hemi.	S. Hemi.	N. Hemi.	S. Hemi.
At 30° of latitude	20·3	18·4	27·3	21·8	14·6	14·6
„ 40 „ .	14·0	12·0	24·0	15·6	4·9	9·0
„ 50 „ .	5·8	5·6	18·1	8·3	7·0	2·9
„ 60 „ .	1·0	2·0	14·0	3·2	15·8	7·6

and precariousness are the words that best describe the biological conditions in the great areas just defined.

*

* *

It is here and there in the northern and southern sub-tropical zones that the climatico-botanical areas most favourable to population are found, regions of irregular winds, temperate climate, and diversified cultivation.

Here there is a very real dissimilarity between the two hemispheres. The distribution of land and sea is by no means the same. The Northern hemisphere is chiefly continental, the Southern oceanic, which affects the astronomical distribution of the solar heat. The mean annual temperature of the Northern hemisphere is the higher, but beyond latitude 30° the mean temperatures for the coldest month are higher in the Southern. Moreover, there is no longer any question of regular zones of high or low pressure; these bands are broken up, so to speak, into fragments, and in their place we find centres of high or low pressure, towards which the winds converge, or from which they diverge violently. This meteorological domain comprises in the Southern hemisphere—South Africa, some parts of Argentina and the South of Australia; in the Northern—the greater part of North America, Europe, and Asia.

In these regions, the seat of rich and powerful civilizations, westerly winds generally prevail, and assure abundant rains and an equable climate in all the western parts of the continents. The eastern parts are not so well off. Moreover, warm currents obliquely cross the Atlantic and the Pacific, chiefly in the Northern hemisphere, and these contribute still more to that equalization of climate which naturally results from the presence of wide stretches of ocean—so much so that the western regions of the continents, already favoured by the constancy of the westerly winds, present positive anomalies due to the action of the Kuro Shiō or of the Gulf Stream; Lisbon has a mean temperature of 53·2° in January and 75·6° in July; New York, in almost the same latitude, a mean of 29·9° in January and 77·5° in July. Thus these temperate lands are warmer and more moist on the West than on the East. But taken as a whole, and leaving out these differences, they are eminently suitable for the development of a varied and abundant vegetation.

Two areas can here be discerned: a forest area, corresponding in the north of the continents to quaternary glacial deposits and, further south, to the beds of ancient seas such as Lake Agassiz and the Sarmato-Pontic sea, and a huge area covered with loess, where trees only grow when inequalities in the ground favour the exposure by erosion of a primitive soil, heavy enough to provide their roots with a firm hold.

There is nothing more monotonous than this zone of bare land; it is prairie, carpeted with a vegetation which comprises, no doubt, a fairly large number of species, but on which the prevalence of certain common plants impresses quite a remarkable aspect of uniformity. But there is no zone whose primitive aspect has been more altered by human toil. Those vast surfaces of loess yield easily to the plough-share of man, or even, in the earlier stages of civilization, to the hoe. Vidal de la Blache has often pointed out very justly how these facilities for cultivation explain many of the facts of population and many an historical evolution. Here, fertility is not the most important consideration. The prairie is fertile throughout. It contains within its borders the vast *Czornosjom* or *Czernoziom*, the black soil districts of Southern Russia, stretching alike into the basins of the Don, the Dnieper, and the Volga, which have an area of more than 300,000 square miles, half as much again as the whole of France, with a depth of vegetable soil varying from 3 to 16 feet and sometimes even from 30 to 60 feet, with no forests or trees—a huge grain-growing district prepared by thousands of centuries of grass. The prairie also includes the Hungarian *Puszta*, whose seas of undulating grasslands with their half-wild cattle and their *Czikos*—mounted herdsmen—were sung by Petœfi, before a sustained effort had succeeded in transforming them into marvellously rich cornlands. Elsewhere we have the Cossack and Kirghiz steppes, arid, with a poor soil sometimes without grass or pasturage, sinister in their winter aspect and little less terrible in summer. Elisée Reclus has left us an unforgettable picture of them in his book *La Terre*, out of date, naturally, but showing what a virile grip of reality he had, and still has.[1] Then there are the Prairies of North America, once very similar before American labour turned

[1] Paris, 3rd edition, Vol. I, pp. 101–2.

them into a kind of immense chessboard of industrialized cultivation, to the Hungarian *Puszta* and the grassy steppes of the Black Lands: but to the west, they degenerate gradually into great arid plains, then into desert. These were all lands easy to traverse, open spaces utilized from the earliest times by human migrations and great ethnic displacements; carts could go over this flat surface drained by nature without encountering obstacles; in the hard clay soil the cart-ruts extended for miles in straight lines; horses, going at a gallop, rivalled the wind in raising clouds of dust and stirring up the debris of plant life.

Quite otherwise is the forest area, where the trees, in the North, grow out of the firm soil resulting from the heavy glacial deposits. It is also absolutely different from the Equatorial forest. Whether copse or grown woods it is never so dense or so tangled in its undergrowth as to present that type of obstacle so often described by the pioneers of the great Amazon and Congo forests. There are no creepers and no climbing plants; the greatest hindrances are the brambles.

For the rest, we must always remember that it is now nothing but a ruin, a faded copy of the ancient forest. At an epoch not very distant from our own, compared with prehistoric and immemorial ages, Gaul was covered with trees from the ocean to the Mediterranean. In Germany, according to Roman authors, the Hercynian forest was a sixty days' march in extent. This is doubtless an exaggeration, but still, the forest must have then been very large: it is chiefly since the sixth century that it has diminished.[1] In Europe, at that period, the contrast it presented with the grass steppes and moorland must certainly have been as striking and complete as the contrast that still remained at the beginning of the nineteenth century, between the *llanos* and the *selvas* of the Amazon and the savannahs and cypress woods of Louisiania. The boundless sea of herbaceous plants succeeded the immense, compact mass of trees and ran parallel to them along enormous spaces. But it is not merely in quantity but in quality that the forest varied.

We are just beginning to learn the mechanism of the transformation of "virgin forest" in Africa or America, into

[1] Hausrath, *Der Deutsche Wald*, Leipzig, 1907.

"secondary" forest by the efforts of man; to understand the way in which those efforts, at first negligible, but continuously prosecuted and multiplied, can have profound results. Very slight causes are sufficient to disturb the unstable equilibrium between light, which promotes rapid growth and young wood, and shade, which is needed for slow development.[1] Taking these differences into account, an analogous process was at work in the forests of the temperate zone. Formerly the *Urwald* was more impassable and more difficult to move about in than our woods of to-day, which have all been more or less humanized. Our rivers are controlled, our marshes drained, our lakes turned into fields; our thickets thinned out into woodland, our forest glades converted into arable land. The whole aspect of the country at the present time, succeeding a previous aspect which betrayed the destructive and debasing power of man rather than his reconstructive and creative capacity, no longer represents in any way "a state of nature", a state purely theoretical, no less difficult to define rigorously with regard to plants than to man. This has been shown in the clearest way, so far as central Europe is concerned, by Gradmann.[2]

Forest, moreover, has not prevented human settlement, and it would not be correct to represent it as the foe of human societies. There are too many remains and too many ruins which prove the contrary—remarkable agglomerations of *tumuli*, of hut foundations in the midst of the woods. Hidden by the thickets and effectually protected by them, it was not merely villages which sprang up in little rudimentary groups. The settlements were larger, and more numerous, than might, perhaps, have been expected. We must not forget that even the dense Equatorial forest, especially in Africa, if not more populous, is at least more generally inhabited, less uniformly dense, and more studded with clear spaces than it was once supposed to be.[3] States, even, have sprung up and been able to grow in the shade of the forest, and under its powerful protection—the original Russian state and the possessions of the Teutonic Order, for example. Moreover, the European

[1] Cf., for example, what Aug. Chevalier says about this, in his various publications.

[2] Gradmann, **XIV**, Vol. VII (1901), pp. 361–77, 435–47.

[3] **XI**, 1908, Vol. XVII, pp. 279–80.

forests, to speak of them only, being composed largely of oak and beech, in their Western and Southern parts of birch, and in their Northern and Eastern of firs and pines, were easy to clear, and had been fertilized by the slow accumulation of organic débris. In every way they provided means of protection and food for man, quite as efficient as the open prairie with its clay soil, if not more so.

*

* *

There is one further zone. Beyond the Boreal forest (for hardly anything similar exists in the Southern Hemisphere [1]) —beyond the folious forest, in which the line where beech ceases furnishes a limit interesting to examine,[2] and even beyond the forests of evergreen conifers, the sylvan plant life gradually changes its character and finally disappears. Its limit, however, does not describe a regular circle round the pole, but is curved in the same way as the isotherms. It is much nearer to the pole in Europe than in the Northern parts of America; in the neighbourhood of North Cape, between 70° and 71° N. latitude, the birch is still found; in Siberia the most hardy larches grow as far north as 68°; but in Labrador the firs do not go beyond 58°. The striking parallelism between the lines which mark the Northern circumpolar limit of trees and the isotherm of 10° in July shows that temperature is above all things responsible for the change, and finally for the disappearance, of forest growth. But the violence of winds, drought, scanty rainfall, and frost, which hardens and desiccates the ground to a great depth, are all secondary factors which augment the effect of the persistent cold. The forest growth no longer benefits by that minimum of 10° mean temperature for five months in the year, which the beech requires for the various stages of its growth. It is replaced more and more, as the temperature gets lower, by grassy tracts of country; a thin border of puny and solitary trees marks the transition from *taïga* to *tundra*, then

[1] We may complete the parallel of the two continents as regards temperature:

	Annual mean.		Coldest month.		Hottest month.	
	N. Hemi.	S. Hemi.	N. Hemi.	S. Hemi.	N. Hemi.	S. Hemi.
In lat. 70° . .	10·1	11·5	7·0	0·8	26·0	22·0
„ 80° . .	16·7	19·8	1·8	6·5	33·5	31·5

[2] Cf. A. Woeikof, "L'extension du hêtre, fonction du climat," *Arch. Sc. phys. et nat.*, 4th period, **XXIX** (1910) and **XXX** (1910).

grass itself gives place to moss and lichens. The size of such woody plants as still survive in the more sheltered spots becomes so meagre that they are no longer trees, except in the botanical sense. Dwarf birches and stunted, diminutive willows are the only representatives of arboreal vegetation to the North of the Arctic circle, where the annual precipitation does not exceed 10 inches, where the ground is perpetually frozen. In Nova Zembla the highest willows reach 8 inches, and these are the giants of the arboreal vegetation of the district, whilst the dwarfs measure less than an inch.

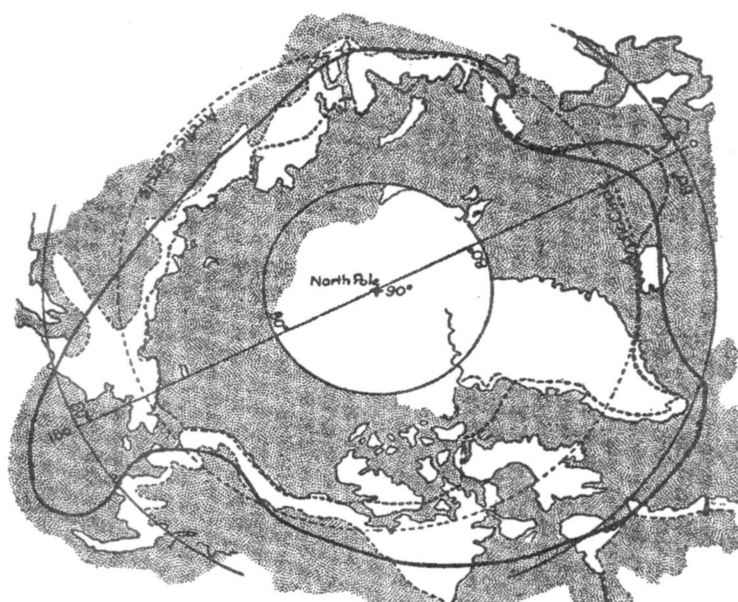

FIG. 4.—NORTHERN CIRCUMPOLAR REGIONS, SHOWING THE NORTHERN LIMITS OF SYLVAN PLANT LIFE.

Shaded area: Wooded vegetation. *Black line:* Isotherm of + 10° in July. *Dotted line:* Limit of human habitation.

Such are the condition and appearance of the *tundra* of Eurasia and the *barren grounds* of North America : miserable regions, with a mean botanical dowry, a mediocre fauna, and, like the desert, with a meagre support for human life.

III

The Symmetry of the Terrestrial Organism and the Distribution of Human Societies

Thus, if we take a bird's-eye view of the world as a whole, we get the impression of a kind of terrestrial symmetry. All its parts are co-ordinated and classified. In the centre is a forest vegetation, so overpowering that it stifles all life except its own, bordered by regions more suitable for human settlement. Then comes a gap, with the belt of sub-tropical deserts following on one another slantwise from continent to continent, beyond which possibilities of settlement again appear, gradually reach their maximum both in quality and variety, then fade away again in the frozen lands of the North and South. Such is the order and the regulation of our world, and the surface of the earth appears to an observer, taking a bird's-eye view of it, as a true Cosmos—an organized and coherent world.[1]

But at this stage our difficulties begin. The temptation to go a step farther is very strong, so strong indeed that few can resist it, and the slope is smooth. It is easy to assert that a special type of human society corresponds to each of these zones, and to give examples. Equatorial societies, the inhabitants of the great forest, thinly scattered, living on the harvest of the woods or more rarely by hunting, isolated and thrown back upon themselves, so to speak, present everywhere the same characteristics, whose monotony reflects that of their environment.

Similarly, there are sub-tropical societies. Amongst the people of the steppes, which border deserts like the Sahara, common features mark all the societies which inhabit those unstable districts. Sometimes, though rarely, a whole tribe takes up its permanent abode on the land and devotes itself to agriculture. Often it is only a small part of the tribe which settles down to life on the land, for the normal life is nomadic. Nearly all these peoples, whether of Berber, Fulah, or Arab origin, are cattle raisers, and move about with their herds as pasturage necessitates, and most of them (we note it without the intention of establishing any definite connexion between

[1] Cf. G. Menedinti, **XI,** 1901, p. 7 ff.

phenomena which are plainly related, but of a different order) live under patriarchal rule and have adopted Moslem monotheism. As conquering peoples, most of them have founded more or less powerful but ephemeral kingdoms.

In the temperate lands, also, we may say that the type of society has been analogous. Here were agricultural districts, where men who settled down quickly proceeded to form states—monarchies or, at a later date, republics—of real and great stability. Natural resources were exploited to the utmost, and manufactures, combined with agriculture, gave rise to great industries of the capitalist order. The continual improvement of means of communication permitted the establishment between different peoples of systematic and regular relations. A single type of material and intellectual civilization tends to develop under such conditions, in spite of the number and even the complexity of the elements which have to be included in it.

Lastly, the polar regions naturally show a characteristic type of civilization. Living a precarious and limited existence, bound to an immemorial routine, entirely preoccupied with combating the cold and with a painful search for uncertain food, all the "Hyperboreans", whether Esquimaux or Samoyeds, fishers or hunters, breeders of dogs or reindeer, exhibit throughout the whole extent of the circumpolar regions a number of common characteristics which suffice to bring into prominence the likeness between them.

And thus it may be affirmed, these great climatico-botanical regions, which it is so easy nowadays to mark off and characterize, have their special human as well as their special plant or animal character. They are not regions void of humanity. Anyone who speaks of "Equatorial countries" or "Arctic countries" thereby speaks of societies of an equatorial type, or, as Ratzel says, "Randvoelker." These statements are made, but they need proof; nor are we, after this kind of general assertion, really much advanced in our knowledge of "that other world, which is man".

It is nearly four centuries since Jean Bodin in his *République* first sketched his system of terrestrial zones, which is now academic. About the year of grace 1560, the theory was new and suggestive, and the deductions promising: "these points established, it will be easier to form a judgment on the nature of the people "[1] . . and so it doubtless is; no one is likely to dispute the classroom value of such a collection of facts. But their value after all is confined to the classroom; and since science implies research, their scientific value, to all intents, is nil.

The proof is this. It is possible for anyone taking a comprehensive view of the Universe to group the geographical facts in a certain number of great regions, which are arranged, so to speak, symmetrically on either side of the Equator.

On the other hand, it is possible to distribute accurately in these regions various types of human societies, noting that there are a certain number of differences between these societies in different regions and a certain number of resemblances within them.

But the real and only problem is this: whether the constitution of these typical human societies is the direct result of the physical nature or, so to speak, of the internal character of the climatico-botanical regions: in plain words, whether the climatico-botanical region is the cause of the particular human society said to be specially adapted to it.

*

* *

A preliminary remark seems necessary. The question we are raising is certainly not a simple one, and the problem we have just stated cannot be solved "by algebra". There is no such thing as a simple human factor. A human society and the life of a human society are not simple matters: to explain them, a thousand complex elements must be coordinated, which are intermingled in a way which is very difficult to understand or to measure. Let us, therefore, simplify them arbitrarily, and first of all simplify our premises. Let us reduce them even to a single one and that the most important. Let us proceed as if for the moment we had to face only the problem of quantity and to study the manner in which the mass of human beings was spread over the surface of the globe according to gross numerical evidence only. Is this great single factor, chosen indeed because of its magnitude, directly and immediately dependent on geographical environment? We see at once the value and

[1] Bodin, **XXXVI**, l. v, 1, p. 464.

general importance which the reply to such a question will possess.

Now whilst these vast regions stretch evenly on each side of the Equator, the people in them are very far from being distributed with any mathematical equality as to the density of each square mile.

On the one hand, if we add to the 448 millions of human beings in Europe [1] the 302 millions of India, the 326 millions of China proper, and the 52 millions of little Japan,[2] overwhelming masses of mankind, amounting to two-thirds of the whole, are grouped on one-seventh of the land surface. On the other hand, the empty spaces are no less remarkable: Africa, as far as one can judge from calculations not likely to be under-estimated, seems to have 140 millions at most, and a density which does not amount to 12 to the square mile. Similarly, in South America it does not exceed 6 to the square mile: and in the Australian continent, that "colosse informe et mal venu", as the geographer Lespagnol somewhere calls it, the population hardly reaches 4½ millions, and the density is not 3 to the square mile.

Can it be truly said, then, that it is the climate or, even more generally, the combination of the climatico-botanical resources and possibilities of different regions which governs and determines such inequalities?

We must not forget that Woeikof, in his memoir of 1906 (**XCVIII**), calculated that more than half the human race (806 millions) live between the 20th and 40th degrees of North latitude, that is to say, in a belt of land from which the whole of Europe is excluded, but in which the greater part of the deserts of the Northern hemisphere are found.

But can we talk of heat or cold—sheer heat and sheer cold, so to speak? Geographies generally agree to place the "pole of cold" at Verkhoyansk in Siberia; and it is a fact that of the three poles of cold which Mohn recognizes in the Northern hemisphere, in his account of the meteorological results of Nansen's Polar Expedition (Eastern Siberia, Central Greenland,

[1] Density per sq. mile, 102.

[2] Respective densities: India 148, China 153, Japan 312. It must be understood that we have reduced the problem to the simplest question of numbers. What a number of commonly neglected elements there are which would render it infinitely more complicated and more striking! We will only mention one: longevity. The average life in India is 23 years, in France it is 47.

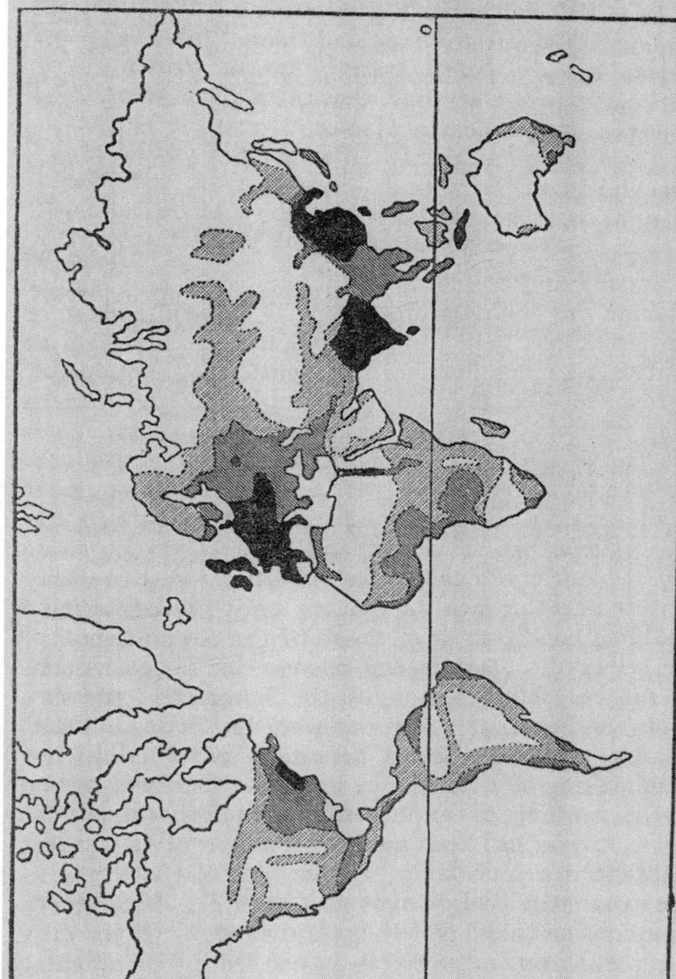

FIG. 5.—DENSITY OF HUMAN POPULATION.

White areas: less than 1 inhabitant to the sq. kilometre; *light-grey areas*: less than 10 inhabitants to the sq. kilometre; *dark-grey areas*: from 10 to 50 inhabitants to the sq. kilometre; *black areas*: more than 50 inhabitants to the sq. kilometre.

and the Polar Region properly so called), Siberia is the chief and the most accentuated. But Verkhoyansk, which is included in it, is an inhabited place with a population of 356 according to the latest census, and the soil there is sown and cultivated every year: indeed, human families live and multiply there under conditions which are elsewhere considered prohibitive, for the January mean is – 51·2°. Inversely, Massowah, on the Red Sea, in the middle of a stifling coastal plain, combines all the extreme conditions of heat which our meteorological treatises define, and is, notwithstanding, a place regularly inhabited (population 7,000).

There is no blind fatality about heat and cold. The extreme North of Canada and Alaska is not inhabited in any regular way, although no temperature below – 54° Fahrenheit or – 47° Centigrade has been recorded there. But near Havre (Montana, U.S.A.), much further to the south, the thermometer has gone down to – 68° Fahrenheit, and not far off in Northern Dakota the winter is as severe as in any Arctic region, yet experience proves that men can live in these parts quite well. If we take account of the fact that for a whole year the number of hours of sunshine is greater in the North than in the temperate regions, where clouds and fogs intervene so as practically to restrict its theoretical duration, we can easily see that it is not the laws of climate only that determine the uninhabited condition of so much of the Arctic region.

Another series of meteorological phenomena has to be considered; the restrictive action of the barometric pressure is well known and evident. Men can work but little, and that with difficulty, under too low a pressure; but this did not prevent the making of a railway in Peru at a height of 13,000 feet, nor the working of sulphur mines on Popocatepetl at 17,800 feet. A road has been made at a height of 18,500 feet in the Karakorum; and lastly, 17 per cent of the towns in Bolivia are situated at a height of over 13,000 feet. In Southern Tibet mountain sickness is felt by travellers, at times very severely, at an altitude of 12,000 to 15,000 feet; but Shigatse is a town 12,740 feet high and Gyangtse stands at 13,000 feet, where a July temperature of 105° has been recorded; whilst from September onward it freezes, and night temperatures of – 16° are frequent, and even normal, in winter.[1]

[1] Sion, **CXCVI,** *passim.*

Here man persistently sets nature at defiance ; and where he does so, can we assert that it is the obvious and direct action of meteorologic conditions which accounts for his absence ?

Is it due to climate or physiology ? To the sheer weight of material conditions which can be expressed in numbers, in degrees of heat, or in yards, or to what is described by the vague word acclimatization, that is, to adaptation and suitability ? Not long ago a geographer quite rightly reproached Brunhes, the author of *Géographie Humaine*, with his relative indifference to medical geography.[1] There is a Polar anæmia, for instance, as there is a tropical one, to which all races are not equally subject. Is not this an important hindrance to population of a different order from what we may call "sheer" cold ?

White men would not be able to settle in polar countries, even if supplied with fresh and wholesome food. The want of light would quickly sap their vitality, by a process which Dr. Cook of the *Belgica* has convincingly proved.[2]

Climate, then, is the question ; but it is only to be considered in relation to the people who are exposed to it ; and nothing is more suggestive than the maps of medical geography in a recent book of Petermann's [3] published by the *Mitteilungen*, for the charts of colonial diseases so often coincide exactly with some great group of biological facts, or with some climatico-biological zone. In the African equatorial forests the effects of endemic malaria may combine with those of tropical anæmia and dysentery. Is this climatic determinism in the narrow sense of the word, or determinism of some distant climatic source, climatic by filiation and transposition ? It may be called, in the full sense of the word—geographical determinism.

The answer is not our own, but that offered by Vidal de la Blache, who, in 1917, at the end of a life of study and wide experience, observed, in the first of his two remarkable articles on the distribution of mankind on the surface of the earth,

[1] Facts have been collected by Semple, **XC,** Chap. II (Indians of the Amazon plains employed in the Andes ; Ladaks of the Himalaya taken down into the plains, etc.).

[2] **XI,** 1901, p. 460.

[3] Wutschke (J.), "Die geographische Verbreitung von Krankheiten," **XIII,** 67th year, March, 1921.

"In truth everything relating to man bears the mark of contingency."[1]

*

* *

How perfectly justified he was in pointing this out and insisting upon it! For "geographical calculations are not at all like those of a farmer estimating the probability of his crop from the richness of his land". Everywhere we find districts neglected which are apparently well suited for man, and everywhere also unfavourable districts occupied by men, where they cling to the soil, and, by force of will and against all probability, so to speak, anchor themselves to it. The diversified and fertile Sudan, where natural districts succeed one another "every hundred miles or so", each possessing special resources and productions, is sparsely peopled. The rich and attractive valley of the Mississippi, with its productive black lands in the south, and further up, its prairie soil well suited for agriculture, was practically uninhabited for centuries, and has still only a small and scattered population. Yet these lands are fertile as any, and sure to give a good return. But "a good return" is the idea of economists and business men, not of "man" as man. Fertility and productiveness are essentially ideas of a botanical order and interest. We should be in danger of gross error if we gave them a human sense.

Anyone who studies the world-distribution, not of men, but simply of animals, must avoid the temptation to assume the truth of deductions drawn from similar ill-understood ideas, and to endow them with an absolute value. Kropotkin has demonstrated this clearly in one of the most striking pages of his *Mutual Aid*.[2] "The number of animals in a given region," he shrewdly remarks, "is determined not by the greatest amount of food which that region can supply, but on the contrary by the produce of the worst years." He points out that in the steppes of Transbaikalia the horses and cattle which pasture there throughout the winter show no regular increase, in spite of the number of births, and do not produce the mighty herds which the soil could doubtless

[1] Vidal, **XCVII.**
[2] Kropotkin, **CXXX,** pp. 74–5.

support. "Throughout the year there is food for five or six times as many animals, and nevertheless their number increases very slowly." It is well worth while to read the very detailed analysis he gives of the reason for this fact. It provides yet another proof of the fallacy and weakness of arguing, in many cases, from numbers only, under the spell of statistics, or of a schematic map, or graphic representations. And this lesson in caution is not needed in zoogeography only; anthropogeography requires it also.

Kropotkin elsewhere shows this clearly when he tells of villages in S.E. Russia where the inhabitants have abundance of food and yet, in spite of birth-rate of 60 per thousand, find that their population remains stationary.[1] The reason is that there is no sanitary organization, that one-third of the infants die before they are six months old, and that out of 100 children only 17 or 18 reach the age of 20.

This appalling natural destruction is related to that which animals experience. Myriads of insects, birds, and beasts fall victims to climatic changes or disease, and the survivors always emerge from the experience with enfeebled health, and with diminished vitality and power of resistance. It is no doubt to avoid these consequences that in surroundings especially unfavourable to man—the Sahara desert—we find, according to Emile Gautier,[2] that the healthy and vigorous population of the Tuaregs never increases, but remains at a fixed number. This people, which has reached limits of destitution beyond belief, and which lives in a "state of nature", almost naked on the arid soil, hardly better equipped than the jackals, exists and keeps vigorous and strong only at the price of a self-imposed reduction of its numbers by the precautionary limitation of the birth-rate. "A cooking pot, a violin, and an irrigator in bone and leather of native manufacture" form the only furniture of their tents. At such a cost the Tuaregs prevent the necessary reduction from being brought about cruelly and brutally by hunger or disease.

Thus, as we have shown, we have here only one great problem, and that relatively a simple one, with its terms apparently all mathematical. The total number of men;

[1] Ibid., p. 73.
[2] Gautier, **CLXXXII**, p. 177.

the relative number of men; the area of the countries; the relation of the first term to the second. But mathematical rules are themselves insufficient to account for facts which one would have supposed very simple. What will it be, then, when we attack the problem in regard, not to human density, but to historical civilization and societies? Indeed, the conclusion arrived at by Woeikof in his treatise on the distribution of population on the earth,[1] that the essential cause underlying the present distribution of mankind is less the advantages or obstacles due to nature than those due to man himself and his nature, might almost be adopted a priori as an evident truth without any attempt to demonstrate that it is well founded and fits the case. The demonstration, however, is no less easy and to this we may now proceed.

[1] Woeikof, in Petermann's *Mitteilungen*, **XIII**, Vol. LII, 1906.

CHAPTER III

Natural Man—An Individual or a Member of Society?

We must not lose sight of the terms of our problem. If we get far enough away to see things in their proper perspective there are only two; the natural regions and man in relation to them. The whole question is, what reciprocal relations link the one with the other?

The regions we know. We have defined them and characterized them shortly as so many vast climatico-botanical unities. But as to men, ought we not to define them also, not certainly in the mass, but in relation to the bounds of those great climatico-botanical areas, whose distinctive features we have just studied and classified? Within these areas we have to place men. The question is—what men?

Let us say at once that we have rejected the abstract, confused, and unanalysed idea of "the Earth", and in the same way we should reject the abstract, confused, and unanalysed idea of "Man". Man as an abstract idea has no interest for the geographer. It seems worse than useless, really dangerous, to raise a belated brother to that *homo economicus* whom economists have had so much difficulty in banishing altogether from their speculations. Of human societies we may speak, but not of "man", not even that absurd species the *homo geographicus* created complete. This is true for to-day, doubtless, but it is also true retrospectively, as we shall endeavour to establish at the outset.

I

The Old Conception: From the Human Pair to the Nation

Man is a political animal. Such is the formula of Aristotle which has been repeated for many a long day. But it is perhaps not so long ago that a precise signification, a real bearing—in Geography at any rate—was attached to it.

Indeed, it is a fact, readily admitted because it would be difficult to deny, that all human beings are naturally members of societies which are politically organized, of great national bodies more or less perfect and mature. A political geography exists which for many years has been based entirely on the study of states and political societies, being indeed nothing but a miscellaneous and arbitrary collection of facts about administration and of statistical details. But from this human geography in its beginnings tended to diverge the more considerably in proportion as it was unable to reconcile at once all the theories on the relations of man with nature elaborated by successive generations of theorists; of whom the latest, at least, imbued with the French ideas of the eighteenth century, always complacently regarded man simply as man, isolated man, man in the abstract—as the first and last term in a series of more or less ingenious analyses. For a long time, as we know, all the theorists have constructed the evolution of mankind on a kind of pyramidal plan.

At the base was "primitive man" quite isolated, selfish, improvident, seeking sustenance for himself only, merciless to others, especially to the weak, the man of Rousseau's *Discours sur l'Inégalité*: "Stripping the being thus constituted of all his natural endowments and of all the artificial faculties which he was able to acquire only by generations of progress, considering him, in short, as he came fresh from the hands of nature, I see an animal weaker than some, not so active as others . . . but on the whole the best organized of all; I see him gorging himself beneath an oak, quenching his thirst at the nearest stream, and making his bed at the foot of the same tree which has furnished his meal, with all his wants satisfied."[1] A truly precious bit of writing, as is also what immediately follows it in Rousseau's *Discours*. Who would dare to say that his singular fortune has altogether ceased to-day?

This original man, this natural man, or rather this man as nature made him, lives alone. There is no such thing as human society at this stage. When society did evolve, it was for long supposed to be a sexual society, first a couple, then a family; the society of Chapter II of the *Contrat social*,

[1] J. J. Rousseau, *Discours sur l'origine et les fondements de l'Inégalité parmi les hommes*, 1st part.

insecure, unstable, migratory: "The oldest of all societies and the only natural one is that of the family: the children as yet only remain linked with the father so long as they need his protection. Directly that need ceases this natural bond is dissolved. The children, freed from the obedience which they owed to the father, and the father, freed from the care which he owed to the children, are equally independent of one another. If they remain united it is a voluntary, not a natural union, and the family exists merely by agreement. The family then, if you will, is the earliest model of a political society."

This is Rousseau, strange as it may seem. But is Jean Jacques really so very far behind, say, Fustel de Coulanges, who describes, in his *Cité antique*, the method of formation and the orderly growth of what he calls " the family in olden times ", which with its " elder and cadet branches, its servants and *clients*, might comprise quite a large number of men " ? [1] When we recall Fustel's opinion that it was of " an indefinite number of societies of this nature that the Aryan race ", as he called it, " would appear to have been composed during many successive centuries," [2] we must remember that many geographers, especially in France, are primarily historians. " These thousands of little groups," he quite logically explained, " lived isolated, having few mutual relations and no need of one another, being united by no religious or political bond; each one had its own domain, its own internal government, and its own Gods." And so for ages the family, the *gens*,[3] was " the only type of society ". But gradually unions of families occurred, from which resulted those groupings " which the Greek language calls a *phratria* and the Latin a *curia* ".[4] Then, from the union of groups of this kind, tribes were formed.[5] Next federations of the tribes were organized and nations were born. The evolution is simple, logical, and quite plausible. There is no question of a progressive enlargement of human society. It " has not

[1] Fustel de Coulanges, *La Cité antique, Etude sur le Culte, le Droit, les Institutions de la Grèce et de Rome*, Paris (rev. ed.), 1923, Bk. II, Chap. X, " La *gens* à Rome," p. 130.

[2] Ibid.

[3] This is the title which Fustel gives to paragraph 3 of Chap X of Bk. II (p. 119).

[4] Ibid., III, 132.

[5] Ibid., III, 135.

increased [in this race] like a circle which expands little by little, becoming gradually larger ".[1] Fustel, with his analytic power, states this clearly: the formation is the cellular one, which is altogether different: a collection of exactly similar societies which are derived from one another by a series of federations; finally, we have the city, which is, properly speaking, a " confederation ".

*

* *

We know how learned contemporaries fought against such a view—to mention one only, Edward Meyer in Vol. I of the second edition of his *Geschichte des Altertums* [2]; but it is still widespread and popular.

The most important fact of social life, for the professors of a certain sociological school, is now, and always, the family circle.[3] To the prime importance of economy or religion, they oppose that of the family—the source of social bonds. And they can find arguments from its ancient constitution. It is certain that the ancient Greek or Roman family was much larger than the present-day family. To the relatives of the father were joined those of the mother, together with a number of dependents of various kinds. It was also much more closely bound together than that of the present day. The indivisibility of the family possessions and the authority of its head over men and property lent these ancient families the aspect of little monarchies.[4]

It was this that made it so easy to presume that from the juxtaposition of similar groups the State was created.

Statistics tend to confirm this. In our social state to-day in contemporary Western countries, the family is becoming more and more reduced in numbers, so reduced indeed that the number composing it is quite minute. Not so long ago, they tell us, things were very different. In the seventeenth century—as the beginning of the increasing limitation of

[1] Ibid., III, 143.

[2] Trans. into French by Maxime David, **LXXXI**, p. 1, pars. 2 to 14.

[3] For example, cf. G. Richard, *Notions élémentaires de sociologie*, Paris, Delagrave, 3rd ed., 1904.

[4] Fustel, *Cité antique*, II, VIII, 94; cf. in Schmoller (G.), *Principes d'Economie politique*, trans. Platon, Vol. II, p. 27 ff., the remarkable description of the great patriarchal family.

births is generally attributed to the middle of the eighteenth[1]—families were infinitely larger than they are nowadays. It is claimed, by the aid of a great collection of figures which, however, rest on no very secure basis, that this is an established fact. We may point out that it is easy to instance more or less remarkable[2] cases of individual fecundity, but that when we can verify the actual averages we obtain very different results.[3] The mirage of "the good old times" is still far from vanishing. However that may be, there are some, even to-day, who claim to have discovered in countries which have remained outside the great currents of civilization undeniable traces of the ancient condition of things.

In the most advanced countries, which Rousseau would therefore have called the most corrupt, the average number of members of a household varies from 3·5 to 4·5, according to the interesting calculations of Salvioni, and in those same countries also the number of households consisting of a single person is worthy of note.[4] But Ireland, on the other hand, shows households with an average of 5 and Bulgaria of 6.

The household is defined as "all those who live by the same fireside". It corresponds, therefore, to one of the ancient definitions of the word "fire"—a word susceptible in old writings of numerous interpretations which are well known to historians interested in censuses.[5] It embraces the family properly so called, the servants, the dependants, and all who lived as they said "à feu et à pot" with the master of the house. Thus we are judging whether the families of old times were larger than those of to-day by the difference between the households of former times and those of the present. These enlarged families formed important groups which entered into relations with similar neighbouring groups; barter was organized between them and soon increased; hence arose an increasing specialization within each unit; division of labour resulted, and from the

[1] Mathorez, *Histoire de la formation de la nation française : les Étrangers en France sous l'ancien régime*, Paris, 1919, Vol. I, p. 9 ff.

[2] Ibid., p. 4 ff.

[3] I would refer to my *Philippe II et la Franche-Comté*, Paris, 1912, p. 107, n. 1, for a very significant example of a "reduction" of this sort.

[4] *Allgemeines Statistiches Archiv.*, Bk. I, Vol. I, p. 191 ff.

[5] On these different uses of the word "feu", there is a note by Sagnac in *Rev. Hist. moderne et contemp.*, 15th October, 1904.

play of these little organizations a complete economic world was definitely formed. These are the classic theories, but they are not altogether satisfactory.

II

The Antiquity of National Groups

It is certainly not very easy, stating the problem in strict and chronological form, to feel sure whether the family is or is not antecedent to the more extensive and complicated groups.

But what are we to understand by family? Has anyone ever found anywhere, in its primitive simplicity, an example of that couple, the instinctive and "natural" union of a male and a female, which some would fain place at the base of the whole social system?

Go back as far as we will, what we find actually is an ordered society of men and women, obedient to regulations which they may not disregard, and with well-defined rights and obligations. Are these obligations "natural"? Do the conditions we are speaking of arise from "Nature" itself, to employ a much too common phraseology?

Scarcely; for, in the first place, they are not the same everywhere for all men, as they should be if they sprang from "human nature"; secondly, what have they "natural" in themselves? Sometimes the children are under the authority of the father only, sometimes of the mother; in one place the eldest are privileged, in another the youngest.

How can we explain these relations between children and their parents except by reference to rights and duties as a whole, which are evidently epigenetic? And how can we explain this epigenesis manifesting itself in the same way and producing the same results within the whole of one group, while different from those that we see in other groups sometimes not far distant?

Where shall we find this primitive couple—a man and woman united "according to nature", producing children "according to nature", the children remaining under the care of their parents "according to nature", and forming with them the "natural" family, the first social "cell"?

They are a pure romance, an illusion of retrospection: mankind took a long time to understand the link or causal relation, which seems to us so simple to establish, between those two acts chronologically so far apart in the human species—copulation and parturition.[1] It is true that, when the idea was once realized, it was used to full advantage and was made to explain almost everything. On this point Meyer's analysis is acute and convincing.[2] He shows us how all these collectivities, these detached groups which some would regard as the primitive cells of the social edifice, are only of a conventional nature, not of natural formation based on consanguinity. He notices all the cases where in all those "primitive" and ancient societies which we can investigate, procreation is not the origin of the family bond, but rather a legal act of a symbolic character: communion by blood, adoption, procreation of the sons by a substitute for the husband.

"Nevertheless," he adds, "the idea is universally prevalent that these groups are based on a real blood relationship, and are consequently the descendants of a common human ancestor; for, to the mythical thought of primitive man, the analogy drawn from procreation forms the readiest explanation"[3]; and he imagines everything that exists, social groups as well as the objects of the outside world, to result from it.

In fact there is nothing simple or "primitive" about the family as we find it in the least advanced societies. It is accounted for, and can only be accounted for, by the active intervention of a collective force, the State.

As Meyer has observed, we must certainly not imagine this word to imply any organized government, but a society whose political nature is characterized only by the restrictions which it imposes on its members in the triple domain of rights, customs, and morals, and by its relative independence of the societies which surround it. This political society, in the wide sense, is found in every place where men exist; under its

[1] In an interesting study by F. von Reitzenstein, see *Zeitschr. f. Ethnologie*, Vol. XLI, 1909, pp. 644–63; "Der Kausalzusammenhang zwischen Geschlechtsverkehr und Empfängnis in Glaube und Brauch der Natur- und Kulturvölker."

[2] Meyer, **LXXXI**, I, par. 13, p. 36.

[3] Ibid., par. 14, p. 36.

action and control spring up the various conjugal unions, families, and village societies, the so-called primitive groups which in reality it fashions, and to which it is, in fact, anterior, since it presides, so to speak, at their formation.

Thus the numerous social groups, varied in form and extent; tribes, phratries, clans, families, which include and intersect one another, are not "the original pre-political forms of social organization—the atoms whose aggregation, at a relatively late epoch in human evolution, has alone given rise to the State",[1] as Fustel de Coulanges was still asserting in the *Cité antique*.

The formation was just the reverse. Neither phratry, curia, tribe, nor clan was ever a State, but, always and only, a subdivision of a State or tribe. "The State is not the product of these groups; it is they, on the contrary, which have been created by the State."[2]

*

* *

Moreover, if the family was a primitive and self-governed organization, one of two things must be granted: either there existed an aggregate of unchanging characteristics inherent in human nature, which would leave their stamp upon all family societies in all places and at all times. Thus no doubt all the analogies which such societies present would be accounted for; but who could then explain the material differences which are observed by anthropologists and sociologists? Or such a collection of common and natural characteristics did not exist; and then how does it come to pass that individual caprices and influences, having free play, have not varied indefinitely the model of the social groups?

In fact, there are no caprices in the social morphology of primitive people; and from the earliest times (as far as we can formulate conclusions on such an obscure subject) there was genuine homogeneity in the industrial products which have been found, often at very considerable distances apart and in totally dissimilar localities.

It is fairly well known that certain pre-historic industries

[1] **LXXXI,** par. 6, p. 13.
[2] Ibid., par. 13, p. 36.

were spread over wide areas: the Magdalenian industry, for instance, extended from Northern Spain to Russia, through France, Belgium, Central Germany, Austria, Hungary, and Poland. Doubtless we cannot be sure about the synchronism of the remains discovered in the different countries we have just mentioned: de Morgan was justified in drawing the attention of researchers to the danger of over-general or over-rash conclusions.[1] There remains none the less a collection of facts which clearly suggest two solutions: one that in very early times there existed very widespread human groups and societies: the other that frequent and regular relations quickly developed between these societies.

Again, the latest and best accepted linguistic studies lead us also, by quite a different road, to the same conclusions. It is not only a historian like Camille Jullian, who, in his *Histoire de la Gaule*, and in his lectures at the Collège de France, saw across the distant millenaries of an uncertain pre-historic age, not wandering and scattered tribes, but peoples already constituted, radiating and conquering from a central home, a mother-nation: "an Indo-European nation," an "Italo-Celtic nation", a "Ligurian nation"; he does not hesitate about using "that precise and definite word 'nation' which has hitherto been reserved for modern times posterior to the Roman conquest".[2] And it is not a question of groups based on identity of race in the physical sense of the word. He asserted a long time ago that these organizations had "no reference to that animal relationship of blood or race".[3] They were really states formed by the will of man, and religion is undoubtedly a proof of this,[4] because the existence of national gods serves first to form, then to maintain nations. Language is a still more powerful factor.

A linguist also like Meillet, speaking as a linguist, uses this same word nation.[5] Where, to-day, we meet with a great variety of languages due to differentiation of peoples

[1] De Morgan, **CLXXV**, pp. 28–9; pp. 68–72, etc.
[2] The antiquity of the idea of a nation (*Rev. politique et parlementaire*, 18th and 25th January, 1913), p. 7.
[3] On this controversy, cf. Febvre (L.), "Le développement des langues et l'Histoire," **XVIII**, Vol. XXVII, 1913, p. 56.
[4] Jullian, op. cit., p. 25, special edition.
[5] Febvre, op. cit., p. 58.

and splitting up of groups, we find, when we go back through the ages to prehistoric times, a single language—an outward sign of the former wide extent of a single social group.

"In early times," says Meillet, "many of these varied idioms of to-day were one, and the further we go back into the past, the greater appear the resemblances which prove this ancient unity."[1]

The greater part of the European languages "belong to the same linguistic group, that is to say, they are variations of a single language known as Indo-European, which belongs to the prehistoric period and whose component elements have long since widely diverged".[2]

Now it requires a certain political unity, or at least a certain unity of civilization, to admit of a common language.[3] "So unified a language as the one which is conjectured from the concordance between the languages concerned presupposes the existence for a considerable time of a nation which was marked by a certain unity . . . A nation must feel its unity before linguistic unity can be created. There is nothing which would warrant our speaking of an Indo-European race, but there must have been necessarily (we do not know quite where or when) an Indo-European nation." This is a logical necessity which must be faced, whatever solutions are accepted for the many problems of detail which also arise; as, for instance, that of the origin of the Germans and of their primitive idioms, which has been lately raised by Feist.[4] For even if we allow that the German language is not of Indo-European origin, the rapid changes in these primitive idioms in the first millennium B.C., as the result of an Indo-European conquest, which is admitted by Feist, would still prove the importance of ethnical groups and movements in distant periods.[5]

Thus in the most remote ages we find that the linguists follow the archæologists and historians in telling us to look not for "men", but for great political groupings and human

[1] Meillet, *Les Langues dans l'Europe nouvelle*, Paris, Payot, 1918, p. 15.

[2] Ibid.

[3] Meillet, *Introduction à l'étude comparative des langues indo-européennes*, Paris, 1912, 3rd edition, p. 405.

[4] Feist (S.), *Kultur, Ausbreitung u. Herkunft der Indo-Germanen*, Berlin, Weidmann, 1913.

[5] Lichtenberger, *Revue des Études anciennes*, Vol. XV, 1913, pp. 185–6.

societies: large and widespread communities, covering vast regions with the same civilization. If anyone is astonished at such a wide field, let him remember that even at the present day the Esquimaux extend from Alaska to the Eastern shores of Greenland, a distance of 5,000 miles, and that in the Pacific region, from Easter Island to the Samoan Archipelago, and from New Zealand to the Hawaian Islands, that is to say over an area about three times as large as Europe, there exists practically only one language: in a few hours a Tahitian is able to understand and even to speak the dialects of New Zealand, the Marquesas, and the Hawaian Islands.

What we may call the prehistoric portion of geography serves also to account, in some measure, for such great or rather for such widespread communities.

III

The Large Homogeneous Human Groups of Ancient Times Corresponded with Large Homogeneous Geographical Areas

The formation of these large uniform groups was no doubt due to the relative sameness of environment. We must picture the primitive world as presenting infinitely less variety than our present one. It was not cultivated, and its original aspect had undoubtedly not been altered by the destruction or creation due to the numberless acclimatizations of plants and animals which human societies effect and multiply as they themselves increase. Might we not expect that these great uniform spaces would induce a common manner of living, and therefore a common culture among groups of men in search of a means of existence?

It will perhaps be objected that man's activity has not consisted in introducing only variety into the general appearance of the earth; far from it. In some ways the labours of civilized societies tend to bring cultivation and production to a general level. Vidal de la Blache admitted some time ago that "the modern European is an indefatigable labourer at a task which tends to render uniform, if not the whole planet, at least each of the zones of the planet".[1] When we look at those immense

[1] Vidal, **XCV**, p. 103.

tracts of North America, where the same crops are now reproduced, so to speak, mechanically, and at those of China which, since they were cleared, have become so many gardens filled with useful crops, wheat in the North, rice in the South; when we think of those abrupt cultural revolutions, over such wide areas, brought about so suddenly and violently by industrial changes in all parts of the world; when we appreciate the obstacles which too great a variety of natural products presents to modern cultivation; certainly all these considerations, and others of the same order, seem to justify the assertion of Vidal de la Blache. We have spoken only of the plant world; the animal world undergoes exactly the same transformations.

There is certainly, among modern men, who are at once masters and slaves of industrial forces, a need of simplification which must be satisfied by some means. Man chooses, but he finds the choice more and more embarrassing; we will instance but one only out of a hundred facts to prove it. If the Equatorial forest escapes his exploitation to a great extent, it is no doubt, amongst other reasons, because the great variety of its products is a source of perpetual trouble, which deters him.[1] The very wealth of vegetation, in a way, prejudices commercial wealth, and contrasts unfavourably with, say, the happy monotony of the Scandinavian lands—Scotch fir, Norwegian pine, Norwegian pine, Scotch fir—no other species leading to complications—just unthinking, straightforward toil. A botanist and explorer, well acquainted with the vegetation of the Sudan,[2] has recently expressed his anxiety about the threatened fate of those West African countries which might, with a little effort, produce such a variety of native fruits. "Instead of endeavouring to bring uniformity into the production of that vast territory," he observes, "it would be better to encourage each district to produce its own speciality which is absent in the other districts."[3]

Such anxiety is significant, and will probably be justified by the event. It is certain that in some ways the primary tendency of civilization is to uniformity. But when that has been remarked, have we got very far? The dead-level of monotony which modern man tends to create, and which

[1] Raveneau, **XI**, 1901, pp. 74–5. [2] Auguste Chevalier.
[3] Quoted by L. Marc, **XI**, 1910, p. 45.

he strives to create with all the most highly perfected means at his disposal, is an artificial limited sameness, nearly always unstable, and, so to speak, superficial. How different from the primitive, natural, and essential sameness which once prevailed over immense territories !

*

* *

There are two sides to every human operation. The Pharaohs who took advantage of their foreign expeditions to introduce exotic plants into Egypt, transplanting them to the Nile valley, and for so doing took to themselves honourable titles which they had inscribed on their monuments, and those who, by systematic and studied acclimatizations, collected within their country that enormous quantity of plants for food, or industry, or pleasure, which Ch. Joret describes in his book on the plants of the classical East,[1] all these created at the same time variety and monotony, for they made Egypt a copy of Western Asia, whose plant resources they turned to their own profit ; they brought about a real similarity of aspect between the two ; and, moreover, they altered the "natural Egypt", if it may be so called—Egypt left to its own resources—to one allied to the neighbouring regions and now chiefly characterized by what it has borrowed.

The same was the case with the Ptolemies in later ages, when they imported certain fruit-trees grown from time immemorial in Western Asia—almonds, peaches, and mulberries. They helped to create a new Mediterranean country where these trees had an important place.

But at the same time they weakened the original character of their country, which had been so long ignorant of Greek agricultural methods—of all which is expressed by the word *φυτεύειν*. Again, to take an example from nearer home and at a later period, the men of the Middle Ages were driven by the necessity of producing unaided, on their own land and in their own cantons, everything which man requires for his bodily needs, so as to have no need of relying on neighbours, or above all on merchants from distant countries. When, for instance, without any regard to the climate or to the

[1] Joret, **CXV.**

resources of the land, they introduced the vine into Andorra and into many villages of Haute Cerdagne[1] or into the barren and sterile mountains of Morvan,[2] or into Normandy,[3] Picardy,[4] or even Flanders,[5] and a hundred other places, they created uniformity. So, too, the farmers of Algeria on the hills between Berrouaghia and Aumale, as Emile Gautier tells us, although the prosperity of their country depended on its being covered with olives, figs, and vines, were "compelled by distress to grow wheat, since unless they could produce it themselves, they had nothing to eat". All these people, in the same way, tacked on fragments of country of one kind to natural regions whose disparity with them was complete. But when we have noted these facts and many others like them, what conclusion are we to draw? Must we despair arriving at any equilibrium?

In primitive times the geological ages were not far distant—that is, epochs when climates were little differentiated. The same plant life then extended over vast areas as, in the case of Europe, when forest prevailed. To-day the contrast is marked. To the north are the great permanent forests, first of deciduous trees, then of conifers; but to the south, in the countries around the Mediterranean, forest has disappeared. Formerly Greece itself[6] and Northern Italy[7] consisted of vast forests extending over mountain and plain. Elms, chestnuts and oaks filled the valley of the Po long before the Roman domination, as has been proved by the excavation of the *terramare*.[8] This is but one example out of a thousand. Monotony of vegetation was the rule; and a second monotony or sameness of landscape—that of the Mediterranean as we see it to-day—has replaced the earlier one, though this is more restricted. It characterizes a small district cut out of a large one, and is of relatively recent origin.

We must never lose sight of the very great length of prehistoric times, noı of their primordial importance and the

---

[1] Sorre, **CCXXX**, p. 219.
[2] Levainville, **CCXXV**.
[3] Sion, **CCXXIX**, p. 149.
[4] Demangeon, **CCXXIV**, p. 254.
[5] Blanchard, **CCXVII**, p. 37.
[6] Neumann and Partsch, *Physikalische Geographie von Griechenland*, p. 357 ff.
[7] Nissen, *Italische Landes-Kunde*, I, Berlin, 1883, p. 431 ff.
[8] Helbig, *Die Italiker in der Poebene*, Leipzig, 1879, p. 25 ff.

extreme value of the heritage they have left us. The olive did not suddenly conquer the Mediterranean area, nor, in its turn, did the vine. So that it was only gradually that olive oil was substituted for animal fat or butter, and wine for beer, and that a new area of material civilization was formed, which increased and expanded up to the limits which climate naturally allowed. The men of the North, alone unable to cultivate the olive and the vine under their cold skies, kept to the use of the foods which they originally had in common with the men of the South.[1] Aristæus, the hero-traveller, took time to complete the planting of the *mare nostrum* with the *olea europæa*. There is no doubt that the dates are uncertain, and there is every reason to believe that Hehn, in his classic book,[2] has exaggerated both the importance and the recent nature of the agricultural debt of Greece to the East—and of the northern countries of Europe to those of the Mediterranean. It is quite possible that the vine, olive and fig-tree were common in Greece (in a wild state, it is true) before the time of Homer; it may be that much of the debt of the Greeks to Asia dates from a considerably more ancient period than we imagine—to the Aegeo-Cretan age[3]; and also that the introduction of cultivated plants into Northern Europe began to some extent before the Roman invasion. Still it is none the less true that we undoubtedly need not go back so very far before we can picture an Italy whose landscape bore no traces of the olive, vine, cypress, plane-tree, oleander, citron or orange.

For the rest, granted the Aegeo-Cretan age, the centuries before the Homeric poems, what we assert is simply this, that Europe—the world contemporary with the origin, expansion, and movements of those vast units in which so many concordant hypotheses lead us to believe—had singularly less variety, less wealth, and fewer contrasts than the Europe of historical times; and that since then there has been some reflection of that monotony and relative though obvious uniformity, easy to understand, in the kind of life led by men and in their institutions and social existence as a whole. It would not

[1] Besnier, art. *Oleum* in **CLXIX,** IV, I, col. 1686.
[2] Hehn, **CXIV.**
[3] O. Schrader, **CXIV.**

be wise then to neglect similar observations when we are trying to understand and explain that remarkable unity of civilization in prehistoric times which is attested not only by the labours of archæologists but by the observations of linguists and students of human beliefs. Thus Frazer estimates, rightly or wrongly, from his careful study of the Saturnalia and similar festivals of which he has found evidence and has described, that in prehistoric times a wonderful unity of civilization prevailed in Europe and Western Asia.[1]

And so antiquity, primordiality, and the remarkable extension of human groups in the most remote past that we can trace, all bring the thoughtful observer to this point: it is not primitive man with whom we have to deal, but properly speaking, primitive society.

IV

The Savage and the Barbarian in their Natural State: Their Wants and Customs

Why, therefore, do so many clever men still persist in advocating, like a kind of logical mechanism, a theory of primitive man and his needs, of which the least we can say is that it in no way fits in with the best known and established facts? Why does so much recent work on the subject still flaunt the outworn rags of Rousseau's old garment? Is it really so difficult to know how the natural savage behaves?

He is pictured as launched into the world intoxicated with his freedom and strength, a being with fierce, unbridled passions. On the one hand are his desires; on the other is nature, his larder, offering him the choice of a hundred vegetable and animal products for speedy and easy use, all equally well adapted to appease his hunger, quench his thirst, clothe his body, shelter and warm him, in short to satisfy all his essential wants. His natural wants,[2] we are told. No doubt the wants are natural, but what about his manner of satisfying them?

The real object of our search is to know how much more primitive man appears to be curbed by nature, harassed by

[1] Frazer, **CLXXI**, Vol. III.
[2] Brunhes, **LXVII**, p. 11.

traditional customs and tied down by prejudices and foregone conclusions than civilized man. The savage is above all a creature of habit, and habit chiefly governs his movements. It accounts, for instance, according to the testimony of Schulz-Lorentzen, who knows the country well, for those migrations which every year take the Eskimos of Southern or Eastern Greenland, some to the North, others to the South [1]; it explains also the very narrow limits within which he satisfies his simple needs: to mention one only, his primary need—food.

In the Homeric period—as Vidal de la Blache loved to recall—people were classified, according to Victor Bérard, according to their food; they were sitophagous, ichthyophagous or lotophagous. There is no doubt that the food of these peoples was monotonous. It was so, because it was not left to each person's free choice, but was the result of collective constraint—of social constraint. How, in any other way, can we account for the negligence of those cattle-rearing tribes who were so long ignorant of the use of milk for food? How can we explain so many extraordinary and well-proved omissions, that unwillingness of the uncivilized to try experiments, or use any new kind of food?

Not long ago no beef was eaten in Madagascar. Drury tells of having seen cattle "which could not walk, some because they were so old, and others because they were so fat". Malagasy folk-lore hands down to us the tale [2] of the King Ra-lambo who saw one day near Antananarivo an ox which was near "dying from fatness". The idea occurred to him of using it for food. Carefully avoiding the lee side of it "for fear that its breath might be fatal", he killed the animal and had the flesh cooked. The smell of the cooking was seductive, but he resolved not to taste it until his slaves had eaten some of it. The anecdote is not without a typical value.

Ra-lambo made an experiment which it was in his power to try. But there are others which are formally forbidden. Savages people the earth with a multitude of souls or spirits which animate plants and trees and all the vegetable world.

Frazer has compiled a singularly rich collection of facts

[1] Beuchat, in **XVI**, 1906, Vol. XVII, p. 181.
[2] E. Gautier, *Madagascar*, pp. 358–9.

and customs [1] which show how profound is the belief of man in the close bond between his own life and the life of plants, and how he persuades himself that he would perish if the plants were killed. The belief in spirits has the same effect. It explains why the Hidatsu Indians of North America never cut down large living trees. When they wanted large pieces of wood they cut them out of trees which had already fallen.[2] In the same way with many natives the destruction of certain trees, particularly those which are useful for food, like the coco-nut palm in West Africa, is reckoned as great a crime as parricide. These ideas differ so much from our own that we obstinately fall back on "utility" to explain everything. Meniaud, speaking of the existence in some Sudanese districts (the Mossi, for instance) of a chief or *naba* for butter-trees (karites) whose office is to guard those useful plants, deduces from it that this exploitation on the part of the natives is not absolutely blind.[3] Doubtless; but it is not its utility that protects the tree, it is religion. Multitudes of trees are considered sacred by the various peoples who cover the earth, and so escape the axe. It is curious to note that in some tribes, when any clearing is required, an excuse is made by alleging compulsion, thus throwing on others the responsibility for felling the trees.

*

* *

Hence it is not at all surprising that "ideas" continually interfere to control man's food; and that social constraint is always at work. On this point, too, the mass of facts collected by Frazer is singularly suggestive and convincing: for example, the ceremonial eating of new wheat at festivals in Europe[4]; of new rice in the East Indies, India, and Indo-China; of new yams on the banks of the Niger; of new fruits amongst the Kaffirs, the Zulus, and the North American Indians. Before the feast of new fruits, writes Frazer,[5] no Indian tastes or touches a grain of the new harvest. Amongst the Coorgs of Southern India the man who is to cut the first bundle of rice is selected by an astrologer. Only

[1] Frazer, **CLXXI,** Vol. II, Bk. I. [2] Ibid.
[3] Meniaud, **CLXXXIII,** Vol. I, p. 265.
[4] Frazer, **CLXXI,** Vol. II, Ch. III. [5] Ibid.

after a solemn ceremony is it permissible for everyone to gather and bring in his rice. And even in France, at the present time, does not something of the same sort remain in the ceremonies that take place at the commencement and end of the vintage? Granted that they are measures of utility and evidently of a practical nature, still it was not very long ago that in the East of France, in Franche Comté, for instance, they still celebrated the "kill-cat" at the vintages according to an immemorial rite, which Frazer describes.

So far we have dealt with vegetation and its curbing, damming and cramping effect on the free expansion of human needs. Next as to animals; what a number of curious facts, here also, throw a vivid light on the relations of man with his environment! We know the history of the bears and the Aïno; the latter live on the former. They eat the flesh either fresh, dried, or salted; they wear the skin, and pay their debts with fur. But when they have killed one, they hold a sort of expiatory ceremony; they put the skulls of the bears they have killed in a place of honour in their huts; and, moreover, they celebrate a solemn bear festival every year. Nor are they alone in this. The Gilyaks, a Tungus people of Eastern Siberia, also feed on bear's flesh; but many precautions are necessary to prevent any risk in the eating. They must deceive the bear when alive by lavishing on him marks of the greatest consideration, and when dead they must honour him by paying respect to the spirit which has quitted his body. Still the Gilyaks and the Aïno kill and eat the bears, reverently, it is true, but without scruple. But the usual attitude of primitive man to animals is different. He does not kill, for he is afraid of spirits. Instances of it are plentiful in connexion with crocodiles, tigers, and serpents.[1] When man kills, however, he excuses himself; and he makes more excuses for himself the more ferocious the animal is—or the better to eat.

It is the harmless animal without edible value which is generally killed without care or ceremony.

These are very general facts and almost universal practices found amongst hunters, as amongst fishers, in America as well as in Asia, Africa, or the Polar regions. Nowhere is

[1] Frazer, loc. cit.

food eaten by savages without thought as to choice. There are prohibitions, restrictions, taboos, on all sides; even when the food is varied there are fixed rules with regard to the order of eating.[1] Amongst the Central Esquimaux it is forbidden to eat the spoils of the land at the same time as those of the sea; it is forbidden to keep in the hut, at the same time, land animals which have been killed and whale, seal, or walrus. At Florida in the Solomon Islands no one who has eaten pork, or fish, or shell-fish, may enter a kitchen-garden. In other places the anxiety not to mix foods is so great that, in certain cases, a ritual purge is enjoined. Amongst the Masai, a pastoral tribe of East Africa, the young warriors take meat and milk alternately, and always purge themselves when they change from one diet to the other.

*

* *

In conclusion. To many economists, economic operations are so many considered actions, all based on utility and profit, and are the result of a whole series of calculations, of valuations, and of comparisons between the want felt and the price to be paid foi the satisfaction of that want. And too often economic science has been falsified precisely by the abstract manner in which economic facts have been regarded and by that invincible tendency of modern civilization to reduce all human progress to simple factors such as "need". There have been some clear minds, Karl Bücher,[2] amongst others, which have seen for a long time that the "economic nature" varies from man to man. It is a matter of education and habit. It is not the same in all men; it is not the same in all classes of society. Need we recall once more the persistent error which contrasts the uneconomical purchasing of the lower classes with the foresight shown by the middle and trading classes in calculating their expenditure? The comparison established between the desire and the price to be paid for its fulfilment does not lead to the same conclusion in the one case as in the other. Geographers must keep all these facts in mind and must not follow economists along a perilous road on to dangerous ground.

Above all, they must cease to let "Man" loose in "Nature",

[1] Frazer, **CLXXI**, Vol. II, Ch. III. [2] Bücher, **CLXVIII**, p. 2.

where he is pictured in a beautiful terrestrial Paradise producing all that is necessary for existence, and where he has only to take in order to satisfy his natural needs from the plants, fruits, fishes, game, domestic animals, milk, etc., spread before him. "Man," "abstract man," the *homo geographicus* who should and could feed on everything without distinction, and take advantage of everything—that man does not exist. The theorist generously offers him beasts and birds, but hundreds of thousands of men refuse these presents and eat only cereals or fish. He offers milk and the butter and cheese obtained from it; but hundreds of thousands of men neglect them, although they are herdsmen.[1] The table is large and royally spread for all. But Jacquemont, in India, when he watched his Sepoys feeding, saw as many stoves, pots, fires, and cooking utensils as there were men. No two of them would eat together or of the same food.

Wherever "man" and "natural products" are concerned, the "idea" intervenes. This last often has nothing utilitarian about it, and governs not only the food of men, but their dress also, and the construction of their dwellings, and in fact all their physical and material being. "On the Malabar coast there are still people who are constrained to go almost naked for fear of being touched by their loose garments."[2] But we need not go so far away, nor search in distant lands and ages. Let us recall a profound remark of Michelet's in that *Histoire du XIX siècle,* which is no longer read, although it is rich in suggestion. The historian is commenting on the supremacy which alcohol and meat had gained amongst foods. "Is it mere sensuality?" he asks; "No, more than anything it is the pleasure of feeling oneself strong, and capable of greater achievement."

But to return to the past: social constraints and religious constraints become confused. Between the desires and needs of man and everything in nature that can be utilized by him, beliefs, ideas, and customs interpose. The origin of cultivation and of animal domestication is intimately bound up with religion and magic. Rites that were also utilitarian processes were the first manifestations of man's industrial

[1] On milk, cf. Hahn, **CXIII,** par. 5: "Die Milch und die Entstehung der wirtschaftlichen Verwertung der Milch," p. 19 ff.

[2] Bouglé, *Régime des Castes*, **XVII,** 1900.

genius.[1] Here we are far from moving in the domain of the individual. An anthropologist like Deniker, in his book on the races and peoples of the earth, very rightly classes everything that concerns the food, dress, and means of existence of men among their "sociological" characters. The question is not a natural and personal one, but social and collective; we are never concerned, we repeat, with "man" but only with human society and its organized groups.

It is just as impossible to isolate arbitrarily "the animal" or "the plant". In their case also we must substitute the idea of the society for that of the individual. It is an animal and vegetable society which confronts human society. This, however, is not the place to study them; it would be beyond not only our competence, but our subject. We will simply remark here that man is not enfeebled because he is confronted with harmonic animal or vegetable aggregations; on the contrary, he is strong for that very reason, because in reality these aggregations are made up—and this is especially true of the plants with which we are chiefly concerned—of antagonistic elements which have arrived at an equilibrium, though a precarious one.

Between these elements man is the arbiter. He is the little weight which just suffices to turn the scale. An insignificant movement on his part is repeated indefinitely, and amplified more and more until it entails consequences out of all proportion to the original expenditure of force. Certain poor negroes take up their abode in a forest, cut down trees, and make one of those clearings of which there are thousands in the great Congo forest. They live there for a year or two, three at most; then, when the land is exhausted, they go away and the trees grow again after their departure. But they do not grow as before. The equilibrium between the species which require shade and those which aspire to the sun has been disturbed by man's action. A secondary forest now takes the place of the primitive one, and is the first term of a series of degradations which follow one another by a strict law. If there were no solidarity among the plants, no reciprocal bonds between them, if there were no vegetable communities, but only individual plants face to

[1] S. Reinach, *Cultes, mythes, et religions*, Vol. II, Paris, 1908, *Introd.*

face with individual men, would the action of the black man lost in the forest have brought about a similar series of consequences? There is no doubt whatever as to the answer.

These remarks should serve to bring distinctly before our eyes the true character of the action of man on the surface of the earth.

It is not the action of isolated individuals. It is the result of great collectivities, which, as far back as our researches and our reasoning allow us to go, impose on masses of human beings laws, customs, and practices which react forcibly on the conduct of those masses in their relations with the power and resources of nature.

Supplied with these definite indications, we can now resume our study of the problem of the limits or boundaries of the great natural areas and of the climatico-botanical regions considered in relation to man and his work, which we have so far only been able to undertake, in some sort, from the outside. We are no longer exposed to the danger of grave misunderstanding as to the tendencies, wants, and forms of human society.

PART III

POSSIBILITIES AND DIFFERENT WAYS OF LIFE

CHAPTER I

Its Bases—Mountains, Plains, and Plateaux

LET us briefly review our argument from its commencement in Chapter II of Part II.

We have analysed the two complexes " the earth " and " man " about which there is so much vague talk.

We have replaced the indistinct and confused notion of " the Earth " by that of a cosmos, a great harmonized whole made up of climatico-botanical zones, each one forming an organic unity and all of them placed symmetrically on either side of the Equator.

Then for the notion of " Man " we have by an analogous process substituted that of human society and endeavoured to explain the true nature of the action of such a society in its relations with the animal and plant communities which occupy the various regions of the earth. The main problem, of the value which the natural regions of the cosmos have for man, remains. We have already confronted it—or rather it has confronted us—without any effort. We must now consider it again.

Let us make clear the terms and the data. Some speak of natural regions—climatico-botanical regions—as reservoirs of forces which act directly on man with a sovereign and decisive power, and leave their mark on every manifestation of their activity, from the smallest to the most important and complicated, and in a great measure are at the same time the cause and the subject of these manifestations. This is the determinist theory. We have already pointed out its difficulties, and have urged that natural regions are simply collections of possibilities for society which makes use of them but is not determined by them. But we had not then formulated a theory of human society and of its special mode of activity; moreover, we had only stated the problem in general terms. We must now give attention to the details.

I

The Vicissitudes of Possibility: Recurring Rhythm

It has been the custom for many years to speak of human society in the great climatico-botanical regions as adjuncts, so to speak, of plant and animal societies, which were themselves, it was assumed, strictly dependent on meteorological phenomena. But these regions, into which man was thrown as a kind of extra, have nothing tyrannical or determinant about them; this we must never tire of insisting on and must demonstrate in every possible way. Although he reviews and criticizes them along with many others, there is no necessity for the historian or geographer to look on the facts, which he retains in his descriptions and on which his studies are essentially based, as component parts of a pre-established order.

Still less have those facts any determining value for men and their existence. Even plant societies, which are less adaptable to environment than human ones, do not suffer exclusive and tyrannical compulsion from external conditions; *a fortiori*, human societies are capable of protecting their own existence from that tyranny.

The temptation is strong, it must be confessed, to form arbitrary classifications and to assert that there exist uniform regions of physical and human geography within which everything, and therefore all living creatures including human beings and human societies, have the same characteristics.

There is Miss Semple, for instance, whose interesting and painstaking book *The Influence of Geographic Environment* we gladly quote, because no other propounds with such enthusiastic and candid good faith the ideas we seek to controvert. She assures us that the shores of the Arctic Ocean form one of those sharply defined regions which we may profitably recognize and study apart from others.[1] There the facts of vegetable, animal, and human life all bear, though indistinctly, the same imprint—that of climate.

[1] Semple, **XC**, Chap. VI.

The Ostiaks, Lapps, Samoyeds, the Hyperboreans of Siberia, having Mongolian characteristics, are all cast in the same mould. But the Esquimaux? To our author it is evident that they have characteristics which distinguish them from the former groups. They present a difficulty, but that does not matter. Whether they are of Mongolian origin or an offshoot of the Indian race, Miss Semple proclaims them in every case " a transition people " and the difficulty vanishes. Their stature, their general appearance, and their colour proclaim them the brothers of the Siberians; but if you collect and examine their skulls they are the near relations of the inhabitants of the other side of the Behring Straits. And so the craze for pre-established regions is satisfied, it must be confessed, at little cost or trouble.

For another example, let us pass from the icy Polar wastes to the hot countries of the sub-tropical zone.[1] There is a region to the south of the Sahara, very clearly marked by its physical nature and its negro population; a narrow territory bounded by the Tropic, with little variety in its relief, and with the same weather conditions affecting a soil that is almost constant in character, and evidencing a monotonous and backward social development, rudimentary agriculture, and only the lowest grades of pastoral life. It is no use objecting to this that the picture is too crude, that it is based on a very superficial acquaintance with the physical and human geography of a land which explorers are more and more depicting to us as being extremely varied in its products, rich in its possibilities, and composed of totally dissimilar " districts " peopled with a veritable mosaic of tribes belonging to stocks originally heterogeneous. We can raise no objections, because objections are worthless to a believer armed with a dogma which may not be discussed.

And this is a Ratzelian dogma: " If the space is limited and not greatly differentiated, the physical and human types found there are monotonous." Our contention is quite otherwise. We admit regional frames in a general sense, but in the collection of physical features it represents we see only possibilities of action. And let us add at once, to anticipate an objection which automatically arises: these

[1] Ibid.

possibilities of action do not constitute any sort of connected system; they do not represent in each region an inseparable whole: if they are capable of being seized they cannot all be seized by men at the same time with the same force; otherwise what would become of the case which we are trying to establish against determinism? Would not the determinant value of geographical regions appear a very real one under another form? In this connexion, as in others, it is useful to remember the old formula of Leibnitz—that all possibilities are not compossibilities.

*

* *

For all the possibilities of establishing a human society which a given region offers do not inevitably exert their influence at the same time or with the same force. The partisans of "geographical predestination" are obliged to allow this. For instance, Miss Semple herself tells us, and very reasonably,[1] that we should distrust misleading generalizations; that as a result of insufficient analysis we may falsify facts by deducing from them summary and defective formulæ; that we are tempted to over-estimate the value of certain factors, because there are many forces to take into account, and we are always inclined to make an arbitrary simplification of the action of each, as well as to reduce their total number. She states that influences are not all of the same value; she means by this that the factors of human geography act with an intensity which varies with the epoch, and she analyses that variation very judiciously, grouping her observations under three chief heads.

In the first place, she remarks, human society has freed itself more and more from the tyranny of the natural regions; the progress of material civilization and of medicine easily enabled either humanity as a whole, or various fractions of this whole, to leave the primitive domain to which we might have supposed them confined, but this has been done by modifications or improvements in clothing, habits, or hygiene. In fact, one of the great advantages possessed by the European is that he alone has been capable, thanks to his varied means of preparedness, of enduring without too much danger

[1] Semple, **XC**, Chap. I.

both Polar winters and the intense heat of Central Africa. "The Indians whom Pizarro recruited at the coast died of cold on the interior plateaux; the porters from the neighbourhood of Mexico City shivered with fever when they went down to Vera Cruz." [1]

In the second place, Miss Semple observes that in a fixed region the conditions may change in weight and value. Thus a civilization in its infancy may benefit greatly from an isolated, confined, and sheltered habitat, but the same habitat (precisely because of its original advantages, which in turn become so many disadvantages) at a later stage of development may prove a real inconvenience to its inhabitants; Egypt, Phœnicia, Crete, insular and peninsular Greece, have all known these vicissitudes. These countries were favourably circumstanced at the outset, but the circumstances soon ceased to be favourable; whereas, on the contrary, the plains of Russia, formerly inhospitable, later became the richest and most important members of a State which was at one time prosperous and great.

Thirdly, and lastly, when we try to estimate the value of a district, the factor of communications must be taken into account. The evolution of the great trade routes and of world communications is of vital importance, as is also that of the network of roads linking one country to another for purposes of reciprocal political, economic, moral and intellectual relations. This hardly needs demonstration.

At the ends or crossings of important routes communities form, grow, and prosper. Every historian dilates on the stimulating influence of roads in all ages—to mention Frenchmen only, Déchelette in the domain of pre-history, Camille Jullian in that of early Gaul, and Vidal de la Blache in the domain of French history.[2]

This is all quite true and calls for no criticism, if one thing is granted; that is, there must be no talk of necessity. There is no strict, rigid, mechanical necessity: once again, the truth is evident—the concord which is established between the earth and its inhabitants consists of mingled analogies and contrasts. "Like all the harmonies of organized bodies," Reclus wisely remarks, "it arises from strife as well as from

[1] Capitan and Lorin, CCII, p. 401.
[2] We shall return later to these questions. See Chapter II of Part IV.

union, and never ceases to oscillate about a changing centre of gravity."[1] There are cases in which communities, often large ones, have sprung up owing to the ease, frequency, and number of their connexions with the outside world; but there are others where extreme isolation, distance from routes, and inaccessibility have been a positive advantage.

The history of Russia furnishes a notable example of this. The southern steppe, that is to say the really rich part—the Black Lands—served both as route and vehicle of the great invasions. But these invasions continued in operation not merely to the Middle Ages, but until modern times. Under their repeated shock, society had not time to establish itself in Southern Russia. Scarcely was a social group installed before it was overrun, broken up, and swept away by a new wave which almost inevitably followed the path of the one which preceded this settlement. Moreover, in the fourteenth and fifteenth centuries all Russia south of the Province of Orel was "an absolute desert".[2] The beginning of the seventeenth century, "the period of disturbance," saw the routes of the Tartar invasions once more in use—the traditional *Chliahs*.[3] The Czernoziom was desert whilst the loess was peopled, and the North itself, wild and wretched as it was, was less wild and less wretched than the South.[4] This paradox ceased to obtain only in the time of Peter the Great.

And so the Russian state was not born in the region of easy passage through the land, the steppes, which were too open to invaders; it was in the poor and out-of-the-way parts of the country, in the clearings—the *polia* or *poliany*[5] which are scattered in the wooded zone to the north of the Black Land, that the old historic towns were founded, Rostov on the banks of its lake; Pereiaslav-Zalêskîi and Vladimir-Zalêskîi—that is to say, "beyond the forest"; Iourev-Polskvoi—that is to say, "of the clearing"; lastly Moscow, surrounded at a distance with an almost continuous girdle of forest.

Here we have a curious dissociation of the ideas of fertility and natural wealth and that of primordial possibilities of

[1] Reclus, **LXXXVII*a***, Vol. II, p. 619.
[2] Milioukov, **CCXXVII**, p. 70.
[3] Ibid., p. 72.
[4] Ibid., pp. 40–1.
[5] D'Almeida, **XI**, 1910, p. 180.

existence ; a curious example also of a sort of inversion of values—but not an isolated one. For the protecting forest has only played the same defensive rôle in the genesis of Russia as was played, in a quite different country and climate, by a long succession of lagoons, of captive waters cut off from the sea by those narrow bands of shore, the *lidi*, and dotted with small habitable islands. The great political state of Venice was founded in the shelter of these lagoons by the refugees from Altinum, Montselice, and Padua, situated in richer lands which had been traversed from early times by many routes, owing to the suitability of its firm, light soil, but which for that reason was repeatedly devastated by invasions, like the Russian plain. These people established themselves at Torcello, Burano, Murano, and further south at Malmocco, and Chioggia, before they finally founded the great political centre of the Venetian Republic in the previously despised soil of Rialto, Olivolo, and Spinalunga.[1]

*
* *

These facts speak so forcibly for themselves that the theorists and the most uncompromising champions of geographical predestination could not do otherwise than confirm them, although they attempt, illogically enough, to maintain at the same time their own fundamental and favourite thesis. But how many analogous cases are there in history ; how many examples of sudden mutations in value and destiny !

We will instance another, the classic case *par excellence*, that of England's "being an island." We are told that it is race—the Norman origin of a portion of its population—which, coupled with the insularity of the country, explains the maritime power of Great Britain. Seafaring was the early instinct of a considerable number of the citizens, and navigation was a vital necessity to the island. Granted. But what is there in common between the England of the Heptarchy and modern England ? Between Norman England and the England of Cromwell ? Yet the environment has not

[1] Molmenti, *La vie privée à Venise*, Venice, 1895, Chap. I ; Diehl, *Une république patricienne : Venise*, Paris, 1913, Chap. I.

altered, nor the composition of a population which had been stable and homogeneous for centuries.

Do not let us shift the problem. It must not be claimed that England, long a country of sailors and predestined so to be, has simply passed through the same vicissitudes (only in an inverse sense) as another great and celebrated maritime nation of antiquity similarly predestined—Greece. Ancient Greece was a great maritime power, whilst modern Greece is only a very small one. But the decline in value is not so much due to discrimination of effort as to a transformation of environment. Formerly, its maritime activity was supreme in the Eastern Mediterranean basin, which then really constituted the whole of the civilized world; to-day it still operates in the same district, but that is now only a small and unimportant province of the great world. On the contrary, the maritime activity of England was at first limited, so to speak, to one side of the Atlantic and to seas of only local importance; hence it was not remarkable. But the maritime revolution of the latter part of the fifteenth century ended by promoting that activity to the foremost rank, which it still retains. It will be admitted that the analogy is quite a false one. Up to the time of Elizabeth English maritime activity was not noteworthy: Richard Ehrenberg has shown clearly in his instructive book on Hamburg and England in the Elizabethan period, how and why that activity began to develop; with him we can follow the way in which the exportation of cloth, monopolized by the guild of Merchant Adventurers,[1] was transformed after the end of the fifteenth century into a transit trade. But before that the old Merry England lived by agriculture and cattle rearing and its life was concentrated on and bound up with the soil of its own island. It was no seafaring nation, mainly occupied in fulfilling a destiny as such, until a great revolution, external and foreign to itself, transferred the seat of maritime activity and supremacy from the Mediterranean to the Atlantic—from a domain more or less inaccessible to British sailors to one which surrounded their country on all sides. The truth is that England has changed its nature, or rather, owing to causes in no way dependent on race or

[1] Ehrenberg, *Hamburg und England*, Jena, 1896, p. 27.

geographical environment, quiescent forces, dormant powers have been awakened from the sleep of ages, and have come into play.

History is full of such awakenings. And more so, perhaps, than that of the peoples themselves is the history of their mutual relations—of the great routes of terrestrial intercourse which hold so important a place in the daily life and welfare of human societies. We shall have occasion later on, in our fourth part, to return to this ; but in future let us note that there is no longer anything inevitable, fixed, or perpetual—nothing, we repeat, but possibilities.

Terrestrial routes, which might be thought unalterable, seem to be subject to a great number of physical and geographical influences which are quite consistent and explicable. The web is continually and rapidly being unmade and made again, with extreme mobility. We have lately seen the great railways of Europe—the great transverse lines from North to South, to the Mediterranean and, beyond that, to the near and far East—competing for the traffic across the formerly inaccessible Alpine regions, and through the heart of that Switzerland which was not so long ago a veritable pole of repulsion for travellers. What a race there was in the construction of tunnels in the years just before the War! What an almost uninterrupted series of borings, each one more expensive and more difficult than the last—and requiring the greatest and most costly labour! After the Simplon, the Austrian lines of the Tauern, the Pyhrn, and the Karawanken opened in 1909–10 ; the Bernese Lötschberg opened to traffic in August, 1913 ; the Hauenstein quite recently finished ; the Nice-Cuneo via Tenda ; and the enormous list of colossal projects—from Mont Blanc to the Splügen and the Greina.

The history of the sea tells the same tale. In the sixteenth century, they tell us, there was a transfer of maritime activity from one domain to another, from the ancient Mediterranean to the young Ocean. The statement needs modification, however. It must not be supposed that immediately after the discovery of America there was anything like a complete "maritime revolution". After 1492, as before it, the chief trade of the Baltic and North Sea ports was with the northern countries. What England and Holland coveted was the heritage of the Hanseatic League. The consequences of the discovery of the New World were slow to manifest themselves: the more so since that world had to borrow nearly everything from us, had scarcely anything to give us, and was very sparsely peopled. The special products of America (precious metals excepted) did not play any considerable part in European economy until the seventeenth century: a dense and economically important European immigration into the new continent was necessary before the Atlantic could become an ocean of numerous and regular routes.

With this reservation, the statement is on the whole justified; for a time the Atlantic traffic outrivalled the Mediterranean. But has not a new phase come with the piercing of the Isthmus of Suez and restored to the old inland sea a new glory? What is the real object of these innumerable tunnels through the Alps? Is it to get into Italy for Italy's sake? The objective, economically speaking, would be inconsiderable. Italy, in this case, is only the gateway to the East, the outpost of Egypt, stretching out its peninsula towards Alexandria.[1] So we have three phases: Mediterranean supremacy, followed by decline, and then renewal of activity. Will not the completion of the Bagdad railway entail disastrous consequences to this revival? Or, on the other hand, will not the increasing development of maritime life and economic activity in the countries bordering the Indian Ocean, the new vigour of the South African Union profiting by the world-war, all this supply of young energy and new productions, will not these compensate Suez for the loss of traffic and above all of travellers due to Häidar Pasha's railway to Bagdad and the Persian Gulf? The promoters of a scheme for a great modern port at Suez, with a petrol refinery and an entrance channel dredged to a depth of 40 feet, must have foreseen the fact.

Moreover, how many century-old routes in Africa, Asia, and the two Americas suddenly become deserted and lie dormant, although the physical reasons for their establishment remain unchanged?

There are perpetual mutations, following each other with increasing rapidity, one would say with an increasingly

[1] Eisenmann, "Les chemins de fer transalpins," *Rev. des cours et conférences*, 1914.

feverish activity. We must follow day by day, and minute by minute, the development of the world's network of routes if we wish never to miss either a project or a revolution. And nevertheless the configuration of the globe, the shape of the continents and their physical relations have undergone no change, neither have the traditional habits of the people. The possibilities would appear to remain identical. In reality, they alternately sleep to re-awaken, and then again to slumber. They are without doubt permanent, but they are not permanently in use, nor all at the same time. They are the keys of a piano ; if we put a finger on one of them the hammer makes the chord vibrate : but we do not touch them all at the same time, equally or necessarily. Some are struck frequently, and being always in use, always give back the same sound. Others are held throughout long centuries, but do not cease to give their note. Yet others remain for a long time idle and untouched, awaiting the re-awakening. And this is due not to mere chance, but to the action of human society.

II

The Definition of Possibility

Having got thus far, let us mark our advance. By successive steps we are gradually narrowing the problem. Natural regions are simply regions of possibilities for human groups. But if these possibilities form definite and permanent systems, what have we gained by our discussion ? Would not the systems of possibilities exactly resemble those collections of forces which were in question previously ? We should have changed the name, but should we not have kept the thing itself ? Would not those possibilities, as like as sisters to the natural powers, have controlled the lives of men with the same stringency ? No : since there is nothing synchronous, necessary, or predetermined in them : but constant variations and mutations, periods of dormancy and sudden awakenings, all due to human activity. But how then, if the possibilities are to play only an ephemeral and intermittent rôle, can we take them into account in a scientific work ?

The real problem can now be succinctly stated. It consists, first of all, in analysing carefully the idea of possibility; secondly, in classifying the regions in order of increasing or decreasing possibilities, or—if that enterprise appears really too ambitious and also too unsafe and ephemeral—to establish some kind of summary but clear order among them. If the regions offer only possibilities, they do not all offer the same number, nor are these all of the same value and quality. As they do not act invariably or, so to speak, automatically, the more numerous they are the greater the probability that we shall find some among them in action at a given moment. On this basis we can build the sort of hierarchy of which we have spoken, but the order is difficult to establish owing to this task of defining possibility.

*

* *

The primordial condition of the foundation and development of a human society in a given region is evidently that it should find at its disposal an animal world and, more important still, a plant world rich enough to supply its wants. But is this correlation the mathematically simple and automatic result of the play of a single factor—the number of species or individuals?

We cannot deduce the advantages and disadvantages which a country offers for human groupings by merely considering its zoological or botanical density. In other words, we can form no conclusion as to the richness or the poverty of a country from the length of a catalogue of its plants or animals. By an apparent paradox—but only an apparent one, as we shall show—extreme plenty often produces the same unfortunate results as extreme want. In certain surroundings, faced by exuberance, an excessive botanical or zoological abundance, man cannot make his abode and succeeds badly in his endeavours. Too much wealth is practically the same thing for him as the poverty he finds in other environments. His life is, as it were, stifled and paralysed by the excess of life which surrounds him. The consideration at the same time or successively of two terrestrial zones as distinct as the polar and sub-polar zones on the one hand and the intertropical zone on the other, proves this conclusively. It is useless, however, to institute a formal parallel between them. In the case of Arctic and Antarctic lands, the fact is generally granted without difficulty and no proof is necessary; man finds a thousand obstacles in his path owing to the scanty resources of those districts. For the intertropical regions, on the contrary, proof is not altogether superfluous.

In former days it was usual to describe those hot countries, their vegetation, and their botanical and zoological wealth, with a most illusory enthusiasm. They were the lands of promise, where nature, generously heaping her treasures on man, saved him from almost all labour, and spared him the trouble and anxiety of clothing, housing, or feeding himself; plenty of nutritious fruits were growing without his care, for which he had only to stretch out his hand, so to speak, and his food was choice and appetizing. A complete psychological picture of the gentle savage of the hot countries was founded on this rather over-idealistic geography. But have such out-of-date fantasies been everywhere and always replaced to-day by more solid ideas? Enthusiastic but over-hasty [1] botanists paint us idyllic pictures of the Equatorial forests of the Amazon and Congo, as the outcome of their steady routine-work. "Nature there is always keeping holiday. These are the blessed regions of eternal summer, where the mighty equatorial plant-life flourishes. In these lands man lives without toil; the produce of two or three trees will suffice to feed him for a whole year, and everywhere he finds the most varied and delicious fruits at his disposal." More than this; enthusiasm for the present overflows and inundates past ages, even to remote antiquity: and we are thus launched into the genesis of man: "primitive man had here less danger of perishing from hunger than in the cold regions, and it is most probable that he spread from thence over the whole surface of the earth." [2] We will leave these visions of Cocagne: so many words, so many errors—as is overwhelmingly proved by the testimony of all modern observers and explorers.

The lofty tropical forest is a difficult place to live in; this is the verdict of all those who have had real experience of

[1] Costantin, *La Nature tropicale*, **CV**, Introd., *passim*. The volume is relatively recent—1899.

[2] *Contra*, amongst others, M. Boule, in **XVI**, 1916 (Vol. XXVII), p. 498.

those enormous, thick, prodigiously high, and crowded trunks, growing up straight as arrows towards a sky of dazzling brilliancy but impossible to see, bound together below, as though cemented, by a formidable network of lianas, creepers, bushes, and thorns, all struggling to climb to the tree-tops and the light which never reaches the undergrowth, in order to put forth their flowers and ripen their seeds.[1] The problem of finding a way through these living and opaque walls is difficult; to find an outlet, if one is not indigenous to these hostile countries and thoroughly trained to the quite special gymnastics which they require, is a hopeless task.

This is all an old story. Many years have passed since Stanley, in one of his letters to the *Daily Telegraph* from Manyenema in Central Africa, dated 1st November, 1876, dispelled the mirage of the virgin forest, fascinating us with an unequalled beauty and splendour when seen from afar from the summit of some hill which overtops the wall of trees—savage, inhospitable, and closed to man as soon as he tries to penetrate it, and, as Stanley said in memorable words, truly overpowering in its silence, its vastness, and its want of proportion and of visible relations with humanity. And our knowledge of the tropical forest has without doubt progressed since Stanley's time; the French expeditions of Chevalier and Commandant A. Bertin, and Count J. de Broy's expedition to Mayambe, both very recent, have given us much more precise ideas on the composition of the forest masses, and also on their relative discontinuity; they have shown us that the density of the forest corridors has often deceived travellers as to the true character of the regions they were traversing, that the open spaces were larger, and the brushwood clearings more numerous than was supposed; there is a kind of mingling of the forest and the real savannah up to the Equator. At the same time there was a sort of parallel reaction against the over-rigid ideas and over-strict calculations which made us look on these countries as veritable deserts. The general map of population in Bartholomew's recent *Atlas of Economic Geography* shows us this reaction perhaps a little exaggerated.[2]

[1] Costantin, **CIV**, p. 194 ff.

[2] Bartholomew, **X**[a], sheet 7. The map gives 26 to 64 people to the sq. mile in the African Equatorial forest, whilst that of Brazil gives less than 1 to the kilometre.

But, when all is said, the best-qualified observers of the African forest zone, after a lapse of years, still re-echo the voice of Stanley. There is Dr. Cureau, the author of a study [1] on the primitive tribes of equatorial Africa, a little too systematic perhaps, a little too worked-up, and a little too schematic also, but full of useful information. It would be impossible to make us feel the contrast between the forest and the plain better than he does—the virgin forest, compact, sombre, silent, monotonous, almost colourless (the general tint of the landscape is green, the ground a burnt-sienna or greyish colour), in the interior of which " the thick roof of foliation, always green, crushes you, the heavy and stale humidity overpowers you, the green gloom tortures you ". Here, there is tangled undergrowth which forms " an obstacle as pliant as it is resistant ", there, there is passage-way where the great trunks crowd on one another, but one has to clamber over the projecting roots and the trunks of the giants which time has laid low, while the feet slip on the thick carpet of dead leaves, and sink deep in the slime of rotting wood. In like manner Dr. Cureau points the contrast between the man of the plains and the " man of the woods " who leads the precarious and suspicious life of a perpetual recluse in his obscure dwelling under those gloomy vaults, and, when drawn from his haunts and brought into the light of day and the open country, " seems as dazed and uneasy as a bat blinded by the light." [2]

Yet that " man of the woods " has apparently all the requisites for prosperity. Dr. Cureau gives a very good idea of the anxious and in many ways undeveloped life which the great forest imposes on its guests, by reason not only of the extreme luxuriance of its plant population, the formidable size of its trees and the struggle to the light of its secondary plants, but of " the terrible plague of every sort of minute creature that creation has produced, devastating larvæ and sharp-jawed insects which bear witness to the unparalleled fecundity of a swarming animal life ". And his conclusion is plain ; there is no gaiety or joy, for nature is there the stepmother of man. " She refuses him the first necessity of life, food ; since the trees bear their fruits at inaccessible heights, and hunting in the forest is a lottery. She refuses

[1] Cureau, **CLXXIX**, p. 30. [2] Ibid., pp. 30, 302.

him the sun, the source of health and good spirits. There is not a blade of grass to rejoice his sight, nor even moss for the repose of his weary limbs." [1]

*

* *

So much for Africa : but when we ask those best acquainted with America about the Amazonian Selvas, their testimony is the same. The first impression is of inexhaustible fecundity. " The earth there is hot, with a heat moist from living matter, the result of incessant fermentations and a thousand prolific putridities," says M. Rivet.[2] But after study the judgment is revised : " the fertility is more apparent than real," says M. Le Cointe.[3] The soil is poor, sand, clay or rock ; above this is a very thin layer of arable soil, which the rains easily wash away as soon as it is cleared ; it is then very evident that the place is nothing but " a desert, covered with verdure, which is only waiting for its chance to reappear ".

This is essentially a vegetable nature, with no smiles for man and no accessory resources ; the balance-sheet is poor. And so, as a natural consequence, the people of Central Africa live under a permanent régime of hunger. " To eat his fill, to gorge himself to the point of indigestion, is the one idea of the negro." [4] What a striking paradox ! We find a perpetual state of semi-famine on a virgin soil which abounds with life and productiveness. Nothing, however, is easier to understand. The game is scarce, of great physical strength, and exceedingly dangerous when it takes the form of the elephant, the hippopotamus, or the wild ox. The raising of cattle is left, so to speak, to the animals themselves, and the domestic beasts, sheep and goats, are small, few in number, thin, tough, and unsavoury. There are no large cattle owing to the prevalence of contagious diseases.[5] Agriculture is rudimentary—some meagre fields of manioc, sorghum, millet, and sweet potatoes in the rare clearings. But even if agriculture were more scientifically managed, the results, undoubtedly, would not be very different. European attempts at cultivation so far have not been very successful. Too many

[1] Ibid., pp. 29–30.
[2] In **XVI**, 1907, p. 83.
[3] *Climat de l'Amazonie*, **XI**, 1905, p. 458.
[4] Cureau, **CLXXIX**, p. 252.
[5] Ibid., p. 258.

enemies lie in wait for the plant, to say nothing of the difficulties of a climate subject to sudden variations, which at one time dries up and destroys the crops, at another uproots and carries them away to bury them under a mass of silt. The natural products of the soil, the tubers, which are dug up in the bush, are "famine food", says the explorer Chevalier [1]; they contain either glucosides or prussic acid, so that a whole series of preparations is necessary before they can be used to any extent. Nature is only prodigal in caterpillars, slugs, and frogs, and such insects as ants, termites, grasshoppers and butterflies, of whose invincible tenacity and perpetual buzzing we, in Europe, would find it difficult to form an idea, so hungry are they, so all-devouring and indomitable that it has been said that "the real ferocious beast of equatorial Africa, and the most to be feared is the insect".[2] But, to redress the balance, the natives, Bandas, Mandjas and others, gather them in basketfuls during the winter season and eat them; termite-fat is a regular article of their larder.[3]

Hence, it is not surprising to find that famines are prevalent in these lands, and that cannibalism still persists there, though, no doubt, this practice is not really connected with their food requirements. It probably originated in a sort of ritual fetishism, which prompted the native to incorporate in himself the qualities of his victim by eating the whole or part of his corpse; but it is none the less true that the cannibal feasts are often a real sustenance to the famished, to those Bandas of Ubangi, for instance, who in times of want, as Chevalier saw, did not hesitate to fish up and feast upon bodies which had been thrown into the water; the negro, we know, does not object to his meat being high, and will even eat decomposing carrion. Dr. Cureau reminds us that "the earlier commandants of the post at Banghi had for a long time to station an armed sentinel in the cemetery to preserve the recently interred dead from the voracity of the natives".[4] We do not eat the smell, says the negro, philosophically.

However, the inter-tropical lands are not all forest. Must we then look in the laterite, that clay produced by the decomposition of the ancient rocks, granite, gneiss and

[1] Chevalier, **CLXXVIII**, p. 112.
[2] Cureau, **CLXXIX**, p. 253.
[3] Chevalier, **CLXXVIII**, pp. 89–90.
[4] Op. cit., p. 257.

diorite, by the action of the copious tropical rains, to find the special facilities for the existence of human groups? Are they in the red soil of the Deccan, Indo-China, Madagascar, or the Congo? Emile Gautier, who has made investigations in Madagascar, tells us that the earth there has the colour, hardness, and fertility of the brick from which it gets its name; artificially hollowed out here and there, it is used as a receptacle, at the bottom of which men sow their seeds in a little vegetable mould. But the absence of forest does not mean the presence of laterite. When a sufficient amount of rain falls on this somewhat less ungrateful soil, does the picture change? Do possibilities of settlement then occur? Yes, but this never happens to an extent that will allow the equatorial regions to compare with those temperate ones which have neither the poverty of the polar and sub-polar countries, nor the illusory riches of the tropical lands.

III

The Supporting Bases of Mankind—Plains, Plateaux, Mountains

We have now determined the first category of such elements as we require for a general definition of the idea of possibility. Two conditions only are needed for the possibility of settlement by communities of men. One is that there should be present sufficient zoö-botanical sustenance on which an existence can be based with confidence for the morrow. The other is that it should be possible to take advantage easily of the natural resources thus placed at the disposal of human society: and especially that the plant and animal societies should be available for man to use freely and advantageously —and in such a way that they are deprived of all excessive, stifling, and, so to speak, blind fecundity.

This implies an absolute condemnation of any grouping which claims to be based on an arithmetical idea of riches or poverty, measurable by the greater or less number of either botanical or zoological species and individuals.

The geographical idea of riches or poverty, as we have shown, is quite different. At the same time let us once more remark that this is just as much a condemnation of any system of bounds based only on climatic considerations. All the more so in that if the necessity for the rearrangement of societies by men appeared evident, it would necessitate the establishment of a new condition of things before it could be attempted. For there are certain plant and animal surroundings which prevent men from playing an active part; they cannot successfully invade a botanical or zoological region to rearrange it, organize it, and adapt it to their needs, unless they first of all establish certain supporting posts favourable to the free development of their efforts.

The idea of such *points d'appui* seems to us of vital importance both to methods and facts. Thanks to it, an element of variety is introduced into the oppressive dullness and stark monotony of the climatico-botanical boundaries. By means of it, the topographical element, so complex and rich in variety and possibilities, reappears along with the biological element which the study of the climatico-botanical regions led us to consider first. But the difficulty begins when we have to give this idea a precise meaning and to analyse its actual content.

*
* *

The division of the surface of the globe into mountains, plains, and plateaux is an old and traditional one. Modern geographers have received it from their predecessors, and have not abandoned it—which is perhaps a mistake. They continue to use the old terms and simply try to improve by analysis the ideas involved. They commonly add also a new "species", that of depressions, and thus raise to four the number of varieties allowed to terrestrial relief, but the general definitions given remain somewhat vague.

Let us turn to one of those manuals which make no claim to originality but which lay themselves out to publish a fair account of the conclusions of others, rather than personal work: the manual of general geography by Lespagnol, a work midway between the great academic manual, which is too full for ordinary students, and the popular elementary treatise. It was published in 1905 under the title *L'Évolution de la Terre et de l'Homme*. It classifies the four forms of relief,[1]

[1] Lespagnol, **LXXIX**, 2nd part, Chap. IX, p. 261 ff.

dividing the mountains into mountains due to dislocation, mountains due to erosion and mountains due to accumulation. The first of these are subdivided into mountains due to folding, and to fracture, and mountains worn down and transformed into peneplains.

It might seem that this attempted analysis would lead us to reject the idea of "mountain" or to reserve it strictly for one only of the categories analysed. But such is not the case; we are told that "mountains represent parts of the surface considerably elevated above the ground"; a very vague formula. What ground does it mean? Starting from what elevation? Is it relative or absolute—i.e. does it refer to the land surrounding the mountains or to the sea-level? There are mountains such as the Alps, the Pyrenees, the Himalaya, the Jura, the Morvan, the mountains of Thuringia, the Vosges, and the Black Forest; but there are also [1] the mountains of Rheims (944 feet) and Laon (593 feet), the Mont des Cats (511 feet), and Mont Cassel (504 feet), and also the peneplains which "geographically" are plains or plateaux [2]; there are also the dunes of the deserts which "may rise to some 650 feet"; how uncertain it all is! The name of mountain is given to low hills which do not rise above 800 feet; it is difficult to fix the number of feet at which a mountain becomes a hill, and a hill becomes a small mountain. In reality the height of mountains is only a relative term, which depends on the general height of the base from which they rise.[3]

Nor is the idea of plateaux more precise. We have already seen that there are mountains, in the genetic sense of the word, which are plains in the geographical sense. What then is a plateau "geographically speaking"? "It is the prevailing form of a region of elevated land ill or little irrigated." Its altitude is undefined: there are no precise limits to it. Usually, plains are limited to a height of 800 feet, "but many exceed that height and on the other hand the Lorraine plateau does not everywhere reach it." [4] Concerning this 800 ft. there are, as we said before, heights of no great importance, and which do not exceed 800 feet to which the title of mountain is given. The statement that plateaux are

[1] Ibid., p. 279. [2] p. 278. [3] p. 281. [4] Ibid.

intermediate between plains and mountains is thus weakened in advance. Further, it is stated that these plateaux, which vary between 800 and 16,000 feet (the Thibetan plateau), hardly ever present flat surfaces, which does not help to clarify our ideas.

Lastly, as to the plains. These are the regions which form the least elevated part of the relief. Some are peripheric, some are coastal, some are inland. But here again, what precise criterion is there to distinguish accurately plains from plateaux — for example, in North America, the "lacustrian plateau" of Labrador from the "lacustrian plain" of the North which adjoins it on the southern border of Hudson's Bay? Is it the relative height or the structural origin? All this is left remarkably vague and confused.

Depressions are regions which lie below sea-level. Here, at any rate, the criterion is clear. But they are also regions which "as the result of fractures followed by subsidence, have undergone such a sinking of level that they are dominated by the neighbouring districts".[1] Are they, therefore, merely sunken plateaux? The idea is a comparatively just one when applied to the Great Basin of the United States or to the Tarim in Central Asia, but elsewhere? "Many other regions, especially in Asia, Africa, and Australia, have the more or less decided character of depressions, and undergo in a variable degree the same destiny." This is a very accommodating "character", as was also the other. Provisionally, it is to be presumed that these indecisive regions enrich the category of plateaux or that of plains according to our choice.

*

* *

Our intention must not be misunderstood. We have no idea of laying ourselves open to ironical, and no doubt very obvious, criticisms. A very difficult problem faces modern geographers—that of reconciling the new and precise ideas which result from their efforts at analysis and still more from their careful observation of the genesis of form, and their researches into structural origins, with the old traditional theories which have kept their sway, consecrated by centuries of custom, which we cannot keep pushing aside from day

[1] p. 283.

to day, or ruthlessly transform. But it is of the highest importance to our task that we should call attention to the lack of precision to-day in the ideas which are based on a whole series of the most ambitious and the most precise historico-geographical theories and considerations.

For the special influence of the mountains, plains, and plateaux is constantly referred to. First of all we are reminded of their evident effect on climate. We are reminded that mountains attract rainfall and also that they form, from the base to the summit, a kind of biological complex in which the most distinct climatic zones, and consequently the most varied zoö-botanical worlds, become neighbours, brought together and, so to speak, juxtaposed in space.

Such a lofty peak as Monte Rosa, for instance, with its 15,000 feet of altitude, is a sort of zonal epitome of the European continent from Lapland to the Mediterranean, whilst on the slopes of Mount Everest, which rises to 29,000 feet, all the climates of Asia, from the Tropics to the Polar regions, are reproduced successively and regularly.

As to the plateaux, the account is somewhat more vague, for the idea of plateaux, as we have seen, does not err on the side of precision. We are told, however, that " the climate there is generally severe on account of its altitude ".

But the relations which people claim to have established between those vague abstractions, mountains, plateaux plains, and the actual realities of climate are of considerable importance to man. Here, then, is the opportunity for us to pass from botany to man, and to compare, from every point of view, the life of human societies in the mountains, the plateaux, and the plains, considering each of these problematical and artificial units as a different supporting base for possibilities ; but we have no agreement as yet for their rank in the series, and the analyses (as is not surprising) are singularly wanting in strictness and logic.

At the time, already distant, but not so distant as some would imagine, when Élisée Reclus wrote *La Terre*,[1] it appeared to him that, of all the mighty masses of the continents, the plateaux were the most important in the history of humanity. He shows them [2] to us standing out from the midst of the

[1] The 3rd edition was in 1876.
[2] Op. cit., **LXXXVII**[a], Vol. II, p. 633 ff.

plains, with their own systems of mountains, rivers, and lakes, with a flora and a fauna of their own, and a climate always cooler and generally drier than that of the low countries; in short, the plateaux were in his eyes a perfectly well-defined order.

But when we come to follow his analysis we see that the importance which he attributes to plateaux naturally varies very much with place and time, and that the part he considers them to play is sometimes a purely negative one, sometimes a very positive one.

On the one hand, he looks on the plateaux, or rather certain plateaux, as so many barriers; they are, he says, really isolating zones, the strongest barriers that can be placed between peoples; for the great ocean, formerly untraversable, is to-day mere child's play to our ships.

The plateaux of the cold and temperate regions are not only boundaries between nations; some of them are absolutely desert because of the aridity of the soil and the rigour of the climate. In South America people dare not venture on the plateaux of the Andes between Chile and the Argentine; even in France the Causses of Florac, Levezou, and Cavalerie are very dangerous to cross in winter.

But, on the other hand, there are plateaux highly suitable for human habitation, especially those which, in very hot regions, supply an element of coolness and salubrity: "vast hanging gardens which are elevated to a height of 3,000 to 7,000 feet," they carry "on their marble or granite pillars as it were a fragment of the temperate zone, with its climate, its productions, and its relatively prosperous inhabitants".[1]

Such are the plateaux of Ethiopia in Africa; and, in America, the Peruvian plateau, the home of the Incas, the high lands of Colombia, where dwelt the Muyscas and other Indian tribes, and the *altos* of Guatemala, Anahuac and the peninsula of Yucatan, the seat of an ancient civilization. The list of Élisée Reclus could be further lengthened. The *tierras templadas* of Mexico, whose habitable zone of warm temperate climate extends at a height of from 3,000 to 6,000 feet between the *tierras calientes* and the *tierras frias*; the mountains of Equatorial Africa, especially that great mountain mass Adamawa in the Cameroons, which rises in places to a height of more than 6,000 feet, and which introduces the savannah into the heart of the

[1] p. 635.

forest region—these are very striking examples of the beneficent and salutary rôle of certain plateaux. Imerina, in Madagascar, also owes to its elevation its salubrity and its immunity from the marsh fevers of the adjacent lowlands.

Thus, in one place the formation of the land produces, in a habitable zone, the roughest and most unfavourable conditions for existence, so unfavourable indeed that they end, in extreme cases, by preventing all possibility not only of the development but even of the existence of human societies. Elsewhere it creates, in an unfavourable region, islands favourable for the establishment of groups relatively prosperous.

What becomes, then, of the idea of the "plateau" as the source of special conditions of existence and the mother of human societies characterized by the imprint of their origin. "According to their latitude and the configuration of the surrounding country, the plateaux have a favourable or unfavourable influence on the destinies of man," was the conclusion arrived at by Élisée Reclus a long time ago.[1] A cautious conclusion, but a strong contrast to his prefatory statement that "the plateaux are of supreme importance in the history of mankind". It means really that each particular case must be considered separately, and carefully studied as to its special characteristics; but there are no general rules, still less is there any necessary and single idea of "plateau".

*

* *

The same remarks apply to the term "mountain", for constant reference is made to the influence of mountains on man, and the special characters which they imprint on mountain societies—characters in every respect dissimilar to those of societies on the plains, being affected by a natural environment peculiarly oppressive and tyrannical.

The method is simple. A well-chosen instance of a mountain community is taken; the most obvious characteristics of the life of its members are noted; their native peculiarities are ignored; and a general rule is set up from the observations thus collected.

Let us take the case of Andorra, which is a region remarkably isolated; so completely isolated, indeed, that it has preserved

[1] p. 635.

a unique political system which has been investigated so thoroughly that we are familiar with all its peculiarities.[1]

In the group of valleys, deeply carved by glaciers and by erosion, which form this interesting country, the inhabitants have established a system in conformity with the possibilities. The shaded slopes, the *ubach*, which are almost valueless,[2] are either waste land or are covered with scrubby fir trees; but the sunny ones, the *sola*, are cultivated at the base and form pastures higher up.

Cultivation only takes place, however, where it is possible to solve the double problem of retaining the soil on the slopes and of irrigating it.[3] The most extensive arable ground, moreover, is situated in districts where the climate hardly permits husbandry, or where habitation is impossible in the winter. In consequence the area devoted to pasture is greatly extended.

Moreover, the flocks, in these valleys, are both the source and the traditional standard of riches. They pass the winter, which is long and severe, in cattle sheds low down in the valleys or on the first slopes, whilst the inhabitants, to banish ennui and to amuse themselves during the inclement weather, betake themselves to work at little domestic industries naturally very antiquated and leisurely. As soon as the snow has disappeared the annual round of pastoral movements begins. The animals are driven towards the heights, where they meet other flocks not from the valleys, which come to share with them the highland pasturage during the summer. Side by side they move on all through the summer in a prescribed order so as to economize the grass. At Michaelmas the herd is broken up. The cattle from other districts go back to their own country, whilst those of the Andorra valleys linger on the less exposed slopes, and slowly regain the lower valleys; by Christmas time all are in the folds—at least all those which the year's provision of forage, augmented by young shoots and tender branches, allows to be kept.

To these migrations quite a series of tiers of houses correspond; the winter ones are collected in villages or hamlets, and are packed full of various belongings in a manner that marks a determination "to crowd as many things as possible, people and cattle, food and firewood, into the minimum of

[1] Brutails, *La Coutume d'Andorre*, Paris, 1904.
[2] Sorre, **CCXXX**, p. 415.
[3] Ibid., pp. 422–3.

space".[1] The summer houses, *bordes* and *cortals*, perched at a height of from 5,000 to 7,000 feet, are surrounded by poor fields of rye and potatoes, which mark the extreme limit of cultivation.

Higher still are the huts of the shepherds, the *orrys* where cheese was formerly made from sheep's milk.

The people move periodically from the winter to the summer dwellings, as the herds do from the sheds below to the pastures above. This peculiar life produces in them very marked characteristics. Its isolation explains why their little country has escaped the clutches of the great neighbouring states, and has preserved a special organization of its own, oligarchic under a democratic guise, to which the Andorrans are attached by all the fibres of their being. For Andorran patriotism is extremely deep-rooted, ardent, and fully developed.[2] And if we study also their social, political, and moral conditions, as M. Brutails has done, we must grant that there is an effective solidarity amongst them and a special development of certain rules in their scheme of government; especially those which relate to common property and grazing rights. Lastly, the Andorrans strike the observer by their serious and grave demeanour, and by a kind of rigid morality, generally assumed, and in reality masking the violent passions which it represses. They are dominated by tradition, are the slaves of old methods, and cherish a superstition, rather than a respect, for the past, for its customs, its forms, and all its judicial and moral legacy. So strong, tenacious, and far-reaching is the hold of ancestral customs, that few escape from it.

Here, then, we have a doubling of agricultural levels and a corresponding doubling of habitations; a combination of a precarious and restricted agriculture with a very full and compelling pastoral life, and with a more or less temporary and unimportant industrial activity; the seasonal rhythm of a life oscillating between a summer and a winter state; a corresponding alteration in establishments, houses, stabling, sheepfolds, and barns; constant autonomy of groups, respect for tradition, attachment to native soil, and a limited outlook. Here are quite a collection of characteristics, but they are not peculiar to Andorra or the Andorrans. In the Pyrenees, first of all, these very characters mark all the mountain regions

[1] Sorre, p. 445. [2] Ibid., p. 462.

of like altitude and geographical conditions—Cerdagne, Capcir, Carlit, with slight variations in the proportion of the constituent elements: "if we study life in the great mountain masses of the Pyrenees, we shall find there no characteristics different from those in Andorra.[1] And when we leave the Pyrenees a similar state of things is found wherever analogous geographical conditions are reproduced, as at Transhumance in the Carpathians, where it has been studied by M. de Martonne. The rhythmic change of life, according to the seasons, was observed in the valley of Anniviers by Brunhes and Girardin; and the staging and variety of forms of dwellings in the Trentino Alps have been described by Marinelli. "We are compelled," is the opinion of Sorre in his very interesting book on the Mediterranean Pyrenees, "to consider the Andorran type of life as a variety of a species spread over the whole of Europe. We find always the same fundamental arrangements and often the same appearances, despite the diversity of place."[2]

*

* *

We have assuredly no intention of impugning the truth of conclusions so abundantly confirmed and, in a general way, so legitimate. Still, some comments are necessary. Keeping strictly within the limits to which a geographer like Sorre confines himself, we may observe that the Andorran facts—divested, however, of all their strictly Andorran peculiarities, for the cultivation of tobacco which predominates on the agricultural soil of its valleys is not a usual highland occupation, any more than smuggling, to which so many Andorrans devote their activities, is confined to mountainous districts—since they are very general, do undoubtedly recur in other mountainous countries, but it would be manifestly wrong to say that they are characteristic of all Pyrenean life.

It may be granted that such is the life in the higher mountains, but we should have to exclude from the mountain district and banish from the Pyrenean region those lands intermediate between the coastal plains of Rousillon and of Ampurdan and the high Pyrenean districts—Capcir, Carlit, Andorra, and Cerdagne—and also the central valleys of Catalonia and of the Conflent with their magnificent adornment of beeches, their

[1] Sorre, **CCXXX**, p. 453. [2] Ibid., pp. 480–1.

sparkling streams, their meadows, their orchards, their mines, their cotton mills, and their industrial country towns. And then, can we ignore race? Granted that the Andorrans are mountaineers, still, as Sorre himself says—not once but twenty times—they are also Catalans, Catalans in language, in their tendencies and relations, in their piety also, and in their culture and character; and their most characteristic features are common to all the Catalonian mountaineers. The only difference is that the Andorrans exhibit them in a greater degree. They are "the type of the majority of the Catalonian mountaineers".[1]

Moreover, if we overstep the limits we set ourselves just now, if we try to generalize more, to create a single universal type of mountaineer, the direct product of a natural unity which is called "the mountains", what an error we make!

"The mountains"; how can we follow so many creators of abstractions, Miss Semple, for example, when they seem to be utterly careless about the difference between one zone or type and another? here, mountain masses and isolated valleys, like lost islets, where a special form of human life is evolved on the spot; there, regions less rugged and less inaccessible, or great countries open to traffic, such as one meets with in the heart of numberless mountainous zones which have seen century after century of human traffic, human migrations following one another along the routes that traverse them.

What is there common between the lands of the Mohawk depression, or the Cumberland gap, and the rest of the Appalachians? What analogy between the Brenner and the wild mountain districts which surround it?

Then "the mountaineer", what shall we say of him—the abstract, typical, universal mountaineer?—the man whose curiosity is necessarily restricted and horizon is limited by a high mountain barrier; the slave from birth of tradition and routine, conservative to his inmost being and rooted in the past; the superstitious guardian of the moral and material heritage left him by his ancestors because nothing occurs to inspire him with a desire for change. Old habits, old costumes, old languages, old religions. Is not this the inhabitant of the Engadine with his Romansh, the Basque

[1] Sorre, **CCXXX**, pp. 450–3.

with his Euskara, the Vaudois with his religious doctrine, the Andorran with his privileges, and, further afield, the Albanian with his dialect and his Islamism ? And for the rest, this theoretic mountaineer is a vigorous, honourable man, living a healthy life in the midst of a patriarchal family group closely united, industrious, frugal, thrifty, and provident, ignorant of luxury, careless of comfort, a hard worker, and a formidable competitor to the people of the plains. On the other hand, naturally also, he is neither scholar nor artist, for do not the mighty bounds of his mountain home stifle and crush the creative genius of man ? The inhabitants of the high Apennines are of the same race as those of the Tuscan hills, but here we find genius, there a rude and unpolished rusticity.

However, we will let that pass. Is the mountaineer backward and slow as compared with the plain-dweller ? Rousseau, and Kropotkin after him, would protest in the name of the "montagnons" of the Jura. Are the astute and cunning Dauphinois of Stendhal less intelligent than the Beaucerons ? These people, who have spread unceasingly as emigrants over the great world routes ; are they rivetted to the soil, deprived of outlook, and wrapped up in routine ? It may be said that poverty has driven them ; but poverty is the other name, or one of the other names, for a mountain environment. And besides, what does the motive power matter ? It is the result that we are considering. Lastly, could we not with the same ease, and, needless to say, the same appearance of truth, sustain the contrary thesis that the mountains are the very best means of habituating man to wide horizons, and that their summits make him, even more than the sailor, a lover of wide spaces ? Scholarship for scholarship, one is as unsound as the other. As for the problem of genius, so dear to the Abbé Dubois, the most prudent course at the moment is to reply that it is no concern of geographers as such, not even if they call themselves anthropogeographers.

There exists a geographical notion of civilization distinct from the historical and philosophic one [1] ; this latter, in the sense which Guizot gave to it formerly, and which it is generally

[1] On this wide question, cf. the useful little book of Niceforo, *Les indices numériques de la Civilisation et du Progrès*, Paris, Flammarion, 1921.

agreed in France to keep to-day, extends to all the elements in the life of a people, economic, social, political, intellectual, æsthetic, moral, and religious. The former is fortunately more restricted ; it consists only in the development by society of the resources which its natural environment offers or which it at last discovers in it ; and it is almost mathematically measurable as so much per cent of the utilization of possibilities. To study its relations with its physical environment is a task quite difficult enough, and there is no necessity to complicate it further. This reply, rude and negative though it is, is better assuredly than a detailed criticism of hazardous assertions. We should be as foolish as those we wish to criticize if we were to argue that Gustave Courbet, who was undoubtedly a painter, came from the Jura, and that Stendhal, who passes for a writer, was a Dauphinois of Grenoble—like Berlioz. For then it would be necessary to find out how the pictures of Courbet manifest the specific influence of the Jura, or the psychology of Stendhal that of " Cularo " as he delighted to call it. And besides that, we should have to show that Ornans in the valley of the Loue, the birthplace of Courbet, and Grenoble on the banks of the Isère, have some claim to represent the mountains . . .

The truth is, there is no sort of mountain unity which would be always found wherever on the earth mountainous elevations exist ; any more than there is one unity of plateau, or one unity of plain ; but simply that analogous possibilities are met with in different places, and that these have been turned to account in the same way, and the civilizations are in consequence comparable—if we omit their individual and truly characteristic features.

When analyses are complete enough and numerous enough, when we can add to the contributions concerning Europe equally careful monographs about the mountainous regions of the other continents, it will perhaps be possible to determine a certain number of typical manners in which human society has adapted itself to the possibilities of the various classes of mountains. At present the attempt is premature ; but the unitary delusion is worse than a delusion ; it is dangerous folly.

CHAPTER II

The Minor Natural Regions and their Bounds
Insular Units

We will not trouble to criticize this fully. It is absurd to try to estimate the number of possibilities contained by each of those artificial unities, mountains, plains, plateaux, depressions ; or the sum of the means which it places at the disposal of human societies. But can we not break up these false and deceptive unities and decompose them into their elements ?

The word mountain, it is true, is a wide one, and not at all precise ; the idea of it is therefore vague and badly analysed. To express the varieties of relief, the great languages of western civilization clearly lack the delicate shading which is found in the speech of certain peoples for whom an exact knowledge of great stretches of country, with no possibility of any mistake, is a vital necessity. They tell us [1] that the Tuaregs, for instance, have fifteen different expressions, which they can apply to as many types of hills, according to their shape, the nature of their soil, their colour or other such details.

It is very curious to note how geographers, when they wish to be more exact about the far too rudimentary ideas which the literary languages place at their disposal, are obliged to have recourse to the local terms used in the daily life of the rustic or traveller, and to introduce profusely into their scientific vocabulary the pithy and appropriate words used in the district: *crêts* in the Jura, *puys* in Auvergne, *ballons* in the Vosges. The list would be interminable.[2]

The mountain is not a unit. But what of the mountain valley ? Is it not the type even of a real little geographical unity, a unity of population, cultivation, and civilization ? When we look on such valleys as we meet with in the Alps, the Jura, the Pyrenees, the Apennines, the Caucasus, or the

[1] Chudeau, **CLXXXI,** Vol. II, p. 20.
[2] E. Gautier has some interesting ideas on this subject in **CLXXXI**^{b}**,** Vol. I, pp. 1–2.

Himalaya, do we not find ourselves in the presence of a veritable topographical community, between whose members we can and ought to institute useful comparisons?

But, in a parallel way, do we not find unities of the same kind on the banks of great rivers, clearly defined, easy to view and to comprehend at a glance, really primitive in their simplicity, in their external appearance, their internal structure, and all their comparable characteristics? Have they not attracted numerous and progressive human colonies, and at times given rise to what has been called [1] an almost amphibious race?

Similarly, have not the lake-shores, and even more the sea-shores, swarmed with dense populations of a distinct type, strongly marked with the stamp of the sea, at all times and in all countries, from the epoch when the Danish kitchen-middens [2] were heaped up, to the present day, when men are crowding to the shores of the Corniche or the Riviera?

And in general, are there not natural bounds of a very simple order, so evident in contour that no discussion about the unity of their character is possible, and which, as they support small human societies, allow us to study their development with regard to the geographical conditions under which they were formed? Such is the idea of the geographer who devotes one part of his *Géographie humaine* [3] to what he calls "The Islands"—not so much the islands of the sea, which he neglects, no doubt because he thinks their case has been heard long ago, but what he calls the islands of the desert, the oases, and the islands of the habitable world, the mountain valleys. He would, no doubt, be willing to extend this notion of insularity to the small coastal plains, limited in area but crowded with inhabitants, of which certain deltas, especially, offer types which are characteristic of all, and similarly to river banks, to those at least which, in the midst of an inhospitable land, attract specially compact and vigorous settlements, such as those of the Nile in ancient Egypt, and of the Euphrates in Mesopotamia. These are so many vast oases, or, one might say, human forest-glades, pushing and extending into the arid districts.

[1] Brunhes, **LXVI**, pp. 191–2.
[2] Vidal, **XCVII.**
[3] Brunhes, **LXVI**, Chaps. VI, VII.

Shall we not find here the really characteristic types of those *points d'appui* we seek to discover? But on the other hand, shall we not be more likely to find ourselves again facing, in a new but always recognizable form, that old illusion which we were combating? It reappears continually, with a variety, a perseverance, and a kind of insinuating subtlety which makes it especially dangerous. Let us see whether the same illusion is not really underlying yet once again the idea of those little fundamental and distinct unities—the islands. Let us select for discussion the case which is the most typical and manifest; not that of the isles in the figurative sense which Brunhes lends to that word, but the real islands, the islands of the sea. Our argument must incur the risk of being monotonous or even tiresome; but it seems to us indispensable that it should be placed before the reader.

I

Insularity from the Biological Point of View

If any one idea is " necessary " more than another it would seem, a priori, to be that of societies in islands properly so called. Islands are the most clearly defined of those " separate but therefore all the simpler unities "[1] mentioned by the author of the *Géographie humaine*.

It is not, however, the theorists pure and simple, like Bodin and Montesquieu, who have remarked on their real or supposed human characteristics, and have put them in what we might call the first rank. Bodin contents himself, in Book V of *La République*, with telling us that, according to an old saying, islanders are people who must be distrusted: " Insulanos omnes infidos habere " is the duty of the wise man; for, he explains, whoever says " islander " says " foreign trader ", a man able to argue with his customer and cheat him, as crafty as Ulysses, the perfect prototype of the travelled islander. As for Montesquieu, he too is very brief on this subject. He limits himself, in a very short paragraph,[2] to reminding us that " island peoples are more jealous of their liberty than continental ones ". Islands are generally, in fact, of small

[1] Brunhes, **LXVI**, p. 71.
[2] Montesquieu, **XL**, Vol. XVIII, par. 5.

extent, so that "one part of the people cannot be so much employed in oppressing the other part" as on vast continents. Altogether, a dozen rather vague and inaccurate lines.

The idea of insularity had not then been elaborated; it was, undoubtedly, the naturalists who evolved it; the forerunners of our contemporary anthropogeographers learnt it from them and from the great travellers of the eighteenth century who endowed the scientific world, so to speak, with the whole Pacific universe and its hundreds of strange and varied islands. The heritage transmitted by them has been only too religiously fostered and preserved.

This biological idea of insularity will be found set out in Wallace's authoritative book *Island Life.*[1] The data on which it is based are very simple. Whatever the type of the islands, to whatever class they belong, they furnish the naturalist with "grandiose experiments",[2] whose results he has only to interpret.

The conditions of the environment, which are both peculiar and monotonous, act with regularity and power on the animal races, which are isolated from their ancestral stock and cut off from regular and frequent association with those of the lands or continents from which the sea separates them, and are thus protected from many dangerous rivals. Such variations as they are able to produce are perpetuated, which tends to the formation of a great number of peculiar species. When we say a great number, of course, we are speaking relatively; for another of the best established characteristics of islands is the small total number of plant or animal species which they harbour. Another, fairly frequent, is their archaism, since these bits of detached land act as so many natural preserves for forms which disappear on the continents. Still another is their dwarfing effect on the animals they shelter, which seem to wish to reduce themselves to the same scale as those miniature continents, the islands. Not only is this the case with wild animals, such as bears in Japan, deer in Corsica and Sardinia, and the now extinct dwarf hippopotamuses and elephants of the Mediterranean islands, but with domestic animals also—ponies in the Shetlands, Falklands, and Iceland, black or white sheep in the Faeroes, the Hebrides, Ushant, the Orkneys, and the Shetlands.

[1] Second ed., London, 1892. [2] Cuénot, **LII**, p. 174.

And the conclusion of the whole matter, it is argued, is that endemism, scanty population, persistent archaism, and nanism [1] are the direct or indirect result of the overpowering insular conditions and of isolation in the midst of the ocean. And the infinitely varied consequences of this isolation present themselves in a remarkable number of forms—for example, in the loss of the power of flight amongst a great number of island insects and birds,[2] which is attributed by the disciples of Lamarck to the direct action of the wind, the violence and frequency of which gradually induces the winged races to renounce the use of their wings, and by those of Darwin to selection, which has left only the bad fliers remaining, all the others having been carried away by the wind and drowned [3] owing to their imprudence.

*

* *

To argue from animals to man is easy and tempting. The means by which such a step can be readily made have already been explained in our *Introduction*, with regard to the followers of Hippolyte Taine. So far as the islands specially are concerned, it is not difficult—indeed it is only too easy—to slip from one to the other. Isolated fragments of the globe, separated from all other countries by the surrounding water, an effective protection, especially in archaic times—when Tyre and Arad, on their insular rock, could defy all enemies except perhaps thirst—ought they not to present, if only in the special character of their flora and fauna, monotonous conditions of existence and resources at once limited, changeless, and insufficiently varied for the human groups that shelter and develop there? Is it not "natural" that they should give rise to societies of a local type, very like one another and easily comparable, which, supporting themselves on similar poor and rather unfavourable foundations, continue indefinitely in the same form that their environment has determined and has marked with its strong imprint?

[1] The facts are set out and discussed in Cuénot, **LIII**, pp. 173, 181, 404, 479.

[2] We are purposely omitting to speak of the botanical characteristics of insular environments, the development of arborescent vegetation, etc. (cf. Costantin, **CIV**, in **XI**, 1898, pp. 195–6).

[3] Bohn, **XIX**, Vol. XVIII.

This idea was suggested quite naturally to the geographers by the explorers who revealed the biological characteristics of the flora and especially of the fauna of islands. Among the first was Cook,[1] who in the narrative of his travels revealed with marvellous skill the peculiar features of Madeira and the Azores.

The authority and renown of these pioneers aroused general interest, and the representatives of the different schools rivalled one another in numbers and eagerness. The economists demonstrated how insular shores were especially fitted for maritime life and commerce. The historians vied with one another in dissertations on the evolution of England and Japan. The jurists too and linguists criticized favourably the special forms which language and institutions assume in islands. In Miss Semple's book,[2] for instance, will be found curious details of, and numerous references to, the penal code of the Isle of Man—to the distinction drawn by that code between thefts of different kinds of animals, and the peculiar charm of a vocabulary borrowed almost entirely from the sea. A judge has to swear that he will be as impartial as " the backbone of a herring ", which always keeps in the middle of the fish at the same distance from each side. Here we have an interesting collection of allusions, trivial statements, and ingenious ideas—but the fundamental question still remains: from these facts and others like them, can we legitimately conclude that there really exists a type of insular societies of a quite distinct character, and similar to one another in their main features, whatever be the climate or the period? In other words, is there, or can there be, for the anthropo-geographer, and therefore for the historian, a class labelled " Islands " to be used under any circumstances? Let us examine the question closely, for it is worth the trouble.

II

Island Coasts: The Idea of Littoralism

There are three distinct notions in the general conception of an island which serve by turns to support those ambitious

[1] Cook, Vol. I, pp. 13–24; Vol. IV, pp. 198–209.
[2] Semple, Chap. II.

generalizations to which we object. The island is, first of all, a ring of coast, a circuit of shores, and therefore the perfect type of a littoral habitat. The island, in the second place, is a surface of the earth over which the influence of the sea has sovereign power; and lastly, the island is a realm doomed to isolation and all its consequences, precisely because of its maritime situation. These are three themes which are easily interwoven; it is but a step from one to another: here we keep them apart, but more often than not we really confuse them without noticing it.

The island is a circuit of shores. For the present we will not advance the preliminary objection to such a conception, but merely remark that it is imprudent, and without doubt not very scientific, to create a category so purely formal. The ignorant man who walks in an aisle with groined vaulting, and then in a nave with pointed vaulting, and sees no difference between them, and feels no desire to distinguish between them because, he says, the profile in both cases is the same—that ignorant man is perhaps within his rights; but his ignorance does not destroy the idea of the arch for those who have knowledge, and who claim to found a science of archæology. To ignore the contents of islands, so to speak, and only concern ourselves with the outlines of their exteriors, is not at any rate to follow the example of the biologists, for they make a distinction between one island and another, and this distinction is based precisely on the contents of the islands.[1] On the one hand there are the continental islands, fragments of ancient and long vanished continents which have thus "become" islands after having formed integral portions of continental land. On the other there are the oceanic islands, islands by nature and by destiny, if we may use the expression, islands which have always been islands, some of coral formation, like the Bermudas, others volcanic which have been raised from the bosom of the waves, like the Hawaiian group and the Mascarenes. But we will not discuss this for the moment; moreover, by considering islands as rings of coast, we bring them, as secondary categories, into the general category of "shores".

That there are littoral societies specifically distinct from

[1] Cuénot, **LII**, pp. 173 ff.

continental ones, economists, geographers, and statisticians even are prone to assert. Definitions such as the following are not uncommon: "The seashores give birth to special populations amongst which the dominant sentiments are respect for the family, a spirit of tradition mingled with love of novelty, and a desire for wandering similar to that of shepherds, but confined to the men." [1] Let us say (to save ourselves from the reproach of irony) that even these definitions are more precise and useful than those we have quoted. That, however, matters little. The essential thing is to know what is comprehended precisely in the idea of *littoralism*, a general idea which includes in part that of insularity, or which at least includes it in so far as islands are looked upon as essentially littoral formations.

The decisive proof that the shores are essential elements in the formation of human groups is to be found, we are told continually, in the maps showing density of population. In the majority of countries which possess shores, not only is the drift of population towards the shores and their accumulation on the littoral borders an evident fact, but moreover, in the greater number of cases, if we draw a straight line from the interior of one of these countries to its coast, we can easily see that this line passes through more and more populous districts as it nears the sea. Sometimes even, as is the case in many small islands—the lesser Antilles, for instance, or the islands scattered over the Atlantic and Indian Oceans (Reunion and Mauritius)—the people are almost entirely coast dwellers, and the interior remains, or at least has for a long time remained, almost unknown and nearly desert, even when its healthy conditions give it an undoubted advantage over the coast.[2]

Are these facts correct? Frequently, no doubt. For certain regions we can draw up charts of the distribution of population which are extremely suggestive, when the distribution is calculated in zones equally distant from the sea with the aid of those lines of equidistance, the theory of which we owe to Rohrbach,[3] and which have since rendered such service to geography. This is the case with Brittany,

[1] Gustave Le Bon, *Les premières civilisations*, Paris, 1889, p. 144.
[2] Reclus, **LXXXVII**[a], Vol. II, p. 645.
[3] Peterm. *Mit.*, **XIII**, Vol. XXXVI, 1890.

for example, which has been represented in such a map,[1] illustrating in a typical way the marked concentration of the population along the coasts. The curves of equidistance are drawn every five kilometres, but the first zone, 5 kilometres in width, has been divided into two parts: one which lies immediately on the coast is only two kilometres wide, the other three. Places of less than 3,000 inhabitants have alone been taken into account, those of more than 3,000 have all been reduced to that mean. We have the following results for the first four zones (the author has calculated eleven) in order from the coast inwards:—

Zone I.	1·24 miles wide, density 458 to sq. mile . .	487,019 inhabitants.
Zone II.	1·86 miles wide, density 272 to sq. mile . .	276,622 ,,
Zone III.	3·11 miles wide, density 207 to sq. mile . .	295,655 ,,
Zone IV.	3·11 miles wide, density 207 to sq. mile . .	242,138 ,,

The case of Brittany is no isolated one. In the older countries, where, however, modern industrial civilization seems to contend more actively than elsewhere against the elementary forces of nature, there is no lack of similar instances. In Lower Normandy, for example, which adjoins Brittany, there are, according to a geographer who has made a special study of the district,[2] within a belt 1,500 metres wide following the coast, 177 inhabitants to the square kilometre on the Northern coast of the Cotentin, 157 on that of Calvados, and more than 100 on the Western coast. To the North of the Seine, areas of considerable density stretch for the whole length of Caux in the cantons bordering the sea.[3]

We will admit these facts without discussion, and consider them as proved. Let us remark only that there is no question of a general rule. If there are undoubtedly littoral regions which are much more populous than the hinterland, and which appear especially to attract men, those which Camille

[1] Robert, *La densité de la population en Bretagne calculée par zones d'égal éloignement de la mer*, **XI**, Vol. XIII, 1904, p. 296 ff.

[2] R. de Felice, *La Basse-Normandie*, Paris, 1907, p. 516.

[3] Sion, **CCXXIX**, p. 432. Similar phenomena of concentration are noticed on the shores of the Lake of Geneva, Lake Maggiore, etc., by Brunhes, **LXVI**, pp. 187–8.

Vallaux, in his very interesting little book *la Mer*, calls concentration coasts, there are others exactly opposite in character, which he calls dispersion coasts (a word which we do not favour because it seems to evoke more or less exact images) and which are less populous than those to which they serve as a sea frontage. The contrast is a sufficient proof to him of what one would have expected a priori—that the simple fact of the existence of a coast is not sufficient to induce a great concentration of population. But if we omit these negative cases, these dispersion coasts, and consider the others only, do the figures which we have given above, and those which could easily be urged in support of them, imply a direct and immediate action of the coast on man, always exercised in the same way? In other words, what is it that makes a coast favourable for human settlement?

*

* *

There is no need to seek very far; it is not so long since Ritter formulated his famous theory of littoral articulation. We have already had occasion to speak of it, and to point out obvious criticisms and objections which it entails.[1] But it still keeps its place in the world, revived, rearranged, and skilfully rejuvenated or simply reproduced in its old form. The superiority of Europe and its foremost place among the continents, considered as so many natural unities, is explained by a "pedantic truth", a commonplace—the number of coastal inlets it possesses in comparison with the other "five parts of the world"; and similarly the long supremacy of Greece, or as Philippson puts it, of the Ægean, is explained by the bewildering and truly disconcerting wealth of that highly indented and broken country of violently contrasted geographical forms[2]: lofty Alpine masses, penetrated by gulfs with numerous inlets; small plains with luxuriant vegetation overtopped by desert limestone plateaux or by ridges covered with fir; a perpetual view of bold mountains enclosing seas of the deepest blue.

All this has been set forth many times with more or less ingenuity and ability, and has been as often refuted with

[1] See above, 1st part, Chap. II, p. 89.
[2] Philippson, *Tectonique de l'Égéide*, **XI**, 1898, p. 112.

a multitude of examples[1]: for amongst the rias and the fiords, the most typical forms of a broken coast, it is not true that the deepest inlets are the most populous; it is not true, as has been remarked, that the maritime development of Germany, with its almost unbroken coast, and of Russia, and even of France, all of which on the whole are only moderately rich in indentations, can be explained by the creeks of Greece or the fiords of that Norway which up to a recent epoch had almost wholly lost the seafaring tastes which it must have had at one time, with its Vikings and its wonderfully broken coast-line. It is not true, in short, that every indented coast-line favours population, and that every unbroken coast drives it away.

In the very midst of civilized Europe there is an island with high, salubrious, and indented coasts, passably rich both in the fruits of the soil and of the sea—Corsica; throughout history it has been in touch with the oldest and at the same time the most modern civilizations in the centre of the western basin of the Mediterranean, quite close to the Provençal shore of France and at the gate of Italy, which stretches out towards it mid-way, an intermediary land, but never has any seafaring population or community of sailors or navigators been known there. Its few ports have been founded by strangers; Bonifacio by the Tuscans, Ajaccio by the Genoese. At the present time the whole of Corsica only musters 1,100 fishermen, who man 300 fishing boats, a smaller number than any one little Breton port usually furnishes.[2] The Corsican remains a mountaineer, shepherd, and husbandman; he turns his back on the sea with the same indifference as those Albanians who have lived since the most ancient times on the Epiro-Albanian littoral, but have never profited in any way by its resources[3]; they are neither sailors nor fishermen. They have no communications by sea along their coasts nor with the lands on the other side of the Adriatic, from which only a short distance separates them. "A striking contrast to the Greeks," we are told: doubtless—but to what Greeks? Those of Laconia, for instance, never had the reputation of being great seamen.

[1] Cf. especially M. Dubois, *Du rôle des articulations littorales*, **XI**, 1892, p. 131 ff.; Vallaux, **XCIII**, pp. 26–7.
[2] Brunhes, **CCXXI**, pp. 471–2.
[3] Cuijic, **CCXXIII**, p. 158.

Does anyone wish for a converse proof? There is a low unbroken coast, bordered by dunes, on which nothing grows but a thin, scanty grass; its soil is so sterile that the most skilful, sober, and industrious of peasants could not make a living by cultivating it: it is the Flemish coast, from Calais to the mouths of the Scheldt, as Raoul Blanchard describes it to us.[1] In its 80 miles there are 7 ports, one to every 12 miles: Calais, Gravelines, Dunkirk, Nieuport, Ostend, Blankenberg, and Zeebrugge, seven successive breaches opened in the most forbidding and unfavourable littoral barrier possible. Can it be said that it is the poverty of the coastal region and its lack of agricultural wealth which force the inhabitants to a maritime life? The rule will not hold, as the coast of Holland, near by, abundantly proves. In the 75 miles from the Hook of Holland to the Helder there is a single and absolutely artificial port: Ijmuiden. The coast of Gascony is 130 miles long, and has only one opening good enough for fishing boats. Can anyone say that the natural conditions are more favourable in the one place than the other? Is the relative disadvantage of the Dutch coast as compared with the Flemish due to its orientation? Does anyone believe that because the latter faces almost exactly south-west, and so stretches in a direction parallel to that of the prevailing winds, which renders it less liable than the former to the formation and increase of a line of dunes of prohibitive width—does anyone believe that all this mass of considerations, however ingenious they may be, is sufficient to explain the contrast we have just stated?

No: however rich a coast may be in inlets, that is not enough to attract men to settle there, and to keep them in plenty and prosperity, if there are no other advantages than a favourable aspect and a perfect articulation of its shores. The excellence of its form has here no absolute determinant value. Shape is not itself creative. There are stretches of coast of admirable structure and admirably equipped by nature to play a great maritime rôle, which in fact they do not play. There are some unpropitious ones, which have, so to speak, everything against them, yet serve as homes for very enduring maritime communities. But may not their productive value enable them to play the rôle for which their form cannot suffice?

[1] Blanchard, **CCXVII**, p. 234.

III.

The Productive Coast

Coasts possess more than one kind of utility; they have their food-producing as well as their commercial value. If they attract men who, in one way or another, devote themselves to the "harvest of the sea", as the Italians say, they invite also those who, taking them for their supporting base, launch themselves across the open sea to more or less distant lands, as fishers or seamen. The Greeks were to a very small extent fishermen, and almost exclusively seamen. The same may be said of the Phœnicians whose vessels preceded them over the routes of the inland sea, as the prototypes of the present-day "tramp". On the other hand, to take a modern example from near at hand, the Bretons are first of all fishermen, and as little as may be navigators. However, for the moment let us consider only the first group of "food production" facts. Are they of such a nature as to justify the idea, which we are now studying critically—the essential and distinctive littoralism of certain human societies?

First of all, it would doubtless be surprising if we should find any close similarity among the societies which profit from the sea and spring up as a result of the wealth of the littoral waters, since the submarine littoral boundary or submerged cliff, which surrounds the dry land to a depth of about 1,200 to 1,300 feet, where the influence of sunlight ceases, varies enormously from one country to another.

Whether we consider the subterrestrial zone, where the terrestrial and marine fauna come into contact, or the littoral zone properly so called,[1] which is uncovered more or less by the tides and according to their height, or again the deep coastal zone which succeeds it, the catalogue of species is singularly varied according as the characteristic appearance is rocky, sandy, or muddy, the force of the waves strong or feeble, the tides of great or small extent, and the plankton as a result rich or poor, the waters clear or clouded, and the heat considerable or otherwise. How, with such a variety of changing

[1] On these differences cf. Joubin, *La vie dans les Océans*, Paris, 1912, p. 162, and Cuénot, **LII**, p. 92 ff.

conditions, could we expect to find communities which are dependent on the sea rigorously modelled on one type ?

Again, a coast is the line which limits the sea where it invades the land, but it is, inversely, the frontier-line of the land where it sinks below the sea. There are two aspects : beyond the coast, according as we take our viewpoint from the one or the other, lies land or sea.

It is evident that a coast which, so to speak, happens to be only the littoral edge of a waterless desert itself will be doomed to a desert state, except in rare cases, only to be explained by a quite remarkable abundance of food supplies in the sea. So with the maritime border of an over-dense forest which is unsuitable for man or unfavourable in some way as a home for him. Sometimes then even the richness and abnormal abundance in the waters does not prevail over the obstacles which the sterility of a hostile soil opposes to man. Coasts of this kind, however, are relatively rare. In the case of the others, which maintain dense human populations, the question at once arises : what is it that attracts men to these maritime borders ? Is it the sea or the land that supports them ?

*

* *

Let us glance at a map showing population density in France. Is the concentration in the thickly populated plain of Bas-Languedoc a coastal one ? The dense human population itself recognizes but one cause, and that " the prosperity of the vineyards ".[1] There is no gradual difference in density from the shore to the interior, analogous to that which Robert's chart of population density in Brittany would seem to establish. There are no homogeneous and regular zones becoming less dense as you go inland : " What difference there is," says a good judge, " is mostly due to agriculture." [2] But the influence of the sea can no doubt be traced. The coasts, or to be more exact, the northern coast of the Etang de Thau, which otherwise enjoys conditions exactly similar to those of the rest of the neighbouring plain of Languedoc, has an unusual density of 430 inhabitants to the square mile, which bears witness to maritime influences reinforcing those

[1] M. Sorre, *La Plaine du Bas-Languedoc*, **XI**, Vol. XVI, 1907, p. 418.
[2] Ibid., p. 420.

due to terrestrial habitat. Now an interesting study by Sabde gives us precise information about the fishing industry along the coasts of Languedoc between Agde and Aigues-Mortes, and the essential feature which it emphasizes is the great variety of groups of men engaged in fishing, especially round about Cette. Of "fishers pure and simple", fishers of the high seas, who live a separate life from the other inhabitants of the country, there is only a small group consisting of a few foreigners; they are all Italian immigrants, Calabrians, Neapolitans, or Genoese, who have established themselves on the strip of seashore.[1] But the inhabitants of the second coast, that of the lagoon, the little inland sea of Thau, with its calm and deep waters, its very varied edible fauna, its two hundred species of fish, its shrimps, prawns, lobsters, etc.—their manner of life differs in no way from that of the husbandmen, the vine-growers of the district. The contrast is not between them and the agriculturists, but between them and the fishermen of the high seas. All of them combine other means of livelihood with their fishing business, cultivating small parcels of ground, whenever this is possible, or, in cases of great poverty, hiring themselves out as porters in the town, as grape-gatherers in the country, as collectors of sea-weed, etc.

There is nothing unusual, moreover, in this type of life. A long time ago Camille Vallaux used very similar language concerning a very different country—Brittany. He denounces in a general way the popular idea which, from the presence of granite, or schist, or sandstone, and from an unfertile land with richly developed coasts, indented by deep inlets, flanked by elongated islands and having an outlook over two frequented and productive seas, would deduce the necessary existence of a numerous race of seamen. On the contrary, he points out that we must not, with imaginative eyes, see a seaman in every Bas-Breton. They are more correctly countrymen who have pushed out to their coasts little maritime advance-guards, little colonies of fishermen quite small in number compared with the total population of Armorica, and "representing only a subordinate element of the social life and economic strength of the district".[2] Bretons who

[1] Sabde, **XI**, Vols. XXIII–IV, p. 31 ff.
[2] Vallaux, **CCXXXI**, pp. 219–20.

live by the sea alone are rare. Nearly all of them are really peasants as well as seamen. The sole exceptions are the men of Paimpol, who go to the deep-sea fishing grounds of Newfoundland or Iceland, the fishers of the high seas, and the tunny fishers of the Ile de Groix : the others are all so many fisher-peasants or so many peasant fishermen,[1] each possessing his plot of ground, as a matter of necessity, which his wife cultivates whilst her husband is away fishing. And when the land is so lean and unproductive that the seaman is unable to be landsman as well, as for example, in the little island of Molène, where 600 inhabitants devote themselves entirely to lobster fishery and to dredging for wrack, when any unforeseen mishap occurs there is a famine pure and simple and it becomes necessary to send food to the starving population by special boats.[2]

This is an instance drawn from civilized people, but does anyone believe that the same thing is not true of primitive populations ? How many preconceived ideas there are about the inhabitants of the Pacific domain, the Polynesians, and the Melanesians, "sons of the Ocean" as they used to be called—the alleged original inhabitants who, as we now know, are only emigrants, sometimes from immense distances—whose whole life is still commonly supposed to be determined by its oceanic environment. There is, indeed, plenty of work in those regions for fishermen and sailors ; but for agriculturists also, or, at any rate, for very skilful cultivators of natural botanical resources of the very first order. The Polynesians are no doubt wonderful fishermen and sailors, but can the presence on their coral islets of the *Coco nucifera*, the most useful perhaps of all the palm-trees, the oceanic tree pre-eminently, be regarded as a maritime fact ? From the milky fluid of its unripe nuts they make an excellent drink ; from the ripe fruit they extract a valuable oil ; from the fibre which surrounds it, steeped, and beaten, they make thread ; its terminal shoot is an excellent food, the famous palm-cabbage of the old explorers ; from the ends of the cut flowers drops a liquid which supplies palm wine, and thence vinegar ; the wood of the trunk serves to build their houses, and to make their furniture, utensils, and boats. But these numerous and remarkable benefits from one tree, which is

[1] Ibid., p. 231 ff. [2] p. 233.

not the only one in these countries to render extraordinary services to men (we might speak of the bread fruit-tree *Artocarpus incisus*, and of the root of the taro *Colocasia succulenta*, and of the sago-palm and of many other useful plants of the Pacific region), do not prevent either the Polynesians or still more the Melanesians, who are poorer in natural plant resources, from devoting themselves to agriculture and attaining real skill at it. It would be a very great mistake to look on them simply as fishermen of a type, as clear-cut of its kind as that of certain shepherd nomads in theirs.

*

* *

The influence of the sea does not really extend nearly so far into the land as the influence of continental life over the coasts, even when it is most powerful and most desirable also. In Brittany, for instance, on the shores of the Morbihan, where the manure obtained from the sea contains just those ingredients of phosphate and lime lacking in the soil produced by the decomposition of the crystalline rocks, the Breton farmers only utilize it within a belt of 10 to 12 miles at most.[1] And summer after summer, the Norman farmer, careless of the sea, which he does not even look at, reaps his wheat up to the edge of the cliffs and knows nothing of the world that lies beyond.

Lastly, we must be clear as to another point. There is much loose talk about the powerful attraction of the sea, and the wealth of the population near the coasts, which is urged in explanation of movement, or exodus, or migration towards the coasts. But, in discussing the traditional theme of a "Ceinture Dorée" in Brittany[2] (in connexion with the article by Robert, which we have already quoted and utilized), Vallaux observes very justly that it is not emigration which increases the littoral population. The Bretons emigrate, but scarcely ever from the "Ar-Coach" into the "Ar-mor", from the interior to the coast. The excess of population must be attributed to the higher birth-rate. But who would say,

[1] A. Choveaux, **XI**, 1920, p. 417.

[2] Vallaux, *A propos de la Ceinture Dorée*, **XI**, 1905, p. 457 ; cf. ibid., Robert, *La Ceinture Dorée existe-t-elle ?*

without hesitation, that this is accounted for by geographical conditions only ? [1]

Man is not made up wholly of appetites and instincts. The need for food, primary though it be, does not explain everything—far from it. Fish, or shell-fish, alone do not account for the greater littoral population any more than do the irregularities and indentations of the coasts. Man is affected as much by his ideas as his wants. He eats as he likes, and what he likes. He may consume the *frutti di mare* with pleasure or, on the other hand, with the emotions of those contemporaries of Bodin, whom the author of *La République* reproves in his *Réponse au paradox du Sr. de Malestroict sur le faict des monnoies*, when he deplores the dislike of the French to eating fish which is " so great, that many of them would rather eat tallow at Easter than a sturgeon ", and says that " the fish eat one another for want of being eaten ".

Moreover, there is something both annoying and puerile in the unwillingness to attribute this concentration of men on the coasts to any but material reasons. We will give two cases in point. This is how a geographer comments on a map of the distribution of races in Dahomey.[2] " In a general way," he remarks, " the number of groups increases as we go from the interior towards the coast. Is this due to the attraction of the sea ? No, but the conquered populations are crowded back from the centre towards the circumference by the victors, who themselves spread towards the coast by a sort of inversion of the supposed law according to which the older populations were pushed into the interior."

And again, we have an historian who studies the littoral society of ancient Gaul, and particularly the shores of Morbihan, into which the sea penetrates deeply with rapid currents, and which it cuts up everywhere into capes, gulfs, and estuaries, " as if it wished to seize it with a thousand arms, and snatch from it everywhere victims and offerings." [3] He, too, notices a considerable concentration, and the presence of great " gatherings of races " along the shores. " The

[1] Or food-conditions: with regard to the shores of Thau, Sabde notes (op. cit., p. 38) that the fishers there have only small families, three children on the average, and differ in no way from most French families of to-day.

[2] Hubert, **CLXXXII,** fig. 85.

[3] Cam. Jullian, **CLXXII,** Vol. I, p. 157.

old inhabitants, I think, remained numerous and thriving in Armorica; the name of one of their tribes, the Osismii of Finisterre, goes back to times long before the conquest."[1] And above all, he points out in that land the enormous number of dolmens, menhirs, and alignments, a singular multiplication of sanctuaries and religions. "It is the imperious neighbourhood of the Ocean," he hazards,[2] "which has attracted towards the capes and the isles this world of ghosts, this aristocracy of the dead which crowns them with its tombs. The ancient peoples of Europe—Celts, Germans, and others—nearly all believed that the immortal dead departed beyond the Ocean which terminates the Earth to other shores in the distant Isles of the Blest. So, to save the spirits of the dead from too long a journey on earth, who knows whether the men contemporary with the dolmens did not inter those near and dear to them on the very shores of that sea which they had to cross?" And it is a fact that, all along the shores of the Mediterranean, there are numbers of well-known tombs attributed to mythical personages.[3] There is a culinary geography of the sea, no doubt, but there is, none the less, a religious geography also.

IV

Island Navigation and Island Isolation

We made a distinction just now between the food-producing function of coasts and their maritime function. We noticed that the seashores attract all those who can use them as supporting bases from which to launch across the open seas and live the adventurous life of the mariner. But, as we said before, an island is commonly regarded as the very type of an isolated domain on the seas. How are we to explain the contradiction? We may say at once that there is nothing to explain; all we have to do is to attack the contradiction, and to try, as a beginning, to explain how the idea of insular isolation arose.

There are, manifestly, islands which are lost in the ocean spaces, far from the great routes and the currents of maritime

[1] Ibid., Vol. II, pp. 487–8.
[2] Ibid., Vol. I, p. 158.
[3] References Strabo, Plutarch, Virgil, etc., in Jullian, **CLXXII**, Vol. I, p. 158, n. 3.

circulation. These may be said, accurately enough, to condemn their inhabitants to almost total isolation and, therefore, to a relatively self-developed and original culture, with at times the formation of a very peculiar physical type.[1] Such is the case in the small islands which we find scattered over all the Oceans, the Pacific, the Indian, and the Atlantic, tiny scraps of land as completely lost as Tristan da Cunha or Trinidad; the Andamans in the middle of the Bay of Bengal, with their Negroes and even their Negritos, the Minkopi, who are kin to those of Malacca; the Marshalls, Gilberts, and Carolines in the more unfrequented parts of the Pacific. But there is no need to go so far away. In the open Mediterranean an islet like Scarpanto, the ancient Karpathos, between Crete and Rhodes, gives the impression of most absolute isolation to the few travellers who chance to land there.[2] These tiny fragments of the continent are, in the words of Élisée Reclus, "prisons or places of exile for the people who inhabit them."

But there are, on the other hand, islands situated on the great routes of the globe, at the meeting-points of the chief lines of communication, and at the ocean cross-roads. How shall we compare them with the first sort—Sicily and Crete in the Mediterranean of old, Malta of to-day, the Sunda and Hawaian islands, Porto-Rico, and Cuba? Evidently the formulæ must be changed. Everything about them reflects and bears witness to continuous, safe, and active communication with the outside world. How many dominations and varied civilizations have certain among them, following and replacing one another on their soil!

Take Sicily, by turns Phœnician (to go no further back), then Greek, then Carthaginian, then Roman, then Vandal, Gothic, and Byzantine, then Arab, Norman, Angevin, Aragonese, Imperial, Savoyard, Austrian . . . the complete list would be interminable. Doubtless a total change of civilization has not followed each of these political revolutions, nor the establishment of a new system of cultivation or material life: this need hardly be said. But each of these successive waves, which have submerged, for a greater or less length

[1] De Martonne, **XI**, 1906, p. 320.

[2] Cf. the facts collected in *Karpathos, étude géologique, paléontologique et botanique*, by Stephani (C. de), Forsyth, and Barbey, Lausanne, 1895.

of time, the ancient Sicilian soil, has left something on the shore when it receded. So many dominations mean so many different experiments at least; but were these societies insular? Who would compare one of these islands at the cross-roads with one of those prison-isles, which seem so many asylums of bygone races, customs, and social forms which have been banished from the continents? Who, to go no further away, would compare Sicily, so coveted, disputed, and repeatedly colonized, with her neighbours Corsica and Sardinia?

*

*   *

Many other distinctions force themselves upon us. We will consider only the more important. How many islands situated at the extremities of the great continents, and how many peninsulas also, serve as refuges? The last waves of human migrations come there to die, so to speak. In them the conquered seek refuge after conflicts of race, politics, or religion; we have only to remember Formosa with its savages, the Kuriles with their Aïno, Ceylon with its Buddhists, the Philippines with their Aetas, the Canaries in old times with their Guachos of Berber origin, and, nearer home, we may mention Ireland.

But on the other hand, how many islands also situated near great continents have, by just the reverse process, played a rôle of initiation or expansion and spread their rule or their civilization over the neighbouring lands? We will mention Japan only, as an example. Here, too, there is diversity, a thoroughgoing diversity, in the place of the rigid sameness of common conditions. Islanders sometimes are oriented to the continent. The possession of a coastal archipelago very often affords a supporting base for descents on neighbouring lands, or at least for piracy, as in the case of the corsairs in the Ægean Sea, as described by Victor Bérard from the *Odyssey*, or the pirates of the American Mediterranean, the filibusters of Tortue, described by H. Lorin.[1]

That an island makes an excellent strategic base needs no demonstration. This was discovered in very early times[2]

[1] Capitan and Lorin, **CCII**, p. 327 ff.

[2] Reclus, "La Phénicie et les Phéniciens" (*Bull. Soc. Neuchatel. Géogr.*), XII, 1900, pp. 261–74.

by the Phœnicians of Arad with their lofty and crowded houses, or of Tyre, the invulnerable. We recall, moreover, the characteristic features of the island of Calypso, that ideal home of the old navigators : its springs with their fresh water : its sea-cave for the shelter of men, bales of merchandise, tackle, or sometimes of a slim barque that was hidden there for the night : a safe refuge where a fire could burn under cover without betraying those who lighted it ; the best hiding place possible from which to spring out unexpectedly on the women or on the flocks who came to drink at the spring ; it is the very type of a "look-out", a post of observation convenient for sally or defence, the dream of pirates and wreckers in all ages.[1] As for the peninsula that is almost island, whose approaches are uncovered by the low tide, and whose flanks are washed by the high tide, preventing both a prolonged assault by soldiers or a close blockade by ships, its military value, and its utility for observation and at times for offence, are not inferior to those of the island.[2]

These were ideal bases for islanders with designs on the continent. The peoples of Tyre and Arad surveyed from their chosen abodes all the opposite coasts. The seafaring tribes, settled on the promontories and in the islands of Finisterre, were more interested in the shores of England and Ireland than in the forests of the interior.[3] Élisée Reclus has well described the kind of attraction which is exerted on the inhabitants of the continental coasts by those lands, whose hazy outlines are seen rising from the waters on fine days.[4]

The isles of the Ægean called to the mariners of Asia Minor ; but only that they might thence pass over to the mainland of continental Greece ; and Cyprus also was looked on by the Phœnicians as a port of call before they ventured on the unknown seas. Quite lately, in his big critical work on the Great Enterprise of 1492 and again in his small book on the true and the legendary Christopher Columbus,[5] Henri Vignaud has illustrated that quite special attraction which was exercised on sailors by the known, suspected, or unknown

[1] Bérard, *Mégare*, **XI**, 1898, p. 363 ff.
[2] Jullian, **CLXXII**, Vol. II, p. 491.
[3] Jullian, ibid., Vol. II, pp. 487–8.
[4] Reclus, **LXXXVII**[a], Vol. II, p. 646.
[5] Paris, 1921, pp. 56, 98, 121.

islands of the Atlantic, those uncertain milestones on the new ocean highway.

*

* *

There are actions and reactions, and here again if we looked for a necessity, a "law of the islands" imposed on men and on human societies, we should find but variety and diversity—evolution, also, and the changes wrought by time.

Long ago, in his celebrated work, Ritter remarked on the changes which the course of history would have undergone if Europe had been deprived of the islands of the Ægean Sea, Sicily, and Great Britain and of the protective part they played as refuges and citadels where the Aryan nations, entrenching themselves, could safely guard their intellectual and moral gains.[1] But we know that these lands played other parts also, not less brilliantly. The islands of the lagoons and the sand-spits of the "lidi" were at first refuges, and nothing but refuges, for the inhabitants of the Roman towns on the mainland from invasions which came from the Friuli side. But it was not long before they became bases for an unequalled colonial and maritime development. Yet we can assert that with regard to any advantages which the site of the city offered the Venetians for such an achievement, there was no geographical inevitability of any kind in their advance along the whole of the Eastern Mediterranean coasts. There are many marshland communities which, like that of the Poitevin Marais described by Clouzot, have never left their original site and have remained sedentary, seeking only to utilize the resources of their own district.

"The sea has evidently its good and its bad districts," its unfrequented and its attractive waters; and the fortunate regions which nature has specially dowered are, as we well know, the small enclosed waters which can be navigated between hospitable coasts and protective islands—such as the shores of Tyre or Cadiz, Carthage or the Piræus, in olden times—those sheets of water, at once open and secluded, from which men derive that security and boldness which give

[1] Cf. Reclus, **LXXXVII**[a], Vol. II, p. 647.

rise to naval supremacy.[1] One necessary condition for this, however, is that the people should have the maritime spirit. They must have a personal knowledge of that difficult art of navigation which, as Ratzel has well shown,[2] was originally confined to a very small number of peoples, and was only slowly imparted to others; slowly and irregularly, and under no strict necessity. In France the Breton coast is doubtless the one most likely to incite its inhabitants to a seafaring life. But "they have no taste for romantic adventure. The round in which they move is as small as that of the peasant of the 'Ar-Coat' and smaller than that of the mountain peasant. The sailor does not willingly lose sight of his village with its narrow streets. . . . Attached as closely to his coast and to his little port as the peasant to his plot of ground, he emigrates but little or not at all—and it is he, in truth, and not the peasant, who is immovable on the Armorican rock".[3] To how many seafaring people would Camille Vallaux's description of the Bas-Breton be applicable? The contrast is striking: it is not the sailor with his domestic instinct who emigrates, it is the peasant, and that not by sea, "since the sea of Lower Brittany leads nowhere and no great shipping line calls at its ports."[4]

It is the vice and weakness of summary generalizations that they are specious and hollow, and that they impoverish living reality. Let us reconsider that miserable islet, that tiny scrap of the earth in the Ægean, Karpathos, the modern Scarpanto. Nowhere is there a more isolated spot; mariners there are rude and coarse, the customs are remarkably archaic—in particular, an unusual modification of matriarchy, the transmission of the heritage in the female line to the eldest girls in preference to all other heirs.[5] Almost all the male population emigrates every spring,[6] as the soil is insufficient for their sustenance. The men go away as carpenters and joiners, for the island used to be wooded, and the pitch industry was predominant; as labourers also, and as masons and stone-cutters. They are to be encountered everywhere in the

[1] Jullian, **CLXXII**, Vol. I, p. 28.
[2] Ratzel, *Das Meer als Quelle der Völkergrösse*, Munich, 1890.
[3] Vallaux, **CCXXXI**, p. 222.
[4] Ibid., pp. 275–6.
[5] *Karpathos*, pp. 18–19.
[6] Ibid., pp. 9, 35.

neighbouring islands, and on the mainland of Asia Minor as far as Egypt. Here we have isolation and emigration, travel and archaisms. Nor need such associations astonish us; if they do so, we are like so many of the Ratzelians, or Neo-Ratzelians, who misinterpret the great, constant, and universal law: man may travel, but if he returns to his place in a community whose traditions are preserved by women and old men it is not he who modifies that community, but the community which recaptures him entirely, reabsorbs him anew every time and for long renders illusory experiences acquired elsewhere.

It is difficult to estimate the part of psychology. And, indeed, when we see how rashly some writers are always sketching a type of islander for whom the free wind is as a perpetual call from the distant unknown, and who from constant contemplation of the sea enlarges his horizon to embrace the ocean, whilst others (or sometimes the same) with the same boldness, embroider ingenious variations on the theme of isolation, on the egoism of the Venetians pre-occupied solely with their Venice, on the narrow views of the Englishman interested only in his England, it is not geography, but psychology, to which we are paying homage. For what finally matters is the idea adopted by the people—the political group—with regard to their geographical position, of its characteristics and advantages or inconveniences, though this idea may be quite wrong or have no basis in reality. Whatever be the range of modern guns or the power and scope of action of aeroplanes, "England remains an island" and the Channel tunnel a project only: and this is ultimately what matters and counts.

V

The Islands of the Desert: The Oases

Perhaps we should now continue our analysis and consider the "islands of the land"—the oases. Isolated, cut off from other habitable places by the perilous solitudes of the desert, they no doubt merit the name. Gautier tells us that every oasis in the Sahara is a kind of prison. Those who live in them are prisoners: how, with their inexperience of the routes and wells, their want of transport animals, and their well-founded fear of wayside brigands, are they to get away? They are bound to their palm-trees as securely as if they were chained.

Observers agree that Gautier's remarks apply also to other desert lands, as, for instance, those of Turkestan. Pumpelly, whilst excavating there, carefully studied the oasis of Anou, a little ruined town near Askabad. His vivid and clear narrative confirms that author's general conclusions: however, we may disagree with some of them; they speak of a closed world which for a long time has received only faint echoes from the outside and presents the rare spectacle of a kind of strictly autonomous development of social life.[1]

Be this as it may, it is none the less true that the old empires, in which the first civilizations were born, were after all only immense oases in the Libyan and Syrian deserts. Every oasis in the Sahara is a sort of prison, says Gautier, but the same author rebuts vigorously the illusion that the desert is a place of perpetual torture of some kind. Around the oases, especially those of the Sahara, there stretches the most favourable soil for the encouragement of mutual human relations. For here are roads, immense, straight corridors of sand, the *feidjs* or *gassis*, which the caravans follow; all around these natural roads of the desert is the soil of a garden alley, the *reg*, raked over by the winds during long ages. There is no surface better suited to the camel, that creature of the plains, with his large, spongy feet which look as if they were shod in slippers or sandals, and are so well adapted to the soft, dry surface of the *reg*, which they do not cut up as sharp horseshoes, for instance, would do; and there is no land, moreover, better suited naturally for wheeled traffic. With us Westerners there is no vehicular transport except on roads artificially levelled. In the desert, or at least on the *reg*, the road is everywhere. "I feel sure," writes Gautier, "that the *reg* bore the first roads." Here, then, we have the oasis, that "end of the world", that prison, that closed world entirely wrapped up in itself, becoming the centre of a wide network of routes, since for vast distances there are no obstacles

[1] **XVI**, 1910, p. 525.

that might fix the tracks in one groove. At the same time the oasis is an objective for the warrior nomad who contemplates its conquest and subjection, whilst the dweller in the oasis, relying on his sure base of fields, wells, and trees, lies in wait for the passing nomad and sometimes retaliates for the raids by seizing his cattle.[1]

This conflict constitutes the whole political history of the oasis regions. And by means of this, however shut off they may be, however remote from the great human thoroughfares and the great currents of commerce and trade—which as a rule avoid deserts and prefer the continuous track of the steppes to the dotted one of the arid regions—the dweller in the oasis and his enemy, the nomad, find themselves linked with the rest of the universe, and concerned, in spite of themselves and much more than they think, in the affairs of the world of which they may know nothing. It is a much more important bond than the economic relations they may establish with neighbouring countries, in spite of everything, by means of transport animals, such as the legendary oxen of the Garamantes in the Sahara, those ancient relatives of the Boer oxen of the Transvaal, or those humped cattle of the Sudan which to-day still visit the Hoggar [2]; the horses which were used for transport long before they were saddled; the asses, even those donkeys of Sali in the Southern Touat which an enchanting vision of the good old times still enables the modern inhabitants of the Southern Touat to see just as they used to be when they moved, loaded with dates, all along the wady Messaoud, which merits its name of "the Blessed", from their oasis to Taoudéni [3]; and lastly the camels, those late-comers to the Sahara, slow, heavy, delicate in health, and yielding comparatively little return.

But side by side with these economic relations there are the political relations or, to speak more exactly, the many and often unforeseen reverberations of distant movements which spread in enlarging circles as far as the oases: direct contacts and indirect reverberations.

In his little book on Russian Turkestan [4] Woeikof explains

[1] Woeikof, **CXCVIII**[a], p. 114.
[2] Gautier, **CLXXXI**[b], Vol. I, pp. 136–7.
[3] Gautier, **CLXXXI**[b], pp. 36–7.
[4] Woeikof, **CXCVIII**[a], p. 113.

clearly that the great incursions of Asiatic nomads into Central and Southern Europe are not really to be attributed to drought, but to the overcrowding of men and cattle in their own locality. Drought is a constant factor and never ceases to play its part in Central Asia. If we may believe some writers, its effect is increasing, as the gradual drying up of Asia has been usually considered an established and undisputed fact.[1] However, the great overflow of Central Asiatics into Western Asia, and into Eastern Europe, always towards the West, has ceased. China has captured the Mongolian territory, Siberia has been slowly peopled. The Russians have advanced, step by step, colonizing and constructing railroads. An outlet, too, has been found for the cattle reared by the shepherds, first towards China and later towards Siberia, which was wanting in the times of Attila and Genghis Khan. The conversion of the Mongols to Buddhism, moreover, had this consequence, that a third or at least a quarter of the men were turned into monks—into Lamas constrained to celibacy; here, religion played once more her part in the limitation of births, and took the place in the arid lands of Central Asia of those physiological precautions known in the wastes of the Sahara to the Tuaregs[2]; and the observation of Woeikof corresponds in a curious way, considering the differences in time and place, with a remark of Cournot on the place of celibates under the *ancien régime*, and the useful counteraction provided by their continence to the over-fecundity of the married.[3] Thus, the great movements, the destiny, the most surprising political fortunes in the lives of these completely isolated populations of Central Asia, these inhabitants of the lofty plateaux which even to-day the railroad dare not enter—which it encircles, and will encircle still more very soon, when a continuous line to the south, stretching from Persia to the Bay of Bengal, rivals the northern line, the Trans-Siberian, of which the Trans-Caspian is only a branch—originate in general historical facts which are even more surprising. And this is more evident still in the case of the Sahara.

[1] On this great problem cf. the recent summing up by F. Herbette, **XI**, Vols. XXIII–IV, 1914–15, pp. 1–30.
[2] Gautier, **CLXXXI**, p. 177.
[3] Cournot, *Souvenirs*, p. 29; cf. also ibid., pp. 7, 20.

In one chapter of his notes on his mission to the Algerian Sahara,[1] supported with illustrations as is his way, and since then in his delightful and comprehensive little book on the conquest of the Sahara, Gautier has shown admirably the unexpected repercussions of the taking of Granada by the Catholic Kings in 1492 on the world of the oases. It was followed by an explosion of religious fanaticism, by conquests and massacres, by the pitiless destruction of the old Berber civilizations, and by the triumph of Islam, which though introduced into the country in the eighth century, did not become dominant until the sixteenth: a complete transformation in manners, ideas, and life, both economic and social; all this connected with an incident in European history which was doubtless never heard of in the Touat and the Gourara. "We have here, evidently, a whole collection of events which our European historical education has never taught us to associate with the last tears of Boabdil, but which are not less real than they." Furthermore, we have here, also, another corrective to the preconceived idea of desert "isolation".

One other feature deserves remark. We talk of oases as typical unities given ready-made by nature to men, on which they have only to stretch themselves as on providential beds. In the Sahara, at least, the word does not imply political unity. Each oasis has its name, its geographical individuality, and its frontiers plainly marked by its isolation as a green spot in the midst of a desert of sand. But it is in no way a body politic. In the same oasis there are often many villages which have no political bond: they do not constitute a State. The Touat, for instance, contains twelve oases, twelve distinct palm groves, each one forming a more or less complete and more or less concentrated whole: the number of villages in each varies; there are twenty-six in Timmi, but only two in Sbaa. In population these villages vary from 25 to 500; but each one has its *djemaa*, or assembly, of the notables of the Ksar, who govern it in a very rudimentary fashion, true; their authority never holds beyond the boundaries of the Ksar; and when the villages have any dispute there is no remedy but force to settle the difference.[2]

[1] E. Gautier, **CLXXXI**ᵇ, Vol. I, pp. 261–5.
[2] Ibid., pp. 267–8.

But how does this fit in with the insular unity of the oasis?

*

* *

But is there such a thing as insular unity? Whether surrounded by sand or by water, the island—that typical region, limited and easy to imagine and comprehend—even when small and homogeneous, does not necessarily constitute a political unity. There are islands which are politically divided and remain so for extremely long periods, and whose "form" does not suffice to create unity. Just think of the chequer-work of Great Britain in ancient times. Cornish, Welsh, Anglo-Saxon, and Scottish: then pass on to Ireland; then further away to Madagascar under other skies and quite different conditions of civilization; then, a few degrees nearer the equator, think of the collection of peoples, manners, customs, and dwellings all different from one another which are found in the great forest island of New Guinea; we give to all these tribes the name of Papuans, but they themselves are ignorant of any common name or any national life. They wage sanguinary wars among themselves. Some in the north of the Island share huts in common, some in the south-east live in families in round huts built on piles, some on the south-west coast in huts made of branches constructed on piles, or in the trees, some in conical huts built on the ground. There is no political organization to bring them together. We are speaking now of a large island, where the rank, dense vegetation of the forest is an obstacle to the formation of communities; but how many small islands of the Pacific present a similar spectacle? Besides, people always reason as if the human societies which we have under our eyes and can study directly were dedicated from all eternity, by an unalterable decree of geographical Providence, to their actual habitat, and as if, though new-comers into a fixed environment, all the peculiarities which they present were the result of an immediate adaptation to that environment.

But the Meuse is not the only thing which is "embanked" where it is in the Ardennes massif, nor the Rhine in the Rhenish massif. There are human societies which "entrench" themselves also where they happen to be, with all their means of existence, and all their materials for civilization, in an environment which is not their native one. Is the reasoning valid which examines those materials in a lump, and studies those means of existence in the mass as if they were the direct products of the actual environment?

Let us return yet once more to the Sahara and to the acute and suggestive observations of Émile Gautier, which show such great power of analysis. We are apt to look on the desert as eternal—a sort of perpetual punishment, an immemorial curse weighing on a fated region. But is this conception a true one?

Is not the Sahara, in particular, a young desert and not an ancient one? Is it not now at the beginning of an evolutionary deterioration, the commencement of which man witnessed at the end of the quaternary period, and which is still going on before our eyes? Gautier shows very clearly by what simple and slow, but natural and inevitable processes the dunes kill the Wadis: that is the way the desert was created: there is no necessity to have recourse to the arbitrary and unnecessary hypothesis of a deterioration of climatic conditions.[1] But, then, in the civilization of the modern inhabitants of the Sahara, in the control of the desert by man—that astounding marvel, when we think of the empty and savage deserts of Australia, or the Kalahari in South Africa[2]—what part are we to assign to ancient conditions, to the heritage of former times preserved, adapted, and gradually accommodated to the worsening conditions of the country? The number of place-names with which that terrible desert country is provided is startling.[3] The existence of the wells which border the tracks is a problem; for to-day, in the conditions of modern life in the Sahara, it would be impossible, in those frightful solitudes, to locate their sources and to bore them.[4] Do not this precise language and this labelling of geographical-shapes bear witness to the laborious efforts of an observant race which is to-day scantily represented? Does not the remarkable construction of the wells point to the existence of former generations who were there during the gradual desiccation, and fought it step by step, following underground the sheet of water which they had

[1] Gautier, **CLXXXI**[b], Vol. I, p. 54.
[2] Ibid., p. 18.
[3] Ibid., p. 19.
[4] Ibid., p. 183 ff.

once known on the surface? Pure hypotheses, no doubt, but they have the merit of throwing light on the present conditions and rendering them comprehensible.

VI

The Idea of Isolation and its Geographical Value

We now come at last to the meaning of isolation. What is this idea, where does it come from, and what does it signify?

For the biologist the notion is perhaps relatively clear. He has no researches to make into the world of ideas; that of the animal and plant forms is sufficient for him. Simple processes enable him to arrive at the solutions of the problems which he has to solve. He tabulates in an inventory or catalogue the exact numbers, or what are supposed to be such, of the plants, birds, and mammals of a certain known date before such and such an event, and of another date after some other event, and draws his conclusions.

The idea of isolation has a meaning for him. He knows the natural resources of the creatures he is studying, and their powers of movement. But is the notion of isolation as simple and plain for the geographer? A thousand times, no. Isolation for the anthropogeographer is a very complex idea, and is not purely and simply a "natural" one. It cannot be translated into mere numbers, any more than distance, which is no longer a fixed notion but varies continually with the progress of means of transport, their multiplication, and their increase in power. Certain facts may be dated with the greatest exactitude: such, for example, as the inauguration of the Trans-Siberian line, or the opening of the Panama Canal and, to-morrow, the use of a new aeroplane of superior stability and safety, all of which may upset the notion of the distance from France to Japan, for instance, or from New York to Callao.

But from the inside of an office, without touching in any way whatever the material agents of distance, the board of administration of a great transport company can alter the actual distance from one country to another by raising or lowering its tariffs, by a deliberate and calculated diminution or acceleration of speed, by trickery or goodwill. Before the war there was competition between Calais and Ostend for the Anglo-Italian traffic. The Ostend passage was favoured by the Germans, who had arranged the services by this route with minute care. When any delay to trains was foreseen at the St. Gothard, the administration of the Alsace-Lorraine railways made arrangements so that the connexion with Ostend should suffer as little as possible, but it was very much more cavalier about the punctual departure of the trains to Calais by Mulhouse-Belfort. A station-master was every day, in some measure, controller for a part of the way of the real distance from the North Sea to Italy.[1]

Isolation varies just as distance does, and in an analogous way. It is not to be measured in miles or by the aid of a compass. It has its paradoxes and surprises. The mountaineer at the bottom of his mountain valley—his "mountain island"—is a type of the isolated man, a recluse shut up in the narrow bounds which the lofty mountain barriers impose on his tiny abode. Does anyone believe, however, that he never leaves his hole? That he passes his life rivetted to the depths of his mountain hollow? For whom, then, do those easy passes, of free and convenient access for man and beast, open across the mountains through the midst of unenclosed land? "Towards the summits the slopes are often less steep, and wide pastures stretch from one hillside to another. Walking in the light, dry air of the hilltops is a pleasure rather than a fatigue."[2] The mountaineer, who is an agriculturist only, as he moves from one level to another, according to the season and his crops, never ceases changing his altitude.[3] He is always on the move, but how much more is this the case with the herdsman. From the depth of the valley, where his house and field are situated and his family is installed, he is always going up to the higher meadows and pasturages. He is more drawn towards the tops than the plains; he has more dealings with the other valleys than with the flat country; on the crests and on the high pastures, wherever grass grows, or flocks live,

[1] For all this cf. Eisenmann's excellent notes, "Les chemins de fer transalpins," *Revue des cours et conférences*, 1914—especially pp. 390 ff., "la Méthode."

[2] All this is taken from Cavaillès' study "Une fédération pyrénéenne sous l'Ancien Régime", *Revue historique*, Vol. CV, 1910, p. 3 ff.

[3] Ch. Biermann, *La circulation en pays de montagne*, **XI**, 1913, Vol. XXII, pp. 270–82.

or man passes, he meets men from opposite slopes; relations with them are established and a social life is developed; exchanges are made and business transacted.

Isolation no doubt exists, the isolation which gives rise to real States extending over mountain districts and ceasing at the border of the plain, but it is relative. So, too, is the isolation which every year, with the regularity of a natural phenomenon, brings into the mountain districts an immense crowd of flocks moving towards higher ground, Spanish flocks fleeing from their burnt pastures, and gradually attaining to the herbage of the French Pyrenees, still fresh and green, or those masses of sheep in Rumania, Italy, and Provence, and of the oxen of the Tarentaise, which have been described by Arbos.[1] Relative also is the isolation of the islander who migrates every year to the nearest continent. But that there is any type of land to which it is peculiar, that it depends especially on the mountain which encloses, or on the desert which interposes its arid sands, and its slabs of stone cracked by the heat, or on the ocean which surrounds with its waves, is still an illusion; for there are plains which isolate every whit as much as mountains.

Cuijic, in his book on the Balkan Peninsula, when analysing the conditions of development of its various ethnic groups,[2] remarks that a well-known plain, without any mountains and free from all obstacles, the great plain of Hungary—the Alfold—has never contributed to the penetration by European civilization of the Balkan region.

"The vast plain of Hungary is regarded as a space to be traversed as quickly as possible, on the way to Central Europe, but never as a place to stay in." Thus, to quote the same author yet further, "a basin predestined by nature to serve as a link between peoples, and to assist the spread of civilization, has remained an obstacle to intercourse and fellowship." Moreover, the language spoken in that open and, geographically speaking, unobstructed plain, is absolutely isolated in Europe; it was introduced there by a fairly recent invasion and it maintains its ground there without any external support. The only European language at all related to it is Finnish, and a skilful linguist can still find conclusive proofs

[1] Arbos, "La vie pastorale en Tarentaise," **XI**, 1912, Vol. XXI, pp. 323, 345.
[2] Cuijic, **CCXIII**, p. 108.

of the common ancestry of the two idioms. Is not this single fact highly significant, and calculated to destroy some of the prejudices about that character of a refuge and asylum of old languages and old customs which is so commonly supposed to be the monopoly of mountain valleys and islands?

Isolation is a human fact, but not a geographical one, where men are concerned. By sea, in the case of the islands, it depends on navigation, which is certainly not a natural fact. By land it depends very often on the will of man—on his ideas and traditions, as we have already seen.

*

* *

To conclude. In all the naturally bounded regions which we have reviewed—mountains, plains, or plateaux, and in greater detail, valleys, shores, islands, oases—there live groups of men who present certain analogies, if not similarities, with one another. Whence do these arise? From the existence in different places of the same kinds of possibilities; but these possibilities come, or do not come, into action, according as other conditions vary or do not vary: the same possibility may come into action at a certain instant, then cease to act, and then later return to action in an unforeseen manner. But there is never any inevitability; an exact analysis always leads to the establishment of the complexity of the phenomenon we are studying and to the feeling that we must not neglect any intermediate stage, but on the contrary follow them all, one after the other, and step by step.

What value, then, have these traditional bounds which we have been successively reviewing: what are they? They are a means, not an end. They would have their full signification and complete value only on the old hypothesis—which not only the Ratzelians, but other geographers more clear-sighted and less bound by clumsy systematizations, have only half abandoned—of a mechanical action of natural factors on a purely receptive humanity. Their value for us is only of a practical kind. They are convenient for study. That is the only way in which they interest us and in which they can help us to discover a series of less superficial and better established relations between the possibilities of an environment and the societies exploiting them.

CHAPTER III

Typical Ways of Living: Hunting and Fishing

THERE are no necessities, but everywhere possibilities; and man, as master of the possibilities, is the judge of their use. This, by the reversal which it involves, puts man in the first place—man, and no longer the earth, nor the influence of climate, nor the determinant conditions of localities.

Living, like all animals, in the bosom of nature, man naturally borrows from her, and cannot but borrow from her, all the elements of his civilization. He makes use of them in their raw form when he is a savage: when he is civilized he still uses some of them in a crude form, but transforms the others. Everything in human civilization is thus "natural", and we may legitimately claim that every geographical condition is, in the same way, a human condition; but the statement is so wide that it leads to nothing. It would be really interesting if the geographical conditions were not only the material but the cause of the development of societies; if the existence of the steppes imposed the pastoral life on man and, so to speak, created it for him: if the marsh gave birth to the pile-dwellings: if insularity compelled England to build and keep up a fleet of the first rank. But we have reached no such conclusion. Nevertheless, to denounce the illusion is not to tilt foolishly at windmills disguised as warriors. The force of habit, the constraint of routine, and the invincible inertia of critical judgment are such, that we find truly surprising contradictions every day even amongst cautious geographers. There is Cuijic, in a book filled with information about the Balkan peninsula, who in one place shows how the call of the sea to the Slavs and Albanians has been in vain, in spite of the most favourable geographical conditions,[1] but who, some pages further on, declares that the Danubian plain, though held by one race,

[1] Cuijic, **CCXXIII**, 158, 357.

and much less broken up than any other part of the peninsula, with little forest and largely under the influence of a steppe climate, has " made " an agricultural people of the population which has been settled there since the early Middle Ages.[1] The poison after the antidote!

We have said and proved that such ideas are all the more arbitrary because when we speak of the fashioning of great human societies by the natural conditions which geographical analysis reveals to us to-day, we really treat them, and ought to treat them, as the fashioning of mankind by human labour. A chain of argument such as the following is unrolled before us with more or less ability: in the central part of Tuscany, on the hills which occupy the whole country between the Apennines and the Maremma, the shrubby plants, the vine, olive, and mulberry, are the main feature of the countryside. But these shrubby cultures are " the natural consequence of the relief of the ground, and of the nature of the soil and climate ". They have, moreover, the social effect of maintaining " community of family and the traditional and paternal position of the owner ". Thus the proprietary rights and family regulations are the result of natural conditions [2]—one thing only is forgotten: namely, that the geographical fact on which it was founded, viz. the abundance of shrubby plants in the region of the Tuscan hills, is a fact in no way due to nature, but to man. It was the will of man and his patient efforts and labour which introduced into that district, which was not their original habitat, the vine, the olive, and still more recently the mulberry, which was brought into Tuscany in the second half of the thirteenth century from Sicily by merchants of Lucca.

Besides this, it would be quite impossible to cultivate other things in the district, speaking not from the physical point of view, but—as is self-evident—from the economic. Once more we must remark that the idea of economic possibility, as distinct from geographical possibility, is by no means of natural or geographical order, but purely of a human order. That other crops are possible in the district, not only geographically, but economically, or if anyone prefers

[1] Cuijic, **CCXXIII**, p. 468.

[2] P. Roux, "Les populations rurales de la Toscane" (*Science sociale*, part 55, 1909, p. 3).

agronomically speaking, is clearly proved by the great abundance of cereals in the country. Their cultivation is combined with that of shrubs, and the two, no doubt, are not inseparable. There is no necessity about the matter; and there is always a danger in human geography of being tempted to exalt facts into necessities. In reality, the Tuscan countryside is a human creation. The predominance of the olive, the vine, and the mulberry in the hilly region of Tuscany is a human fact of civilization. The study of the operation of this fact is very interesting. It is, for the most part, of a geographical order, for geography is, before all others, a science of ways and means. It is very instructive to examine how two different human societies in two different countries, having conceived a certain design for the satisfaction of certain wants and under the influence of certain ideas, utilize and ingeniously combine the materials which are offered to them by the different regions to which they are adapting themselves. Here once more the chief element is, as usual, human design.

I

A Geography of the Needs of or the Manner of Life

Design or need? This is the great question: because there are geographers who, having perceived the necessity of altering the centre of gravity of human geography, so to speak, and making it pass from "the earth" into "the man", have commenced with the essential wants of the human animal. A happy beginning, no doubt, granted that there is no question of "natural" wants, or rather that it is understood—if the want is natural, the means of satisfying it is not.

To go into details: man must breathe: man must sleep: man must eat and drink.[1] We have already seen how man-made ideas and decisions come between these necessities and their realization; and the taboos on food are not ineffective to-day.[2] But it is the same with all the "needs". The essential condition for all productive human activity is, not "peace", which is an ideal, but "security", which is a con-

[1] Brunhes, **LXVI**, ibid., p. 50 ff. [2] Cf. above, p. 192 ff.

dition, and one preliminary to others; first of all, to assure his existence, then to procure the means of existence. But between these two kinds of concern a real antagonism is always arising. Suppose that men are establishing a group of dwellings. If there is security, they are free to choose for their establishment an open land, easy to move about in, unobstructed, sunny, and abounding in choice of materials. But if there is war, or a threat of war, on the contrary, they will have to adapt their dwellings as well as they can to sites which are devoid of all the qualities we have just enumerated, but which possess instead the essential virtue of "ensuring security". Hence arose the lake dwellings, among unstable, moving and unhealthy marshes, in the midst of obstacles, troublesome to the enemy, but how much more so to the inhabitants themselves, who depend on the waters, the reeds, and the mud for defence against any attack. There is nothing natural about the ideas and considerations which come between man and nature.

In the same way the need for trade is primordial. It explains and contains the germ of the development of regions, nations, and states. True, but trade in what? The oldest trade dealt in articles not strictly necessary to life: amber, gold, or even tin; for it is a question whether the war material of Neolithic man was really inferior to that of the Bronze age. In any case, peace and war intervened very early between men and natural conditions. At the present time, between the deposits of tin, gold, and Baltic amber, and the distant countries which require them, there intervenes "civilization", a vague word which includes thousands of different things, fashion, luxury, religion, imitation, none of which are peculiarly geographical. As a matter of fact, nature does not act on the needs of man, it is man who by choosing two or three out of several means of satisfying his needs, and by clinging obstinately to what he has chosen, acts in the long run on nature, digs into it a trench, so to speak, always the same and in the same direction, of no great volume at first perhaps, but ever growing deeper and wider. In other words, what has to be brought out clearly is the manner of life of the various human societies.

In two remarkable articles in the *Annales de géographie* [1]

[1] XI, 1911, Vol. XX, 15th May, 15th July.

in 1911, Vidal de la Blache forcibly elaborated this idea so full of interest for geographical research. But the idea was an old one to him; and the germ of its development in 1911 can easily be found in the most characteristic passages of his lecture in 1902 on the geographical conditions of social happenings.[1] "It must be remembered," he had already warned us, "that the force of habit plays a great part in the social nature of man. If, in his search for perfection, he finds himself essentially progressive, it is especially along lines which he has already traced; that is to say, in the direction of the technical and special qualities which his habits, fixed by heredity, have developed in him." And he adds, with foresight and justice: "it often happens that amongst the geographical possibilities of a country there are some obvious ones which have remained sterile or have only been exploited at a late period. We must ask ourselves, in such cases, whether they were in harmony with the manner of life which other qualities or properties of the soil had already caused to take root there." We see then that even at that time Vidal de la Blache had found the idea and the words, and already foresaw the necessity of executing a kind of volte-face, or more exactly a "transfer", which the articles of 1911 realized. In them, taking for his text the powerful efficacy of "organized and systematic habits making their rut ever deeper and deeper, imprinting their mark on the mind, and turning all progressive forces in a certain direction", he shows us that the geographer had been duped by an illusion, which tempted him to say: "this nature, which we see, implies a certain kind of life," whereas such as it is, it is partly the result of a certain kind of life.

In fact, the habits of life formed in certain surroundings quickly acquire sufficient consistency and fixity to become forms of civilization; and these forms constitute types which we can separate geographically, and which it is possible to group, classify, and subdivide. But how and on what principle is this to be done? In other words, what are these different ways of life? How are we to make a list of them and to enumerate their species and varieties?

[1] XI, 1902, Vol. XI, pp. 22–3.

II

The Classifications of the Economists: The Hypothesis of the Three States

"Ask the historians and the economists," it will be said. "The problem is an old one for them, and they have long found the solution." But is that really true?

We know that the old authors had very clear ideas about the classification of peoples—ideas so plausible, indeed, that they have been piously handed down by successive generations, almost without modification, until a few years ago.

According to the historians and political theorists of antiquity, all peoples had passed through three successive phases. First they lived by hunting and fishing, next by cattle-rearing, then by agriculture. A regular and normal chronological sequence; for was it not natural and probable that hunting and fishing preceded the pastoral life, which was itself succeeded by the agricultural? All peoples had then passed through these three states in turn in the simple and inevitable way in which all individuals pass in turn through youth, maturity, and old age.

But this chronological succession was also a social advance. Hunting and fishing were the occupation of rude peoples, with very little civilization, not far from the savage state. From this stage great effort and great progress raised them to the rank of pastoral populations; but to attain to the dignity of agriculturists, firmly settled on a cultivated soil, was the very final stage of progress and human ambition. Three chronological phases, no doubt; but three ladders also, to the third of which none could hoist themselves without having first climbed the other two; the order was unchangeable, like that of the three ages of stone, bronze, and iron. As late as 1890, an original observer like G. de Mortillet, in his *Origines de la chasse, de la pêche et de l'agriculture,* showed himself a convinced disciple of the old theory.

It is only in the last thirty years that its insufficiency has begun to be felt. To begin with the presumption of what we may call the linear evolution of mankind was recognized for what it is, "a presumption," and even doubly a presumption. Then the multiplication of observations, and the growing mass of scientific evidence about primitive peoples, showed the necessity for distinguishing a greater number of " states ", or, to speak more precisely, economic types of human society less arbitrary than those of fishers, hunters, herdsmen, and agriculturists, which have remained for so long in sole possession of the field.

Steinmetz, for instance, who classified the results of a long series of previous researches—to which particular attention had been devoted by Eduard Hahn, an ingenious but imaginative and very unequal author,[1] whose text never fails to be well seasoned with paradoxes—found the necessity of distinguishing not only three, but six or seven quite distinct types of human society. First of all are the gleaners, who live on plant produce and the small animals they meet by the way but use no instruments, whether tools or arms. Next come the hunters, who form a very varied group, some " collecting " or gathering along with their hunting the natural produce available, others being hunters pure and simple, while some alternate between fishing and hunting and some add elementary agriculture and a primitive kind of cattle-raising to their hunting. A third group, the fishers, naturally fills into the same subdivisions. The fourth group consists of the agricultural nomads or hunter-agriculturists; the fifth of settled agriculturists of a lower grade who devote themselves also to hunting, carrying burdens, or tending cattle. Sixthly, we have the superior farmers, who understand the use of manure, irrigation, and agricultural implements; and lastly, the nomad shepherds wandering with their flocks.

Of what use in themselves are all these categories? They have a kind of logical strictness and at the same time a schematic roughness which cannot fail to excite some alarm. The " simple gleaner " is evidently a creature very satisfying to the mind; but there is reason to fear that he is nothing else than the " first man " of the *Contrat social*, and has no more real existence than he. As to all that complicated apparatus of hunters who are partly fishers, farmers who are hunters in their spare time, or hunters who are occasionally

[1] 1895, his *Haustiere*; 1896, and his *Demeter und Baubo*, **CXIII**; more recently, *Das Alter der wirtschaftlichen Kultur der Menschheit*, Heidelberg, 1905.

farmers, one cannot help feeling that there is something childish in its exposition, and that it would have been better to have said at once what seems actually to be the case, that there are very few fishers and still fewer hunters and farmers who are "purely", continuously, and exclusively devoted to one and the same species of economic activity; but that all men have the sense to keep two strings to their bow in case of necessity; that the different economic types come nearer to one another when compelled by want—and that, in fine, there is not much use in multiplying categories more or less arbitrarily.

In reality, if we put on one side the purely hypothetical category of the "gleaners" who are gleaners only, no new distinctions of any value have been brought into the debate other than those of Eduard Hahn, if (following others) we subdivide[1] the agricultural group into three, and contrast the agriculturists properly so called—the modern Western agriculturists, the great producers of cereals equipped with cattle and plough—with the primitive cultivators (who used mattock and hoe) of South America, Central Africa, and the Indonesian islands, and the patient and meticulous agriculturists of the old Asiatic civilizations of Japan and China. But two things require special notice.

In the first place, there is no compulsory passage of the different peoples from one phase or state to another.[2] Sometimes links of the chain are missing; the cultivators of America before the time of Columbus, the men of the great native civilizations, whom the conquistadors met and destroyed, never passed through a pastoral phase, and this may have been due to the fact that they had not the necessary animals. Sometimes there exist in the same group of men and at the same period two manners of living theoretically quite distinct; this is the case particularly in all those societies where men and women live a separate economic existence,[3] and in which the division of labour between the two sexes causes the man, for instance, to live on the animal products of his hunting or fishing, and the

[1] The idea of farming with the hoe is already found in the works of Nowacki, previous to the publication of Hahn's *Haustiere*.
[2] Cf. for instance Hahn, **CXIII**, pp. 4–7.
[3] Cf. Bücher, **CLXVIII**, *L'Economie des Primitifs*.

woman on roots or the fruits she gathers, or on the vegetable produce of a rudimentary agriculture. Sometimes, indeed, the regular order of succession of the three traditional phases is, or seems to have been, reversed.

Roscher had already set the fashion of a prudent opportunism, and suggested that as a fact hunting had appeared first here, cattle breeding there, and agriculture elsewhere, according to circumstances or the climate.

Nowacki, later, set himself to demonstrate that the raising of cattle could not be in any way a direct result of hunting; that during long periods the only existing agriculture was not that perfected agriculture which we can scarcely imagine except in its most triumphant stage, but a rudimentary system of work with the hoe, without the aid of cattle or primitive plough; and that the domestication of cattle appeared not, as the old theory asserted, amongst the hunters, but amongst those who practised hoe culture and who would have been the ancestral stock from whom agriculturists in the modern sense of the word derived, and amongst the nomad herdsmen who were shepherd peoples in other districts. These are, in sum, the ideas which Hahn [1] adopts and develops in his pamphlet of 1896, *Demeter und Baubo*, in which he proposes the following scheme of evolution:—first of all, cultivation by the hoe, *Hackbau*, the first and most ancient form of labour on the earth,[2] which produced for the inhabitants of the pile dwellings the millet, whose nutritive importance has long excelled that of all cultivated plants.[3] Then came the domestication of cattle, first of all from religious motives, afterwards for economical reasons. Next appeared shepherds and nomads, driving their flocks before them over the steppes, and directly afterwards the invention of the cart.[4] It was at first a religious machine, a holy utensil. The ox was soon used to draw it, and later to draw the plough, and this was the beginning of true agriculture. The expansion was slow, however, but it seems that the historical beginnings of the process took place in Babylonia about 5,000 years B.C. It was then in full swing,

[1] Nowacki (A.), *Jagd oder Ackerbau*, 1885.
[2] Hahn, **CXIII**, p. 568, *Die erste und ursprünglichste Stufe aus der alle andern hervorgehen müssen, ist der Hackbau.*
[3] Hahn, *Haustiere*, **CXII**, p. 410 ff.
[4] Hahn, *Demeter*, **CXIII**, p. 30 ff. (*Der Wagen*).

with all its essential characteristics and different main kinds of culture.

This is not the place to examine or criticize such ideas, but we notice them because they also tend, like all the other facts we have just mentioned, to upset completely the notion not only of a chronological but also of a hierarchical succession of the ways of life and the traditional social types.

And this is the second remark we have to make. The less accomplished type of agriculturists, those who scratched the soil laboriously and unskilfully with that primitive instrument, the hoe, and planted in it occasional seeds or roots, using no manure and no method, do not appear, from the narratives and experiences of travellers, to have formed societies superior to those of the fishers and hunters. And again, are shepherds less civilized than many unskilled agriculturists? It is questionable. A settled existence gives us the impression of being a higher existence than nomadism; this, however, may be but apparent, and the impression might vanish quickly in contact with reality. But all these remarks, however just they may be, have one common fault. They only touch the surface of the question.

*
* *

Can we, or can we not, extract from the authors of the classifications a ready-made list of the "ways of life", whether they distinguish three or five or seven or more still, and whether their distinctions are well founded or not? That is the whole question. And the fact that people do not generally ask it, that they find it easy to draw freely from the work of Hahn or of one of his rivals, certainly does not prove that they are right. Let us note at once that all these distinctions and classifications are in fact of an economic order. They are founded entirely on the manner in which men procure for themselves the first material for their sustenance, and they neglect every other consideration. This is perhaps legitimate and allowable when we know the real intentions and design of their authors. But one thing is sure, and that is that he who speaks of an economic type does not speak of a social type; for in that case it would follow that everything pertaining to man depended absolutely on his food—and we have not combated the idea of a strict and rigorous determinism of the soil to fall, in the end, into a determinism, equally strict and vigorous, of victuals.

Peoples who are widely different in their domestic habits, in their moral character, and in their political organization, are classed under the same economic heading—that of shepherds, for example. And when we speak of the manner of life of a people we speak just as much of the inevitable consequences of a particular habitat as of the necessary result of their manner of feeding themselves. Either the idea of the ways of life has no meaning, or it admits in the first place the consideration of the habits of men—of those men who, from the most remote ages, influenced both by a very strong traditionalism, which is itself only a result, and by their very limited experience, always direct their efforts towards the same objects, and always employ the same means to overcome the same difficulties. To tell the truth, it is not the difference in their food which causes the distinction between men; it is that diversity in habits and tastes which impels such human groups to seek one sort of food rather than another.[1] It is not game in one place, and yams in another, which should be the origin and starting-point of classifications: it is the whole conglomeration of aptitudes, traditional tastes, ideas, and customs which forms the contrast between the Pygmy hunters and the Negro farmers, and prevents their intermingling, although they live side by side and in touch with one another. In other words, we must carefully place man on the highest plane in this case also. And where would be the use of our having proclaimed this fact, and having considered the elaboration and acquisition of the idea of "ways of life" as a great advance, if at the same time, by a sort of natural inconsequence, and for want of the indispensable critical examination, we fell back simply into the determinist illusion—into the same error which we had thought to dispel by the aid of this very idea of "ways of life"?

Geographers may, if they will, use the categories of economists. They may talk of hunters, fishers, hoe cultivators, and nomad shepherds; nothing could be more legitimate. But they must understand that these categories cannot have,

[1] See above, p. 161.

and ought not to have, the same strict meaning for them as for the economists. They must not allow themselves to be led by them to the determinant necessity, and at the same time to an obsession by the idea of food supplies as a dominant factor of the same order as that of climate or soil. Economists must consider economic conditions; geographers must study and give the first place to human conditions. On the strength of these remarks let us proceed without further delay to the consideration of different types of human societies.

In what order shall we take them? If we begin with the hunters and proceed to the fishers we may as well state at once that in so doing we do not propose to take any part in the controversy as to the actual genesis of the various manners of living. If we did take part in this, we should certainly not hold with the old classical theory, which is rejected now by everyone. The sole reason which determines our choice is the fact that on the stage of history and on the earth's surface the hunting and fishing communities have played smaller parts than the shepherds and cultivators.

III

The Hunter Peoples

We will leave out those "mere gleaners", the simple collectors of plants, shell-fish, insects and worms, with no weapons for hunting or tackle for fishing, the rude recipients of nature's bounty to all comers, whom it has been usual to place on the lowest rung of the human ladder. The fact that their existence is more or less hypothetical is of little importance on the whole to our present design. Let us begin our review simply with those hunters and fishers who were regarded for so long as the most primitive of all human beings.

Hunters—the word takes us back to the most distant periods we can reach, to those men of the stone age whom Déchelette pictures to us,[1] who built their fragile huts of branches of which no trace remains, near the streams, and carried on their war with the animals with flint weapons,

[1] Déchelette, **CLXX,** I, p. 62.

heavy clubs, or snares, and pits for the larger animals.[1] Against the birds they used stones, thrown at first by hand, then by a sling, later by a bow—in which case the stone first took the shape of a triangular blade with the apex inserted in the wooden arrow shaft. It was still used in the Neolithic Age over part of the future Western Europe, and only gradually gave way to the arrow tipped with an almond-shaped flint, hafted at the broad end and striking with the point.[2]

These were poor arms on the whole, but still they showed remarkable progress, when we remember that the bow and arrow have remained unknown to the Australians, the New Zealanders and many of the inhabitants of the Pacific. They were calculated rather to put animals to flight by causing pain than to deliver them over, dead or severely wounded, to their human enemies; and it is probable that men learnt in very early times to smear their arrows with the juice of certain poisonous or stupefying plants.[3] But the inadequacy of these weapons strikes us less when we read in the descriptions of pre-historians that the men who used them wandered in small bodies over a soil where, on the bank of great rivers similar to those of the New World, there flourished luxuriant vegetation rich in natural produce; since they were omnivorous, they must have possessed other food supplies than those furnished by the chase.

But let us leave these conjectures which are drawing us away from our subject. To-day, in the world as we see it, and yesterday in the world which history reconstructs for us with the aid of documents, hunting is for many people a means or rather one of many means of gaining their livelihood. For others it is their whole life, their only care and occupation.

For want of having separated these two categories, students have often made many mistakes, and incorrect generalizations. Hunters who are exclusively hunters are rare. They nearly all have the same distinctive characteristic as the Pygmies, that dwarf people rather below 5 ft. in height, with woolly

[1] Ibid., p. 77. Déchelette mentions hunters of the Chellean Period. De Morgan considers this unjustifiable, since only in the Moustierian layers does the abundance of animal bones encountered leave no doubt as to the kind of activity pursued by the troglodytes; they were hunters and fishers (de Morgan, *Prehistoric Man*, p. 170).

[2] For types of flint-headed arrows, see de Morgan's figure 41 (**CLXXV**, p. 97).

[3] De Morgan, p. 170.

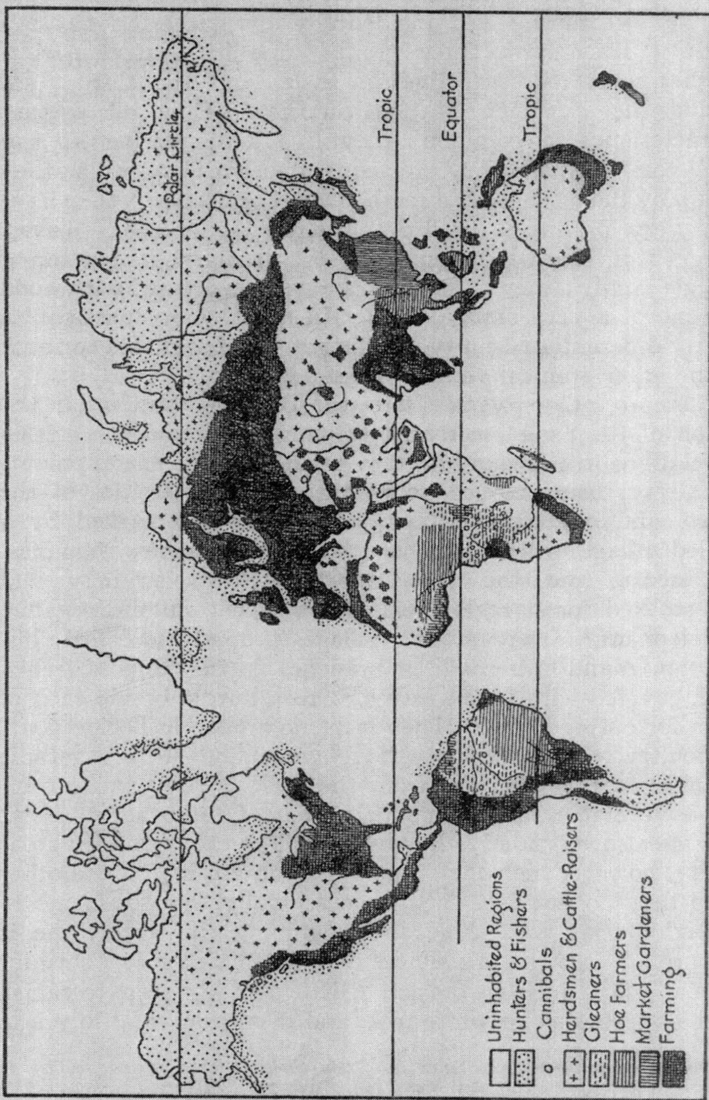

FIG. 6.—DISTRIBUTION OF DIFFERENT MODES OF LIVING (according to E. Hahn, in *Die Haustiere*, 1896, map shown in the text, and E. Friedrich, *Allgemeine Wirtschaftsgeographie*, 1904, map 2.)

hair, broad shoulders and short lower limbs, among whom not a single tribe adopts agriculture or cattle-rearing, but all live by hunting and incidentally by gathering nature's crops.[1] They form three groups; one in Central Africa, another with representatives in Asia, and the third comprising the Bushmen of South Africa. They all present characteristics in common: they live a wandering life, in small communities; they are acquainted with fire, which they obtain by the most ancient method, that of friction; they have only very primitive dwellings, shelters under rocks, caves, refuges from the wind, round or semicircular huts sheltering a single family; they have bows, and arrows pointed with wood or bone of a very archaic type. In short, they constitute a clearly differentiated unity which forms a remarkable contrast to the other ethnical groups of humanity.

There are other Pygmies also, the Babenga who live in the region of the Sanga, and who differ widely from the settled populations in whose midst they reside. Their encampments are always being moved according to the necessities of the chase, and oscillate between two poles, one marked by a settled village which supplies them with manioc, bananas, and maize, and the other marked by a swampy and well-stocked forest region, beloved by their favourite game, the elephant.[2] They have no villages properly so called, but only low round huts made of branches, in the form of trellis-work covered with broad leaves, with a hurdle beside each of them for curing meat.[3] They have no crops, no flocks, goats or poultry. For food they have game and such vegetable produce as they can get from the bush. The yam is their stable vegetable, as the manioc is that of the other natives; they are also very fond of honey, and climb the trees with great agility, however high they may be, to obtain it; on the other hand they do not fish, though occasionally the women go to a neighbouring water-hole and, damming the water, run it off through basket-work sluices and thus catch a few shrimps or small fish. Such are the active little men who seem to vanish at the appearance of white folk, and disappear stealthily into

[1] For their customs, cf. Schmidt's *Die Stellung der Pygmaenvölker in der Entwicklungsgeschichte des Menschen*, Stuttgart, 1910.

[2] All this information is taken from an interesting study by Dr. Regnault, in **XVI**, Vol. XXII, p. 260 ff.

[3] Cureau, **CLXXIX**, p. 264.

the bush, where they hide and are extremely timid and difficult to get hold of.[1] Their neighbours, the settled tribes, speak of them contemptuously as the "beasts of the bush". A very curious fact is the sort of domestic agreement between the two. The Babenga furnish the others with the spoils of the chase, and they in exchange give manioc, maize and bananas to the Babenga. Each of these settled groups has its hunters, who, moreover, often change their patrons and accept more seductive offers to go elsewhere. There we have a remarkable instance of human symbiosis—hunters accommodating agriculturists, but each keeping to their own profession and never uniting in any other way.[2]

These characteristic features of the Babenga are reproduced by many other similar peoples[3]—one might say by all the Pygmy populations of Central Africa.

They also are found, this time in South Africa, amongst other "little men", the Bushmen, whose whole lives are centred in the chase: armed with bows, whose strings are made from the sinews of animals, and which they use also as musical instruments to imitate the noises made by moving animals—for all their thoughts are concerned with game[4]—they devote themselves entirely to the hunting of wild animals, and when these fail them they have recourse simply to their luck as "gleaners" of roots, mice, insects, or termites' eggs.

They have no huts, only light shelters of grass and branches. They have no political organization, but wander in bands; they have neither chiefs, warriors, crops, nor domestic animals; their patience and ingenuity is proof against everything, and they will lie in wait for hours, or even for days; and have wonderful skill in creeping along and approaching animals without disturbing them. A successful hunt is followed by a feast at which they gorge and dance: their life is summed up in procuring and eating their food.

Moreover they have no notion of economy, but shamelessly squander everything. These same essential features characterize all these savages whom some consider to be the

[1] On the mentality of the hunters, cf. Cureau, p. 185 above; also later, p. 255.

[2] This is corroborated by Dr. Poutrin, in **XVI**, 1911, Vol. XXII, p. 421 ff., especially p. 454; id. in Bruel, *L'Afrique équatoriale française*, 1918, p. 199.

[3] Cf. what Hutereau says of the Batuas, the Pygmy hunters of the Belgian Congo (**XVI**, 1910, p. 221).

[4] **XVI**, 1917, Vol. XXVIII, p. 603.

direct descendants of our quaternary ancestors,[1] and who, in any case, have preserved the culture of the latter almost unaltered.

But one question, difficult of solution, now arises : how are we to account for this exclusive taste for hunting, which constitutes a sort of monopoly in favour of the hunters ?

Dr. Decorse, the author of a very interesting study on hunting and agriculture amongst the inhabitants of the Sudan, has no doubts.[2] He sketches the innumerable difficulties in the path of the hunter, the heavy toil which the search for game entails for him, the circuitous tracking of the spoor which by night is scarcely discernible in the tangle of the bush, the long journeys to recover a lost trail, the sudden surprise or the immovable watch in the presence of a beast at bay, the pursuit of the wounded quarry,[3] and the danger.[4] He also shows how the Negro prefers to feed himself otherwise, scratches among the bush to attempt a rudimentary agriculture, fishes on occasion, or gathers the shell-fish in the rivers. " The Negro is never a keen hunter except in case of necessity. When he hunts it is for the sake of food." Elsewhere he says " the name of hunter is applied perhaps somewhat gratuitously to certain ethnic groups which are simply poorer and less favoured by nature than others ".[5] For the peoples who hunt most are just those whose very wooded country makes the clearing of the land and agriculture very difficult. And again " the hunting instinct is not peculiar to any ; it is the conditions of their existence which drive certain peoples to make hunting their chief occupation ". The same universal thesis is seen under different forms.

But does it hold in the case of the little men, the Pygmies, who are the hunters *par excellence* ? It is not want, apparently, that forces them to the chase. At any rate with them hunting is not a sort of occupation of despair, a last resort after every other possible means of existence has been exhausted. The Babenga and their fellow dwarfs of the Central African forests

[1] Schmidt's theory, op. cit., cf. also **XVI**, 1918–19, Vol. XXIX, p. 121.
[2] Decorse, 19, **CLXXX**, p. 457.
[3] Sometimes poisoned by an arrow, cf. for the Bushman, **XVI**, 1917, Vol. XXVIII, p. 603.
[4] On the courage of the Babenga, their boldness in elephant-hunting, cf. Bruel, *L'Afrique équatoriale française*, p. 236.
[5] Decorse, **CLXXX**, p. 467.

are not herdsmen or agriculturists, ruined and compelled by the temporarily bad results of their chief occupation to have recourse to a ruder and less agreeable means of avoiding starvation—viz., the chase. As we said at first, we must carefully distinguish between the hunters who are simply and exclusively hunters and the others. The others may be more or less clumsy farmers, like the Sudanese Negroes, to whom the somewhat too schematic remarks of Decorse apply: for other observers are more precise, and Bruel, for instance, in his recent work on French Equatorial Africa, throws much light on the subject of hunting when he tells us that it is seasonal.[1] The Negro farmers only take to it when the dry season is well established; they then leave their villages and make for territory which is theirs by custom, reserved by a whole code of oral laws unknown to us, where they hunt, and profit also by the annual grass fires which give them the opportunity of immense battues.[2]

These occasional hunters may also be wandering herdsmen, none of whom fail to avail themselves of the sport and the accessory profit of the chase whilst slowly following their herds.[3] But whether herdsmen or farmers they have not the hereditary vocation and the exclusive ardour of those Babenga or those Bushmen who have good and bad huntsmen in their midst, but say of the latter, according to Regnault, "they are not true Babenga."

The real hunters are few in number. They have little importance in the world either physically or morally, consisting of a few tribes of dwarfs scattered here and there, as we have said, in Africa, Asia and certain of the Sunda islands, to whom we may add some historic groups of the type of those buccaneers of the Antilles, who devoted themselves to the hunting of oxen and wild pigs, whose skins they tanned and whose flesh they dried. These are close groups, and evolution does not affect their manner of life. We do not find that cattle-raisers are usually developed among them. But, on the other hand, hunters and farmers also can be evolved from cattle-raisers.

From statements of this kind it by no means follows that

[1] Bruel, op. cit., p. 234.
[2] Ibid., p. 235.
[3] Ibid., Chap. IV, p. 325.

hunting is an altogether inferior occupation within the reach of the less highly evolved types of humanity. The life of hunters certainly does not tend to bind them to the soil by any close tie. Amongst their most striking characteristics are the mobility of their little groups, the unsettled nature of their abodes, and that ignorance of ceramics which they share with all nomads, Australians, Fuegians, certain Esquimaux and Mongols; all discard pottery doubtless because it is too fragile for the use of wanderers. Still this is not a sure indication of inferior culture. The dishes and utensils of the Mongols, considering that they are not made of clay but of iron, wood, or leather, are of very good workmanship, and the Polynesians, who do not make pots, are nevertheless superior in many ways to the Melanesians. It is an exaggeration to speak of the hunters as though they were entirely without organization, and that because of their way of living; for hunting is an organized enterprise, and always involves co-operation.

Search for game, following its tracks and pursuing and encountering it, involves too much work for a single man when that game is large and formidable. It is always carried out by parties, with recognized and complicated ceremonies. In the district of Ugogo[1] they prepare for an elephant-hunt by buying amulets and practising the throwing of a spear with a broad-pointed head, protected by a talisman which usually consists of a strip of snake-skin. For a week they dance and drink; drums are beaten, howling women beat pieces of hollow wood with stones, whilst the dancers of the tribe mimic the gait of the elephant. Then after a series of feasts in which drunkenness plays its part the men set out. Whilst they are away the women must behave with the strictest austerity, the success of the chase being partly dependent on the propriety of their conduct. An elephant is singled out and surrounded, the "mganga" throws the first spear and all the others follow his example. They take off the tusks of the dead elephant, eat the pulp of the dental cavity and feed on the fat which surrounds the intestines, and then the tribe returns with the ivory, the skin, and the meat of the victim.[2]

[1] Burton, **CLXXVII**, *bis*, pp. 607–9.

[2] Similar descriptions in Cureau, **CLXXIX**, p. 260; Meniaud, **CLXXXIII**, Vol. I, p. 185, etc. For Bushmen, **XVI**, 1917, Vol. XXVIII, p. 603.

Such a society is naturally unstable. If the numbers of the tribe increase, if game becomes scarcer on the hunting-grounds, the group must split up and separate in order to live. But we see that hunting is really a kind of industry and that it tends towards a higher civilization by the community of effort which it expects and demands.[1]

The conditions of their life naturally leave their mark on the character and customs of the hunters. There is something special about the kind of ownership which they acknowledge. Truth to tell, the land in itself does not concern them, only the hunting rights; in this sense it is incorrect to speak of the "territory" of the Comanches, of the Algonquins, of the aborigines of Australia, of the Bushmen, or of the Bechuanas[2]: it would be more correct to speak of their ranging grounds. As to their character, observers agree in depicting them as rude and uncommunicative people, fond of solitude and silence, patient, clever, and daring—but touchy, defiant, and extremely double-faced. Is it hunting or their environment which is most likely to give rise to such striking characteristics? Decorse puts the question in the study we have already quoted: "If the hunter is rude and uncommunicative," he says,[3] "it is no doubt on account of the silence and solitude to which the chase has accustomed him—but it is above all because distrust and fear lurk in the forest and the thick bush. Life there is one continual tension of the senses; in front of him is always the mysterious and troublesome barrier of underwood; there is no horizon, nothing but dusk; the sharpest eye is deceived by fancies; man, who is born to use his sight, has only his ear to depend on; less fortunate than the animals, whose nose replaces the eye, he is aware of his inferiority; he lives on the defensive, with watchful eye and straining ear."[4] It may be so. In reality the matter is of no importance. Whether they are what they are because they are hunters or because they are foresters—seeing that they are foresters because they are hunters and vice versa—it is certain that the hunters do form clearly differentiated groups which lead a special kind of life.

[1] Bücher, **CLXVIII**.
[2] Semple, **CX**, Chap. III.
[3] Decorse, **CLXXX**, p. 467.
[4] Cf. also Cureau, **CLXXIX**, pp. 28 ff., 34 ff.

IV

The Fisher Peoples

Fisher peoples are much more fixed to the soil, and have been so from the earliest times: the Danish kitchen-middens, the shell-mounds and heaps of fish, bird and animal bones in the bay of San Francisco,[1] the shell-heaps which mark all the shores of the Atlantic, the Argentine "paraderos", the Brazilian "sambaquis" are there to prove it. These enormous accumulations of debris, nearly all of marine origin, show that relatively numerous groups have lived from remote ages on the borders of the sea, that great purveyor of abundant sustenance.[2] Moreover, the discoveries of archæologists have brought to light the fishing instruments used by these prehistoric fishermen; they show us a type of civilization which has not yet disappeared and may be found to-day among many communities of uncivilized fishermen, such as those on the Ubangi or on the shores of Lake Tanganyika, whom Burton describes.[3]

But fishing seems to be an exclusive occupation, though in a lesser degree than hunting. It also has, undoubtedly, a fairly complicated and special technique, which needs experience. It also demands collective effort and the effective co-operation of men belonging to the same group or the same village. In Equatorial Africa, for instance, the whole available population takes part in the great fishings as in the great battues; they are not only undertaken for the provision of food, but as picnics and pleasure excursions too.[4]

The very considerable labour required for the work undertaken demands the active co-operation of many men—as, for example, when it is necessary to fix a kind of stockade of wattle-work across a river in order to compel the fish to leap through a single opening into the net. At the same time the women, too, must combine to dam the small streams when the water ebbs, and to empty them with their calabashes. On the banks of the Upper Niger, also, the Malinkas band together to fish

[1] On the shell-mounds, cf. **XVIII**, 1910, p. 216.
[2] On fishing in general, see de Morgan, **CLXXV**, 163 ff.
[3] Burton, **CLXXVII**[a], pp. 413–14.
[4] Cureau, **CLXXIX**, p. 263; Bruel, op. cit., p. 237 ff., etc.

by torch-light during the dark nights of March, April and May, when all the men go into the river-bed with torches of straw in their hands and nets made of osier, with which they capture the fish which have been attracted by the light.[1] Collectively also these same Malinkas or the riverside population of the Congo, near its confluence with the Sangha, poison the waters with the leaves of narcotic plants, which stupefy the fish, and render them an easy prey.[2]

But, notwithstanding the existence of so many common characters, there is a notable difference between fishing and hunting. The former is very much easier to combine with other modes of life—particularly with hunting.

The negritoes of the Andaman Islands are typical of those mixed populations who, though fishers, add hunting to their staple industry. Their settlements are very widely scattered (for in that land of tangled jungle concentration would ruin the hunting just as it would the fishing), and consist of small communities of twenty to fifty people, or a hundred at most, which are, in a sense, large families—they are beginning, however, to embrace the idea of larger groups of the clan type, which, though still undeveloped, already possess forests and seas exploited by the different family communities.

In many cases the alternation of hunting and fishing is regulated by the seasons. In America, as a rule, hunting is a winter occupation ; fishing a spring or summer one. The Zahlta Indians of British Columbia hunt during the winter in groups of two families, with bows and arrows, spears, and snares ; fishing takes place in summer, when the whole village reunites.[3] In Alaska, about Fort Egbert, the natives who, before the coming of white man, lived a nomadic life in tents made of skins and were themselves clothed in coats and trousers of skin devoted themselves in winter to hunting caribou or bear, which they drove into enclosures or hunted with the spear ; in spring they fished for salmon, which they dried and carried off to their villages on sledges drawn by huskies.[4] In other cases the division is not seasonal, but sexual. Amongst the Esquimaux in the North of Labrador, the men hunt the seal and the walrus, whilst fishing is left to the women ;[5] this

[1] Meniaud, **CLXXXIII**, Vol. I, 243.
[2] Chevalier, **CLXXVIII**, p. 17.
[3] **XVI**, 1913, Vol. XXIV, p. 108.
[4] **XVI**, 1911, Vol. XXII, p. 98.
[5] **XVI**, 1911, Vol. XXII, p. 720.

division of labour is frequent, and has been reported as equally common in Africa.

Much more characteristic, however, and more interesting, is the mixed life of the peoples who couple agriculture with their fishing. They are so numerous that it would be correct to say that the only peoples who devote themselves exclusively to fishing are those to whom agriculture is either unnecessary or impossible owing to the climate. Those privileged countries where man has, naturally and without labour, an abundant vegetable food supply at his disposal are in the former case. Cook has described the life of the people of Tahiti in 1769: he speaks of their using an extremely varied diet without any labour or cultivation. Being fishermen and collectors of the sea-harvest, they had fish, lobsters, crabs and shell-fish in abundance. Their meat consisted of pork, dog and poultry, which multiply rapidly there without any special care. For vegetable diet they had in the first place the bread-fruit, coco-nuts and bananas, and in case of scarcity the fruit of a shrub called nono, the roots and leaves of an edible fern, and a native root;[1] all these plants grew wild and were sufficient in themselves to support all the domestic animals—including the dog, which in Tahiti was a vegetarian. It was unnecessary, therefore, to organize systematic agriculture; it was enough if every native planted during his life ten bread-fruit-trees, which represented about an hour's work.

In this case it is abundance which makes men exclusively fishermen. In the sub-Polar regions it is the scarcity of plants which has the same effect; it inclines all the human tribes towards the simple and monotonous pursuit of fishing. But these are only exceptional cases. Since fish forms only part of their food,[2] a greater or less part according to circumstances, very often we find among primitive peoples a sort of sharing of functions between the sexes, the man undertaking the fishing or hunting, the woman the gathering of the plants or the cares of a more or less rudimentary agriculture. The division is such a natural one that we find it still, in our own time, amongst many civilized coastal societies; in Brittany,

[1] Cook, **CCV**, II, 445–65; cf. also above, p. 217.

[2] In the little islands of Micronesia, the Carolines for example, the staple food is of a vegetable character. Cf. **XVI**, Vol. XXIX (1918–19), p. 594.

for example, as we have already mentioned.[1] Thus, fishing may pass into agriculture at any stage.

The contrary evolution would seem to be less natural if we take into account the real repugnance to fish which is often found amongst many inland peoples and agriculturists. The ancients themselves remarked[2] that according to Homer no fish appeared at the well-served tables of people of rank. The men of the Homeric period certainly knew all about fishing—lines, nets and harpoons. But the heroes only had recourse to the fish thus caught in case of necessity and when no other food was procurable. If the companions of Ulysses, when detained in the Island of Helios, and those of Menelaus, becalmed in Pharos, consented to eat fish, it was only because they were famished. Fish was an inferior diet, good for a semi-pastoral people, such as the Greeks still were in reality, and for poor people who had no cattle.[3] It is curious to find in old France exactly similar prejudices, when we read the exhortations of Bodin to his fellow citizens, and the vigorous campaign which he undertook in order to induce them to eat fish and not to despise it as an inferior food.[4]

Fishing, less restrictive as a way of life than hunting, also tends to widen the culture of those employed in it. It constrains them to quit the seashore either for deep-sea fishing or for the great river fisheries. Hence a necessity for boats arises. Cook has carefully described[5] the construction of canoes at Tahiti. The piragua with its outrigger, and other kinds of more or less perfected boats, play a considerable part in the lives of all riverside or seashore peoples. It was probably the murex fishery which started the Phœnicians on their maritime career; the Baltic fishery was the origin of the maritime and commercial development of the Hansa; it was the fishermen who in Elizabeth's day helped to direct England towards her maritime and colonial destiny; and lastly it was from the fishing fleet of Japan, the only one left in 1624 after the systematic destruction of her merchant fleet, that the present Japanese navy has sprung.

[1] See above, p. 215.
[2] References in Daremberg and Saglio, **CLXIX**, V, Piscatio.
[3] Helbig, *L'Épopée homérique*, transl. Trawinski, Paris, 1894, p. 546.
[4] See above, p. 218.
[5] Cook, **CCV**, Vol. II, p. 492 ff.

Some of the fisher peoples are attracted so much to the sea that floating villages exist in the Far East, and there are nomads of the sea in the Philippine region—the Moro-Bajan in the Sulu Archipelago, who live chiefly by fishing, and pass their lives in boats, each containing one family, five or six of which form a community. These are extreme cases. But on the other hand there is frequent combination of extreme mobility—that of the navigator which is born of his way of life, so varied and free—with the essentially sedentary existence of the cultivator of the soil.[1]

[1] Semple, **XC**, Chap. X.

CHAPTER IV

SHEPHERDS AND HUSBANDMEN

Nomadic and Sedentary Populations

IT was not, however, the fishers and hunters who were the conquerors of the earth, the first makers of history, and the founders of civilization. The peoples who created and spread over the world the early civilizations, so complex, varied and rich in every way, were pastoral or agricultural peoples. Let us study them, each in turn, while leaving severely alone that wide and thorny question of their possible interrelation or mutual derivation, which is both beyond our competence and outside the scope of this book.

I

Domestication and Nomadism

It is a fact, the admission of which requires no lengthy dissertation, that the life of man was profoundly transformed by the domestication of a certain number of animals. But where, when, and above all how, for what reason, or by what means did this domestication take place? There are few questions still so obscure, notwithstanding all the study and labour and the progress realized during recent years.

Even the idea of domestication is anything but clear. In what does domestication consist? It has been defined as a degeneration. Captivity reacts at once—and powerfully—on the sexual life of animals.[1] The difficulty has never been in keeping wild animals alive in the dietary sense, whether captured in the chase or otherwise, as ancient peoples prove. The American Indians were fond of menageries, which they filled with birds and little pet animals; the Egyptians and the

[1] Caullery, **CXXVI**, p. 159.

Assyrians kept martens, long-tailed monkeys and lions; instances of tamed foxes, bears, and boars living amongst men are not uncommon in Northern countries. But these are animals caught young and brought up amongst dwellings, not born in captivity, and collected not for utility or profit but for amusement or sacred uses, or for the pleasure of company. There are people, as Schmoller somewhere remarks, who keep fowls only for their feathers, and who rear dogs which they do not utilize for hunting.[1]

In other words, we must not confound the penchant and aptitude of man for taming wild beasts with real domestication, a much harder and more complicated operation. The difficulty, as we have said, is to get large animals to breed in captivity. This result is so difficult to attain that even now, after centuries of effort, they have not succeeded in India in the case of the elephant. It is easy enough to blame the civilized man's want of skill in domestication, as E. Gautier does somewhere,[2] and to instance the failure of zoological gardens to domesticate the zebra, the vain efforts of the Germans and the Belgians to break the African elephant, and the unavailing attempts of the colonists of Upper Senegal to domesticate the ostrich.[3] It was not only want of skill in all these cases; and perhaps we are concerned with more serious difficulties than the psychological misunderstanding between our civilized man and the animal. For we must remember that out of the hundred thousand or more species of animals whose domestication is theoretically possible and whose utility would certainly be profitable, man has succeeded in really domesticating some fifty at most, and that only after prolonged efforts.

Modern people are not the only ones who fail. We know that in Egypt, for instance,[4] experiments in taming and domesticating several species of wild animals were tried during a long period in the Old Kingdom. Monuments dating back to 4,000 years B.C. show us gazelles, antelopes, and hyenas held in leash by slaves or brought up in the stable; and on the bas-reliefs of the tomb of Mera, at Sakkara, we see

[1] Schmoller, *Principes d'économie politique*, transl. Platon, I, 481.
[2] Gautier, **CLXXXI**, pp. 104–5.
[3] Meniaud, **CLXXXIII**, Vol. I, p. 222 ff.
[4] Gaillard, **XVI**, 1913, Vol. XXIV, p. 527.

jackals, gazelles, wild goats, and hyenas, undoubtedly being used in hunting. The experiments were evidently being continued.

What is certain is that domestication was the result of a long series of attempts, many of which were abortive and remained unproductive. The spontaneous crossing of animals captured by men with other animals of a kindred species, themselves also in confinement, by reason of that sort of tendency to promiscuity which captivity seems to develop in animals, doubtless gave considerable aid in the solution of the problem [1] so far as the successful cases were concerned. We must not forget that our present domestic animals are not simple creatures, but, as they have been called, " synthesized beings," the issue of repeated crossings of wild species more or less related.

Some naturalists consider that the big Northern races of dogs (Esquimaux, Danish, and German mastiff) were the result of a cross of the wolf with the domestic dogs descended from the *Canis pallipes* of Hindustan ; and that Egyptian dogs were related to the jackal.[2] Nothing is more complicated or more uncertain than the hypotheses of scientists on the genealogy and relationships of our most familiar companions and we are astonished, when we read them, to find from how many different elements these seemingly simple species have been formed.

It is difficult also to give any precise idea of the time or order in which these " conquests " of man occurred. It seems certain, in any case, that the time does not go back beyond the period characterized by the appearance of the older Neolithic remains (the shell heaps).[3] It is then that the dog, no doubt the oldest comrade of man, first appears.[4] Afterwards in the late Neolithic period (polished stone) the goat, the sheep, the pig, and the ox are found simultaneously.[5] The horse would seem to have come last. These six species are generally found together in the lacustrine stations at the epoch of the pile-dwellings. Others were of much more recent origin ; the cat, for instance, was domesticated much later than the dog, and its diffusion was slow : it was only introduced into France

[1] Caullery, **CXXVI.**

[2] Trouessart, *Biologica*, 15th Sept., 1911. Note on the prehistoric origin of domestic mammals.

[3] Following Déchellette's classification, **CLXX.**

[4] De Morgan, **CLXXV**, p. 166.

[5] Trouessart, op. cit.

and the North of Europe in the Middle Ages. As for the reindeer, of which the Magdalenian artists have left us such striking pictures, it is difficult to fix the time when they became the companions of man rather than game.[1]

Lastly, the fowl, which was destined to show so brilliant a record, is still found wild in India. It was worshipped by the followers of Zoroaster, and became the sacred bird of Mazdaism ; it no doubt owes its domestication and its spread over Persia to religious considerations. Its advent into the Mediterranean districts of Europe appears to date only from the historical epoch.[2]

As for the inhabitants of the American continent, or rather of the two American continents which as we know form two distinct zoological regions separated by a zone of transition, or rather of mingling,[3] which includes Guatemala, Mexico, Texas, and California, they domesticated the turkey and one of the camelidæ, the llama, which, however, they never employed in agricultural work.

Fundamentally, although the dog is the oldest and most faithful companion of man, he is not the most important one in the general development of civilization. The ox is of much greater economic importance. Hahn tells us [4] that its domestication was the result of religious ideas ; it may have been associated in early times with the very general worship of the moon—perhaps because of the analogy between its horns and the lunar crescent. Probably wild oxen were at first enclosed, so that they might be sacrificed to the goddess worshipped by the agricultural peoples, the adepts at hoe-culture, and from such enclosure domestication would gradually result. Similarly the milk of the cow, first of all offered to the goddess, then reserved for the priests and kings, would finally become the food of common mortals, at least among some peoples. Thus the domestication of the bovine race would be the work of the first sedentary cultivators, those husbandmen of the hoe whom we still meet with to-day in Asia, Africa, and South America.

*

* *

[1] De Morgan, **CLXXV**, p. 168.
[2] A. J. Reinach, in **XVI**, 1910, p. 75.
[3] Cuénot, **LII**, p. 61.
[4] Hahn, **CXIII**.

The domestic animals of most economic importance are those of the herbivorous group, and their favourite habitat must have been the steppe. Under a dry climate, we are told that every plain naturally becomes a steppe, whether high or low, provided it is exposed to dry winds: the plateaux of Central Asia, Persia, Arabia, the Sudan, the Sahara, South Africa, Australia, the llanos and pampas of South America exemplify the fact: grazing grounds, the grass of which is, however, quickly exhausted by voracious ruminants. So long then as men did not create artificial meadows or establish reserves of forage; they were bound to move their flocks, and themselves with them, in search of provender. Nomadism is thus the natural result of cattle-raising; it is allied to it and is its inseparable companion. Such is the idea of Miss Semple [1] especially.

Things do not really work out so simply. America, Miss Semple's own country, bears eloquent testimony to this. Pastoral nomadism has never existed there, although all the requisite conditions are realized there just as in Eurasia. In North America there were steppes and animals suitable for domestication, bisons in default of goats and wild sheep, which are almost entirely lacking.[2] In South America, where these species are equally lacking, there are vicuñas, guanacos, alpacas and llamas. And yet there was no pastoral life in the New World. If it is the product of migrations and movements of Asiatic peoples, the excess elements which succeeded in crossing over did not take with them the tradition of pastoral nomadism. The American steppe has remained empty of domesticated flocks, whilst agoutis, spotted deer, civet-cats, pumas and jaguars make it their home.[3] It was only much later, very much later, after the introduction of cattle and horses from Europe by the Spaniards, that nomadism made its appearance. Then the llanos and the pampas became the domain of stock-breeders, who lived in tents like the Kirghiz or the Tartars, subsisted almost entirely on meat after the manner of the Huns, and were characterized by the possession of new implements devised for the capture of horses —the lasso in particular.

[1] Semple, **XC**, Chap. XIV.
[2] Cuénot, **LII**, pp. 61–2.
[3] Humboldt, **LXXII**[a], Vol. I, pp. 17–20.

We must not then look on a pastoral and nomadic life as a necessary step in the history of humanity. Special conditions, such as the absence of certain animals, may so influence the history of a people that it does not pass through the phase of pastoral nomadism. But even this statement of the case has a taint of determinism. If from cultivation by the hoe, the "Hăckbau" of the Germans, there arose by progressive differentiation, as from a common mother, not only horticulturists of the Chinese or Peruvian pattern, but cultivators using the plough, and shepherds moving about with their flocks, something must be accounted to the free will, traditions and customs of the different groups of men, at least as much as to natural conditions.

Let us repeat again, although the question was no doubt settled long ago: we must get rid absolutely of the old and persistent idea that pastoral nomadism is a way of life inferior to those based on a sedentary existence. Ratzel, in the first edition of his *Anthropogeographie*, has already noted the fact that "a fairly high degree of civilization may co-exist with the nomad life—and some primitive peoples, on the other hand, are sedentary".[1] The history of North Africa affords us, amongst so many other means of refuting a very old error, one which is admirably to the point. Nomadism was held in great honour there at the epoch of the Berber domination.[2] During the Roman period it lost ground, to revive again after the Arab conquest. The temptation is strong to argue from this that nomadism means retrogression. But it would have to be proved both that the nomads do not make as good use of the resources of their environment as the settlers and that the tent, which is often costly and luxurious, is less comfortable and less dignified than the humblest hut;[3] and that, in a general way, the wretched settler of the French oasis is much superior to the rich nomad in material and moral development.

But we know all about it now: the Ksourians of the oases were formerly nomads.[4] Having lost their flocks and been

[1] Ratzel, **LXXXIII**, 1st ed. (1882), Vol. I, p. 447.
[2] Bernard and Lacroix, **CXLVII**, p. 153; cf. also Bernard, **CLXXVII**, p. 142.
[3] Above, p. 246.
[4] Bernard and Lacroix, **CXLVII**, p. 152; cf. Vidal de la Blache, in **XI**, 1910, p. 75.

reduced to an inferior condition, they became settlers and producers of wheat and dates; isolated behind their enclosures, without animals to carry their produce, and unable to leave their narrow prison of irrigated verdure and shade, they had fallen into a most miserable and pitiable condition. At the present day, freed and protected by the peaceful rule of France, and increasing little by little in wealth, they are gradually returning to their old manner of life, and, masters of the means of communication, they are trying to regain their old privileged position of nomads—an evident proof, if there ever was one, that pastoral nomadism may and often does mean an advance upon a passive and humble sedentary life.

II

The Characteristics of the Pastoral Way of Life

Let us now try to fix precisely the most characteristic features of the manner of life of pastoral nomads, and the various influences which this way of life has on the general civilization of the peoples who have adopted it.

All pastoral people look for their livelihood to cattle-raising. Their flocks and herds form the chief riches of them all. Their great problem is to keep them in good condition. The tundra supplies lichen for the raisers of reindeer, the grassy steppe offers favourable conditions to the rearers of sheep or cattle, for raising stock. But these conditions imply nomadism, since the animals soon exhaust the pasturages and must be moved to fresh grazing grounds.

Such is the usual way of stating the primordial facts from which all the others follow; and it is not incorrect. But nevertheless it is undoubtedly rather too general and of an exaggerated simplicity. It ignores too much the differences in culture, and even in ideas, which make the contrast between the different nomad tribes.

Hahn felt this when, in a study published in 1913, he drew a comparison between the pastoral peoples of Asia and Africa.[1] He contrasts the life of the latter, based essentially on the rearing of cattle, with that of the former, who own those powerful

[1] "Die Hirtenvölker in Asien und Afrika" (*Geogr. Zeitschrift*, XIX, 1913).

means of transport and locomotion the ass, the horse, and the camel. The possession of these animals accounts, according to him, for the brilliant historical expansion of the Asiatic shepherds ; by the aid of these they were able to extend their migrations and to develop the warlike qualities which they displayed in their renowned conquests. The African shepherds, on the contrary, being less mobile on account of their lack of transport animals for great distances, looked on their flocks in a miserly spirit, as treasures to be carefully guarded. They added to their pastoral activities a rudimentary agriculture—though they did not rise to the use of the plough—which rendered their type less pure and distinctive than that of the Asiatic shepherds.

There are weaknesses, no doubt, in this parallel of Hahn's—gaps and prejudices. The picture which the author draws of the African shepherds in no way depicts the Moor or the Tuareg, if it is not quite so unlike the Kaffir and the Hottentot. There would be much to say, besides, as to the value which the author of the *Haustiere* places on the ass, an animal of feeble powers, only useful for short-distance transport ; and we must not under-estimate the long-distance powers of oxen, of which the African herds chiefly consisted. These animals, though small, are swift. Chevalier tells us[1] that amongst the Kredas of the Chad region the transport animal, the entire ox, will do a trek of 20 to 25 miles a day, carrying a load of 120 to 130 lb. besides its driver, and the stages are perhaps longer if it journeys by night. It is none the less true, however, that Hahn's article has the merit of drawing attention to the very varied ideas which the shepherds of different countries and ages may have of their herds and of their value.

"The wealth of the shepherd is in his flock," is an aphorism continually repeated. But "wealth" is not a simple idea, nor is "flock". There are a hundred ways of considering wealth, and also of estimating the economic value of flocks. The raising of cattle and sheep, with us, to-day, is a careful, almost industrial, utilization of all the products of domestic animals : meat, skin, milk, wool, hair, horns, bones, everything is considered ; everything is utilized and sold. With

[1] Chevalier, **CLXXVIII,** p. 387 ff.

primitive man, the flock is more often a reserve. This is the word which Meniaud uses continually in the sketch that he draws of the existence and way of life of the pastoral populations of the Nigerian Sudan.[1] He describes this cattle-rearing as very extensive, and as causing very considerable migrations. During the dry season the herds, sometimes consisting of several thousand head, are brought down to the banks of the rivers, streams, pools, and lakes; in the rainy season they return to the plateaux far from the streams and the sodden ground. In December the Moors come down from the Sahel towards the pools which lie in the circle of Nioro and the basin of the Colombine; in the same way, during the very dry season the Tuaregs keep their cattle on the banks of the Niger; after the rains of July and August they wander towards the north or sometimes to the south, then return to the river at the next dry season. Nature alone feeds the herds, according to season; quite fat at the end of the winter, they grow thinner and thinner during the dry season. But the most characteristic feature of these Moors, Tuaregs, or Fulahs is that they never sell their growing animals; their cattle are not a realizable capital, but a reserve which they never touch unless compelled; they let the beasts grow old in the herds, which contain many old, lean cows, or old sheep whose wool is coming off in patches. This, by the way, and the obstinate preservation of all the females up to decrepitude, gradually brings about a notable diminution in the value of the stock.

This is all the more remarkable as their pastoral occupation does not necessarily save the nomads from famine.[2] Whilst a large part of the herd is dying of old age, they are striving to get food for themselves by other means, and take to hunting. Meniaud tells us that "it is safe to say that amongst the nomads of the Sudan, Tuaregs or Moors, all the men are hunters,[3] except the servants who guard the herds".[4] In particular the Moorish Kuntas and the Tuaregs, especially the Auelimmiden, hunt the giraffe and antelope mercilessly. They often sow a little millet (*Penicillaria*), as do the Kredas

[1] Meniaud, **CLXXXIII,** Chap. II, p. 16 ff.

[2] See also above, p. 163, Gautier's account of the late utilization of oxen for food in Madagascar.

[3] Meniaud, **CLXXXIII,** Vol. I, p. 185.

[4] Chevalier, **CLXXVIII,** p. 387 ff.

of the Chad region of whom Chevalier has given us a full account. Sometimes even, after sowing, they go off on their wanderings and return for the harvest. Still, the milk of their animals, which is their chief food, the produce of this meagre husbandry, and what millet and dates they can buy from the neighbouring settled peoples do not prevent them from having to seek on the veldt for really famine foods—grass seeds, which they pound into semolina, acacia gum, wild fruits, water-lily roots, and orobanche heads.

The testimony of Chevalier confirms that of Chudeau,[1] who also tells how the nomads, in the same region of the Sudanese Sahara, are driven to eat the poorest sort of food and to consume bitter flour made from dried orobanche, grass-seed, and, in case of extreme necessity, grain taken from anthills, which are systematically robbed.

Now let us transport ourselves far away into quite another world—that Asiatic world which Hahn contrasts complacently with the African one. We have a description by Cahun of the Turk of bygone times, when he was a nomad in Asia, reluctantly diminishing his herd by the slaughter of a fat colt or a sheep for feast days and gorging himself on the flesh. At other times he ate no meat except that of the decrepit or dead animals.[2] He too did not live on his herds but by their produce only.

We see then how weak mere formulæ are and why we must agree as to the true meaning of the words before we speak of the wealth which the cattle of the nomad represent to him.

*

* *

With these reservations let us continue our study of the manner of life led by pastoral nomads, making use of some classic descriptions.

It used to be the fashion, after having shown the prime importance of herds to pastoral populations, to refer to the relatively unsettled nature of their dwellings. Their way of life, it was said, prevented them from having a fixed and stable weatherproof dwelling. Then a picture was rapidly sketched,

[1] Chudeau, **CLXXXI**[b], Vol. II, p. 179.
[2] Cahun, **CLXXXVI**, p. 50.

including examples provided by the nomads of all times and all countries. If nomads pure and simple were under consideration, their home was the tent; the numerous studies which have been devoted to that mobile and rudimentary kind of house show it to be more or less the same everywhere, apart from some slight differences in detail of the kind that Huc described when he compared the hexagonal tent of Eastern Thibetans with the *iourte* of the Kirghiz.[1] The wagon is an advance upon the tent, in that it implies an already relatively complex industry, but it allows less mobility; it corresponds to the stage of nomadism represented by the Germanic invasions of the first century B.C., the migrations of the Middle Ages, and the trekking of the Boers in the Transvaal and the Orange River Free State in the nineteenth century, at the slow pace of yoked oxen. When nomadism becomes less, the dwelling takes on a hybrid character. Over a permanent substructure the men place a covering of branches or any chance material; frail as it is, it is enough to shelter its inhabitants during their sojourn: such were the huts of the Si-Fou,[2] and in our own day the *gourbi* of Africa Minor.[3] When at last nomadism disappeared, the completely permanent house appeared; but it is curious to note that it often bore traces of the old nomad life of its builders. It has been remarked that in Spain the Saracens, who were skilful workers in stone, carved it in the same way as their ancestors used to carve wood when they were nomads in Africa; in fact, the appearance of some of the marble slabs in Granada or Cordova recalls that of the carved doors of the pulpit in the great mosque at Qairwan; and elsewhere the plastic arts of these same Saracens have recourse almost exclusively to the motives used in carpet-weaving, the art of the nomad *par excellence*. For the whole furniture of a tent consists of mats, rugs, and a few wooden or metal vessels, rarely earthenware ones.[4] Such poverty is obligatory, since the baggage must always be capable of being folded quickly, and the goods to be carried must not be either very bulky or very fragile.

[1] Huc, **CLXXXIX,** Vol. II, p. 156.
[2] Huc, Vol. II, p. 157.
[3] For Morocco, e.g., cf. Bernard, **CLXXVII,** p. 149 ff.
[4] Ibid., p. 153.

All this is, on the whole, very true. But we must not attach to this outline, though faithful enough and of an instructive nature, the value of a complete picture. We must be ready to accept the facts which may and do run counter to such generalizations, which are necessarily only approximate. There are no rigid categories in life. Even if all nomads live in tents, not all the dwellers in tents throughout the world are nomads. This is a remark made by Augustin Bernard, who mentions the frequency in Algeria of cultivated land near which no fixed habitation exists [1]; and notes that in Morocco many of the inhabitants of the Tell, who are not nomads, make use of tents; some live alternately in tents and *gourbi*; as they hold lands in several places, they work them one after the other, and their movable dwelling is convenient for this temporary change of abode. He sums up: "We can no more separate absolutely the dwellers in tents from the dwellers in huts than we can separate shepherds from farmers; there are transition stages and gradations between them." [2] The same author tells us that the well-to-do natives sometimes build houses on good land in token that they have taken possession of it; but they do not stop moving about on that account. The substitution of the house for the tent is not, moreover, a sure sign of progress. The tent is relatively costly. Many abandon it for the *gourbi* simply as an economy and because they have lost their flocks and herds.

However, let us return to our subject—material life. It is a commonly admitted fact that the economic activities of nomad shepherds are very restricted. Not that all industries are banished from their communities. Those which they practise originate in the necessity for providing all the articles required for their mode of life without having recourse to problematical or non-existent purveyors of such articles. But this industry, naturally, cannot pass beyond the stage of a strictly family one. Pottery, when they have it (which is rarely, since hunters and shepherds seldom use it), wooden utensils, articles of leather and metal work, are manufactured by specialists; the number of these articles is small, for all encumbrances are forbidden; everything else, clothes, the material of which the tents are made, the carpet (that great

[1] Bernard and Lacroix, **CXLVII**, p. 161.
[2] Bernard, **CLXXVII**, p. 154.

and only luxury of the nomad), are the work of the family itself, chiefly of the women.

Whenever things are arranged otherwise it is certain that we are in the presence of a people who are settling down: this is the case in Tunis with the inhabitants of the region of Qairwan or El Wady. There is a great difference, however, which cannot escape the notice of the most careless observer, between native products intended for home consumption and those which are produced by organized industry for sale outside. Trade, owing to the scarcity of objects for barter, is naturally rudimentary. It consists almost entirely in the exchange of the products of stock-raising for vegetable foods and a few manufactured articles. Such, for example, is the trade of the Kirghiz; and such was the trade of the Jews, according to Biblical traditions, when they went to buy corn in Egypt. But the nomads have another sort of business, transport. Their movements make them the natural intermediaries between the peoples who live on the edge of the steppe lands bordering the desert and those of the oases. Thus, the Ishmaelites of old transported into Egypt spices, balm, and aromatic gums. The caravan routes and traffic centres, such as Timbuktu, Baghdad, Damascus, Samarkand, and Tashkent, have all been carefully studied. This kind of traffic by the nomads is often so necessary that under certain political regimes it is imposed on them. Forced labour on the routes (oulah) between China and Lhassa was the heaviest and almost the only burden laid on the nomads. The presence of pack-animals suited to the steppes (horses and more especially camels) facilitates this sort of commerce; but it exists even in parts where the porterage has to be done by men: Burton made careful observations amongst the Myamwesi, that curious people of porters.[1] It is well to notice that this occupation is not connected with pastoral nomadism only. All trade is, or rather has been for a long time, a sort of nomadism. In a large measure it has remained so up to modern times in the very heart of European societies. There was something of the mariner in every merchant of antiquity.

[1] Burton, **CLXXVII**[a], pp. 295–8, 302.

III

Institutions and Religion of Pastoral Nomads

Let us now attack some even more difficult problems. Are there any institutions which are specially characteristic of nomad peoples?

In theory it seems as if it would be to their interest to have large patriarchal families—and it is not wrong, as we know, to speak of the patriarchy of the shepherds as a well-established institution.

The domestication and care of animals are regarded everywhere, we are at once told, as essentially the task of men, and of men only—such important labours transferring to the man the authority and position which hoe-cultivation necessarily gave to women in the agricultural societies. Moreover, we can easily see the special advantages to nomad shepherds of a patriarchal family rule in which the children, the wife, and the servants are strictly subordinate to the father, the head of the family, thus assuring the supremacy of regulated toil over instinctive idleness; using the abilities of all the members of the family as compulsory economic helpers and taking full advantage of the strength of all for the necessary work of the family.[1] But it is permissible to think that, in the first place, many of those who talk about the patriarchal family do not know the exact value of the words they use; it is certain, moreover, that the patriarchal family system is at least as suitable for an agricultural system as for cattle-breeding, and that, in the next place, patriarchy is far from being the rule amongst the nomads. We give only one instance: the Tuaregs are all under a matriarchy; the womb, they say, "holds the child," that is to say, it belongs to its mother and is ignorant of its father.[2]

In fact, as regards family life the nomads are by no means all alike. We know that, among different peoples and in different times, their institutions have been very varied. Polygamy flourishes among the Arabs, as it did formerly among the Jews; but it does not exist among the Bedouins,

[1] On the economic value of the large patriarchal family, cf. Schmoller, *Principes d'économie politique*, transl. Platon, Vol. I, p. 28 ff.; Vol. II, p. 37 ff.

[2] Gautier, **CLXXXI**[a], p. 334.

amongst whom there is rather a tendency to polyandry and the infanticide of girls. Everything depends on the wealth of the nomads, on their present circumstances or past experiences. Some have large families and find it an advantage; others practise restriction, in one way or another, and are forced to it. We must never forget that "the desert" is not a simple geographical condition; it is a zoö-botanical complex which might almost be considered as the limiting domain of a particular manner of life.

Much and long investigation has been devoted both to the character which nomadism imparts to communities and to the political aspects of such a characteristic manner of life.

A nomad race is a warrior race: innumerable classic memories force the analogy on us. Is there a people who, with nomads for their neighbours, have not had to struggle to protect themselves against their raids? And what a wealth of precautions, always the same whatever the time or place! There is the wall that Sesostris built between Pelusium and Heliopolis; and the great wall of China; and that continuous entrenchment which the French at one time thought of making in Algeria; and that network of small forts, oppida and castella, which the Romans erected at irregular distances under a burning sky along the frontier of the Euphrates against the perpetually wandering Semites and Saracens or the Parthians with their long lances barked with iron and leather; there are, lastly, those fixed bounds of the Empire, the Rhine and the Danube, with their continuous wall and fosse. In our days we have the mobile wall of fast expeditionary columns which can go anywhere, and which is so difficult to locate, or the aeroplanes of the aerial police; the object to be attained is always the same, and the nomad danger is still there.

Whence does it arise? There are a score of reasons to account for it. Considering the climatic irregularities, which compel the nomads to leave their usual territory suddenly and bring them into collision with the peoples whom they meet with on their way, the necessity of obtaining the supplies which have unexpectedly failed them and which they must obtain from those who have them, the danger of being attacked or threatened by neighbours who have turned robbers—we can very well understand why the nomads have been led to form a military force and to use it.

Let us, however, be quite clear about their warlike activities. It must be said that, although a robber, the nomad does not behave like a beast unchained; he must always treat his victims in such a way as not to exhaust one of his sources of livelihood. Except in extreme cases where they feel or believe themselves menaced, the Tuaregs do not destroy caravans. They content themselves with escorting them and pillaging them on the road. With regard to the settled peoples, their attitude is a double one; on the one hand, they extort from them a large part of their harvests; on the other they protect the oases which supply them from the attacks of other nomads.

Their life from infancy, like that of all similar peoples, is really a military one. The tribe is always organized, like an army: the march of the caravan and the complicated operations of loading and unloading the animals must be effected with the greatest possible order and rapidity: if not, what a fine opportunity it would present for an ambuscade by a watchful enemy!

Their way of life thus creates, little by little, a special mentality. A warlike spirit, a sense of discipline, the supreme authority of the tribal chief—such are the essential characteristics of nomad societies; and they are sufficient to give to them a considerable relative strength and the best possible power of action against settled peoples. And so when they are not compelled by the insufficiency of natural resources to divide themselves into minute communities—as is the case in the region of Lob Nor, or in the Kirghiz country—the nomads succeed easily enough in establishing great empires. That of the Arabs and that of the Fulahs are good and typical examples—but these empires are ephemeral.

Nothing new is ever attempted. The nomad conquerors keep themselves distinct from the conquered; at the most, they assimilate a few of the characteristics and typical elements of the civilization of the latter: but they make no attempt to improve on it. The only well-known example of improvement introduced by a people of nomad origin into a conquered land is furnished by the Arab agriculture in Spain. Usually the victorious nomad camps in the midst of the conquered people, but he founds nothing solid; he is at the mercy of historic accidents which ruin his ephemeral domination: the successive empires founded and destroyed in the Asiatic steppes, and the vicissitudes of the Sudanese kingdoms are good examples of this process. The study of these vicissitudes justifies us in insisting on the important part played by the nomads in history and in regarding the belt of steppes, with their specially active record, as the "historic zones" *par excellence.*

Observe that a physiological fact helps to account for the frequency and extent of the mutations which befell the nomad empires. Being accustomed to live in small communities, those who were temporarily united to form these realms generally retained a very marked spirit of independence. As soon as a group larger than the tribal group was formed, authority rested on persuasion. That of Mahomet, as of all other chiefs, who, at a certain crisis, have assumed the command of considerable ethnic groups, was based on personal prestige and force, and on the power of eloquence, all of which are essentially personal and transitory factors.

Thus it is that, amongst the shepherds, societies are made and unmade, the quarrels and conflicts of the tribes easily assuming a vehemence and bitterness unknown elsewhere. Enmity and mistrust are handed down from generation to generation and prevent the establishment of any stable policy.

* * *

Does their manner of life, however, exert any real influence over the moral ideas and intellectual development of the nomads? Miss Semple, who has made a lengthy study of the virtues and vices of the "children of the desert and of the steppe", points out how their courage and hardihood are linked with a warlike disposition which itself results from their mode of life. Her sketch of ethnic psychology is worth just as much as all sketches of that kind, such as we have already often noticed—and criticized. But to keep to concrete and easily proven facts, it is certain that the nomadic way of life does not tend to the creation of libraries, and prevents the record of acquired knowledge. Chudeau, in his report on the mission to the Sahara,[1] tells us of a marabout of the Adrar who possessed a library celebrated throughout the Sahara, because it represented "three or four camel-loads"—evidently a great luxury and rarity. It is most probable that their unstable mode of life entails, almost of necessity, an extreme simplification of intellectual knowledge. Oral tradition, which for a long time was the only kind existing among the nomads, is crystallized into a few books, which are at once encyclopædias, legal codes, medical treatises, philosophical and theological works, and poems. The Bible and the Koran are examples. Still, we must not exaggerate: the tendency to compile similar encyclopædias is strong at all times when the conditions of intellectual work are unsettled; we have only to remember the vogue in the Middle Ages for the *Sommes* and the *Miroirs du Monde*; and it would be difficult to find out whether this need was born of material conditions only, or if it did not in some measure depend also on special spiritual conditions, such as the very strong hold of some creed or religion on the mind.

However that may be, the intellectual development of nomads is usually rather limited, and their attitude towards such libraries as they come across is fairly well known. In addition, they are by choice fanatics and men of a single book. All this has been said repeatedly, and no doubt it is true to a certain extent. Still, we must guard against all exaggeration. When people formulate such statements, they always have Islam or the Koran in their minds. A map of the expansion of Islam over the world corresponds almost exactly with a map of the steppes and deserts of Eurasia and Africa, which are especially fitted for nomad life. But all those who know much of the affairs of Islam warn the uninitiated to exercise a prudent reserve in their judgment. Some of them point out to us a domain in the Sahara annexed to Islam recently and incompletely or, to speak more exactly, superficially.

It was only in the sixteenth century that the influence of the Moslems expelled from Spain by the Christians brought about the real triumph of their religion in that Africa Minor

[1] Chudeau, **CLXXXI**[b], Vol. II, p. 52.

where it had been introduced in the eighth century.[1] And yet the triumph has been more apparent than real, since the Tuaregs, Berbers particularly unsympathetic to Arab influences, are a very degraded order of Mussulmans without mosque or clergy who neither pray nor fast : their reputation for absolute impiety is a by-word amongst their neighbours and enemies the Moors.

Let us glance now at the other end of the Islamic world, at the heart of that Asia where Cahun depicts for us in their historical life the Turks of old, and the Mongols, and the Manchus. Was this Islam ? In appearance, yes. In reality, no. In temperament and ideas they were much more inclined to Buddhism. To tell the truth, they allowed themselves to be converted to various religions " very tamely, without enthusiasm, and without any great repugnance ".[2] They became fire-worshippers, Manicheans, Nestorian Christians, or Mussulmans, in a somewhat haphazard way, not understanding much about the matter, and without ardour or any taste for theology; though conducting themselves as loyal and conscientious followers of the creeds they had been made to adopt. Still they kept, at heart, the remembrance of the more ancient original religions whose undercurrent is still felt in the legends, poems, and popular superstitions of the Kirghiz, the Tartars of Siberia, and other Mohammedanized peoples,[3] in spite of all the efforts of Mussulman strictness: with the result that the greatest religious wars of the Middle Ages were waged against Europe by nations who had no quarrel with Christianity and who had even very slight regard for the religion whose very essence they were supposed by the Western peoples to incarnate.[4] A singular paradox—but a warning also that we must distrust appearances and a certain map-making schematism which is a pre-eminent source of error.

There remain the Arabs properly so called. And it is a commonplace to extol their creative imagination, and equally to cite the purity and dryness of the desert air, and the monotony and uniformity of the steppes and sterile solitudes

[1] Gautier, **CLXXXI**, Vol. I, p. 262 ff.; cf. Bernard, **CLXXVII**, Chap. III, p. 85 ff., p. 108 ff., p. 196 ff.
[2] Cahun, **CLXXXVI**, p. 66.
[3] Ibid., p. 68.
[4] Ibid., p. 119.

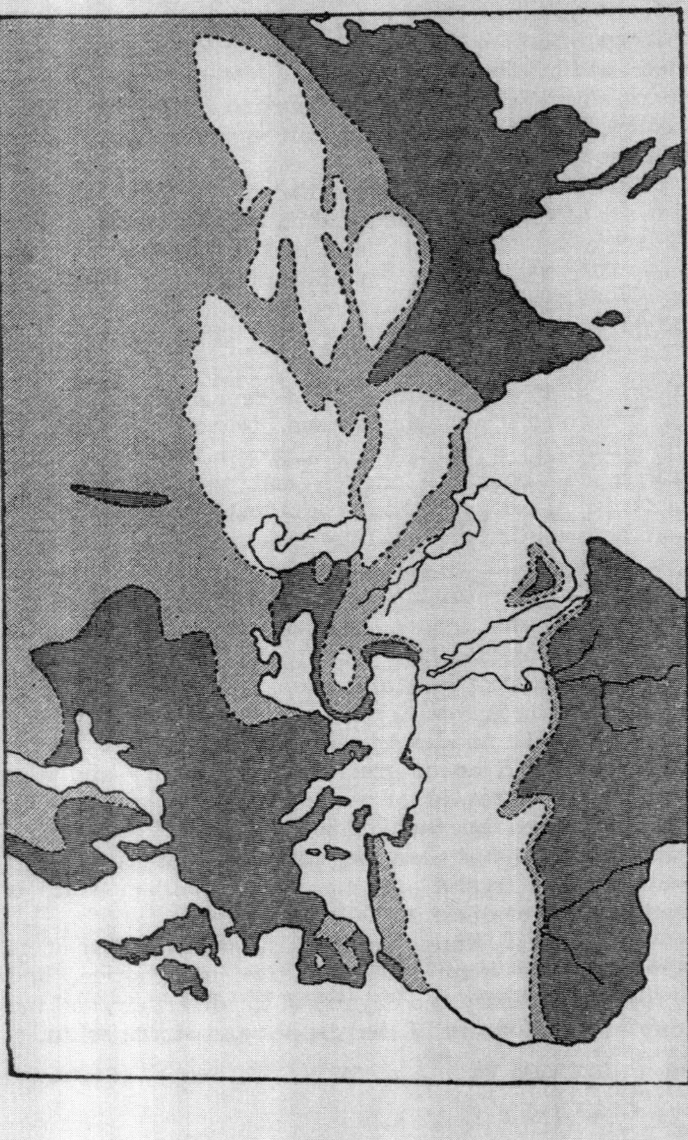

FIG. 7.—REGIONS OF THE NOMADS: DESERTS AND STEPPES OF ASIA AND OF AFRICA.

Dark-grey areas: more than 500 mm. of rain per annum; *Light-grey areas:* between 250 and 500 mm. of rain per annum; *White areas:* less than 250 mm. of rain per annum.

of Arabia, in order to explain how they have given birth to Islam. That is as it may be; but it would be an advantage to know whether there is as much imagination in the Koran as many people suppose, and if, moreover, Islam is an original creation or one built up of borrowed materials. Was not the work of the Arabs limited to taking simple ideas from the peoples with whom they came into contact, which they afterwards expanded? No doubt, the constituent and fundamental ideas of Jewish monotheism were the most likely of all to appeal to a man like Mahomet, and he seized upon them. But what had the Arabian landscape and the nomadic way of life to do with it?

IV

The Oscillations of Nomadism

To-day it is a fact—if not a mark of progress—that nomadism is declining. Little by little the tendency to sedentariness is increasing in all countries, and for various reasons but especially owing to the increasing enterprise of the industrial civilization of Western Europe and America, which, through the medium of their colonies, affects the whole world. In many countries pastoral nomadism has given place, and is giving place more and more, to what Bernard and Lacroix have very justly declared to be the absolute negation of true pastoral nomadism: the moving of the animals under the care of trained shepherds, who go with them alone, whilst the owners of the flocks no longer accompany them.[1]

Now this is a most interesting fact for us to bear in mind, and it is fitting that we should repeat it now at the end of our sketch of the pastoral nomad type of life for it proves decisively that we must not look for the "cause" of this type of life in particular geographical conditions—in the "climate" which brings about "the steppe". What really alters and restricts nomadism is a modification not in the natural but in the human factors of existence; it is the substitution in regions where war, insecurity and economic difficulties formerly prevailed of a state of relative peace or,

[1] CXLVIII, p. 164.

we might say, of "police". This is a most important factor, the influence of which is clearly illustrated in the work of Bernard and Lacroix, which we have already often quoted, for it is due to the pacifying action of France, carried out at so little relative expense and by the aid of psychological and moral agencies wonderfully described by Gautier,[1] that nomadism in Africa Minor has been gradually diminished, in so far, these authors tell us, as it was due to insecurity. But to what else could it be due? To the general economic condition of the country? No doubt. It is plain that the activities of the nomads must be affected by the greater ease with which they can obtain in a stabilized Sahara their various necessities of life as well as a wider and an easier outlet for their own special products. And now, leaving the Sahara, we will return to the evidence of Woeikof concerning Turkestan, and his very credible and ingenious explanation of the causes which render the nomads of the central plateaux of Asia less mobile and less formidable than of old—less fitted to band themselves into immense hordes of devastating conquerors. We have mentioned these causes before: they are the gradual absorption of the Mongols into the sphere of attraction of the sedentary Chinese, and the opening of new outlets for disposing of their animals, not only in China but in Siberia, which is rapidly increasing in population.[2]

The progress of pacification, the general stabilization of human societies under the influence of the great industrial states, whose wants they must supply—not that these states are the inveterate opponents of war, as they have only too lately shown, but because it is essential to them that nothing should stand in the way of their increasing exploitation of a society they regard as inferior to their own—the resulting development of an economic system which is attractive and convenient for nomads as well as for sedentary peoples, and from whose irresistible attractions very few peoples escape altogether at the present day; these all form a chain of connected facts which leave little room for geographical factors properly so called. But can anyone completely gauge the gradual, universal, and subtle power of conquering and expanding their industrial civilization possessed by the

[1] Gautier, **CLXXXI.** [2] Woeikof, **CXCVIII**, p. 113.

great modern states? The history of the consequences which the war of 1914–18 has entailed on the so-called inferior societies, and the tale of the difficulties in which it has involved those societies, nearly all of which are to-day dependent in some way on Europe or on Europeanized America, would be a lesson and a revelation. Let us remember that at the present time in Micronesia the natives of the Western Carolines at Yap and Palau use imported matches,[1] and that in 1917, when the Danish ships no longer brought them the tobacco, matches, wire, firearms, knives, and the steel-spring traps which were essential to their mode of living, the Esquimaux of Smith's Sound experienced a terrible crisis and had to resort for a living, as best they could, to their ancient tools and their old bone, ivory, or flint weapons.[2] How many facts must there be of this sort, which it would be useful to collect and which would show us what a hold our industrial economy has taken to-day on the whole world! But why restrict ourselves to industrial economy? Agricultural economy is equally far-reaching.

Among the causes which explain the diminution of nomadism, the progress of agriculture and its invasion of the open steppes as the result of an increasing population, or simply of a higher economic value, undoubtedly play an important part. Quite recently, in 1917, the Lappland reindeer-breeders met together and held a congress[3] to protest against the incessant advance of colonization, which was continually reducing their rights of pasturage. In hot countries the progress of dry-farming has a similar effect, and tends in certain districts to a kind of revolution of "enclosures" which are particularly obnoxious to the shepherds. Man's work, man's calculation, man's movement, the perpetual ebb and flow of humanity; these are always the prime influences, not the soil or the climate. All this is evident; and yet some of those who recognize it and are the first to acknowledge it seem to give the lie to their own judgment, being apparently recaptured over and over again by the force of the old routine, the traditional commonplaces, and the inherited way of thinking. Just now we recalled the

[1] **XVI**, Vol. XXIX, 1918–19, p. 594.
[2] Ibid., p. 190.
[3] **XVI**, Vol. XXVIII, 1917, p. 601.

conclusion of Bernard and Lacroix in their work on the evolution of nomadism; they were right in considering the "French peace" to be a matter of supreme importance in the world of the Sahara. But in a later book on Morocco, by the former of these writers, we read that "North Africa is a land of mountains, where families, even weak ones, can settle and defend themselves—and of steppes, over which the most powerful tribes are forced to roam from pasturage to pasturage".[1] *Forced!* There is an eternal power in old ideas clothed in deceptive formulæ!

*
* *

It is actually true that they are "forced" so long as the economic conditions are not changed. They obey the law of the steppe, by which they are ruled. But who subjected them to that law, if not man himself? Once for all we should cease to regard or even to appear to regard nomadism and its supposed opposite, sedentariness, as two variable conditions. Nomadism is not a life sentence, as Gautier said in his picturesque manner, when speaking of the communities of the Sahara. Bernard, again, confirms the testimony of Gautier and comments upon it in his own manner. "It must be noted," he writes,[2] "that the natives pass with relative ease from the nomad life to the sedentary, and inversely." The history of the tribes is full of such changes, both recent and temporary: for although it may appear that once the natives are settled they will remain so for ever, it is only an appearance. It is certain that if they had no animals they would be unable to revert to the nomad life; but they are not so stable as is thought. If their trees are destroyed, or if other natives seize them, there is no longer anything to attach them to the soil, and nothing to prevent them from becoming wanderers, as they were before. In Turkish the word for wanderers is Kirghiz. The name of "Kirghiz-Kazak", Cahun tells us,[3] is made up of two words, the first meaning wanderer, and the second, when separated

[1] Bernard, **CLXXVII**, p. 141; cf. above, pp. 236–7, Cuijic's equally inconsistent declarations.
[2] **CLXXVII**, p. 146.
[3] Cahun, **CLXXXVI**, p. 48.

from the name of the tribe, meaning flock: an animal which has left the herd, or a man who has fled from his tribe, is called a "Kazak", which we pronounce "Cossack". Here then we are transported from the Sahara to the steppes of Central Asia, and there we find the same spectacle almost exactly: a perpetual "General Post" of conditions—tribes living by turns as well-to-do cattle-raisers, often possessing arable lands and good walled towns; then as shepherds wandering over the steppes, or living the hard, wild life of outlaws, of "Kazaks", prowling over the desert. A perpetual succession of violent contrasts, of ups and downs; a kind of hot and cold douche of fate: Cahun was not indisposed to attribute the notable contrasts in the character of the Turk, the most adventurous and at the same time the most apathetic of mankind, to these alternate freaks of fortune.[1] This, however, is a question we must not pursue. It follows then that people do not live in "the wilds", when they can live elsewhere, even if they are Kirghiz and if they have, in fact, a choice of the steppes which permits them to realize all that is best of steppe life.

It follows also that once the nomad has been in touch with the settler he cannot do without him. It is possible that there may have been nomads who with their flocks lived entirely to themselves—but such have never been seen in historic times. The Bedouins, Mongols, Kirghiz of to-day, and the Turks of old, lived on cereals.[2] They obtained grain from the settled peoples, giving them in return the produce of their herds. And when they were able to establish themselves in a fertile land they gladly became "taroutchi" husbandmen. But if the settler withdrew his market, if a pestilence destroyed the herds which were given the expressive name of "mal" (capital), if some powerful neighbour fell on the tribe, put its men to the sword and carried off the animals, the survivors still had to live. So the weaker party emigrated, as Kirghiz, into the steppe, and took to the desert as adventurers, as Kazaks; when they became again the stronger party, or considered themselves to be so, they took their revenge: for we must realize the tumult of passions which "the sight of the blue mountains, the fertile plains, and

[1] Ibid., p. 49. [2] Ibid., p. 50.

the silver streams of running water "[1] would awaken in the soul of the armed and mounted nomad—of the Turk surveying the immensity of China from the extreme edge of the plateau —in order to understand that nomadism is not, and cannot be, in Asia, any more than in Africa, a perpetual condition, a sort of divine curse weighing hopelessly on a reprobate race.

*

* *

This is the danger of those " pictures " which are constructed, in the classic manner, of portions borrowed from various models. They have their use—or more correctly, perhaps, their convenience. But we must never allow ourselves to be deceived by them, nor take their synthetized epitomes for even a likeness of the reality. That would be to deprive geography of all life, and make of it a kind of dry repetition for schoolroom use.

Above all, we must never forget what we said at the beginning of our study : economic types are not social types. We find ourselves faced in the Sahara, in two quite separate regions, with Tuaregs on the one hand, and on the other with Arab nomads, the Moors. The geographical conditions are common to both. The same climate affects both equally. The soil on which they both have to live is similar. And yet we find between them the greatest differences in language, in culture, in manners, in customs and in equipment. Undying hatred separates them. But history tells us that this deep ditch was dug only yesterday : on either side of it is the same Berber race,[2] but whereas one group has been wholeheartedly converted to Islam, the other still retains a large pre-Islamic inheritance. This example, such as Gautier alleges it to exist, is warranted to " give furiously to think " to those who are tempted to let themselves be deceived by the old illusion.

V

Hoe-Culture, and the precarious Nature of a Sedentary Existence

" Faced with nomadism, European imagination runs riot. It has been regarded sometimes as a phase of human develop-

[1] Ibid., p. 51. [2] Gautier, **CLXXXI**^{b}, Vol. I, p. 335.

ment, sometimes as a matter of race . . . It seems to me that in the Sahara at least the nomads are a financial aristocracy."[1] In this airily paradoxical remark we have no difficulty in recognizing the voice of Gautier. It is valuable for its own sake and for the light it sheds on the Sahara. But it draws attention also to the part played by economic considerations—the desire to get rich—in the evolution of manners of living, and especially in the transition from the nomadic to the sedentary state.

But there is one question preliminary to the consideration of the change from nomadism to settlement—when a people is settled, has there always been a previous state of nomadism? At one time this view was accepted: to-day it is out of favour. And that on the facts of the case. There have always been and are still a considerable number of peoples who devote themselves to a certain extensive but rudimentary agriculture, whose most striking feature is a total ignorance of the use of domestic animals—notably of oxen. This is the agriculture which the Germans call "Hackbau" or hoe-culture, because the implement used is not the plough, but a bent tool with a short hatchet-like handle, which obliges all who use it to bend low over their work. It was originally made from deer horn,[2] or from the piece of a tree, hooked-shaped, left on the branch where it is taken from the trunk, and hardened by fire; at a later date it was armed with metal, and lastly made in two parts—an "iron" and a wooden handle. This is the tool of the Negroes of the Sudan, or rather of the Negro women, since agricultural work is almost entirely done by the women[3]; the man reserves himself for harder tasks, or at least those which require strength and skill, such as the clearing of the forest and the felling of the great trees, among the fallen branches of which the manioc cuttings will be planted by the women. The hoe is such an important tool that the iron head serves not only as a regular article of barter in the country but actually as money, when it is not used agriculturally but circulates from hand to hand until it gets lost or quite worn out.[4]

[1] Gautier, **CLXXXI**, p. 167.
[2] Claerhout, on Agricultural tools of Neolithic Man (*Ann. Soc. roy. archéol. Bruxelles*, Vol. XXVI, 1912).
[3] Cureau, **CLXXIX**, p. 265.
[4] Ibid., pp. 300–1, and Plate XIV.

The soil is not turned to any depth. The Negro merely scratches its surface.[1] He traces shallow furrows, or piles up the earth in little ridges, on the top of which he sows.[2] But, having no animals to assist him, neither has he dung-heaps nor any manure at his disposal. His poor farming exhausts the soil by over-use.[3] Thus, to compensate in some sort of way for the want of manure, he resorts to the crude method of burning the bush from the end of October to the end of December.[4] This accounts also for his frequent changes of abode: after a few harvests, alternated as best he can, he has to seek new ground. He burns or cuts down the large trees according to the circumstances.[5] He sows any kind of seed without selection or preparation, and without that choice which really constitutes agriculture, that choice which Isis made when she singled out wheat and barley which were growing " together with the other plants ". Then when he has harvested he moves elsewhere. Sometimes a whole village will move within a short radius, following the mobile plantations.

There are none of the better kind of cereals. Millet is the characteristic plant of this sort of cultivation, whose methods are strangely alike in all the continents. The Aztecs of Mexico knew and practised no other; they, too, had only an implement of bent wood [6] with a copper head permitting them to trace furrows, a hardwood spade for shovelling the soil, and a copper reaping-hook to lop off the branches of trees (the Central African Negro has also a sort of cutlass for the same purpose).[7] They also practised burning, in the absence of animal manure, and they worked doubled up close to the soil, which they carefully cleaned, broke up and collected, like the Negro, in little ridges: for soil was a precious substance, not to be buried under sand or lost. Sometimes it was carefully collected and heaped up on wooden or reed hurdles which served to construct those floating gardens or " chinampa " whose secret was known to the Chinese—and to Europeans.

[1] Decorse, **CLXXX**, p. 472.
[2] Bruel, *L'Afrique équatoriale*, p. 243.
[3] Meniaud, **CLXXXIII**, Vol. I, p. 374; Bruel, p. 130.
[4] Chevalier, **CLXXVIII**, p. 62; Bruel, p. 130; cf. Hahn, *Die Brandwirtschaft in der Bodenkultur.*
[5] Cureau, **CLXXIX**, p. 265.
[6] Capitan and Lorin, **CCII.**
[7] Cureau, **CLXXIX**, p. 280.

In the case of all these populations, there can be no possible question of a " passage from pastoral nomadism to sedentary cultivation ", because for one thing they had no cattle, they knew nothing of them and did not seek their help, an impossible state of ignorance for a shepherd people turned husbandmen, and for another, their sedentary state is relative. It is by no means firmly rooted to the soil, and, what is still more important, it is not at all firmly rooted in their spirit. We referred further back to those Central African villages which can be readily moved about within a short radius, following cultivation or clearings. The economic causes which are usually alleged—the rapid exhaustion of the soil and the necessity for clearing fresh ground—would not account entirely for these migrations. We must remember that the village, as we rather pompously call it, of the sedentary people in these regions in no way resembles our European villages, those permanent centres of general interests and true historico-geographical individualities, which have their own life independent to a certain extent even of the lives of their inhabitants.

The Negro village is an individual creation.[1] The man who founds it separates himself from the original stock of his family in order to create for his own family of wives, children and slaves a new shelter which will last his lifetime, but not longer, for when the chief dies the village generally disappears ; it is abandoned and reconstructed some distance away.[2] This is not only because, when the chief has gone, the thread is broken and its beads scattered, but because the idea that death is the result of witchcraft, and that the only escape from it consists in flight, is frequent and normal amongst the Negroes.[3] We have, besides, very little insight into the recesses of these primitive minds, so different from our own ; and we must always remember the extreme impressionability of savages and semi-savages, especially of those whose homes are in the woods ; such as, for instance, the denizens of the Moï jungle of whom Maître, in his strange book,[4] gives us many typical examples. He shows us these poor people, with ideas so often incomprehensible to our minds, terrified by the fear of the possible consequences of some wild and inexplicable deed or some insane murder committed without

[1] Cureau, **CLXXIX**, 214.
[2] Ibid., 217.
[3] Bruel, *L'Afrique équatoriale*, 210.
[4] Maître, **CXCII**ᵃ.

any apparent cause, fleeing suddenly in a panic, taking to the jungle and abandoning their wretched huts and their mean villages, won with hard toil from the forest. There are physical and economic factors, but there are moral factors also. There is a *moral precariousness* about the sedentary life in its early stages, clearly distinct from the physical one, but undoubtedly involving equally important geographical consequences.

VI

The Transitional Types

In reality human societies are never simple. The pure types, or those supposed to be pure, are very exceptional; transitional types are the general rule. There are shepherds more than half sedentary, whose herds only are nomads, and who live in special communities generally united to a village of cultivators like the Fulahs and the Tuculors of the Niger,[1] contenting themselves with getting into the saddle from time to time and visiting, for eight or ten days, the herds which they have entrusted to hirelings; similarly, there are cultivators who live a half-nomad life, such as the peasants of the plain of Hungary, the Alfold,[2] in the very heart of old Europe. During the summer they go to live for months on their domain, far from the permanent houses of their villages, contenting themselves with uncomfortable casual shelters, which they leave when winter comes.

In the same way, there are shepherds who are half agriculturists, including those who sow during the spring in suitable places, go away, and return in the autumn to harvest the produce, and those semi-nomads of the Iranian plateaux described by Richtofen, who spend the winter in fixed dwellings, sow in the spring, then go up to the mountains where they pass the summer and come down again into the plain for the harvest. There are Kirghiz whose diverse conditions Richtofen[3] has also carefully analysed, populations who all live, as he notes, in the districts bordering the mountains or cut up by hilly ground. It may easily be seen how these physical conditions

[1] Meniaud, **CLXXXIII.** [2] De Lagger, **XI,** 1901, p. 441.
[3] Richtofen, *Vorlesungen über allgem. Siedlungs u. Verkehrsgeographie.*

can assist the transition from pastoral nomadism to sedentary agriculture.

But similarly there are agriculturists who gradually acquire beasts, and thenceforward tend to approach, not to the type of the pastoral nomads, but to those Fulahs and Tuculors who move as little as possible themselves, but possess herds which wander over the steppe. These last conditions of transition make a curious study. It would seem as though they must be due to some agricultural necessity, and that these cultivators, without farming animals, were obliged to obtain a supply of them and to improve their methods; but this is by no means the case. Gautier shows us the nomad, the "financial aristocrat", lording it over the settled peoples, and, in the Sahara, compelling them to work for his benefit. Inversely, Meniaud describes for us the manner of life led by the Malinkas and Bambaras of the Niger,[1] cultivators fixed to the soil and practising a traditional primitive agriculture, but still gradually acquiring herds of cattle and flocks of sheep by exchanging their grain for the animals of the Fulah, Moorish, or Tuareg shepherds. This is their way of investing their savings and making them fruitful, or rather of capitalizing them, for their methods of cattle-rearing are quite as rudimentary as those of the nomads, and they never dream of making meadows, or even of gathering in the bush during the hot weather dried up grasses, which make excellent hay. Moreover, what would be the use of money to them? It is a useless form of wealth, difficult to keep, and it brings no return. This explains why we see in Central Africa peoples like the Dinkas of the Bahr-el-Ghazal, who possess immense herds of horned beasts, sheep and goats, which fraternize with all the antelopes, giraffes, ostriches and elephants.[2]

This is their wealth, and they are ever trying to increase the number of their beasts.[3] But it is unproductive wealth, from which they do not attempt to make profit. They are not anxious to sell; for what good would money be to them? And besides, they have it—they produce it themselves. And so the Arab dealers who try to create trade in cattle in the

[1] Meniaud, **CLXXXIII,** Vol. II, p. 16 ff.
[2] Ch. Pierre, **XII,** Vol. XXVI, 1912 (II), p. 123.
[3] For similar endeavours among the Hottentots, see Demangeon, **XI,** 1908, pp. 324–5.

Dinka country are reduced to a single method of doing business—an exchange of beasts—offering to the Dinkas cows and heifers brought from Kordofan or Abyssinia by way of the Nile. The cow is the instrument by which the herd increases, and the Dinka desires cows so ardently that the Arabs regularly obtain five bullocks for one heifer.

The Malinkas and the Bambaras, whose whole labour is employed in the production of rice, water melons and cotton, look on the acquisition of cattle by exchange as the best of all forms of investment. But they do not sell their animals when they are young and vigorous any more than the pure nomads do; they leave them to grow old amongst the herd; it is a form of capital which is lasting and increases slowly without any trouble; they like to feel that they have it behind them, and they manage it like good fathers of families, never selling out that they themselves may profit momentarily and without regard for the morrow.

It must be remembered also that there it would be difficult for them to practise true stock-raising in our sense of the word, because their agriculture does not lend itself thereto. Progress in agriculture alone admits of the improvement of the herds and true stock-raising. When agriculture scarcely produces enough to feed the men, little care is bestowed on the beasts. The herd must feed itself, taking its chance of weary and perpetual wandering over wild country; but this is all changed when by means of skilled farming the land is made to produce a rich harvest. Thus, considering matters from this point of view, there is no antagonism between agriculture and cattle-raising; on the contrary, there is interdependence and a necessary connexion between the two—at least, as regards "agriculture" and "stock-raising" in the modern sense of the words. But the whole difficulty arises from the fact that we describe as cattle-raising or agriculture a general procedure altogether different from that which the words imply in a civilized country. The mere complacent possession of a herd, to which no other value is attached than that of a reserve fund of unemployed capital, small portions of which are to be parted with prudently in case of extreme necessity, is not cattle-raising at all, no more, indeed, than a lean Senegalese chicken is a fat Bresse pullet, or a Sudanese ox is a Charolais bull. Mere words may deceive those who do not trouble about realities, and prove the source of numberless errors and misconceptions.

The different conditions under which human society exists are infinitely varied, and the true relations between one society and another are infinitely more complex than is imagined. To take two extreme cases, that of the Norman peasant of to-day, for instance, and that of the Bedouin following his wandering cattle in Arabia, is a cheap method of contrasting two ways of life and declaring them radically antagonistic. But to build up a theory on this basis, and to reduce all history to the so-called "eternal combat between the nomad and the settler", is childish. For we must particularize before we can generalize. Every science starts from a given complex quantity which it has to explain and, if possible, reduce to unity. It can never start from a presupposed unity.

*

* *

Cattle-raising, nomadism, cultivation, settlement, are vague and empty words which express no clear ideas. The realities are more varied than one would believe to be possible. We have just spoken of that curious "Nomad cultivation" which quite gives the lie to the old ideas. But neither this nor the hoe-cultivation practised by the unstable settled tribes of Central Africa have anything in common with that garden culture—*Gartenbau* [1]—of the Chinese and Japanese, who make up for their want of animal manure by a plentiful use of the human variety, and for the imperfection of their implements and the small amount of cultivable ground by exceptional manual dexterity. Of 1,000 millions of acres in the whole of China, only 125 millions are available for agriculture, all the rest being locked up in the form of forest, pasture, royal preserves, pagodas, or townships.

And this garden culture, for which man does not utilize the assistance of animals but his own strength and skill exerted to the utmost,[2] differs in its turn from our European agriculture based on the economy of human labour, powerfully aided both by animal labour and by the use of perfected implements,

[1] Cf. Hahn, "Die Rolle des Gartenbaues in der Geschichte der Menschheit" (*Gartenflora*, 59, 1910, p. 346 ff.).
[2] Reclus, CXCIV, p. 483.

beginning with the plough and ending with the modern agricultural machines. This form of agriculture, moreover, becomes more and more scientific; plants are adapted to our soil and climate, the losses of the soil are repaired by abundant and skilful dressing with carefully prescribed mineral and animal manures, and finally a relatively small number of species is selected for cultivation and different methods of exploitation of the soil, which elsewhere remain the specialities of distinct human groups, are combined for the benefit of man.

Then it is hardly worth our while to talk of a sedentary way of life. What chiefly gives it birth is the cultivation of useful trees—a culture long in maturing, which requires great care and constant watch both against the crafty hands of men and the voracious teeth of animals. The tree, protected by a hedge, or a fence, or a dry stone wall, gradually evokes the first feelings of property, and of a home soil.[1] But the practice of irrigation afterwards completes the process of fixing man to the soil: irrigation of the surface by flooding, a simple, easy and primitive labour which was practised by the rice-growers in the East of India, an idle and backward people before the active intervention of the British; irrigation by canals, a much more complicated and delicate operation, the true foundation of that garden culture which is the source of the amazing prosperity of China, the most striking example of a country of sedentary "cultivators", firmly rooted to the soil and finding in agriculture the most honoured and noble of occupations.[1]

The many consequences on human societies entailed by the establishment of such a highly perfected system of agriculture and such a fixed rule of life are too well known and obvious to require enumeration here.[2] It is sufficient to have attempted to show that, in the earlier stages of the evolution of human society, the reality was too wide and varied to allow us to accept rash and much too summary theories.

[1] Richtofen, **CXVI**, p. 171 ff.
[2] Cf. Hitier, "L'évolution de l'agriculture," in **XI**, 1901.

PART IV

POLITICAL GROUPS AND HUMAN GROUPS

IN the foregoing chapters we have studied the action of natural conditions on human societies. We have sought for inevitable geographical laws, and found none. We have observed everywhere a great variety of possible combinations of which some only become realities.

At the beginning [1] we stated our opinion that the political problem and the human problem are one. In commenting on Ratzel's statement that " society is the bond by which the State is united to the soil ", we pointed out that we could not regard society merely as a sort of Jack-in-the-box enclosed in a fixed case—the State—and there sometimes expanding, sometimes contracting.[2] We have, in fact, tried to study by themselves the social groups established on their own soil and obtaining their living from it. Such a study is all the more necessary because the State generally arises from the exploitation of the soil, and thus its origin is largely geographical. In principle there is no need, then, to construct a geography of States distinct from economical geography, which itself is closely connected with physical geography. Neither is there any need, in our opinion, to investigate the influence which the geographical environment exercises on States independently of that which it exercises also on men, on the human societies of which States are only one of the expressions or, we might say, one of the faces.

Nevertheless, it will perhaps be interesting to review certain facts which are really political, so as to mark the nature of their relations with the constant geographical factors, if only for the sake of clearing the ground of a certain number of obstructions. To this review we now devote the chapters of this fourth and last part.

[1] Introduction, Chap. II, paragraphs IV, V. [2] p. 25.

CHAPTER I

The Problem of Frontiers and the Natural Bounds of States

If there were really such a thing as historical geography; if that name had not been usurped by uninteresting lists of names applying to localities, determinations of political boundaries and simple sketches or else dry descriptions of administrative history,[1] the chief problem confronting it would be the very existence of the great nations of the modern world.

To us they appear, and justly so, like actual historic and moral personalities. They have their inner life and their own character, but also their physical individualities, their exterior shape, and their material figure, which is so distinct and familiar that we never think of them under any other aspect than their present one; their shapes seem to us to-day to have a sort of eternal necessity. France, Italy, Spain, Great Britain are so many fundamental facts, which we accept as such without ever analysing them. When we look at a map of ancient France, such as a map from the Atlas of Longnon which shows us the shape of the Kingdom of France in the thirteenth or fifteenth century, representing the actual territory it once occupied, we do not really examine it in itself; still less with the idea that it represents a certain state of things, a combination of causes and effects following no inevitable laws, one simple possibility amongst a hundred others, which has become a reality, for a time at any rate, by the action of causes so numerous and so varied that, instead of searching them out, we find it easier to call them a " series of chances ". On the contrary, we instinctively contrast in the back of our minds the France of St. Louis or of Charles VII with the picture of an ideal France which we always carry about with us—not the present France, even, but France as bounded by its " natural frontiers ".

[1] Cf. Tourneur-Aumont's sensible remarks in this connexion, *L'Alsace et L'Alémanie*, Paris, 1919, *passim*, especially p. 65 ff.

I

The Theory of Natural Frontiers

For the whole problem is, or appears to us to be, a question of boundaries. Within us, so deeply implanted that we no longer notice its hold on us, there is a certain idea of the "natural limits" of the great States which causes us to think of their boundaries as things in themselves, having an actual value, a kind of mechanical virtue, and a compulsory and at the same time a creative power.

The definition and enumeration of these boundaries was formerly the first care of the old geographers and historians. "This country is bounded on the North . . . on the South . . . on the East . . . on the West": an obligatory salute to the four cardinal points; as to the interior of the country thus marked out, it was the geographer's task, as we said before, like that of the perfect cook, to cut them up carefully into slices leaving nothing over.[1] The Departments of contemporary France came into being just at the right moment to satisfy those ingenious needs which all "historical geography" seems to arouse in the breasts of officials of the Ministry of the Interior. Ancient France had its "old Provinces", which were adjusted to all needs.[2] So to crown the edifice an admirable geometry was brought into play and superposed on the accepted divisions. It offered to the learned various combinations of shapes between which they could choose. Was France more of a hexagon or an octagon? The uncertainty seemed cruel. On this important point there was much violent argument.

And the boundaries, the frontiers with which they started, were not mere lines. Their value was not temporary and relative. It was not a matter of boundaries as such, but of "natural" boundaries. A whole philosophy of history was comprised in that word "natural". When we speak of natural boundaries, we mean those fixed by destiny, ideals to conquer and realize. Between actual and natural boundaries there is often a divergence. This is annoying. It will —it must disappear! The historian who looks at the map of

[1] Febvre (L.), "L'Histoire provinciale," *Rev. bourg. de l'Enseignement supérieur*, Dijon, 1912.

[2] Brette, A., *Les limites et les divisions territoriales de la France en* 1879, Paris, 1907, Chap. III, pp. 57 ff.

the kingdom at the death of Philippe le Bel knows that it must disappear, and that the Rhône cannot always be the frontier of France, that Dauphiné, Savoy, and further north Bresse, as well as the Franche-Comté, Alsace-Lorraine, etc., must necessarily come to " take their place in the French unity " ; for the rest, if Navarre, marked on the map as one of the vassal countries or as governed by the Capets, overlaps the natural frontier of the Pyrenees well into Spain, he knows that it is an anomaly which, moreover, is provisionally compensated at the other end of the chain by the provisional absence of Roussillon.

It is very interesting to classify these natural boundaries. First of all there are arms of the sea, and oceans. These seem to be the most obvious of all possible frontiers, so to speak, and the most indisputable. The fact that Great Britain remained for centuries divided into rival kingdoms and different hostile nations could only be an unfortunate chance, a sort of historical scandal which must of necessity some day come to an end. But more commonly in the countries of Western Europe it is the mountain chains or the rivers that are promoted to the dignity of natural frontiers.

It is curious to notice how all notions of physical geography were formerly influenced by ideas of boundary. Mountains were nothing but " chains " of heights, difficult to climb over and interposed between countries like so many walls built by Providence. An obstacle only, and a wall, mountains were never considered in themselves and studied on their own account ; they formed a frontier, and not a district. Those who went into the customary ecstasies over the Pyrenean wall, so admirably fashioned to separate France from Spain, a perfect type of the natural frontier, " the most obvious of features, the plainest of lines, designed by nature in her boldest manner,"[1] never thought of investigating whether the Apennines, which are also a chain of mountains and a wall, had played in Italian history a similar rôle as barrier between rival powers, or, on the contrary, had at all times seen numerous states stretching East and West from its ridge, like a bag bulging in two on the shoulders of a strong man.

The theory of river-basins surrounded by lines of mountain

[1] J. Calmette, " La frontière pyrénéenne entre la France et l'Aragon," *Rev. des Pyrénées*, Vol. XXV, 1913.

heights called "watersheds", a theory which was favoured by Bauche in 1782 in his *Essai de géographie physique . . . sur l'espèce de charpente du globe*, and of which L. Gallois in his fine book *Régions naturelles et noms de pays*[1] has written the history and described the rôle, served to strengthen the current prejudice, and rendered so necessary the intervention of mountains in any attempt at delimitation, that when there were actually none they were invented without scruple. True, there was another resource for the historical geographers, and that was furnished by the streams.

*

* *

From the earliest times rivers have alternated with mountains in forming the natural boundaries of States. When we read again the beginning of the first book of Caesar's Commentaries, a book of such singular historic value in all respects, we find that rivers are the only frontiers mentioned: *Gallos ab Aquitanis Garumna flumen, a Belgis Matrona et Sequana dividit*; the Germans, as we know, are those who *trans Rhenum incolunt*, a celebrated statement which has caused much blood to flow in the past. Still the idea persists that a stream of water, even a tiny stream of water easy to cross, is a boundary; that a stream, which we do not see as it is—a narrow thread of water amongst meadows bordered by peaceful willows—but which we imagine to ourselves according to the map as a line only, is necessarily a boundary, an indispensable and ineluctable boundary which must not even be discussed; it persists with so much force even in our own days that not even the most powerful and evident interest in so doing so is able to banish it.

A typical example of the persistence of such an illusion would be furnished by an examination of the maps of sectors on the French front, at the beginning at least of the world war. Anyone who wishes to close the approach to a valley against an enemy camped at its entrance must evidently entrust the care of the two slopes of that valley to the same unit and the same leader, all the more so because as a rule the right-hand slope can only be effectively protected by fire from the left-hand slope which flanks it, and reciprocally.

[1] Gallois, **XXXIV**, pp. 30 ff.

A self-evident and obvious truth; but it was of no avail against the force of an instinctive prejudice which, since a stream is a boundary, made the sectors begin and end almost invariably on one side or the other of a quiet and insignificant little brook which happened to occupy the bottom of a valley, the defence and possession of which was often of the greatest importance.

Let us take another and more geographical example from a good observer, Hubert, who was in charge of the mission to Dahomey. In the region of the Niger, he tells us, "geographical accidents" have always played the rôle of "natural frontiers".[1] We have an example in the Niger, which the Djermas from the East had reached, thus overlapping the Sonraï, but had not crossed, the same Niger which the Fulahs, who are allied to the Djermas, were also unable to cross, being "prevented by the river, which thus forms a natural boundary"; and another example in the Couffo, the Tou, the Weme, and the sea which strictly delimit the territory of the Fons (whether in our eyes or in the eyes of the Fons is a question) just as the Marne, the Seine, and the Oise surround and limit the Ile-de-France. Let us admit the truth of these statements. But we may at least be a little sceptical on the subject of these "natural frontiers" when we read, a few pages further on in the same book, "As to the rivers, except for the Niger and the lower Weme, they form no defence in the dry season as they have no water in their beds."[2] Moreover, are there not true Nigerian communities living in the islands and on the banks of the great river, for whom the Niger is consequently not a moat, but a link? For instance, there are the Dendis, who inhabit both banks of the river and the islands between Bikini and Gaza. And that is not all.

In the same book the author gives a psychological and political explanation of the facts he reports which is quite different from his physical explanation and has no connexion with this mechanical action of natural boundaries; he states it (p. 545) when he tells us that the victorious races seem "to have no wish" to extend their domination (which had no doubt become too precarious) beyond certain geographical limits, formed by the rivers

[1] Hubert, **CLXXXII**, p. 544. [2] Ibid., p. 548.

Atacora, Niger, Weme, and Couffo. A very reasonable and wise remark. For the doubtful point is not the bare fact that certain "geographical accidents", as Hubert calls them, coincide with tribal boundaries, but the bald and mechanical explanation of that fact by the existence of so-called "natural boundaries", effective in themselves. Here, as everywhere else, we must take into account the ideas of men, and the fact that certain groups of them may wish to have such a physical accident for their boundary, or else, from political or economic prudence, may content themselves with the possession of another on the hither side of it. Directly we begin to deal with the existence of human societies we at once fail to recognize how great a part is played by the psychology of individuals, or, to an even higher degree, by group psychology.

II

Linear Boundaries or Frontier Zones?

Since geography has begun to shake itself free from nomenclature and to assert its claim to be regarded as a science, there is no doubt that, whatever may survive and persist, the old idea of natural boundaries has begun to arouse criticism and provoke attack.

Mountains, rivers and forests, now studied for their own sake and as special subjects, are gradually and slowly revealing their secrets. They are often undoubtedly boundaries in so far as they are really obstacles. But they are also bridges, centres of expansion and radiation, little worlds with attractive values of their own, linking together the men and the regions on either side of them. In any case they are never boundaries "of necessity".

Rivers may be boundaries; but with regard to the famous saying of Cæsar about the Rhine which divides Gaul from Germany, who will separate the truth from the illusion, whether psychological or political? The question of the Rhine is much too large and too difficult for us to do anything here but recall its existence; a whole volume would be required for its consideration. But how many "valleys" are recorded in history occupying both banks of a river or stream; how many riverine societies, possessing their own life and character, supported by the river, and deriving from it their subsistence and reason for existence?

Whilst descending the course of the Volga, Brunhes remarks on the small interest that such a descent possesses for a geographer.[1] It reveals nothing of the country beyond. This is because "the river is an active geographical phenomenon which transforms and recreates in its own way the districts bordering its course; it makes its valleys and it makes its banks: by following its course we know the river, the valley, and the banks, but nothing more". Each river is a special little world—whether we speak of the great Russian rivers with their contrasting banks, the one steep, the other low, sandy, and covered with shrubs, islets and swamps, or of the Saône enclosed between two rows of damp and feverish "vaivres",[2] or of the Rhine, which in Alsace, for example, is not a line but a zone, a sort of miniature jungle, with its swampy brakes, its bramble thickets, its islets and double arms forming rings about them, and all its special resources for man—fish and wild fowl, grains of gold among the gravel, not to mention the efficient protection of its waters and its thickets[3]: so much of a separate world is it that, being outside Alsace, so to speak, it has naturally served as a frontier to cover those fertile belts whose dovetailing, or rather collaboration, make the wealth and power of the country—those "Ried" and "Hart"—agricultural terraces between the Ill and the sub-Vosgian hills; vineyards as foreign to the Rhine as the vine-country of Burgundy is to the Saône; and lastly, the Vosges mountains, eternal comrade of the men of the plains.

Can these mountains be considered a boundary? They are a natural region, certainly, a huge forest and pastoral domain important for the sake of its own resources, whose luxuriant pastures have excited from the earliest times[4] the covetousness of rural populations both to the east and west, but a domain which does not live a solitary life of its own, shut in from the rest of the world; Tourneur-Aumont says very truly[5] that the

[1] Brunhes, XI, 1903, p. 79.

[2] Febvre, "Les régions de la France: la Franche-Comté," *Revue de synthèse historique*, Paris, 1905, p. 19 ff.

[3] Tourneur-Aumont, *L'Alsace et l'Alémanie*, Paris, 1919, p. 71.

[4] Boyé, **CCXVIII.**

[5] Op. cit., pp. 75–6.

mountains, for Alsace, are a source of national strength like the Ardennes in the Walloon country, the Jura in the Romance country, and the Alps in Rumanian Transylvania. "The Vosges give easy access to the plain. There is intimacy between the mountain and the plain which the Rhine does not share. The plain has more connexion with the Vosges than with the Rhine." But the Jura, near at hand, forming such a clear-cut bound to the Swiss plain, with that long terminal ridge to the East facing the Alps above the lakes and plateaux of ancient Helvetia—they have never served as a frontier,[1] but for centuries have been a tilting-ground where those uncomfortable neighbours the Comtois and the Swiss have quarrelled over the pastures and the woods, the "Chaux" and the "Joux". With regard to the Pyrenees, that steep, straight, continuous wall "which is pierced by one or two gates, but remains a wall", the same author, a historian unfamiliar with geographical matters, puts the question in these words: "If a human frontier could have been immovable during the few centuries of our brief national history, would it not seem that the frontier of the Pyrenees should have been that one? Far from it, there has been, on the contrary, a whole history of the Pyrenean frontier—a complicated active history."[2] To tell the truth, we are not surprised. Have we not had occasion to speak before, with Cavaillès and Max. Sorre, of those Pyrenean confederations which united the valleys on either side of the range and bound them together by treaties?[3] Have we not drawn attention to the force and continuity of that regular and rhythmic tide of cattle migrating to the highlands, and descending to the valleys, which is no respecter of our prejudices as unconscious champions of "natural frontiers"? And our instances came from near at hand, and are easily verifiable; but if we look elsewhere we should be puzzled to know how to choose—among so many. Has not Sion, for example, in his work on Southern Tibet,[4] pointed out the relations which the movements of the cattle bring about between the two slopes of the Himalaya? And has not Martonne remarked similar facts in the Carpathians, and Cuijic in the Balkans?

[1] Febvre, *Les régions de la France : la Franche-Comté*, pp. 19–21.
[2] Calmette, op. cit., p. 2.
[3] Part III, Chap. II, p. 282.
[4] Sion, **CXCVI**, p. 32.

Forest is also said to be a boundary. But on the other hand, a number of states have originated in settlements in the heart of forests. We have already quoted and commented on the most famous example of this phenomenon, that of the Russian plain.[1]

Then, the most unkind territory, the wildest deserts, are not they, at least, boundaries? But Chudeau, who knows the Central and Western Sahara intimately, asserts that "the most sterile part of the desert, in which there is nothing but gravel and stones—the *tanez roufts*—forms no serious barrier to the Sahara tribes. Although these form a belt at least 125 miles wide from the Tagant to Egypt, they nowhere coincide with an ethnic frontier; numerous tribes have pasture lands north as well as south of this arid region".[2]

Thus our ideas are gradually modified—to our great advantage. We cease to consider so many geographical complexes as simple linear boundaries. And we also become aware that ancient boundaries were never, so to speak, linear; more often they were zones. The Gaulish cities, for instance, were not territorial enclosures with fixed boundaries, drawn with a tape, like the boundaries which population and the ever-increasing appropriation of the soil force on us. "The Gaulish peoples occupied inhabited zones separated by forest zones,"[3] thus they were neighbours, though not in actual contact; according to those ancient customs, found amongst all peoples at a certain stage of development, the forest stretched between them as a march or natural territory. But the forests, as we have already said, were not boundaries only; they often formed true territorial units, with their own particular names: hence it happens that when the forest has disappeared, the name remains attached to the village which it sheltered and provided with a livelihood. Strictly speaking, Bray is the name of a forest; we may say that the place-name of Bray carries with it the stamp of the forest, and similarly that many villages whose names have the suffix "Thelle" might lead us to believe in the existence of a region so called; such a region existed, but the name refers to a forest, which disappeared long ago.[4]

*

* *

[1] Part III, Chap. I, p. 207. [2] Chudeau, **XVI**, Vol. XXIV, 1913, p. 185.
[3] Demangeon, **CCXXIV**, p. 427. [4] Ibid., pp. 428–9.

Thus the notion of a linear frontier is attacked on two sides and breaks down. Elementary ideas are modified, as well as general ideas. The notion of predestined bounds disappears. We no longer see any unavoidable constraint laid on man by nature, or on policy by geography. Man simply adapts himself to possibilities. This idea is evidently much more satisfactory and much more promising than that of "natural bounds", but it still has one great defect. It allows finalism to usurp a place which it should no longer be able to occupy. For it is a question of explaining, not of justifying—and too often justification only is offered.

We start from the present when we endeavour to picture to ourselves the whole of the very long period of evolution which we desire to explain—from the present, considered as a fixed quantity rather than as a passing moment. The entire past is determined by the aid of the present. Obsessed by it, we reject a whole series of latent possibilities which might perhaps have been realized, and which evolution in its course may one day offer again to men, in the garb of necessities.

Let us take the history of a province which is well known to us, the Franche-Comté. According to the usual argument of historians, the Comté, being merely three French departments, is just the French Comté, the Comté predestined to take its place in the bosom of that unity which is France. And certainly many attempts have been honestly made to explain in passing why it was so capricious and for so long unfaithful to its true vocation; geographical reasons have been sought for its frequent separations from its predestined motherland; but the point was not pressed; these are merely the adventures of the prodigal son wandering far from the fold, whose inevitable return is taken for granted, and that is all that matters.

But when a historian has studied the Burgundian wars and the numerous projects which followed the division of the Comté between various masters, the views of the Bernese on that rich country, and the idea so frequently expressed then (and since) of the Comté forming a Swiss canton, and then proceeds to write [1]: "If Nicolas of Diesbach had not died of gangrene at Porrentruy when under forty-five years of age, if ill-fortune had not carried off the best general

[1] Toutey, *Charles le Téméraire et la Ligue de Constance*, 1901, p. 225 ff.

and the most statesmanlike brain in the Cantons, the Comté would undoubtedly have been invaded, taken and kept by Berne," he will very probably be regarded as having acted outrageously in thus presuming to remake history. But is it less of an outrage to construct, according to the present circumstances of a province, a complete picture of its evolution in the past ?

III

The Part Played by Psychology

We now reach a third stage, when we explain, but never under any circumstances justify. We may introduce into this explanation, not a finalist notion from the point we have reached, but the idea of successive stages diversely characterized. We do not study, once for all, a country whose history has been unfolded through the centuries and which has known many and strange vicissitudes—and will know them again, since it is fortunately not in our power to arrest and congeal vitality. Nor do we apply to the Paris of Louis XVI the ideas which served to explain the city of Philip Augustus or the Emperor Julian. Lastly, and above all, we do not confine ourselves to the country that we are studying, but examine it in relation to neighbouring ensembles, which are in perpetual flux throughout the centuries. And we must always remember that such and such a forest, which was a boundary and a defence at one epoch, may be a bond and a bridge at another. We shall not determine the past by the present, and conversely we shall remember that, even if a precedent throws light on the present, it does not condition it. This is really a task to be attempted only in careful, minute, and laborious monographs. It is not a task to be despised, for it is really work of the most delicate description. Well carried out, it is the necessary preliminary to those comparative labours which alone will permit us to study the share geography has had in history, and to work out, if occasion arise, a few outstanding constants.

But how far we are still from the necessary frame of mind ; how slowly new ideas spread, and how tenacious of life is the old routine ! Supposing an historian, starting out ready equipped with the theory of natural frontiers and linear boundaries between countries, perceives that historic reality puts the greatest strain on that theory in the typical case of the Pyrenees, will he reject it and draw the legitimate conclusion from his researches? Not a bit of it! Two pithy sentences will fully enlighten us on that subject: "In a region whose profile is not well marked (such as Northern France), it would be difficult, perhaps, to teach children the exact force of that expression 'natural frontier'. The term speaks for itself, on the contrary, in the case of the Pyrenean Range, which is a perfect type of the natural frontier."[1] Here we are warned—the idea of the natural frontier is for "grown-ups" only. We see that the times are not yet past when the good Longnon worried about the delimitation of the Ile-de-France and, after having stated that it was contained in the angle formed by the Marne and the Seine to the South, and by the Oise to the West, felt the imperative need of completing his unfinished figure to the North, so as to close the last side of the quadrilateral, and could find nothing better to do than to add the names of the tiny Thève and the inglorious Beuvronne.

After this, we are not surprised to find in otherwise excellent works from the pen of experienced linguists certain lamentations which are at once ridiculous and heart-breaking, and in which they indulge, often enough, when they have to admit that to their great surprise certain particular well-defined territorial units do not coincide with the linguistic, morphological, or phonetic boundaries they were trying to establish, and above all, to explain. They are within an ace of renouncing geography as a failure, so strongly rooted in their minds[2] is the belief in a kind of geographical fatality or, in other words, the absolute determinism of natural conditions. The fact that a certain estuary, river, or chain of mountains is not a linguistic boundary does not constitute any condemnation of geography, which, happily, no longer believes in the direct and overwhelming influence of surface relief or hydrography on the complex conditions of human life. The Eastern Pyrenees do not form a linguistic boundary; at no point do

[1] Calmette, op. cit., p. 1.

[2] Febvre (L.), "Histoire et linguistique," **XVII**, 1911, Vol. XXIII, pp. 142–3.

the Alps mark the line of demarcation between different patois [1]; no more do the mouths of the Loire and Seine. What then does geography claim if rivers and mountains are not necessarily boundaries? It is content with a possibility and is right in so being. It is not geography that makes mistakes: it is the linguist who makes mistakes about geography.

In other words, every historical unit, every regulated society, seemed to form *ipso facto* a geographical personality in the past. We, fortunately, have a wider outlook. In the North of France there are three provinces, Picardy, Artois, and Cambrésis. But we pass from Picardy into Artois and from Artois into Cambrésis without noticing any difference. All three are countries where the fields, the streams, and the villages resemble one another, countries of the same physical and human aspect, because they are of the same structure and constitution.[2] They are not geographical units, nor can geography take account of them as such. A geographical unit must have its peculiar aspect: that is the rule. If there is a contrast between two types of villages, dissimilarity between corn-land here and grass-land there, a boundary exists there—a geographical boundary that no geographer would be so childish as to expect to find definitely marked on the surface of the earth in the shape of a stream or a chain of hills.

Under these conditions, the problem of boundaries undergoes a singular change in form and importance. It is no longer a question of finding at all costs a network of lines, a definite bound enclosing with more or less success a piece of territory: it is not the definite bound or frame that is of prime importance, but the thing framed or bounded—the expressive and living centre of the picture. The rest is only a margin.

Let us add one more word. Nothing is more important than the chronology of boundaries. We must never build an argument on boundaries considered as constants. Some of them were originally enforced on men by geographical conditions. The boundaries of French dioceses generally followed those of the Gallo-Roman cities, and the latter very often those of the Gaulish cities, themselves conditioned

[1] Dauzat, *Essai de méthodologie linguistique*, 1906, p. 221.
[2] Demangeon, **CCXXVI**, *passim*.

in many cases by the existence of forests, marshes, obstacles, or natural accidents. Anyone who studies them finds ultimately, at the end of his study, a sort of geographical residuum. But in general those frontiers lost their natural character very quickly. They became conventional lines separating men and things which gradually grew more alike. A hundred new territories were carved out of them at the will of successive governments, continually altered, completed, and cut up, until it became impossible to recognize any underlying stable natural cause. There is no more geography in the boundaries of royal Artois than in those of the Pas-de-Calais or the Somme.[1] And the truth is, once again, that we must look beyond material symbols and find out the desires, the beliefs, the human and psychological factors which constituted their solid and effective basis. Rauh was right in his remark [2] that when a people fixes a natural frontier for itself, it is simply a limit which it sets to its desire for expansion. Every "natural" frontier can be violated. The sea did not prevent William's Normans from attacking Harold's Saxons in their island. What a number of purely artificial frontiers, on the other hand, are safe, or at least respected!

In his little book on the Sahara, Gautier gives us one very good example [3] of this when he tells us of that frontier of Bechar which an order from Paris was sufficient to create, and which immediately became, for a long time, the inviolable frontier of a lawless country.

IV

The State is never Natural, but always Man-made

The bound frame, or margin, matters little. The inside is the important part, and must receive the chief consideration. In other words, the problem of frontiers must be investigated from the inside, never from the outside.

And similarly, when we are studying a state, the chief interest consists in disentangling two ideas of the first

[1] Demangeon, **CCXXIV**, p. 120.
[2] Rauh, **XXVI**, p. 63.
[3] Gautier, **CLXXXI**, p. 70.

importance, that of the germ from which it has grown and that of its economic solidarity.

There is no little provincial state which has not had its germinal, its geographical starting-point; there is no durable political formation in whose origin we cannot discover a combination of forces, a kind of armature around which other territories could build themselves up like the soft parts round the bones of a skeleton. We say "a combination of forces". Quite a long time ago, in 1898, Vidal de la Blache himself wrote in an article, "a solid nucleus around which the parts annexed have grouped themselves by a sort of crystallization"[1] —and he ended, "States in this sense are like living beings." Further on, Vidal clearly expressed his idea of the solid nucleus, a rather dangerous term, by pointing out how interesting it is for the geographer to seek "to discover, in the combinations which we call a State, the initial force which, in time, formed the centre of attraction".

At the beginning of the development of the Ile-de-France, Brandenburg, the Duchy of Moscow, and the State of New York, he recognized distinctly "the action of certain local features which, step by step, set other influences in motion".

So Vidal had seen clearly the danger of that term, "a solid nucleus." This is because the germ of a State is not, as a matter of fact, one of those little natural units with strongly marked characteristics, whose traces the patient geographers are attempting to find everywhere in our old complex States. There is no State, however small, which can be reduced to one of these units, or whose boundaries coincide or did originally coincide with those of a "district" in the geographical sense of the word, the sense that was so well defined lately by Gallois.[2] The proof is easy; we have only to take the districts of France, which are the most typical, have the most marked characteristics and are the best determined: we shall easily see that they never formed historical units.

Morvan,[3] for instance, has never existed as a state nor possessed its own administration, any more than Brie, Beauce, or Limagne. The little natural region which it forms has never served as the bounds enclosing a province or independent

[1] Vidal, **XCV**, p. 108. [2] Gallois, **XXXIV**. [3] Levainville, **CCXXV**.

historical group: and yet its individuality has impressed men in all ages, and it is still well marked in the economic life, the agricultural activity, the general appearance, and the basic conditions of existence of this fragment detached from the central mountain mass, this humpbacked country with its worn-looking topography, poor soil, rude climate, difficult approach, and essentially rural population. In a way, the impossibility of building up a state on a district with no variety—one of these very distinct yet very monotonous little units—becomes greater and greater as we go further back into the past, because it was necessary then that each state should be self-sufficing, and consequently the consideration of prime importance was the possession of different kinds of soil and a variety of products. All States consist of an amalgam of fragments, of collections of morsels detached from different natural regions, which complement one another and become cemented together, and which make of their associated diversities a genuine unity.

Man does in the political world very much what he does in the botanical world. In the latter he breaks up the vegetable societies and from their disjointed elements forms combinations to suit his requirements—fields or meadows. In the former he breaks up the natural units, the districts, to construct other political ones from the detached pieces. We have often referred to the rise of the little State of the Franche-Comté and the happy combination of plains and forests, corn-land and vineyards, woodland and pasture on which it was founded in early times and endured for long centuries.[1] Camille Jullian, too, in his brilliant History of Gaul,[2] has drawn a suggestive distinction between countries inhabited by one tribe—primordial units of agricultural units, with their borders protected by forests, marshes, or mountains—and regions infinitely more complicated, true strategic and economic units, formed of complementary lands, territories, plains, and mountains, forests, and arable land, opening on to the same routes, converging on to the same river, commanding one another, and finding it necessary to agree in order to exchange their produce and their means of defence: in short, societies for mutual protection and moral and physical solidarity.

[1] Febvre, *Philippe II et la Franche-Comté*, Paris, 1911, p. 39.
[2] Jullian, **CLXXII**, Vol. II, p. 30.

We only refer to them in order to note that man was no more content with passive adaptation in the creation of states than in the arrangement of his material life.

It follows quite naturally from this that there should be some places on the earth specially suitable for the birth of living political groups, regions favourable for bringing them to maturity.

When we look at a map, we see that such regions do in fact exist; they are found, as we should have expected, a priori just on the borderland of differing natural formations (steppes and savannahs, savannahs and intertropical forests), and at the meeting-points of these formations. This happened in Asia, where the belt bordering on the steppes forms a veritable centre of political activity; this region witnessed those continual oscillations in power between the nomads and the settled tribes, which we described a little farther back.

It happened also in Africa, where it is well known how fruitful of political movements the various regions of the Sudan have been in the course of their stirring past, and how they have given rise to a series of successive dominations, the result of the same conditions, which have stretched between the two extreme limits: the Sahara to the north, and the tropical forest to the south. Lastly, it happened in America, in the time of its curious pre-Columbian civilizations, with their distinct and vivid character.

*

* *

However, we must not go too far. It is necessary to know where to place limits to reasoning by analogy, even when it is to all appearances most accurate and legitimate. For what is true of States at a certain stage and of a certain kind of formation is not inevitably true of more advanced States of other and more complex formation. The transition between limited provincial States like the Franche-Comté, Burgundy, or Lorraine, for example, and a great national State like France could not possibly be made without considerable difficulty if we supposed it to follow the same course which allowed the Gaulish *pagi*, *pays*, or districts to become the territories occupied by tribes, and later still the domains of the Celtic nations. It is evident that the process is not the same, and that an explanation by the union of complementary units does not hold in this case.

In other words, if the new problem does contain certain geographical elements, they are of another nature. Quite different elements and considerations intervene. Sentimental issues intervene and play a most important part, prevailing over economic interests or geographical connexions. Durkheim, taking for his theme the feeling of moral unity always possessed by the various countries which, when reunited, together made up Russia, proceeded to the conclusion [1] that individual States are formed by a phenomenon of differentiation in the bosom of large societies, all the members of which feel themselves united by bonds of ethnical or moral relationship. And if after they have been formed and separated from one another they feel later on the need of drawing closer together and uniting, this tendency has its roots in the most distant past. The sentiment of unity then is only a remembrance, an echo, if we will, of an ancient sentiment which has never disappeared. Panslavism has existed since the beginning of Slav societies, like the Pangermanism of to-day or the Panhellenism of former days.

This suggestion certainly leads us to a better understanding of some curious and troublesome facts, such as the existence in a Gaul divided into rival and hostile tribes of that extraordinary Gaulish sentiment of patriotism which takes us by surprise when we see it bursting out in the time of Vercingetorix. We must certainly not exaggerate or put too much confidence in Durkheim's opinion, or we shall run the risk of arbitrarily diminishing the rôle which geographical factors play in the birth of great states. We shall have occasion to return to this shortly. But it is certain that the rôle is not exactly the same in the case of the great states as in that of more elementary forms, those of the second rank, such as provincial states. Durkheim's remark ought to be treasured, if only for the sake of the warning. But it certainly has other interesting points. In particular, it is a useful reminder of what we have previously said about the precocious appearance of large human groups—even exceedingly large ones. It also warns us against the ever-recurring illusion

[1] Durkheim, **XVII**, 1902–3, pp. 449–50.

about man, which cannot conceive of the development of societies except as a series of additions: the man plus the woman plus their children = the family; a family plus another family plus more families still = the tribe; a tribe plus other tribes = a people; peoples united = a great nation—formations all built on the same plan and developing themselves by a series of successive propagations in a direct line. We have already shown the danger of such explanations.[1] But the error has deep roots, and naturally enough it springs up again without any effort.

V

The Natural Regions of States

In fact, these highly specialized creations, the great states, which are characteristic not of the forces of nature but of the intellect of man, ought to be compared with similar formations. In this way we can, and must, admit that there are what may be called "natural regions of great States" on the earth's surface. This time we do not refer to privileged zones or to organisms which are still simple and easy to break in pieces, but true political, intellectual, and moral consolidations of power.[2]

The great states do not live isolated, bound up in themselves and jealously shut up behind walls.[3] They are bathed, so to speak, in the vast international or, if anyone prefers, intersocial environment which envelopes them. Each of them lives in a perpetual state of becoming and of decay; elements are continually being detached from it which go to increase neighbouring states; and inversely, elements come from them which it absorbs in its turn, and incorporates in itself. There is an exchange, not only of people, but also of ideas, sentiments, and beliefs. Thus vast groups of States are formed, in constant intercourse, tending more and more to resemble one another in their general character; and thus have arisen the great comprehensive civilizations

[1] See above, Part II, Chap. III, p. 149 ff.
[2] Cf. Durkheim, **XVII**, 1906–9, Vol. XI, p. 8.
[3] Meyer, **LXXXI**, par. 40, p. 87, "Aires de civilisation." See also ibid., § 111, p. 215.

which we call "worlds", a word which is intentionally vague but very comprehensive: the Eastern world, the world of Islam, the Asiatic world.

There are actions and reactions: the same peoples who tend thus to resemble one another more and more every day, imitating one another, unconsciously influenced by one another, taking each other as a pattern and diffusing a common civilization, as a sort of subtle emanation, these same people are striving no less ardently and no less actively to separate themselves more every day from their neighbours, and by carefully cultivating their special gifts to accentuate as much as possible their characteristic features. There is no doubt that the conflict between these two tendencies is one of the dominating facts of history. But which of the two is the more strictly due to geography?

Ratzel, for his part, considered that it was the second. In his opinion, the individuality of states was the result of geography. To debate the question is useless. There is no need to banish geographical considerations from the study either of the first or the second of these two great processes, any more than there is need to proclaim them in one case sovereign, in another case powerless. It is perhaps wise to study them without any foregone conclusions before talking much about them. After all we shall find that they have each about equal right to a certain pre-eminence. The life of human societies has nothing in common with a distribution of prizes; and the question is not to find out whether the sociologist, the economist, the psychologist, or the geographer shall have "the first prize". Men can never entirely rid themselves, whatever they do, of the hold their environment has on them. Taking this into consideration, they utilize their geographical circumstances, more or less, according to what they are, and take advantage more or less completely of their geographical possibilities. But here, as elsewhere, there is no action of necessity.

CHAPTER II

COMMUNICATIONS : THE ROUTES

STATES are usually formed by methods which imply the existence of routes and of various means of communication. For, without routes and communications, how could men succeed in reconstructing, out of the débris of the natural units they have broken in pieces, homogeneous ensembles to suit their convenience?

But, at first sight, it would seem that the existence of a network of routes necessarily implies the active and earnest co-operation of nature and man; that the very structure of the country must determine the tracks in advance, and make them into regular channels; in other words, that the problem of routes must be a geographical one. After all, it does not appear that those geographers whose ideas we are discussing and criticizing have really thrown much light on this subject. The Ratzelians especially have given little attention to such questions. They have devoted themselves to studying the movements of peoples; and whilst doing so they have had occasion, no doubt, to point out that some valley, some depression, or some pass was a route, or that some mountain, some arm of the sea, or some desert, on the other hand, was an obstacle to the movements of peoples; but it is evident that what interests them is not so much the ways by which a single traveller or a few small caravans or at most an old time army could pass, but the great natural openings capable of allowing an entire population to emigrate *en masse*. The simple communications probably only interest them in exceptional cases, those which are strictly dependent on natural conditions; the reason being that they are before all anxious to prove, or, more precisely, to justify a theory already elaborated and expounded. However, the method they have followed has attained very poor results, and the conclusions arrived at are generally somewhat puerile.

I

The Track and the Terrain

It does not need much science to establish the fact that the plains, in different degrees at different times, offer favourable conditions for circulation, whilst the great rivers, the mountains, the deserts, and the seas are generally hindrances. But too much weight must not be attached to such statements, since here also we must make distinctions. In the case of peoples with a gift for navigation, rivers, far from being hindrances, will quickly become routes of exceptional value. If such peoples have a commercial spirit, the mountain routes will not frighten them, but will lose or gain in importance according to circumstances. And we are not speaking of more special reasons which may induce men at certain times to put up with many inconveniences and to frequent inhospitable lands, nor of those scientific revolutions which may suddenly upset old habits or create new ones. The Alpine routes fell into disuse after the invention of railways and the piercing of the great Alpine tunnels, but the increased use of automobiles has restored them to life again; thus there have been changes of routes although the natural conditions remain the same. Here, as elsewhere, it is not a matter of actual necessity; only of possibilities.

In how many different ways, for instance, may a river be utilized? It matters little whether it be used for transport by boat, or by sledges, like a road, in winter when it is frozen, or if it is never deserted, as in mountainous countries, because its valley cuts through the hills, and in desert countries, because its course, either visible or subterranean, furnishes travellers with their sole supply of water, for in all these cases the man has to conform to the natural track of the stream. It is for these reasons that the Nile, the lower Volga, the Irtish, the Indus, the Niger, and the Amazon are routes; that it is very difficult to travel in Turkestan unless the Syr-Daria is followed; that Livingstone had to keep along the dry course of the Makoko, marked by springs, in order to cross from the Orange River to Lake Ngami; and lastly, to choose a few significant facts from the immense supply we have at our disposal, it is in this way that the St. Lawrence and the Great Lakes have formed an excellent means of penetration into the central parts of North America, as the whole history of the discoveries and explorations of the seventeenth and eighteenth centuries serves to demonstrate. And the same thing may be affirmed about the valley of the Hudson and the Mohawk gap.

Similarly, the valleys in mountainous countries determine the routes in advance: the passes attract the roads from afar. The nature of the ground prohibits transit in certain mountain districts, certain specially difficult belts, and on the other hand ordains that certain parts of a chain may be crossed by numerous routes. For well-known physical reasons, the chief lines of communication between Spain and France are not found in the centre of the Pyrenees, but at the two ends. The Alps in some parts are very forbidding, great stretches of mountains being almost impassable. Between the Grimsel Pass and the Upper Rhône, and between the Simplon and the Great St. Bernard there are regions which it is nearly impossible to cross. This explains why the important passes have remained unaltered throughout history. The routes of antiquity and of the Middle Ages [1] already went by the Hinter-Rhein and Coire, to reach the Danubian country by way of Ulm. The Brenner served as a route for the Cimbri and the Teutones, and the Emperors always passed this way when they visited Italy for coronation or in pursuit of state policy. From the time of the Romans, certainly, and doubtless long before that, the routes over the Alps between Gaul and Italy were exactly the same as those chosen by motor-cars to-day; the via Aurelia traversed the Corniche; the Mons Matrona (Mont Genèvre) was used to cross from the Dora Riparia to the Durance; and a wave of civilization has never ceased to flow and expand over the north and the entire east of France by way of the Saint Bernard, then by the Bas-Valais and Saint-Maurice d'Agaune, the key to the route, and by the shore of the Lake of Geneva and the gap of Pontarlier.

The historic rôles of the Khyber Pass and the gate of Herat, the Darial Pass and, nearer home, the time-honoured pass of

[1] Maillefer, "Les routes romaines en Suisse," *Revue histor. vaudoise*, 1900; Œhlmann, "Die Alpenpässe im Mittelalter," *Jahrb. f. Schweizer Gesch.*, 1900, III, pp. 164–89; IV, pp. 3–324.

Belfort, which Vidal de la Blache calls the Burgundian gate,[1] are explained by similar considerations.

In fact, when men wished to establish means of communication to suit their convenience they generally fell back readily upon the old tracks and the ancient thoroughfares. The Erie canal follows the Mohawk gap; the canal from the Rhone to the Rhine and the railway from Mulhouse to Lyons naturally pass through the Burgundian gate. In the same way the prevailing winds and ocean currents have played a part of the greatest importance in the story of the seafaring nations, and mark the stages of the road they took. The coming at different periods of Esquimaux racial elements to Europe brought hither by the Gulf Stream, the arrival in Madagascar of numerous Indo-Malayan tribes driven by the Monsoons, and the gradual advance of the Portuguese in their Oceanic discoveries as they moved on from island to island are well-known illustrations.

*
* *

Yet all this only demonstrates possibilities; men did not always passively submit. It was they who adapted routes to their various needs, even when these followed old tracks. They modified them so as to avoid dangers or difficulties. The floods of the Isère made it almost impossible to establish a route at the bottom of the valley at the level of Grenoble, so the Romans took their road half-way up the slope across the flank of the Casque de Néron: again, electric eels were found in great numbers in a small stream, and the horses, benumbed by shock, were often drowned, so the route was deflected across the steppe of Urituca.[2] There are winter routes and summer routes, not only in the mountains, but even in flat countries; in Northern Germany the route followed the *Geest* in winter and the *Marsch* in summer.[3]

These were slight modifications strictly dependent on natural conditions. But man is gradually freeing himself from the bonds of subjection which tie him to the soil; or

[1] Vidal, **CCXXXII**, 234.
[2] Humboldt, **LXXII**[a], Vol. I, 29.
[3] Rauers, in **XIII**, Vol. LII, 1906, pp. 49–59.

rather, he does not always choose the same possibility out of the many which are offered him. So long as it is only pedestrians and beasts of burden which have to move about, there is no need for wide roads; man's sole care then is simple enough—he is concerned only with the length of the journey, the shortest way from one point to another, and the avoidance of uneven ground and too many fords. Roads for wheeled traffic and *a fortiori* great highways have other requirements. The consideration of gradient then becomes important, because of the question of traction and because the channelling of the surface by rainwater is in direct proportion to the slope. If the traffic is slow and the vehicles are innocent of springs, the road may remain narrow and broken with impunity. Quick traffic and perfected springs, however, require roads to be broader, better kept, more regular in gradient, with their surface and camber more carefully engineered. The possibilities are not the same in both cases.

However, it is well known that the problem of gradients is presented—and solved—in very different ways for motor traffic, for ordinary railways, for cogwheel railways, and for those worked by a lateral drive by means of a third rail.

The possibility of piercing tunnels and of constructing viaducts greatly affects the conditions of the construction of lines. Here again it is of small importance to know whether man is more or less firmly attached to his environment; what is certain is that a track which serves for the necessities of one epoch may be useless at another, and again be suddenly restored to favour and new life. Such revolutions in trade routes are common; there are many notable instances, especially the desertion of the Mediterranean by the great maritime traffic after the Portuguese discoveries at the beginning of the sixteenth century, and its sudden recovery of fortune in the nineteenth, after the piercing of the Isthmus of Suez. But land routes have known corresponding changes. The caravan tracks in Syria and in Mesopotamia, which were abandoned for a time after the construction of the Suez Canal, have regained their former importance since the Europeans have constructed railways and roads in those countries. On the other hand, in the old countries the roads were neglected after the construction of the network of railways;

the development of the motor-car was necessary before their value could be restored and attention attracted to them.

In a well-defined region, moreover, we can recognize very clearly the different roads which correspond to the different stages of civilization.

The region of the Côte in Burgundy offers a typical example. There we may clearly distinguish the old road of the Middle Ages, which passes at the highest level on the hillside and commands the country; a favourable position in times of general insecurity. Lower down are the roads used by the diligences, much wider and more regular. Still lower, and quite on the flat, are the railway and the national road which connect Dijon with Lyons.[1] Three different possibilities were in turn utilized during three different epochs.

II

The Functions of Roads: Trade Routes

Much more interesting than the study of the natural conditions under which routes were established—since this only leads to conclusions that a child might grasp—is the consideration of their value. Of all the tracks which each might take it is found that there are one or two which have been chosen by preference and have remained longest in favour. But why did men follow them? That "why" must be understood in the most finalistic sense—"to what end?" In reality, human activity cannot be analysed beyond a certain point, and it is useless to try to dissociate the track of a route from the nature of the traffic which it carries. And from this point of view we may distinguish routes of different types, and, adopting an easy classification, review successively trade routes, religious routes, and political routes.

The first are found in all civilizations, even the most archaic and rudimentary. The patient labours of pre-historians [2] are causing us to realize daily that we must look further and further into the past for the creation and origin

[1] Sketches in Vidal, **CCXXXVI**, p. 243, map No. 45; cf. also Jobard (G.), *L'archéologie sur le terrain*, Dijon, 1903, p. 121 ff.

[2] De Morgan, **CLXXV**, Part III, Chap. IV; Fig. showing the old trade routes, p. 270.

of the great trade routes. Routes, and the barter that presupposes routes, not only during the bronze epoch of civilization in Europe, but long before, in the age of polished stone,[1] are now commonplaces to us. We are not only familiar with the fact of their existence, but we can trace their effects. Certain signs and indisputable inferences throw a curious light on the economic activity of the very distant past. We are familiar with the strange distribution of megaliths in different parts of the world: they are found in Western Europe, from Scandinavia to Spain, on the shores of the Mediterranean and the Black Sea, and in India, Southern Japan, and Korea.[2] Obviously, we must needs distrust hypotheses which are too rash and ambitious, but an English scholar[3] has lately made it clear that if we mark on a map, along with the megaliths, the lodes of metallic ore and precious stones and the banks of pearl oysters in India and the Pacific world, we see the most striking coincidence. Thence the conclusion that the megalithic civilization was spread by a race actuated by the desire for riches; to put it more precisely, that the race was none other than the Phœnician. We must necessarily reserve our judgment on such a bold conclusion, and regard this Phœnician intervention as a romance until there is proof to the contrary; since we know nothing or next to nothing about this people. Nevertheless, coincidences such as these open the way to many new studies and much profitable research. They are big with future knowledge.

In any case, as soon as written records appear we find ourselves on solid ground, even when these texts have to be interpreted and to a certain extent guessed; this is conclusively proved by the researches of Victor Bérard on the spread of the Phœnicians in the Mediterranean. A glance at the history of antiquity and of the Middle Ages is enough to show that the maritime routes had not changed during those periods. It may be objected that this permanence is explained by the fact that the trade routes in question, being the only ones known, were the only ones on which people dared to venture. But we may just as well say that they were

[1] Ibid., p. 238.
[2] Ibid., distribution map, fig. 147.
[3] W. J. Perry, cf. **XVI**, Vol. XXIX, 1918–19, p. 133.

the only ones known because they were the only useful ones. If new ones are created, their origin is always due to economic interests; men seek easier means of access to the countries which produce the desired commodities. There was no other reason for the great maritime discoveries of the fifteenth and sixteenth centuries and the adoption of the new trade routes which they opened up. It is a common error on the part of historians, when explaining events, to place factors of very unequal importance on the same footing, since some—the spirit of adventure, the progress of navigation, etc.—are merely favourable conditions, whilst commercial requirements are, on the contrary, the immediate and effective cause of discoveries. We have only to consider the economic profit which the Spaniards and the Portuguese derived from the new routes, the disastrous influence which these routes had on the trade of the Venetians and Genoese, and the difficulties created by the Venetians and the Arabs for the Portuguese in the Indian Ocean, to convince ourselves of the true meaning of those adventurous voyages. After that time the same thing happened in the Atlantic Ocean as had happened long before in the Mediterranean. Definite routes were created, resembling those of to-day in every respect. In the sixteenth and seventeenth centuries, for instance, there were sailings between Europe and South America which followed well-marked and highly specialized routes, such as the official route of the galleons from Cadiz to Carthagena and Porto Bello in the Isthmus of Panama, the routes of "vaisseaux de registre", the smugglers' routes frequented by the St. Malo pirates and the English. These last arrived at Peru via Buenos Ayres or by doubling Cape Horn; the registered ships also followed them; everything depended on trade necessities.[1]

Similarly, because rivers were excellent trade routes, they became frequented routes and have played a well-known part in history. The Ædui owed their power to the position of their state astride the Soire, the Allier, and the Saône. The possibility of using those waterways and of levying heavy tolls on foreign merchants who utilized them was a source of wealth and supreme power to them. Their neighbours

[1] Girard (A.), "Les voies de commerce dans l'Amérique espagnole pendant l'époque coloniale," *Bibl. Americ.*, II, 1912, p. 289 ff.

realized it when they combined to deprive them of these advantages; it was for the possession of the Saône tolls that the struggle took place between the Ædui and the Sequani.[1] And this is no solitary case. The Gaulish cities were for the most part consolidated all along a river,[2] with a view to keeping possession of both banks, because complete possession of a river route is not effected unless both banks can be held and policed. Thus the water is generally a central line, and very rarely a terminal line or boundary.

Exactly the same may be said of land routes.

Whether we are speaking of caravan tracks in the steppes or the desert, or of the roads that lead to the fairs of Champagne, or of the great iron roads of modern commerce, the value of the routes in all cases and in all ages lies not in the track followed, but in man's need of it. Demangeon, in reviewing the recent book of Marcel Blanchard on the great routes of the Western Alps,[3] remarks that the decisive reason for the Cenis route was that the Alps can there be crossed in a single effort, as the route comprises only one ascent and one descent. This may be granted; but the explanation, at most, admits of a comparison between the Cenis route and that of the Genèvre, which necessitated first an ascent from Italy, then a descent into the valley of the Durance, then, in order to leave that valley to the west or north-west, another climb, either by the Lautaret valley or via the Bayard Pass and the Champsaur. And yet this relative ease of the Cenis may have had some importance formerly when the traffic was by caravans of pack-mules; it may have retained a little of this importance when the railway was constructed, because this line is already old, being one of the first to cross the Alps; but it is quite otherwise to-day. Have we not witnessed, during the years just preceding the war, the mad race of the great commercial Powers to get tunnels[4]—each one wanting, nay insisting on boring its way through, turned back by nothing, undismayed by the greatest geographical difficulties, not hesitating at the most audacious projects? Against these economic interests, which are so powerful that they

[1] Strabo, **IV**, 3, 2; Cæsar, **IV**, 10, 3.
[2] Jullian, **CLXXII**, Vol. II, 26 ff.; 223 ff.
[3] **XI**, 1921, p. 128.
[4] Eisenmann, "Les chemins de fer transalpins," *Rev. des cours et conférences*, 1914, notes, pp. 191–3.

constrain men to overcome impossibilities at enormous sacrifices, how can we set the small advantage which the relative simplicity of its track may give to the Cenis as a route?

*

* *

Anyone who attempts to classify the trade routes on a rational basis should dwell, not on the details of the track, nor on considerations of place or situation, but on the importance and nature of the traffic which feeds the route. This is so true that there are industries which have created their own network of routes for themselves.

The most typical is undoubtedly the salt industry. There are many districts like the Franche-Comté, where we find a special arrangement for the convenient distribution of that most necessary of products, a whole system of linked roads or "sauniers", of which the centre lay at Salins. "Viæ salariæ" have existed everywhere—even in the heart of the Sahara—and, since the beds of rock-salt lay near the metallurgical centre, as was the case in Noricum, Lorraine and the Franche-Comté, for instance, the salt-ways were also metal routes, of a dual nature, military and commercial. For the possession of salt beds, like that of mines and rivers, gave rise to bitter strife and never-ending conflicts. But do we not often hear of the amber and coral routes, and those of spices and silk? To consider only the itinerary of these routes, as if that itinerary showed the reason for their existence, would be (to take an obvious comparison) as absurd as to classify ports according to their geographical position. To distinguish the coastal ports from the river ports, and to divide the former into ports situated on gulfs, bays and fiords and the latter into ports situated on estuaries and terminal ports situated at the navigable limits of a river,[1] is in our opinion much the same as making a psychological study of the members of a family from their descriptions on a passport, "nose medium, chin round, face oval." That there are people characterized by oblique eyes or flat noses and that there are quite a number of ports actually situated at the terminal point of river-navigation are two facts of great interest and utility; but the

[1] For these divisions, cf. Assada, "Les types de ports, essai de classification"; **XII**, Vol. XXVII, 1913 (I), p. 262 ff.

second can no more instruct us as to the actual trade of these river ports, than the first can instruct us as to the psychological character of the different peoples with oblique eyes and flat noses. Marseilles and Genoa are both ports on a gulf, but the one, hitherto cut off from any hinterland, is only a sort of bazaar or emporium with an outlook seaward only; the other, on the contrary, is an outlet to which the products of great industrial and agricultural regions are brought for exportation. And yet for two ports like these, which have an undeniable physical resemblance, which moreover lie on the shore of the same sea, in the same zone of economic activity and in the same small area of a particular civilization, there are countless ports, between which, up to the present, the ingenuity of geographers has not found the slightest sign of a purely geographical resemblance!

It would be no easy task to find the geographical likeness between ports of distribution like Bombay, Hong-Kong, and Zanzibar, and ports of call like Aden, Dakar, and Algiers; or between those outlets of industrial regions, Boston, New York, Barcelona, Rotterdam, and Antwerp. Moreover, it would be deceptive. Whoever establishes a port must evidently take the geographical conditions into account, even though it is only to surmount them. For there are ports created at the present day, in spite of geography, which man constructs in their entirety by violating nature, because he finds there an economic interest of the highest importance. The case of Zeebrugge is one of the best illustrations. It is a human creation in every sense of the word. Not only was there no site which seemed to suggest a port on the inhospitable coast where men have placed it, but there was no pressing necessity for its creation; that is, there was here no industrial or commercial centre which, up to that time, had been without a convenient and sufficient outlet or opportunities for expansion commensurate with its importance, and which was impatiently waiting for them to be made. Bruges was no such centre; it showed no such superabundant energy straining towards a maritime trade. On the contrary, Bruges, a sleepy town, bethought itself one day of its traditional connexion with maritime affairs and decided that a new port might perhaps restore to it some life and prosperity. Hence Zeebrugge was created to be " a means placed at the disposal of the trade of

Bruges with a view to its restoration and future growth". In the words of an admirable judge,[1] it was a lever for a future revival, but in no way an indispensable outlet for present prosperity.

But the construction of a port, even in spite of nature, is an easy matter for modern engineers. Only "it is not the same thing with a port as with a manufacturing industry which, immediately the mills are set up, commences work automatically, and whose only care is to place its products in general circulation". The clientele of a port has to be created, and that is no small matter in a world where trade is jealously kept and controlled by so many trusts, pools, and other organizations formed to hinder the free play of economic forces, and able, as we know, to nullify the greatest geographical and natural advantages. Hence the conclusion that "it is only by slow and persistent effort that Zeebrugge can be created and developed". As a final analysis, its prosperity does not depend on nature, for she is hostile; nor on an economic geography with a natural basis. It is personal and individual action which will make this creation of the engineers succeed or fail.

Hence we see clearly that ports are above all human products —the living work of man becoming more and more independent of geographical conditions. If we wish to make a useful classification of them, the chief point to consider is their true economic function, or better still the proportion of values they possess, the special combination of the various characteristic functions of ports[2]; it is better, moreover, not to attach too narrow or too strictly material a meaning to the word "economic". Ideas and "speculation", in the original meaning of the word, are fundamental elements in all financial affairs. It is generally admitted that capitalism, in a certain sense, is only a system of ideas. Assada, the author of an interesting study on types of ports, is quite right in saying that economic conditions alone do not suffice to account for the real nature of a port, but must be considered along with the social conditions. And he gives an example[3]: "It may

[1] J. Nissens-Hart, "Les ports et leurs fonctions économiques," in *Société scientifique de Bruxelles*, Vol. IV, Louvain, 1909, pp. 179–80.
[2] Concerning these functions, cf. de Rousiers, **CLXVI.**
[3] Op. cit., p. 226.

seem strange," he says, "to attribute the export of wheat on a large scale to social causes. As a matter of fact, this exportation depends as much on the degree of civilization and on the manner of life of the rural inhabitants of the hinterland as on the fertility of the soil. And if Odessa, for instance, specializes more and more in the exportation of wheat, it is as much because Russia is still a young country, where the population is small compared with the area, and the needs of the bulk of the population are very simple, as because it is the outlet of the black soil region."

*
* *

In reality, the study of all these subjects has still to be begun. In connexion with highly civilized countries, it is not impossible to utilize statistics, especially those of the railways, for finding out the importance of any particular trade; strictly, preferential tariffs, where they exist, should help us to identify a particular traffic, though the task is always a delicate one; but if we want to use other figures which are less clear, such as those of port statistics, we find a thousand difficulties in the way. For the importance of a port is measured by three different calculations: the gross tonnage of the ships visiting it, the import and export tonnage, and the figures for the value of the trade passing through it, which are never in agreement; from which it follows that a classification made from one of these calculations is never the same as those made from the other two. But not all ports give us in their general statistics the three necessary figures obtained by the same method; and so we are misled by most of the formal lists. We are dealing here with complicated organisms, and with trade items between which it is difficult to discriminate. But even when the historian, the geographer and the economist are dealing with the simpler civilizations, the difficulties are great.

It would be very interesting to arrange them in groups, for we should see then that the explanation of these facts often lies in technical considerations not as a rule understood.

Let us take as an example the routes of the Sahara. In a sense, these are veritable sea routes—or were, to be more exact, since very little of this Sahara traffic now survives. They stretched between two opposite coasts, that of Africa Minor to the north and that of the Sudan to the south, across a sort of sandy or stony sea which separated them, and had to be crossed with the minimum loss by damage. Two lines of "ports", a northern and a southern, served as termini for caravans coming across the desert; on the one side Tenduf, Tripoli, Benghazi; on the other Timbuktu, Kano, Zinder, Kuka, Abech, El Fasher. These towns had all grown from a nucleus of nomad Berber middlemen,[1] those great organizers of transport in the Sahara, which was usually augmented by Arab elements from the Mediterranean towns. These middlemen warehoused what the caravans brought from the north: cloth, glass beads, perfumes, sugar and paper; in exchange they gave the same caravans the products received from the Negro kingdoms—gold, ivory, feathers, and above all, slaves. At the ports of call, in the course of their journey, true products of the Sahara were added to these Sudanese or Mediterranean products: salt, especially, created a fully organized traffic, which was sufficient in itself, and still suffices to-day, to attract men to the desert and retain them there: recent researches give us precise information about the remunerative character of this trade, and the chief routes which it follows.[2] But, in a general way, the traffic across the Sahara is only the shadow of what it used to be when processions of 10,000 to 15,000 camels were strung out along the tracks, from Timbuktu to the Tuat and thence to Tafilet or by Ghadames to Tripoli, or again from Kano and Zinder to Ghat and to Murzuk, or from Abech to Benghazi by Kufra. Why are the desert routes now almost lifeless?

The disappearance of slavery, and consequently of the chief article of trade between the Sudan and the Mediterranean, has been alleged as the reason. There is no doubt of the fact; but must we not take into account another factor which Meniaud has made very clear? Fifteen thousand camels can carry nearly 1,500 tons net weight.[3] That was a considerable tonnage in former times. In the fifteenth century the largest ships displaced only 400 to 500 tons. In the time of Elizabeth, the *Great Harry*, of 1,000 tons, was a monarch among ships. Hence the caravans of the Sahara of the fifteenth and sixteenth centuries represented a trading fleet comparable with the

[1] Meniaud, **CLXXXIII,** Vol. I, 175.
[2] Cf. especially an interesting and accurate study by Cortier, **XII,** Vol. XXV, 1912 (I), p. 91 ff.; particularly 97–8, on the conditions of the Bilma traffic.
[3] Meniaud, **CLXXXIII,** loc. cit.

best European merchant fleets. But to-day? The medium-sized liners which plough the routes to South America, Africa, Australia and the Far East displace from 6,000 to 12,000 tons, with a speed of 14 to 15 knots. As to the merchant vessels, some cargoes are of huge dimensions—up to 20,000 tons—but the majority are between 3,000 to 10,000 tons and the largest iron sailing-ships displace from 1,500 to 5,000 tons.[1] Is it not very instructive to compare these figures with those we have previously given? And have we not grounds for the conclusion that the sea-going ship had everything in her favour to enable her to dethrone "the ship of the desert"? As soon as the communications penetrating from the coasts to the interior from the Gulf of Guinea as well as from the Mediterranean were developed and modernized, maritime trade was able to play a rôle of ever-increasing importance in the commercial life of the Sahara and the Sudan.

To sum up: in the matter of the establishment of trade routes, it is of secondary importance whether the nature of the ground favours them. The necessary condition is the need for communication, and if that exists, no obstacles or difficulties will prevent men from making them. Marshes, snow drifts, the wildest mountains, the desert itself will be braved and conquered.

III

Religious and Intellectual Routes

What is true of commercial routes is equally true of religious ones. Men do not move about solely from reasons of a material or economic nature. As far back into the past as records permit us to penetrate, we find them making their way towards the great centres of religious and intellectual life. Need we recall, for instance, the pilgrimages of ancient Greece, the throngs that assembled at the time of the great festivals from all parts of the country, so that at certain dates Delphi, Corinth, Nemea, Olympia, Athens and Delos became the real centres of the whole Hellenic world? This type of travel was certainly quite independent of geography. The pilgrims,

[1] Vallaux, **CCXXXVI**, p. 280.

it is true, chose in preference the most practicable routes, but their movements themselves were quite independent of physical conditions, which influenced neither their cause, their fervour, their seasonal variations nor the vicissitudes experienced in the course of years. This social phenomenon of pilgrimages has been constant throughout history. We know, moreover, how important it was in the Middle Ages, and how at that epoch it created, supported, and developed special roads known as pilgrim ways, marked by monasteries, hospitals, and almshouses, and described in special guides and route books.

The great pilgrimages of the age, the major pilgrimages, led to Rome and Jerusalem on one hand and to Santiago de Compostela on the other. We know what routes the pious travellers took to Rome [1]: the Great St. Bernard and the Val d'Aosta; the valley of the Arc, the Cenis and the Dora Riparia; sometimes, but more rarely, the southern ways: Mont Genèvre, the Tenda Pass, or the shore-route of the Corniche; thence they passed on to Rome by the Cisa Pass or, further east, by the passes of the Apennines between Forli and Arezzo.[2] The port of embarcation for the Holy Land was usually Brindisi, but sometimes Venice, Genoa or Pisa.[3] It concerns us very little that these routes were chiefly frequented in summer, and that they crossed the mountains at the points which were most convenient geographically—the passes; the dominating fact for any study of them is that they were essentially religious routes, and that all their other features were subordinate to this; that as such they essentially lent themselves to foot traffic, and that this traffic took place, sometimes at a fixed date, as at certain festivals, sometimes at no definite date, in which case the choice of seasons naturally affected it. We are not here dealing with an urgent and permanent traffic, such as is the case when it is a question of the transport of provisions and the necessaries of life.

The routes which took pilgrims from all over Europe to Santiago de Compostela, in Galicia, are equally familiar.[4] We

[1] Bédier, *Les légendes épiques*, 2nd ed., Vol. II, 1917, p. 143 ff: "Les chansons de geste et les routes d'Italie," map, p. 153.

[2] Male, "L'Art du moyen âge et les pélerinages" (*Rev. de Paris*, Vol. CLV, 15th October, 1919, p. 718).

[3] Bédier, op. cit., p. 266.

[4] Bédier, op. cit., Vol. I, 1914, p. 366 ff.

know that in the tenth century the pilgrimage to Santiago was already prosperous; and that its popularity increased suddenly in the first third of the twelfth century "owing to the action of an able and ambitious man, Diego Gelmirez, Bishop and afterwards Archbishop of Compostela"—again we see individual initiative at the source of these great collective streams, and such creations of the human will as sanctuaries, ports, or industries. We know, too, what the "launching" of such a pilgrimage would mean: for instance, the making of roads—the famous roads of Saint James—and along these roads the formation of "hospitia" in quite incredible numbers, and hostelries or shelters for the night at suitable intervals; the creation almost everywhere of special brotherhoods; the upkeep of a religious and military order devoted to the protection of the main army of pilgrims.[1] And all this took place not only along the roads to Santiago and Rome, where the "Romieux" crowded in such numbers, and in such long processions, especially in summer, that the roads received the exclusive name of *strata publica peregrinorum* as though merchants, soldiers, ambassadors, monks and students did not also throng the old and still firm Roman highways![2] A hundred other Christian sanctuaries attracted voluntary or penitent visitors from afar, such as, in France alone, Chartres, Clermont, Le Puy, Tours, Poitiers, Saintes, Conques, Moissac and Toulouse. We can easily understand that the determining elements of the routes they made were the facilities for resting-places at convenient intervals all along the way, and the possibility of visiting on the road as many sanctuaries as possible.[3]

However, we must not think that these phenomena of strictly religious travelling were peculiar to Christian mediæval countries. Camille Jullian tells us of the activity of the sanctuaries and the great religious assembling-places of the Celts; they were commonly, like our own abbeys of the Middle Ages, centres of economic and especially of industrial activity.[4] The metallurgical importance of Alesia is well known, and "it was not chance that led Alexandre Bertrand to believe that

[1] Bédier, I, p. 367.
[2] Ibid., II, p. 148.
[3] Male, *Revue de Paris*, Vol. CLVII, 15th February, 1920, p. 774 ff.
[4] Jullian, *Rev. des Et. anc.*, Vol. XXII, 1920, pp. 211–12.

the working of iron was bound up with the Druidical organization". And, in the same way, these sanctuaries had their commercial side; a business connexion was established between them; the common life, economic, religious, and linguistic, whose existence we can trace back to the first iron and bronze ages, may be partly explained by these links, these routes from sanctuary to sanctuary. But later still? A recent work points out[1] how the area of distribution of *clocca* (Fr. *cloche*)—portable ecclesiastical bells—supports the hypothesis of a Celtic origin for both the word and the thing, for they are found in the North of Italy, the Engadine, France, the Asturias, and Portugal. The Irish monks are said to have introduced both word and bell on the continent, and their propagation is supposed to have taken place along the pilgrim route which goes from Bobbio to Santiago de Compostela. Of the intellectual or artistic, as distinguished from a material, expansion we have, moreover, ample knowledge through the labours of Bédier, Male, and many others.

Much the same thing can be seen in Mohammedan and Buddhist countries. One must have been present at the festivals of Mouloud in one of the great sanctuaries of Islam such as Mecca, Kairwan, or Tlemsen, to understand the importance of the pilgrimages in the eyes of the faithful. The pilgrim caravan routes to Mecca have been studied carefully as well as the Buddhist pilgrim routes to Lhassa. But we need not look so far afield. Is it not enough to examine the traffic on some of the French southern railways to be aware of the part which is played in the movement of traffic in a great modern country by such a pilgrimage as that to Lourdes or in a less degree to Our Lady of Auray? The Lourdes example is full of significance. Lourdes is privileged in its situation. It is, moreover, an old historical site. We find there a spring known from the very earliest times. There is also an isolated steep rock, level at the top, and marvellously adapted for fortification. All round are fertile and variegated fields. A rural market centred round a spring at the foot of a fortress—Lourdes was a little rural metropolis rejoicing in all the advantages of such a position. Then a pilgrimage was started—we know how. To-day it is on the way to becoming a sort of capital of the Pyrenees.

[1] *Rev. des Et. anc.*, 1920, pp. 3–9.

Let us remark that these religious routes have very often a double function, since we may also call them intellectual routes. The great games of ancient Greece took place at the time of the religious festivals, and included literary, artistic, and musical competitions. The great sanctuaries of the Middle Ages were the beginnings of great intellectual centres, as at the present time the celebrated mosques of the Islamic world are the home of the schools of the " tolba ". Need we refer to the theories of Bédier on the origin and spread of the Chansons de Gestes, and the connexion his researches have established between literary production and the radiance emanating from the great centres of mediæval pilgrimage ? There seems to be no doubt that in the gradual evolution of society a distinction arose between intellectual and religious centres. But what happened in the case of the religious centres also came to pass as regards the Universities ; they became a point of convergence for all those concerned, whom they attract from afar ; they gave rise to, and supported, a special traffic along the routes which led to them. The attraction exercised by the University of Paris during the whole of the Middle Ages is well known ; it is also well known that towards the end of the Middle Ages, in the time of the Renaissance, the practice of making the tour of France or even of Europe—in any case, the tour of Italy—prevailed in the student world. And still at the present day, in Germany and Anglo-Saxon countries, certain Universities are really international centres of travel and intellectual activity, drawing students from all parts of the world.

IV

Political Routes and the Genesis of States

Commercial, religious, and intellectual routes there are, but not the least among them all are the essentially political routes which have produced or maintained States and Empires.

A State can only exist when a certain number of individuals desire to belong to the same collectivity, and to share the common interests of its other members. Routes, then, play a necessary and sovereign part in the life of political units; a varied part, however, which is not exactly the same at all times nor in all cases; but of such a character that a study of the network of roads in a country at a given epoch, and a comparison of it with the network in a neighbouring country at the same period, or even with the network in the same country at a previous or later period, throws much light on the character, nature, and aims of the State which governs the country. Vidal de la Blache has shown this admirably at the end of his *Tableau de la France* as far as that country is concerned: there is nothing more striking than the comparison he draws between the maps of the Roman roads in Gaul, of the royal roads at the end of the eighteenth century, and of the modern railways. He brings to light, above all, the important fact that political routes, unlike the others in many cases, always form a system. They show a considered "combination" of ways and means of communication, with the view of permitting the State the free and adequate use of its resources and power and ready communication with those neighbouring countries with whom it has vital relations. This is no doubt true of France and of its roads, which were calculated to serve the centralizing policy of its monarchy. It was certainly very true, in ancient times, of the systematic network of the great Roman roads, or of the royal roads of Persia in the time of Darius. It is still true of the network of railways in most modern states. By careful study we can easily distinguish the strategic and military railways from the great passenger and goods lines. It is true also of certain maritime routes; the well-known route to India, by the Mediterranean, the Red Sea and the Indian Ocean, studded with British possessions, is the most typical example.

It is not geography, then, but politics and history which find direct expression in these systems; it is a question of the actual forging of armour of the strongest possible material by men anxious to maintain and hold together the constituent elements of a national organization. Such work is always difficult and cannot be improvised, but demands special agents to render it serviceable. For absolute necessity is absent in the case of a State in the making, in that it has not acquired that special character which only a long series of trials and cruel vicissitudes of success or misfortune borne in common gives to the creations of history and politics.

Above all, there is at first no necessity—that is, no geographical necessity—about the amalgamation or association of certain districts which form a group to make a State. We can always imagine, instead of the grouping which actually takes place, others which could or might have been made without any impossibility or illogicality. At times even geographical convenience is disregarded in a most unexpected manner. Vidal de la Blache, in the thoughtful and powerful book which we quoted above, says very justly: " If the union of the different districts of Gaul had not been an accomplished fact before historic life awoke in the Germanic North, who knows if other combinations might not have seemed more attractive ? Between the basins of Paris and London, between Lorraine and Swabia, there is less difference from the geographical point of view than between those districts and the French Mediterranean provinces ?"[1] It is a great and suggestive thought, that no country is born from itself—has been able to do without external influence in its birth, development, and establishment. " The impulse comes from without. No civilized country is altogether the creation of its own civilization. Or at any rate it can only produce a limited civilization, like a clock which goes for a time and then suddenly stops. In order to arrive at a higher degree of development, its life must be in touch with a wider sphere, which enriches it with its own substance and instils into it new ferments."[2] In other words, at the cradle of every State there is a " route "—not at first one of those man-made roads, one of those fixed and calculated routes which belong to a system and combine with others to form a strong political armour, but the first little trickle of general life, the forerunner of a broad and powerful current.

Vidal de la Blache speaks in one place of " that almost immaterial thing which is called a way of communication ".[3] It is in this sense that there is always a " route " at the origin of great countries, of great national entities: at first a sort of electric spark which runs across a series of districts, puts them into communication, traverses the whole line, and by

[1] Vidal, **CCX**, pp. 53–4. [2] Ibid., p. 17.
[3] Ibid., p. 52.

creating an obscure kind of solidarity between them, singles them out to the exclusion of other possibilities. A great work, of the highest importance. But, in order that the effects may be lasting, there must be superposed on this immaterial road a material one—a hard highway of stone and cement. "Italy only became a nation when the Appian and Flaminian ways were combined to link its extremities together," and France only when the Celtic roads, the ancestors of the Roman roads, distributed over the country great currents of intercourse which gave birth to, developed, and have since maintained the unity of France.

This is a singularly vivid conception on the part of that great geographer, steeped in history and prehistory, and accustomed to meditate on and perfect an idea which all the empty pedagogic categories put together were incapable of containing. There is no constraint, nothing essentially determinant in those influences of soil and geographical environment which he appreciates, moreover, with such subtle acuteness and insight. He was not the man to confound a country like France with a jumble of provinces mechanically united like the stones in a pavement. He knew too well that those great masterpieces of man's work, States or Nations, elaborated during a long period of infancy, full of hazard and peril, were the fruit of deliberate activity, creative intelligence, and a stout will fighting against the obscure influences of environment and striving to utilize them and adapt them to its needs, but submitting to them passively—never.

CHAPTER III

Towns

I

Exaggerated Interpretations

SOME excellent treatises on towns, written by geographers, have appeared in France during the last few years. We shall have to return shortly to the conclusions arrived at in these treatises. But there have also appeared—generally outside France, and particularly in Germany—studies of groups, whose authors propose to class and catalogue towns, to divide them up into genera and species, and to group them according to their geographical types. Some of these authors, like Ratzel, whom they all follow,[1] based their work on the situation, others on the plan, others again on the aspect, the materials, the shape, and the external appearance of the houses and buildings of the place.[2] Lists have been made, divided into families, arranged in categories and types. It is a great work, amusing at times in its results—at any rate, in its manner; its utility is unquestionable, provided its authors recognize that it is provisional and that they avoid certain rash generalizations.

Here are four towns—Zurich, Lucerne, Thun, Geneva.[3] All four are situated at the end of a lake, astride the river which drains the lake; do they not form a natural group? May we not, in connexion with them, legitimately utter that fascinating word "type", which gives such play to the imagination? Certainly, if we please. But what interest is there in the comparison? What relation, what analogy between the insignificant Thun and the powerful Zurich, the industrial capital of Switzerland—between Lucerne, the little town of hotels and foreigners, and Geneva? Does the situation of these towns, so entirely different from one another, or rather

[1] Ratzel, **CLXII.**
[2] Hassert, **CLIV.**
[3] Brunhes, **LXVI**, p. 245.

does the geographical peculiarity which they have in common create any analogy in their functions? None whatever. In this case again it is the function which is of primary importance; it is by their function that towns should be classed and catalogued, as we said just now of ports and routes, if we wish to obtain a really useful classification. Otherwise we might as well classify mental types by arguing from the length of the nose or the shape of the ear of the individuals who are being studied.

Function may certainly react on the shape, aspect, or plan of a city,[1] but the opposite is never true. And, moreover, a clear understanding on the first point is necessary. When we are told that " Venice, Amsterdam, and Danzig are towns built on the sea or near the sea, which have the common characteristic of being canal towns; they certainly deserve to be grouped and compared ",[2] we evidently cannot but subscribe to the statement. But does the comparison which it is proposed to make carry anything useful or merely something that may be interesting? Towns built on the sea, or near the sea, canal towns—and after that? What inference are we to draw? Not every comparison is valuable in itself, and to class the kings of France as fat and thin, tall or short, is not to contribute very effectively to a knowledge of their reign or their character.

The author whom we are quoting adds[3]: " the great advantage of such groupings, which are based on intrinsic qualities, is that they allow us to compare with those perfect and homogeneous types, portions, even small portions, of other towns which share the same geographical nature." And to quote in support, pell-mell, Hamburg, Bruges, Metz, and " Strasbourg with its *Klein Frankreich* quarter "—by which is understood the quarter of tanneries and mills where the Ill divides into five streams, one of whose quays, recalling many sad remembrances as little "national" as may be, takes its name from the tumbledown hospice " Zum Franzœsel ".[4] But, with the best will in the world, what is there in the least " geographical " about the resemblances of those various

[1] Hassert, **CLIV**, *Das Stadtbild*, pp. 93–112.
[2] Brunhes, **LXVI**, p. 246.
[3] Ibid.
[4] Seyboth, *Strasbourg historique et pittoresque*, Strasbourg, 1894, p. 581.

quarters? To speak of the mill district of Strasbourg as Venetian would certainly be rather farcical. If we are told the "water-side" quarters of European towns resemble one another, in the sense that they all have the sky above, houses, and water, we will admit it readily. But if this triumph of science is to be labelled "geographical" we are at a loss to understand what is meant or else the word "geographical," being used to convey too much, conveys nothing at all. It goes without saying that we can compare certain quarters of certain towns in appearance and planning, but what is at the bottom of such likeness is the technical consideration of trade and of man's labour. What do resemble one another at Metz, Strasbourg, Bar-le-Duc, and a score of other towns in the east of France are the special buildings with vast drying rooms which are traditionally required for the tanning industry formerly so widely distributed—an industry which the still waters naturally attracted. So that we are led to conclude that, in these countries, men have brought to like technical problems like solutions; as in these problems of architecture, that is to say of the utilization of both ground and materials in such a way as to meet certain industrial needs. But what has geography to do with it, if geography is, or is to be, regarded as a science? It is a mystery.

In reality, Vidal de la Blache here again propounded the true problem of the geography of the town and solved it at the time when he wrote: "Nature prepares the site, and man organizes it in such fashion that it meets his desires and wants."[1] This is the evident truth. But we must in addition and at the start introduce a supplementary distinction.

"Nature prepares the site." A non-temporal formula, if we may so call it, and hence suspect by the historian. For it may allow us to confuse, as the geographer did whom we have just quoted about the towns of the lakes and the towns of the canals, what Camille Jullian, an historian, distinguishes carefully as the two contributing elements to a town's vitality—its formation and its growth.[2] For it is precisely the absence

[1] Vidal, **XCV**, p. 107.

[2] Jullian, "Rôle des monuments dans la formation topographique des villes," *Rev. des cours et conférences*, 22nd year, 1914, No. 8, p. 729 ff.; cf. by same author: "A propos de géographie urbaine," *Rev. des Etudes anc.*, Vol. XXI, 1919, pp. 112–14.

of any distinction between these two that renders any assimilation of different towns, such as those mentioned above, both incomplete and difficult to accept. It is possible that the particular situation of Zurich, Lucerne, Thun, and Geneva, at the end of a lake, astride the river that drains the lake, played a part in the genesis and primitive establishment of those four towns; that in all four it has been a contributory element in their original establishments—a "formative element". And if this is true, if a careful study of the origin and of the development of those four cities confirms it, it is quite evident that it is a very good thing to point it out. But simply to say, without any more details, after having named those four towns, that "from their mere position towns belong to the same type"; no. For long ago the physical peculiarity in question must have yielded place, in the development of these urban organisms, to factors of quite a different nature and of infinitely more importance: to factors of growth or, as Jullian calls it, of enlargement.

II

Fortress Towns

Let us return again to some of our facts and try to group them by the aid of this useful distinction; never losing sight also of the necessary consideration of the functions of towns. For it is evident that there are certain topographical peculiarities which lend themselves better than others to certain uses; there are, we may say, sites easier to adapt than others to a particular one of the many functions which towns fulfil.

Now, when we think of these functions of towns, we naturally think first of their military value. Is not its circle of ramparts the very emblem of a town, its mark, its symbol? But besides walls built by the hand of man, natural sources of strength are not wanting. They are many and various. A steep mountain, a hill with precipitous sides, a rock commanding the surrounding plain is an excellent base for a nation to hold which requires a strong place of refuge or a military centre, as in the case of the Acropolis at Athens or the Acrocorinthus or Mont Auxois or the plateau of Gergovia or the lofty Mont Beuvray on which stand the ruins of Bibracte or the African Cirta. If the bend of a river, in addition to the mountain, affords the protection of an impassable fosse, the site is better still; such a one as has made from Celtic times, and perhaps even earlier, the military fortune of Besançon, the ancient Vesontio. An island is an excellent refuge, easy to defend, as in the case of Tyre or of the Parisian "Cité". It is unnecessary to multiply these examples as the facts are not in dispute. Still it may be noted that, as time goes on, towns that are merely defensive are becoming more and more rare; we must not, however, conclude from this that our civilization no longer knows the fortress-town; in the east of France there are Langres, Toul, Verdun, and Belfort which still play an almost immemorial military part on the French frontiers. But what is important to remark, on the other hand, is that there was never any geographical predestination about any of these towns.

They were not the offspring of a rock, of a river bend, or of a girdle of water or a marsh; but essentially of man's will.

For one thing, a favourable site is not indispensable to the creation of a fortress which will satisfy the need of a human society for defence and protection. When that need exists, man profits by any advantages the ground can give him. If there are in the neighbourhood any natural elevations, or rocks, or hills, he organizes them for defence; if there are none—he does without.

Walls, palisades in form of a fraise (*plessis*), a *ferté* or "strong place", the fosse and vallum, were so many means of defence which sometimes supplemented those which favourable ground offered, sometimes made up for their absence.

Man, however, has often no choice. He has created towns, in times of peace and security, for trade and barter, and therefore established them in open and healthy country, sunny, easy of access, rich in choice of materials. The political situation changes; there is a threat of war and invasion.[1] Great merchant cities, built on the open plain without thought of danger, have to be defended, hastily protected and fortified; for it is not always convenient to abandon them or remove them to a better position. Cross-roads and the point where

[1] Cf., for example, Blanchet, *Les enceintes romaines de la Gaule*, Paris, 1907, p. 5.

several roads converge cannot be moved. When barbarian invasions threaten, when the Roman peace is weakened, when great commercial towns, which have sprung up at the intersection of several Roman roads, have to be hurriedly fortified, there is neither time nor means to remove them. It was not of their own free will that the inhabitants of the coastal towns of Friuli and Venetia fled from Altinum, Padua, and Ravenna to bury themselves among the protective lagoons, returning almost to the old shelter of the prehistoric pile dwellings in the midst of insalubrious marshes and reeds, devoid of means for building.

Poitiers, placed at the intersection of eight Roman roads, could not be moved; nor Tours, situated at the centre of a network whose threads reached out to Orleans, Le Mans, Nantes, Poitiers, and Bourges. If there is a favourable spot near, it is utilized; in this way changes of name are explained, showing changes, which Jullian notices, in the importance of districts, and to which we shall refer again. But there is not always such an emplacement at hand. Artificial fortifications are then constructed. Man's ingenuity is pitted against nature. Yet, after all, there are, in flat countries, many purely military towns, military entirely in origin and design, which have never known defences other than walls and moats in the manner of Vauban.

Yet, all the time, there were plenty of sites thoroughly adapted for defence, which man neglected, or at least which were never adopted for towns. Here it is that those elements of growth or enlargement, of which Jullian speaks, come into play, and which are far from all, or even chiefly, geographical or natural. The development and life of an urban community are chiefly conditioned by its political and international relations at different periods, even in the case of a place which is purely military. A frontier may be changed, recede, or be modified by some treaty, but there is no modification in the topography and no diminution in the material advantages which the citadel, rock, or the river moat offers for defence: yet here we have a predestined site which can no longer support even a simple village. We need only think of such ruined and vanished towns as La Mothe, which for so long incarnated the Lorrainers' spirit of resistance, or of the towns to-day reduced to the state of mere museums of military architecture—

Semur-en-Auxois, for instance, or Carcassonne : it is increasing security and the disturbance of frontiers which have gradually deprived them of life and animation. But, even to-day, do not towns which are certainly not military only, and which have other reasons for their existence besides a girdle of forts or a strong garrison, pass through a critical time owing to a change of frontier such as the reincorporation of Alsace in France ? And do not the towns of Alsace find themselves confronted with formidable difficulties which in no way have their origin in the towns themselves or in Alsace ?

III

Formative Elements and Elements of Growth

The creation of a military town is, we see, simple only in appearance. It may appear to be so if we confine our attention to that formative element constituted by its hill or river bend ; it ceases to be so when we look also into the elements of its growth. But the same difference is found everywhere. Many towns, as we know, owe their origin to a spring. Such, for instance, was the beginning of Nîmes ; it is a famous spring which still exists to-day, and which the ancients revered and worshipped, faithful to the teaching of the elder Pliny, who says that " springs make towns and create divinities ". It is quite certain that the spring *Nemausus* determined the birth of Nîmes ; it was really the cause of it ; if there had been no spring, there would undoubtedly have been no town, for what other reason could there be for fixing one there ? This is no isolated example. And the old creative virtue of waters has not yet disappeared. Do not the hot springs, the great healers of diseases, the thermal waters, account for the birth of Bourbonne, Luxeuil, Aix-la-Chapelle, etc., as in our own day for the birth of Vichy, Luchon, Dax, etc. ? But Nîmes once created—that is to say, the houses built around its spring—that spring cannot account for its later history. Other factors come into play, precisely those factors required to transform a small collection of houses, which might vegetate as such for centuries, into that vigorous organism —a town.

Amongst these different factors, the possession of a centre of barter is one of the most important. A fortress is often at the same time a market. It sometimes happens that under the shelter of its walls and within the great area they surround (Bibracte was more than three miles in circumference and had an area of 350 acres; and Gergovia a circumference of 2½ miles and an area of nearly 200 acres) one of those open market spaces is installed which the Romans called a "forum" and the Gauls *magus*, and which have left numerous traces behind them in French place-names.[1] But this is neither the rule nor a necessity. In times when markets had only a temporary existence[2] analogous to that of the fairs or "pardons" of to-day, it was not necessary to shelter them behind permanent fortifications, since a whole series of special institutions[3] provided, amongst all nations, for the general safety of the merchants in the old sense of the word, that is to say, the buyers and sellers. We may add that, in old times, the particular market for the sale of provisions was specially reserved for women to the exclusion of men.[4] The latter could only join in the business when, along with the provisions, goods of other kinds appeared on the sale ground; for then the market began to participate in long-distance trade, which was more or less of a military nature and of man's province.

In any case we may surmise that many townships, open or fortified, owed their origin to commerce. Jullian has studied a certain number in ancient Gaul.[5] He observes that these localities were, for choice, situated on the boundary of a city at the point of contact of two differing groups of producers. Such was the case with Nijon near Bourmont (Noviomagus), between Lingons and Leuques; with "Mosomagus", the market of the Meuse, now Mouzon, near the frontiers of the Remi and the Treveri; with "Tornomagus", Tournon (in the Indre), on the border of the Turones, the Bituriges, and the Pictones. But these places have ceased to play an important part in economic life and do not even exist any longer as towns; a clear enough proof, if one were wanted,

[1] Jullian, **CLXXII**, Vol. II, p. 238.
[2] Huvelin, **CLXV**, p. 9.
[3] Ibid., Chap. XIII ff.
[4] Lasch, "Das Marktwesen auf den primitiven Kulturstufen," *Zeitschrift für Sozialwissenschaft*, 1906.
[5] Jullian, **CLXXII**, Vol. II, p. 238.

that without any predetermination, men simply chose from among the different places which might serve as economic centres those which were best adapted to the needs of the moment. In the same way Tongres during the Roman period and Quentovic, Tiel, and Durslede during the Carlovingian were the only commercial centres of the Low Countries. Liége, Louvain, Malines, Antwerp, Brussels, Bruges, Ypres, and Ghent [1] only appeared at the beginning of the Middle Ages.

The interest men have in frequenting certain markets varies with the general state of civilization, the nature and method of production of the manufactured articles, the state of the roads, the means of transport, and, above all, the conditions created by domestic and international politics. Nearly all these factors are historical even more than geographical, and through them the influence of society on locality is exercised. There are many instances of markets gaining and then losing importance, although they themselves were in no way modified. The decline of the Champagne fairs; the substitution of Atlantic for Mediterranean ports at the end of the fifteenth and the beginning of the sixteenth centuries; and, finally, the substitution of Cadiz for Seville, of Havre for Rouen, are all so many illustrations of this commonplace truth. It is useless to pretend that great discoveries have been made because certain facts, which have not been really co-ordinated nor systematically presented, have been included in an abstract formula: for here we are in the domain of history.

There is another class of towns whose existence depends more on travel than on trade. We mean those which owe their origin to what Jullian calls "wayside episodes", features of the road such as fords and bridges, the entrance to a defile or a forest region or a specially difficult country, the foot of a steep gradient, the first halt on the plain at the bottom of a mountain descent, the meeting-place of several routes, cross-roads, and, perhaps, ports; for after all a port "is simply a stopping place, the end of a stage on a main route; it is the place where sea routes end and land routes begin, where disembarkation and loading take place, and, we might almost say, a 'relay' station." These features

[1] Pirenne, **CLXI**, pp. 2–4 and 15.

are all frequently formative elements in the history of towns; but the important thing is, that they are all, as a rule, important elements of growth in the same history.

For the increase or decrease of towns is due in the first place to routes; they sometimes change their sites owing to routes; it is due to routes that they become centres of accumulation and storage of the agricultural or industrial products of a whole district, or, again, centres of distribution for distant and exotic products. Nothing has more influence than the history of routes on the destinies of towns, whether their origin depends on a route, a spring, a sanctuary, or a hill fortress.

Moreover, the creative power of routes is not extinct, even to-day. We can still name communities which have been created directly by communications. The little towns which have been founded at the entrance and exit of Alpine tunnels; those which have sprung up at the chief junctions of railways, at the points where they meet, or where two lines cross; such places as Laroche, or Saint Germain des Fossés, with their special population of hotel-keepers and railway employees; all these curious formations bear ample testimony to the fact. But it must be noted that all these towns are quite independent of normal geographical conditions. The tunnel towns do not occupy sites comparable with those of the "towns of the passes", to which the Ratzelians attach so much importance; nor do the railway towns, the towns which result from a great railway station, a junction, or a terminus of routes. The agglomeration springs up how it can, and where it can, round the iron road and with a kind of life which it sometimes creates artificially in absolute defiance of all favourable geographical conditions.

It is the same with industrial towns. We are told that the situation of these is fixed by the special resources of the district. But here again we may be allowed a certain scepticism. Mines attract a mining centre. That is evident; but mining business never assumes a character of permanence or perpetual immutability. It changes frequently from causes of an economic or political kind which depend much more on the general state of civilization than on strictly geographical conditions. The use of bauxite or of fluor-spar is recent. Oolithic minerals have less and less interest for metallurgists; phosphorated minerals, useless till quite recently, interest them more and more. All these are so many causes of immense changes in certain regions, and are due to devèlopments of science, to the progress of technical knowledge, and to the appearance of new wants: causes, all of them, unconnected with geography. There is no more interesting study than that of the local reasons for an industry and for the communities which it fosters; but how are we to explain how Clermont-Ferrand, for instance, owes its real growth to the indiarubber industry? The surrounding country, besides being very badly served by both land and water communications, possesses none of the chief requirements of that industry. Here we are concerned with an absolutely artificial creation,[1] due to the energy of a few men; and here again natural conditions are of less importance than the utilization by man of possibilities, the greater part of which are not even possibilities of geographical origin. Need we speak now of political capitals, of the great religious centres, or of the cities of learning? No doubt the importance of the routes which they command explains in part the rôle and development of the great capitals. It is an undeniable fact that the situation of Paris is unique in respect of the easy communication which it allows with the rest of France; that Berlin is favoured in its aspirations by its position at the junction of the great waterways of Germany, is another; but the position of a capital never explains its size, its permanence, nor even why it became a capital. How many towns, even in Europe, have suddenly become, or ceased to be, capitals, for historical and political reasons which have no connexion with their situation? Versailles owed its birth to a royal whim, and its fall was brought about by no geographical considerations.[2] In reality, the capital is made by the State, the prosperity of which creates the prosperity, and the decline of which entails the decline of the town which it has chosen as its chief seat. Historical and political events have infinitely more influence on the development of the capital than the physical conditions under which it was established.

As to centres of learning or religion, need we recall the

[1] Bataillon (L.), "Clermont-Ferrand ville industrielle," *Action Nationale*, 25th Oct., 1920.

[2] Foncin (M.), "Versailles, étude de géographie historique," **XI**, Vol. XXVIII, 1919, p. 321 ff.

fact that the number of students in a given University in Germany varies with the arrival or departure of such and such a professor? And if Kairwan and Tlemcen have become great towns which attract thousands of pilgrims, if Lourdes has increased, as we know it has, is it by virtue of some physical predestination? There are tourist towns, the great examples of marked geographical determinism? A traveller of world-wide celebrity, or an interested doctor, or a well-known sportsman has only to make the place the fashion, and the birth of a town follows; it develops and increases in size, and takes root on ground sometimes as little suited as possible for the development of a town. . . . And we may see, in times of trouble, how the mere fluctuation of the exchanges assures prosperity or brings ruin to the place.

IV

Man and Urban Possibilities

The true and only geographical problem is that of the utilization of possibilities. But it is so complex that it is evidently foolish to try and solve it by the aid of a very simple formula or some supposed geographical law. It is the great merit of the urban monographs, of which we spoke at the beginning, that they have proved this. One of the most typical and striking seems to us to be that which Blanchard has written on the town of Annecy in the *Recueil des Travaux de l'Institut de géographie alpine de Grenoble.*[1]

Annecy, which its situation, in touch with various districts of small extent, and at the mouth of a narrow, winding, and difficult pass, did not predestine to any very great destiny, does not occupy a simple position. Its site is formed by the union of a certain number of different elements.

A rocky ridge, the Semnoz, commanding the lake and the surrounding country, is suitable for defence. A low hill, that of old Annecy, with fertile soil and facing due south like a fruit wall, is well adapted for cultivation. The shore of the lake is dangerous on account of floods, treacherous, and unhealthy; but it supplies fish; it permits easy and

[1] Vol. IV, 1916, Fasc. IV.

extensive communication by water; and it has its value as a defence. The Fins, unbroken, plain, dry, and of light soil, favours movement, agriculture, and population. Lastly, a river with constant and regular current offers great facilities for industry.

All these constituent elements of the site of Annecy have their advantages, and all have their inconveniences. Not one of them is capable, by itself, of definitely stabilizing an urban organism. It is also a fact that among these different elements the town has wandered, that it has changed its situation from one to the other of them, fixed for a moment by the particular qualities of one of these elements, attracted the next by the different qualities of another, moving from the lake to the Fins, from the Fins to the hill of old Annecy, jumping from the hill to the Semnoz, coming down again to the banks of the Thion, wandering over all the attractions of its complex site, according to the necessities of the hour, that is to say, according to the necessities of its history. But every time what was created was a poor, mean, badly constructed organism. The strictly modern town must be visited to see how, on so complex a site, there can develop an urban community which is no longer content, like the series of former Annecies, with occupying and utilizing such or such an element of its site, but takes possession of them all and derives profit from them all simultaneously. The shores of the lakes attract by their beauty; the easy and open Fins plain becomes covered by convenient dwellings; the distant hill of old Annecy is clothed with villas and country houses; the ridge of Semnoz still marks the centre of the town; and lastly the Thion is more than ever the soul of the new industrial city. And so the complete utilization of the resources offered by the site and position has at last ended by making Annecy into a large fine city, whose prosperity, founded on various elements, appears capable now of withstanding the shocks of destiny.

A very instructive and quite typical monograph.

A remark made lately by Camille Jullian supports in the most opportune manner these conclusions.[1] If towns or places have very often changed their names, it is generally, he tells us, owing to the fact that, because of changes in the popu-

[1] Jullian, *Rev. des Études anciennes*, Vol. XXII, 1920, p. 53.

lation or in their habits, some hitherto subordinate quarter with a distinctive name has taken front rank and so given its name to the whole. Lemincum, for example, has not become Chambéry. For Lemincum still survives. To-day, the high ground to the right of the road is Lemenc, and Chambéry lies lower to the left of the road; but when Chambéry, having increased in importance, dominated the group, its name also predominated and became the common name for the whole group. " Do not say that the name of Fleury-sur-Loire has been changed to Saint-Benoit; as the name of a group, yes; but Fleury still exists as a quarter of the commune which has taken its name from the neighbouring quarter of Saint Benoît." [1] In fact, no study is more interesting than that of the separate formation and the union of these active organisms and busy cells formed by city quarters. In his lectures at the Collège de France, Camille Jullian has already, for some years, set the example of such researches [2]: after studying the formation of the French towns, and then analysing the organs which permit of their fulfilling their various functions, he has tried to bring out the part which monuments play in the formation, and the transformations also, of the various urban quarters. His recent remarks on the combination of quarters in producing a town seem to us very fruitful of ideas: they certainly open to historians quite a new field for research into the past of towns.

We say " to historians ". This certainly is not meant to exclude any willing helpers nor to start one of those petty " shop " quarrels, which are a disgrace, if not to science, at any rate too often to scientists. But it is because such researches in reality are so far from having anything geographical about them that, when we read those which experienced geographers have carried out on the subject of certain towns, we are apt to think that after all some " human geography " is perhaps nothing else but history revivified at its sources, rejuvenated in its methods, and happily revolutionized in its subjects.

[1] Ibid.

[2] Jullian, " Rôle des Monuments dans la formation topographique des villes," *Rev. des cours et conférences*, 22nd year, March, 1914, No. 8.

V

Is the Action of Natural Conditions on Man Weakening?

An example like that of Annecy, we may remark in conclusion, permits us to ask, usefully, an old though rather idle question: is the action of natural conditions on man weakening? In our opinion, it is one to which the answer "yes" or "no" cannot be given. It is easy, certainly, to build up on scanty facts two contradictory theses to argue about, and by taking the opposition to the one most generally accepted to demonstrate by examples that modern civilization subordinates itself to the conditions which nature imposes on it in various parts of the world better than did former civilizations. Does not progress, in fact, save man from having to oppose the natural agriculture of the regions he inhabits, and to force the soil to produce, in defiance of climate, fruits which it can only grow by constraint? Is not the town of our days anxious, as we have just seen, to seize on and utilize to the utmost, for its different purposes, all the elements of its natural situation? Does not the mountain, for its part, find its pastoral vocation strengthened, now that man is no longer obliged to struggle with the cultivation of his cereals, since he receives what he requires from a distance and he can therefore devote all his time and care to the pastoral industry? Thus the slopes of the valleys are becoming, throughout their whole extent, immense grazing lands dotted with haycocks. As Arbos says, in his work on pastoral nomadism, "The advance of civilization has only made use of the economic method determined by the natural conditions." These facts, which could be multiplied without profit, support those we have already alleged in drawing attention to the unmistakable tendency of our civilization to uniformity.[1] They also reinforce all those furnished by the recent history of economic colonization, of the taking possession of new lands. There, man, at first, feels his way. He does not adapt things all at once. He does not know which soil or aspect to select. He makes mistakes; but gradually the will of man prevails and his object is realized. Why enumerate examples? It would certainly be better to try to interpret correctly all those which at once occur to our minds.

[1] See above, pp. 157–8.

Must we then conclude from such facts that they establish the subjection of man to nature? The statement has been made without hesitation by, among others, the author of a quite recent work of urban geography about Marseilles.[1] He shows very well how the site of the great town was destitute of real advantages. The land was very broken, with deep ravines in places; there was no flat ground easy to build on, except quite out of the way in the south; a series of steep knolls literally enclosed the deep fosse of the port; there was no water; the climate was disagreeable; the rainfall was slight (20·5 inches) and badly distributed (over 55 days); the mistral was violent, parching in summer, very cold in winter; all round was an amphitheatre of very arid limestone hills, dipping suddenly into the sea to the west, and forming a great obstacle to communications. In reality the sole factor that fixed a city there was the typical port, the old Lacydon.

There is no better example than this, we may remark, of the importance and determinant value of those formative elements of which we spoke previously—of those "germs of towns" we might say, as we spoke before of "germs of states".

The case is by no means an isolated one. Blanchard has shown that Grenoble was established on its site, in defiance of climate, of the rough and biting north wind, and of the constant danger of inundation at the only point in the valley, known as the Graisivaudan, where the Isère could be forded near its confluence with the Drac; and has not Toulouse also braved the terrible floods of the Garonne to keep its place at the point on the river where great routes cross? But what conclusion are we to suppose that the author draws from all these facts? That man is never the slave of nature? That he defies it, that he mocks it, that he braves all its rigours whenever a purely human design urges him to do so? Not at all. The geographer we quote concludes: "Man must, then, submit to the laws of nature."[2] Whereupon, seeing that Marseilles has quite naturally taken advantage of the easiest

[1] G. Rambert, "L'agglomération marseillaise, étude de géographie urbaine": *La Vie urbaine*, 1919, No. 3.

[2] p. 314.

positions for building in order to expand, and that it took care to " occupy all the depressions which it could find ", he adds that this ordinary fact, this proof of common sense, forms " a remarkable instance of the influence which nature exercises on man ". It is true that, the lower parts having once been occupied, the steady growth of the town made it necessary to scale the heights and to perch large modern houses on hills formerly considered as impossible to build upon. The conclusion is that we have here " an equally striking example of the reaction of man against the forces of nature ".[1]

Do we not see, once more, the evident ravages which all this childish dynamism, all this philosophy of " influences ", all this familiar intercourse of " nature " with " man ", make in the minds of otherwise intelligent people, labourers whose labour is, as it happens, and as is undoubtedly the case with this monograph, quite accurate, useful and praiseworthy ?

There is only one way of getting out of these Byzantine controversies : is it " nature ", which . . . ? is it not rather " man ", who . . . ? Let us simply conclude : the problem is not " is the grip of natural conditions on man becoming weaker ? " which is nothing else but the old problem of " influence " bequeathed by the soothsayers, the astrologers, and the disciples of an obscure and primitive naturalism, to the historians, who have themselves bequeathed it to the geographers. The real problem is : " is the grip of man on the earth becoming stronger ? " Of the answer to that there can be no doubt.

It is not the cadets of Saint Cyr only who " learn, that they may conquer ". The civilized man, thanks to the continuous triumphs of science, and thanks also to the steady improvement in his technical equipment, is no longer content to deal with nature somewhat furtively, as did his ancestors of old, using fire—using, let us imagine, great conflagrations of forests and prairie fires which, to that poor man, so destitute of appliances, were a formidable agent in the transformation of the globe, although for the enormous destruction which accompanied it he received but very little profit ; it was much the same thing as burning his house in order to cook an egg.

[1] p. 315.

The civilized man directs his exploitation of the earth with a mastery which has ceased to astonish him, but which, when we reflect on it for a moment, is singularly disturbing. There is no "nature", ready-made and established, which he accepts as a whole and which he bends as such to his will. He scatters it and breaks it up. Without any regard to the "natural nature", if we may so express it, of a region, he introduces a certain cultivation, banishes a certain plant, upsets a certain established economy, not once but ten or twenty times in half a century, because he is driven himself by the great driver who dominates everything, the great modern industry of capitalist type, which demands, unweariedly and unceasingly, products, raw materials, plants, and animals to grind, to break up, and to transform.

Here, for instance, are the successive revolutions in Ceylon during the last thirty years. Ceylon was formerly, by age-long tradition, the island of cinnamon and cardamom, the land of spices. But, when the cultivation of spices ceased to be remunerative, Ceylon became the island of coffee. However, man having introduced the cultivation of coffee on a large scale into Brazil, and that cultivation having spread very widely, Ceylon abandoned coffee for tea. But attempts at the acclimatization of the hevea of Brazil having been made, and the necessary experiments having given excellent results, and rubber being much more remunerative than tea, Ceylon has become the island of rubber. So much so that the cultivation of the hevea has been almost abandoned in the very country whence it came to Ceylon, in South America where the Peruvian forests produce very little now—just as they have ceased to supply the world with quinine since the chinchona has conquered Java. Yet this is not the end, and to-morrow perhaps Ceylon will be the island of cotton; and the day after to-morrow?

It all depends on the climate and the soil, it may be said. If they did not suit the cultivation, it would be impossible. Irrigation, we may answer; natural or artificial manures, scientific methods of cultivation, of forcing, and also of transport. There are evidently limits, and one would not think of growing pineapples in Greenland. But within each of those great climatico-botanical zones which we have defined there is room for a hundred cultures which, so far as land and climate are concerned, are equally possible, not for that irritating abstraction "man", but for modern industry, the devourer of raw material obtained at the lowest possible price, that is to say, always in bulk ; in quantities for manufacture, as they say. And for reasons which have nothing "natural" any longer, but are entirely of an economic and financial order. For in the new countries to which civilized man lays claim, just as to his own lands, what madness it would be to think that "natural" conditions of production controlled the distribution of cultivation ! In such a country as Nyassaland, for instance, noticed by Ratzel long ago, there were found, at the time when he wrote his *Politische Geographie*, the oleaginous cultures collected in the lowland regions and near the sea, whilst coffee, tea and indigo were plentifully scattered about the plateaux away from the sea. Was this due to suitability of soil, or to climatic influences ? By no means. Simply to cost of carriage. Coffee, tea, and indigo are fairly valuable and not very bulky, whilst oleaginous products are heavy, of small value, and are only remunerative when near to ports for shipment. Gain, the calculation of the returns, these are what govern the world to-day, and not "nature".

But is the study of this transformation, of this material and moral revolution, the province of geography ? Undoubtedly. But with a reservation.

Now, as formerly, man, his works, the material traces which his labours leave on the ground, all these still form an integral part of the geographical physiognomy of the globe. As Vidal de la Blache said, quite a long time ago, man, "by the establishments which he creates on the surface of the earth, by his dealings with rivers, even with the forms of the surface relief, with the flora, the fauna and the whole equilibrium of the living world, belongs to geography." Only, he plays in it more and more the part of cause, not of effect.

He shows himself as a being essentially endowed with initiative, so well armed that he can confront the forces of nature without fear, and with the certainty of succeeding in the end—and of piercing the Isthmus of Panama after that of Suez, and of making a tunnel under the Channel when he wishes, and of freeing himself by the aeroplane from the restriction which the ground places on the movements of men or goods, and, with better reason, of transforming the Nigerian " Mesopotamia " into a vast cotton producing region as soon as he finds it to his industrial interest. His interest alone regulates his formidably armed and increasingly narrow egoism.

So man, civilized to-day, banished from geography as the patient, reappears in the very forefront of it as dominant agent.

CONCLUSION

THE TASK BEFORE US

BIOLOGICAL METHODS

GEOGRAPHICAL METHODS

WE do not consider that a book such as this needs a long conclusion. It is not a manual, nor a complete study: it is simply a critical discussion, which has tried to come to a conclusion at every stage, and any summing-up would be vain repetition.

Before bidding farewell to our readers, however, it may not be out of place to recur to one point in order to answer certain possible objections. Every critical work exposes its author to a double suspicion—that he creates the trouble for the pleasure of denouncing it, and that he only supplies a sterile and confusing negation. We think we have deserved neither of these reproaches.

*

* *

It may be objected that all this talk about geographical determinism is a windmill which is being mistaken for an army, and that no one believes in it or talks about it nowadays. Various books will be quoted, all correct and irreproachable, and all containing a condemnation of a blind and strict determinism. No doubt. But let us always remember that passage from Ratzel which we quoted almost at the beginning of our book; and Ratzel is no insignificant new-comer. Quite recently certain French geographers pushed him to the front with the greatest goodwill—for reasons which we need not inquire into here. It is worth while to repeat once more that sentence about the soil which, " always the same, and always situated at the same point in space, serves as a fixed support to the changing aspirations of men." This it is, says Ratzel, " which governs the destinies of peoples with blind brutality " ; which, when they happen " to forget what underlies them, makes them feel its power and reminds them by serious warnings that the whole life of the State has its roots in the soil ". And the final axiom, which we must not forget, asserts " a people should live on the land fate has given them ; they should die there, submitting to the law ".

Happily for the godfather of anthropogeography, his work, often precise and well packed with solid facts, does supply something which gives the lie to such crass assertions. And besides, Ratzel alone was not the whole spring-time of geography. And Vidal de la Blache, who was not wont to be carried away by theory, but thought and expressed his thoughts with a vigour altogether his own, has repeatedly criticized such extravagances in the full sense of the word. It is none the less true—we have said this also before—not only that the world still contains a fair number of Ratzelians and Neo-Ratzelians, many of whom, under pretext of correcting their master's ideas, exaggerate them, but that geographers who are themselves the strongest opponents of geographical determinism are continually being caught in the very act of contradicting themselves, at any rate in words—so strong is the hold of the old system, and so dangerous is the survival of the old doctrines, all the stronger and more dangerous when one is not on guard against them, since they act secretly—like " influences ".

*

* *

Hence no one has the right to say that we are contradicting ourselves when we defend human geography against the criticisms of social morphology — or to be more exact, vindicating its right to a free and independent existence—although throughout the book we have used our best efforts to criticize it. The charge collapses. It is not against human geography, as such, that our criticisms have been intentionally directed, but against a vicious and puerile conception of its nature. And it will be observed that we have nearly always based our study on the eminently suggestive work of a great mind which certainly did not invent anthropogeography (who, by the way, did " invent " it ?). A great mind, which, without allowing itself to be deceived and carried away by the ambitious and bold generalizations, the bankrupt ideas disguised as philosophic verities, and all the worn-out panoply of Ratzel's theorizing—so often oblivious of facts and realities !—, has itself patiently, modestly, and without advertisement built up, little by little, by original thinking and meditation, a sound and fruitful method of research into the problems of " human geography ".

There is no need to warn his disciples and fellow-workers, nor the inheritors of his ideas, nor those who carry on his modest and useful work, against excess, extremes, or feeble and at the same time dangerous simplification. Still less are we thinking of those so-called geographers who have seen fit to set up in public an ambitious and jerry-built edifice, an immense temporary hangar, without foundations or beams, filled with wind and phantoms, good only to impress the ignorant or lead amateurs astray—they know very well what they are doing. Our words of caution, our objections and critical remarks are meant for students in good faith, more especially for those who, as historians, are the conscious or unconscious heirs of the problems set by their predecessors—problems we are stating for them. They are meant also for all those who, without seeing the danger or suspecting the difficulty, still instinctively speak of " influences ", and who pick out here and there, from the work of geographers, a striking parallel or a seductive conjecture, and proceed to deduce therefrom so many first principles and positive consequences for their studies in the history of politics, literature, or art in the good old way of Taine.

The problem is ill-stated, and the method ill-arranged. As yet, we have not enough thorough-going researches and really exhaustive monographs, and too few of the possible comparisons. That, in fine, is what we must say, and say again, and not allow ourselves to be seduced by those showy stucco edifices which encumber the ground and turn the heads of the simple.

* * *

We can never repeat too often that the object of geography is not to go hunting for " influences ", such as that of Nature on Man, or of the Soil on History. These are dreams. Such words in capital letters have nothing to do with serious work.

And the word " influences " is not to be found in the scientific dictionary: it is an astrological term. Let us then leave " influences " once for all to the astrologers and other " charlatans ", as good old Bodin would say—Bodin who was steeped in them himself.

In fact, we must either walk round and round in a circle repeating truisms promoted to the dignity of laws by virtue of the use of a few abstract words, demonstrating that Man is subservient to Nature, or Nature to Man, or else attack the real problem resolutely. It is a problem of " relations ", not of " influences ". " Relations " is a sane word and its past is not wrapped in fog and obscurity or steeped in occultism.

What are the relations between human societies of to-day and their present geographical environment? That is the fundamental problem, and the only one which human geography sets itself.

Not without design do we say " the only one ". For it is usually thought that we must distinguish two problems. On the one hand, it is said, the mission of human geography is to show how, and to what extent, man is a geographical agent, of the nature of water, wind or fire, working upon the surface of the earth and modifying it as they do. On the other hand, human geography ought to prove that geographical factors, soil, climate, etc., play a decisive part of the greatest importance in the life of human societies. The difference is really a frivolous and a purely academic distinction which leads to nothing.

To act on his environment, man does not place himself outside it. He does not escape its hold at the precise moment when he attempts to exercise his own. And conversely the nature which acts on man, the nature which intervenes to modify the existence of human societies, is not a virgin nature, independent of all human contact; it is a nature already profoundly impregnated and modified by man. There is perpetual action and reaction. The formula " the mutual relation of society to environment " holds equally good for the two supposed distinct cases. For in these relations, man both borrows and gives back, whilst the environment gives and receives.

*

* *

But he who would do useful work upon the study of the mutual relation between environment and human society ought, doubtless, to have an intimate acquaintance with that environment, and an exact knowledge of the true nature and the real character of human societies.

"An intimate acquaintance with the geographical environment! that goes without saying," we shall be told. Not at all; on this we must insist. For what we require is not that calm and tranquil sort of acquaintance which we get by reading treatises and the manuals, however excellent. We mean a scientific acquaintance—with all that this implies in the way of risk and devotion, uncertainty, ingenuity, and ardour. We must remember that physical geography was only born yesterday; that it is quite a new and recent science; that it is, moreover, strictly dependent upon a whole series of other sciences which are themselves young and are every day making discoveries in the fields which they are patiently clearing. For the future it is not from superficial, second-hand study, but only from personal, minute, attentive, and direct study of the environment, of its different elements, and of its principal or secondary characteristics, that decisive progress in the study of human geography can come.

There is an enormous amount of work to be accomplished both in research and hard thinking. Much work must be done in physical geography in the first place, for everything depends on that. How can we argue about the relations which may exist between such and such a climate or surface modelling, and such and such a mode of grouping, of activity in a human society whether in a particular region or in the world at large, if, for one thing, this or that fact of climate or relief has not been minutely isolated, defined, and studied in all its aspects, not by climatologists or geologists, but by geographers, according to methods proper to geography and for ends that are definitely and uniquely geographical? But this work of investigation of the physical universe by geographers is still only in its infancy. What is thirty years of useful labour, when we think of the immensity of the work to be accomplished? Moreover, whole districts and enormous stretches of territory continue to evade the grasp of our scientific instruments. There are lands without laboratories, meteorological stations, or means of easy access, with no maps, which a sparse network of scientific reconnaissance and exploration is only just beginning to cover; and these are precisely the countries where, according to a theory which demands constant interpretation, as we have seen, the examination of the relations between the natural environment and human society would be, in a certain sense, both easy and profitable.

Scientific progress in this direction cannot grow out of the spontaneous and brilliant intuitions of a genius. It can only be the fruit of long and painstaking collective toil, that other form, and not the least useful one, of human genius. To toil on and patiently await the harvest is here, as elsewhere, the only possible programme.

*

* *

As to the real understanding of the true nature and character of the different aspects of human society, here also we must know our own minds.

We do not demand that those desirous of studying the relations between contemporary societies and their physical environment should be endowed with an encyclopædic culture which would cram their heads with ill-digested ideas gleaned from ethnology, psychology, sociology, history, ethics, and even philosophy, thus leaving them incapable of accomplishing fruitful original work.

On the other hand, were we to proclaim that they should know about man nothing but what concerns geographers—analysts of the landscape, whose business it is to study human societies, as it were, only from a "scenic" point of view—our programme would really be an impossible one. For it would mean a study not only of all the characters which have been written about, but also all the possible morphological or geographical interpretations of every sort of human fact, in so far as, being concerned with the earth's surface, it is capable of graphical representation.

It is not the encyclopædia which is wanted, but intelligence.

Between man and his natural environment, ideas are always creeping in and intervening. No human facts are simple facts. Natural facts, on the other hand, never exercise a purely mechanical, blind, and fatal action on the life of man. This must be repeated all the more persistently because those who know it best are continually allowing themselves to relapse into a kind of unconscious " naturalism " whenever they speak of man and human society and of their activity on the surface of the earth. One would say that, for many geographers, the nearer man is to the brute, the more " geographical " he is, as if it were not precisely the action of the most civilized and best-equipped societies which places before us the highest problems of human geography.

It is not only sociologists who sacrifice, if they do sacrifice, to the obsession of " primitive man " and the " savage ".

And, therefore, the two fundamental bases of all serious and useful human geography are an intimate first-hand acquaintance with the natural environment and a general understanding of the conditions of man's development.

*

* *

But the problem of historical geography differs in no respect from the general problem of all human geography, of real historical geography, be it understood, which has nothing to do with the nomenclature, and lists of divisions, and administrative boundaries of a Longnon, for example, or some other such savant whose work—however commendable it may be for its intrinsic qualities—should not lay claim to the title of geography.

What were the relations of human societies of bygone times, at different epochs in the various countries of the world, with the geographical environment of their day, so far as we are able to reconstruct it ? This is our problem simply transposed from the present to the past. It also demands from those who wish to work at its solutions, some of which are particular, others general, the knowledge described above, and, naturally a knowledge of the theory and practice of historical research and investigation. For it is by the aid of texts and documents that they will generally have to reconstruct in part the state of these vanished civilizations, whose relations with the " landscape " they seek to discover—the condition of which, whether topographical or climatic, has generally altered much since those days.

It matters little whether those who undertake such research be labelled at the outset geographers, historians, or even sociologists—"social morphologists" at that. But in every case they will have to start from the existing condition of affairs—that is to say, to take their stand firmly on the conclusions of human geography: and these will be sound in proportion as they rest on a sound study of physical geography—the indispensable basis and animating leaven of all that is worthy of attention in human geography. The greater the progress made by this latter study—the greater the multiplication of careful, methodical, and close analyses of environment decomposed into its complex elements—the more valuable will be the conclusions of human geography, and therefore of historical geography, that species of a singularly extensive and comprehensive genus.

Once more, in conclusion: toilers in this field must work and know how to wait. And yet, cautious as they must be, they must not disregard hypothesis, however rash such hypothesis may seem, provided it is treated as such, that is to say scientifically. Brückner is quite within his rights in investigating whether oscillations in climate, with a periodicity, it would appear, of roughly thirty years, do or do not exert a precisely similar influence upon the movements of population in Europe and North America, through the medium of variations in the size of the harvest depending on summer rainfall and temperature. But on the other hand, it is illegitimate at once to magnify the hypothesis and to argue from it eloquently that all mankind revolves to the rhythm of the hygrometer and the thermometer. Nothing must be excluded from sheer prejudice, of course. An open mind, an aptitude to welcome ideas and to institute comparisons which nourish and vitalize a young science are to be encouraged. But all ambitious generalizations and childish amplifications, all those "philosophies of geography" which recall with even less substance and reason the worst of the old "philosophies of history" must be put aside, together with all that worthless glitter, those great determinist machines, those world-systems in which everything is co-ordinated according to the measure and limitations of little minds empty of inspiration, but nothing whatever is really explained.

*

* *

When we plead thus for a radical change of method; when we ask that the era of sophisticated philosophies should be closed for many a day to come, are we going with or against the general sense of those sciences which can best supply us with a model, and strengthen the young science whose outline we wish to stand out clearly from the shadows?

We shall very soon be reassured by a glance at the evolution which has taken place in the domain of biology during the last few years.

Not so very long ago the renowned and hoary theory of adaptation reigned there undisputed. It sought in utility the explanation of those characters which seemed to adapt a living being to a function, or to render it capable of fulfilling that function, should it be called upon to do so. According to that theory, the present condition of a living being was the inevitable and mechanical result of the action of exterior agents on that being. This was what both Darwin and Lamarck believed, the one alleging natural selection, the inevitable result of the struggle for existence, as the explanation; the other, need. But the result was the same, and, from this point of view, the theories need not be described as "quite different", as Cuénot makes them out to be. For the same conception of life animated them both; that mechanical conception which has been so very prolific in the history of the sciences, and which has owed its fecundity entirely to its extreme simplicity and narrowness. To make out that living beings were destitute of that initiative, that faculty of making a fresh start in an unchanging environment, which truly constitutes life, is a convenient artifice, of which science has made a wide use—with plenteous results. But after a considerable number of discoveries had been made on this basis, there came a time when scientific men felt the necessity of allowing some place in biology to that which Bergson in his own domain and about the same time called the impulse (*élan*) and creative power of life. Cuénot's theory of pre-adaptation was a characteristic manifestation of that state of mind in the biological world. Under cover of this theory, there reappeared in scientific studies a vitalism which revived, to the great scandal of a number of scientists brought up in the blind and uncompromising mechanist faith, the fruitful and by no means unscientific idea of chance—that idea to which Henri Berr, in his book *Synthèse en Histoire*, has given so much prominence.

The choice must be made. Either the living being is more or less passive under the action of the natural forces of its environment, and we can calculate its reaction with certainty and therefore foresee it by measuring its power of resistance to the measurable forces which opposed it. Or else the living being is endowed with an activity of its own and capable of creating and producing new effects, in which case there is an end of determination, in the true sense of the word; and in its place we have only approximations and probabilities. We lose, on the one hand, much of the beautiful simplicity and certainty of the mechanical explanations. We gain, on the other hand, as Lafitte observed some time ago, a richer and more complex view, better matched with the exact complexion of the phenomena of life. A balance has to be struck, and a balance sheet prepared—without there being any occasion to substitute one fetish for another, to burn impetuously to-day what was worshipped yesterday, and to deny gratuitously, for example, the possibility of adaptations in the traditional sense of the word, or of specializations due to a gradual modelling by the environment and the way of life. Only, the fact ought not to be believed a priori, nor schematically deduced from principles admitted without any discussion. The fact must be studied in itself, carefully verified, apart from any theory, by observation and experiment, and without the fatal intervention of any " philosophy of Nature ".

*

* *

We have said that the theory of pre-adaptation was one of the characteristic manifestations, in biology, of this new state of mind. But was not the theory of ways of life, in geography, as Vidal de la Blache formulated it, also a fitting translation of intellectual needs of just the same, or at any rate of very similar character, whether its author was fully conscious of it or not ?

It is not biology alone that is faced with the task of effecting a great change in method, and a gradual transition from the metaphysical age of general systems to the age of observations and hypotheses verified by experience. The idea of admitting that chance has some share in the development of life, and that consequently chance is a subject for scientific research, should not alarm any historian or geographer, nor should he be guilty of the ridiculous fear manifested by the disciples of the "moral sciences" with regard to their confrères of the physical and natural sciences—that fear of not being strictly orthodox. This time they have behind them the authority of well qualified scientific men.

"The structure exists first," writes the American biologist Davenport, quoted by Cuénot, "and the species seeks or finds the environment suited to its particular constitution." Man exists first, the geographer should say, utilizing and elucidating Vidal de la Blache's theory of kinds of life. His habits, his special character, his way of life, are not a necessary consequence of the fact that he is placed in this or that environment. These are not the product, to use that bald formula of the environment. He carries them with him, he transports them with him. They are the consequences of his own nature. We must not say blindly that "Such and such a region necessarily constrains its inhabitants to adopt such and such a way of life", but rather that under the powerful action of organized and systematic habits "gradually deepening their ruts, and thus imposing themselves with greater and greater strength on successive generations, stamping their mark on minds, and giving a definite trend to all progressive forces" the aspect of a country may be completely transformed. In a great measure this aspect is due to the activity of the inhabitants themselves. Here is another side of the truth which geography has no right to neglect, either for its own sake, since it would then lapse into a sterile routine, to the monotonous chanting of old Ratzelian litanies or of astrological formulæ inherited from the remote past, or even, as we are justified in insistently repeating, for that of history, whose progress is very closely connected with its own, and which has need of it in order to advance in her turn.

We have only reached that stage of the Genesis when the light begins to be distinct from the darkness. An immense perspective of toil stretches before us, both historians and geographers, to an indefinite future. This is not the time to fall asleep in idle admiration of the poor, little, mean, and sterile system which some of our forerunners have erected, at the cost of hard toil whose beauty and personal value we shall never dispute, on the insecure basis of a determinism which is half arrogant, half ashamed. There is another and a better thing to do than to linger over it—to work.

BIBLIOGRAPHY

Note.—The following Bibliography makes no claim to completeness either as regards the infinitely varied relations between human societies and their geographical milieu, or even in respect of the chief questions raised in the present work. The list contains no more than a brief indication of the principal works or articles which will enable the reader to pursue the study of these questions further or which have been specially referred to. This book is perhaps less suitable than any other in the series for a methodical bibliography, however summary. An endeavour has rather been made to provide the reader with a choice of references as varied as possible.

(*a*) ATLASES

H. Berghaus, *Physikalischer Atlas*, 1st edn., Gotha, 1849–52, 6 fasc., f°. New edn., Gotha, 1887–92, 7 fasc., f°. (*a*) *Geologie*, by Berghaus; (*b*) *Hydrographie*, by the same; (*c*) *Meteorologie*, by Hann; (*d*) *Erdmagnetismus*, by Neumayer; (*e*) *Pflanzenverbreitung*, by Drude; (*f*) *Tierverbreitung*, by Marshall; (*g*). *Völkerkunde*, by Gerland . **I**

J. G. Bartholomew, *Physical Atlas*, vol. iii; *Atlas of Meteorology*, by Bartholomew and Herbertson, Edinburgh, n.d. [1899], f°, vol. v; *Atlas of Zoogeography*, by Bartholomew, Clarke, and Grimshaw, Edinburgh, 1911, f° . . . . . **II**

A. Stieler, *Hand-Atlas*, 9th edn., Gotha, 1905, f° [10th Centenary (1821–1921) Edition in course of publication] . . . **III**

P. Vidal de la Blache, *Atlas général, historique, et géographique* (last edn., revised), Paris, 1921, f° . . . . . **IV**

H. Kiepert, *Atlas Antiquus:* zwölf Karten zur alten Geschichte, 6th edn., Berlin, 1876, f° . . . . **V**

K. v. Spruner, *Hand-atlas für die Geschichte des Mittelalters u. der neueren Zeit*, 3rd edn., text by Th. Menke, Gotha, 1880, f° **VI**

G. Droysen, *Allgemeiner historischer Hand-atlas*, Bielefeld and Leipzig, 1880, f° . . . . **VII**

F. Schrader, *Atlas de géographie historique*, Paris, 1896, f° . **VIII**

R. L. Poole, *Historical Atlas of Modern Europe from the Decline of the Roman Empire*, Oxford, 1896–1902, 4° . . . . **IX**

J. G. Bartholomew, *Atlas of the World's Commerce*, London and Edinburgh, 1907, f° . . . . **X**

J. G. Bartholomew, *Atlas of Economic Geography*, London, 1914, 4° . . . . **Xa**

(*b*) PERIODICALS

Annales de géographie, Paris, from 1891 (with separate annual parts devoted to Geographical Bibliography, published under the direction of L. Raveneau, 1st Bibliography, 1893) **XI**

La Géographie, Bulletin de la Société de Géographie de Paris, Paris, from 1900, 8° XII

Petermann's Mitteilungen aus Justus Perthes Geographisches Anstalt, Gotha, from 1855, 4°. Separate parts, Ergänzungshefte, grouped in volumes, Ergänzungsbände (Band I, 1860–1) XIII

Geographische Zeitschrift, edn. by A. Hettner, Leipzig, from 1895, 8° XIV

The Geographical Journal, including the Proceedings of the Royal Geographical Society, London, from 1893, 8° . . XV

L'Anthropologie, Paris, from 1890, 8° XVI

L'Année sociologique, Paris, from 1896, 8° XVII

Revue de synthèse historique, Paris, from 1900, 8° . . . XVIII

Scientia (Rivista di Scienza), Bologna, London, Paris, from 1907, 8° XIX

(*c*) Method

H. Berr, *La Synthèse en histoire*, Paris, 1911, 8° XX

H. Berr, *L'Histoire traditionnelle et la synthèse historique*, Paris, 1921, 16° XXI

E. Durkheim, *Règles de la méthode sociologique*, Paris, 7th edn., 1919, 16° XXII

H. Hauser, *L'enseignement des sciences sociales*, Paris, 1903, 8° . XXIII

P. Mantoux, "Histoire et Sociologie" (*Rev. Synthèse*, 1903) . XXIV

F. Rauh, *De la méthode dans la psychologie des sentiments*, Paris, 1899, 8° XXV

F. Rauh, *Études de morale : la Patrie*, Paris, 1911, 8° . . XXVI

Ch. Seignobos, *La méthode historique appliquée aux sciences sociales*, Paris, 1904, 8° XXVII

F. Simiand, "Méthode historique et science sociale" (*Rev. Synthèse*, 1903) XXVIII

P. Vidal de la Blache, "Le principe de la géographie générale" (*Ann. de géogr.*, iv, 1895–6) XXIX

P. Vidal de la Blache, "Des divisions fondamentales du sol français" (in *La France*, vol. i, of *Cours de géographie*, by Vidal de la Blache and C. d'Almeida, Paris, 1897, 12°) . XXX

P. Vidal de la Blache, "Les conditions géographiques des faits sociaux" (*Ann. de géogr.*, vol. xi, 1902) XXXI

P. Vidal de la Blache, "La géographie humaine, ses rapports avec la géographie de la vie" (*Rev. Synthèse*, 1903, vol. vii) XXXII

P. Vidal de la Blache, "Les caractères distinctifs de la géographie" (*Ann. de Géogr.*, vol. xxii, 1913) XXXIII

L. Gallois, *Régions naturelles et noms de pays*, Paris, 1907, 8° . XXXIV

(*d*) The Problem of Environment : Historical

J. L. Heiberg, "Théories antiques sur l'influence morale du climat" (*Scientia*, vol. xxviii, June, 1920) XXXV

J. Bodin, *Les six livres de la République*, revised edn., Lyon, 1580, f° (Book v, ch. i, pp. 461 sqq.) XXXVI

R. Chauviré, *Jean Bodin, auteur de la République*, Paris, 1914, 8° XXXVII

J. B. Dubos (abbé), *Réflexions critiques sur la poésie et la peinture* (1719), Paris, 7th edn., 1770, 8° XXXVIII

M. Braunschvig, *L'abbé Dubos, rénovateur de la critique au XVIIIe siècle*, Paris, 1904, 8° (Paris Thesis) XXXIX

E. L. Montesquieu, *De l'Esprit des Lois* (1st edn., Geneva, 1748; used for the London Edition, 1757) XL

J. Dedieu, *Montesquieu et la tradition politique anglaise en France: les sources anglaises de l'Esprit des Lois*, Paris, 1919, 8° (Bordeaux Thesis) XLI

Buffon, *Œuvres choisies*, vol. i, Paris, Didot, 1861, 12° . . XLII

Lamarck, *Philosophie zoologique*, Paris, 1809, 2 vols., 8° (reprinted, Paris, 1908, 8°) XLIII

J. Michelet, *Histoire de France: Préface of* 1869, and Book III, *Tableau de la France* XLIV

Cam. Jullian, Introduction to the volume of *Extraits des historiens français du XIXe siècle*, Paris, 6th edn., 1910, 18° . . XLV

H. Taine, *Histoire de la littérature anglaise*, Paris, 1864, 12° . XLVI

H. Taine, *Philosophie de l'art*, Paris, 1881, 2 vols., 12° . . XLVII

P. Lacombe, *La psychologie des individus et des sociétés chez Taine, historien des littératures*, Paris, 1906, 8° . . . XLVIII

P. Lacombe, *Taine historien et sociologue*, Paris, 1909, 8° . XLIX

Ch. Darwin, *The Origin of Species* (French transl. by Barbier, Paris, 1876) L

F. Brunetière, *L'Évolution des genres dans l'histoire de la littérature.* I: *Évolution de la critique depuis la Renaissance jusqu'à nos jours*, Paris, 1890, 16° LI

L. Cuénot, *La genèse des espèces animales*, Paris, 2nd edn., 1921 LII

(*e*) The Problem of Milieu: Physical and Ethnical Data

E. de Martonne, *Traité de géographie physique*, Paris, 3rd edn., 1921 LIII

A. Supan, *Grundzüge der physischen Erdkunde*, Leipzig, 6th edn., 1916 LIV

E. Suess, *Antlitz der Erde.* E.T., *The Face of the Earth.* French transl., *La Face de la Terre*, by E. de Margerie, Paris, 1897–1901, 3 vols., 8°, in seven parts (one of tables) LV

A. Penck, *Morphologie der Erdoberfläche*, Stuttgart, 1894, 2 vols., 8° LVI

J. von Hann, *Handbuch der Klimatologie*, Leipzig, 3rd edn., 3 vols., 1908–11 LVII

J. von Hann, *Lehrbuch der Meteorologie*, Leipzig, 3rd edn. (Süring), 1915, 8° LVIII

O. Drude, *Manuel de géographie botanique*, Poirault's translation, Paris, 1897, 8° LIX

A. F. W. Schimper, *Pflanzengeographie auf physiologischer Grundlage*, Jena, 2nd edn., 1908 LX

A. de Quatrefages, *Introduction à l'étude des races humaines*, Paris, 1887–9, 2 vols, 8° LXI

J. Deniker, *Races et peuples de la terre*, Paris, 1900, 8° . . LXII

E. Pittard, *Race and History*, Paris, 1922, 8° (L'Evolution de l'Humanité, no. 5) LXIII

L. Gumplowicz, *Der Rassenkampf.* French transl., *La lutte des races*, Paris, 1895, 8° LXIV

(*f*) Human Geography and Political Geography

(*General Works*)

W. Bagehot, *Physics and Politics,* French transl., Paris, 1885, 8° **LXV**

J. Brunhes, *La géographie humaine*, Paris, 1910, 8° (2nd edn., 1912) . . . . **LXVI**

J. Brunhes, " La géographie de l'histoire " (*Rev. de géogr. ann.*, vol. viii, 1914, part i) . . . . **LXVII**

J. Brunhes and C. Vallaux, *La Géographie de l'histoire : Géographie de la paix et de la guerre sur terre et sur mer*, Paris, 1921, 8° **LXVIII**

C. Cherubim, *Flüsse als Grenzen von Staaten und Nationen in Mitteleuropa*, Inaug. Diss., Halle, 1897, 8° . . . **LXIX**

Lord Curzon of Kedleston, *Frontiers* (Romanes Lecture, 1907), Oxford, 1907, 8° . . . . **LXX**

Huckel, " La géographie de la circulation selon F. Ratzel " (*Ann. de Géogr.*, vol. xv, 1906, and vol. xvi, 1907) . . . **LXXI**

A. von Humboldt, *Cosmos*, French transl. by Faye, Paris, 1855–9, 4 vols., 8° . . . . **LXXII**

A. von Humboldt, *Tableaux de la nature*, 3rd edn., Stuttgart, 1849 . . . . **LXXIIa**

E. Huntington, *Civilization and Climate*, New Haven, 1915, 8° **LXXIII**

C. Jullian, " L'ancienneté de l'idée de nation " (*Rev. pol. et litt.*, Jan., 1913) . . . . **LXXIV**

O. E. Junghaus, *Der Fluss in seiner Bedeutung als Grenze zwischen Kultur und Natur-Völkern*, Leipzig, 1899, 8° . **LXXV**

H. Kraemer, *Der Mensch und die Erde*, Berlin and Leipzig, 1905–13, 10 vols., 4°, French transl. by Schalck de la Faverie : *L'Univers et l'Humanité*, preface by E. Perrier, Paris, n.d., 5 vols, large 8° . . . . **LXXVI–VII**

K. Kretschmer, *Historische Geographie von Mitteleuropa*, Leipzig, 1904, 8° . . . . **LXXVIII**

G. Lespagnol, *L'Evolution de la terre et de l'homme*, Paris, 1905, 16° . . . . **LXXIX**

A. Meillet, *Introduction à l'étude comparative des langues indo-européennes*, Paris, 3rd edn., 1912, 8° . . . . . **LXXX**

Ed. Meyer, *Geschichte des Altertums.* In French : *Histoire de l'antiquité*, vol. i ; *Introduction à l'étude des sociétés anciennes : Évolution des groupements humains*, transl. by David, Paris, 1912, 8° . . . . **LXXXI**

A. Penck, " Klima, Boden, und Mensch " (*Jahrb. f. Gesetzgebung*, Ed. by G. Schmoller, 1907, pp. 577 sqq.) . . . . **LXXXII**

F. Ratzel, *Anthropogeographie*, vol. i, 3rd edn., Stuttgart, 1909. Vol. II, 2nd edn., Stuttgart, 1912 . . . . . . **LXXXIII**

F. Ratzel, *Politische Geographie* (*Geographie der Staaten, des Verkehrs und Krieges*), Munich and Berlin, 2nd ed., 1903 . **LXXXIV**

F. Ratzel, *Kleine Schriften* (Helmot), 1906, 2 vols., 8° . . **LXXXV**

F. Ratzel, *Le Sol, la Société, l'Etat* (Année sociol., 1898–9) . **LXXXVI**

E. Reclus, *Nouvelle géographie universelle : La terre et les hommes*, Paris, 1875–94, 19 vols, 4° . . . . . **LXXXVII**

E. Reclus, *La Terre*, 3rd edn., Paris, 1876, 2 vols., 4° . . **LXXXVIIa**

E. Reclus, *L'Homme et la terre*, Paris, Librairie Universelle, n.d., 6 vols., 4° . . . . **LXXXVIII**

C. Ritter, *Die Erdkunde*. In French: *Géographie générale comparée*, transl. by Buret and Desor, Paris, 1836, 4 vols., 8° . **LXXXIX**

E. Semple, *Influences of Geographic Environment*, London and New York, 1911, 8° . . . . **XC**

A. Siegfried, *Tableau politique de la France de l'Ouest sous la 3e République*, Paris, 1913, 8° . . . . . . **XCI**

W. Sievers, *Allgemeine Länderkunde*, Leipzig and Vienna, 6th edn., *Europa*, by Philippson, 2nd edn., 1906. *Asien*, by Sievers, 1893. *Afrika*, by Hahn, 2nd edn., 1901. *Nord-Amerika*, by Deckert, 3rd edn., 1913. *Süd-u. Mittel-Amerika*, by Sievers, 3rd edn., 1914. *Australien, Ozeanien, u. Polarländer*, by Sievers and Kukenthal, 2nd edn., 1902 . **XCII**

C. Vallaux, *Géographie sociale* : le Sol et l'État, Paris, 1911, 16° . **XCIII**

J. Vendryes, *Language*, Paris, 1921, 8° (L'Évolution de l'Humanité, no. 3) . . . . **XCIV**

P. Vidal de la Blache, "La Géographie politique d'après les écrits de M. Fr. Ratzel" (*Ann. de Géogr.*, vol. vii, 1898) . **XCV**

P. Vidal de la Blache, "Les genres de vie dans la géographie humaine" (*Ann. de Géogr.*, vol. xx, 1911) . . . **XCVI**

P. Vidal de la Blache, "La répartition des hommes sur le globe" (*Ann. de Géogr.*, vol. xxvi, 1917) . . . . . **XCVII**

A. Woeikof, "De l'influence de l'homme sur la terre" (*Ann. de Géogr.*, vol. x, 1901) . . . . **XCVIII**

A. Woeikof, "Verteilung der Bevölkerung auf der Erde unter dem Einfluss der Naturverhältnisse und der menschl. Tätigkeit" (*Peterm. Mit.*, vol. lii, 1906, pp. 241–51, and 205–70 ; 4 maps, pls. 17–20) . . . . **XCVIIIa**

(*g*) Man's Exploitations : Vegetable, Animal, and Mineral

A. Bernard, "Le Dry-Farming et ses applications dans l'Afrique du Nord" (*Ann. de Géogr.*, vol. xx, 1911). Republished in a revised form by Widtsoe, **CXXII** . . . . . . **XCIX**

R. Billard, *La vigne dans l'antiquité*, Lyon, 1913, large 8° . **C**

J. Brunhes, *L'irrigation . . . dans la Péninsule ibérique et dans l'Afrique du Nord*, Paris, 1902, 8° . . . . . . **CI**

A. de Candolle, *L'origine des plantes cultivées*, 2nd edn., Paris, 1896, 8° . . . . **CII**

Costantin, *Les végétaux et les milieux cosmiques*, Paris, 1898, 8° **CIII**

Costantin, "Biologie de la végétation tropicale" (*Ann. de Géogr.*, vol. vii, 1898) . . . . **CIV**

Costantin, *La nature tropicale*, Paris, 1899, 8° . . . . **CV**

P. P. Déhérain, *Les plantes de grande culture*, Paris, 1898, 8° . **CVI**

Th. H. Engelbrecht, *Die Landbauzonen der aussertropischen Länder*, Berlin, 1898–9, 2 vols., 8° . . . . . . **CVII**

Th. Fischer, "Der Œlbaum, seine geographische Verbreitung, seine wirtschaftliche u. kulturhistorische Bedeutung" (*Peterm. Mit.*, Erg., no. 147), Gotha, 1904, 4° . . . **CVIII**

Th. Fischer, "Die Dattelpalme, ihre geographische Verbreitung und kulturhistorische Bedeutung" (*Peterm. Mit.*, Erg., no. 64), Gotha, 1881, 4°. . . . . **CIX**

L. Gallois and Lederlin, "La culture du coton dans le monde" (*Ann. de géogr.*, vol. vii, 1898) . . . . . . **CX**

C. L. Gatin, *Les palmiers* (Encycl. du Dr. Toulouse), Paris, n.d., 12° CXI

G. Gibault, *Histoire des légumes*, Paris, 1912, 8° CXII

Ed. Hahn, *Demeter und Baubo* (*Versuch einer Theorie der Entstehung unseres Ackerbaus*), Lübeck, 1896, 8° . . CXIII

V. Hehn, *Kulturpflanzen und Haustiere in ihrem Uebergänge aus Asien nach Griechenland und Italien, sowie in das übrige Europa*, 8th edn., by O. Schrader, Berlin, 1911, 8°. Cf. Schrader's critical remarks in *Die Anschauungen V. Hehns von der Herkunft unseren Kulturpflanzen und Haustiere im Lichte neuerer Forschung*, Berlin, 1912, 47 pp., 8° . . CXIV

Ch. Joret, *Les plantes dans l'antiquité et au moyen âge, histoire, usages, symbolisme.* I: Les plantes de l'Orient classique, Paris, 1897, 8° CXV

F. v. Richthofen, *Vorlesungen über allgemeine Siedlungs u. Verkehrsgeographie*, edn. by O. Schluter, Berlin, 1908, 8° . CXVI

E. Risler, *Géologie agricole*, Vols. I, II, III, IV; Paris, 1884-97, 8° CXVII

G. Roché, *La culture des mers en Europe: piscifacture, pisciculture, ostréiculture*, Paris, 1898, 8° CXVIII

W. Roscher, *Nationalökonomik des Ackerbaues u. der verwandten Urproduktionen.* 13th edn. by H. Dade, Stuttgart and Berlin, 1903, 8° CXIX

H. Semler, *Die tropische Agrikultur, ein Handbuch für Pflanzer und Kaufleute*, Wismar, 1866, 3 vols, 8° CXX

Van Someren Brand, *Les grandes cultures du monde, leur histoire, leur exploitation, leurs différents usages*, transl. from the Dutch by F. Rode, Paris, 1905, 4° CXXI

J. A. Widtsoe, *Le Dry-Farming*, transl. by A. M. Bernard, Paris, 1912, 16° (preface by Aug. Bernard) CXXII

E. de Wildeman, *Les plantes tropicales de grande culture*, Brussels, 1902 CXXIII

A. Woeikof, "La géographie de l'alimentation humaine" (*La Géographie*, vol. xx, 1909) CXXIV

A. Woeikof, "L'étude des sols" (*Ann. de Géogr.*, vol. xvii, 1907) CXXV

M. Caullery, "Animaux domestiques et plantes cultivées" (*Ann. de Géogr.*, vol. vi, 1897) CXXVI

V. Groffier, "La production de la soie dans le monde" (*Ann. de Géogr.*, vol. ix, 1900) CXXVII

Ed. Hahn, *Die Haustiere und ihre Beziehungen zur Wirtschaft des Mensches: eine geographische Skizze.* Leipzig, 1896, 8° CXXVIII

R. Hesse and Fr. Doflein, *Tierbau u. Tierleben*, vol. ii: *Das Tier als Glied des Naturganzen*, Leipzig and Berlin, 1904, 8° . CXXIX

P. Kropotkin, *Mutual Aid.* In French: *L'Entr'aide, un facteur de l'évolution* (transl. by Bréal), Paris, 1906, 16° . . CXXX

R. Muller, *Die geographische Verbreitung der Wirtschaftstiere mit besonderer Berücksichtigung der Tropenländer*, Leipzig, 1903, 8° CXXXI

L. de Launay, *L'or dans le monde*, Paris, 1907, 18° . . . CXXXII

R. Launay, *La conquete minérale*, Paris, 1908, 18° . . . CXXXIII

Ed. Lozé, "Le charbon dans le monde" (*Economiste français*, 1904-5) CXXXIV

Ed. Lozé, *Le minerai de fer dans le monde* (ibid., 1906) . . CXXXV
Ed. Lozé, *Le fer et l'acier dans le monde* (ibid., 1906–7) . . CXXXVI
A. Mengeot, " Du pétrole et de sa distribution géographique dans le monde " (*XVIe Congrès Soc. franç. de géogr.*, Bordeaux, 1895) CXXXVII
G. Villain, *Le fer, la houille, et la métallurgie à la fin du XIXe siècle*, Paris, 1901, 8° CXXXVIII
M. Zimmermann, " Les foyers de production de l'or dans l'antiquité et au moyen age " (*Bull. Soc. géogr.*, Lyon, vol. xx, 1905) CXXXIX
Bourdeau, *Histoire de l'habillement et de la parure*, Paris, 1904, 8° CXL

(*h*) Circulation of Man and his Products : Human Installations

K. Andree, *Geographie des Welthandels*, edn. by Fr. Heiderich and Rob. Sieger, Frankfort, 1910–13, 3 vols., large 8° . . CXLI
H. Baulig, " Sur la distribution des moyens de circulation et de transport chez les indigènes de l'Amérique du Nord " (*Ann. de Géogr.*, vol. xvii, 1908) CXLII
J. Bédier, *Les légendes épiques : recherches sur la formation des chansons de geste*, 2nd edn., Paris, 1914–21, 4 vols., 8° . CXLIII
F. C. Huber, *Die geschichtliche Entwickelung des modernen Verkehrs*, Tübingen, 1893, 8° CXLIV
P. Huvelin, *Essai historique sur le droit des marchés et des foires*, Paris, 1897, 8° CXLV
P. de Rousiers, *Les grands ports de France, leur rôle économique*, Paris, 1909, 16° CXLVI
A. Bernard and N. Lacroix, " L'Évolution du nomadisme en Algérie " (*Ann. de Géogr.*, vol. xv, 1906) CXLVII
L. A. Fabre, " L'exode montagneux en France " (*Bull. géogr. hist. et descrip.*, 1908) CXLVIII
R. Gonnard, *L'Emigration européenne au XIXe siècle, Paris*, 1806 CXLIX
P. Leroy-Baulieu, *De la colonisation chez les peuples modernes*, 6th ed., Paris, 1908, 2 vols., 8° CL
R. Blanchard, *Grenoble, étude de géographie urbaine*, Paris, 1911, 8° CLI
R. Blanchard, " Annecy, esquisse de géographie urbaine " (*Rec. trav. Institut géogr. alpine*, Grenoble, vol. iv, 1916) . . CLII
P. Dupuy, " Le sol et la croissance de Paris " (*Ann. de Géogr.*, vol. ix, 1900) CLIII
K. Hassert, *Die Städte geographisch betrachtet* (vol. 163 in the collection " Aus Natur und Geisteswelt "), Leipzig, 1907, 16° CLIV
A. Hettner, " Die lage der menschlichen Ansiedlungen " (*Geogr. Ztsch.*, 1895) CLV
A. Hettner, " Die wirtschaftlichen Typen der Ansiedlungen " (*Geogr. Ztsch.*, 1902) CLVI
J. Levainville, *Rouen : étude d'une agglomération urbaine*, Paris, 1913, 8° CLVII
E. Masqueray, *Formation des cités chez les populations sédentaires de l'Algérie*, Paris, 1886, 8° CLVIII

P. Meuriot, *Des agglomerations urbaines dans l'Europe contemporaine*, Paris, 1897, 8° CLIX

D. Pasquet, "Le développement de Londres" (*Ann. de Géogr.*, vol. vii, 1898) CLX

H. Pirenne, *Les Anciennes démocraties des Pays-Bas*, Paris, 1910, 18° CLXI

Fr. Ratzel, "Die geographische Lage der grossen Städte" (in *Die Grosstadt*, Dresden, 1903), 8° CLXII

A. Meitzen, *Siedelung und Agrarwesen der Westgermanen und Ostgermanen, der Kelten, Römer, Finnen, und Slawen*, Berlin, 1895, 4 vols., 8°, atlas CLXIII

Ministère de l'Instruction publique. Comité des travaux historiques. *Enquête sur les conditions de l'habitation en France, les Maisons types*, Introduction by d'A. de Foville, Paris, 1894, 8° CLXIV

Ministère de l'Instruction publique. Comité des travaux historiques, vol. ii, with a study by J. Flach : *L'origine historique de l'habitation et des lieux habités en France*, Paris, 1899, 8° . . . . CLXIVa

(i) Human Societies: Monographs

(a) Prehistory and Antiquity

H. d'Arbois de Jubainville, *Les premiers habitants de l'Europe*, 2nd edn., Paris, 1889–94, 2 vols., 8° CLXV

V. Bérard, *Les Phéniciens et l'Odyssée*, Paris, 1902–3, 2 vols, 4° CLXVI

M. Boule, *Les hommes fossiles : éléments de paléontologie humaine*, Paris, 1921, 8°. E.T., *Fossil Men*, 1923 CLXVII

K. Bucher, *Études d'histoire et d'économic politique*, transl. by Hansay, Brussels and Paris, 1901, 8° CLXVIII

Ch. Daremberg and Edm. Saglio, *Dictionnaire des antiquités grecques et romaines*, vol. iv., Paris, 1877, sqq., f° . . . CLXIX

J. Déchelette, *Manuel d'archéologie préhistorique, celtique, et gallo-romaine*, Paris, 1910–12, 6 vols., 8°, incl. two appendix vols. CLXX

Sir J. G. Frazer, *The Golden Bough*. In French : *Le Rameau d'or* (from the 2nd edn.), Paris, 1910–11, 3 vols., 8°. . . . CLXXI

Cam. Jullian, *Histoire de la Gaule*, Paris, 1908–20, 6 vols., 8° . CLXXII

A. Meillet, *Aperçu d'une histoire de la langue grecque*, Paris, 1913 CLXXIII

J. de Morgan, *Les premières civilisations : études sur la préhistoire et l'histoire*, Paris, 1909, 8°. CLXXIV

J. de Morgan, *Prehistoric Man* (L'Evolution de l'Humanité, vol. ii), Paris, 1921, 16° CLXXV

(b) Africa

H. Barth, *Reisen und Entdeckungen in Nord und Central Afrika* (1849–55), Gotha, 1857–8, 5 vols., 8° CLXXVI

A. Bernard, *Le Maroc*, Paris, 1913, 8° CLXXVII

Sir R. Burton, *Lake Regions of Equatorial Africa*, 1860. In French : *Voyage aux grands lacs d l'Afrique orientale*, trans. by Loreau, Paris, 1862, 8° . . . . CLXXVIIa

A. Chevalier, *L'Afrique centrale française* (1902–4), Paris, 1908, 8° (account of voyage of the Chari-Tchad mission) . . CLXXVIII

Dr. Ad. Cureau, *Les sociétés primitives de l'Afrique équatoriale*, Paris, 1912, 18° CLXXIX

J. Decorse, "La chasse et l'agriculture au Soudan" (*Anthropologie*, 1905) CLXXX

E. Gautier, *La conquête du Sahara*, Paris, 1910 (2nd edn., 1919) CLXXXI

E. Gautier, "Etudes sahariennes" (*Ann. de Géogr.*, vol. xvi, 1906) . . . . CLXXXIa

Gautier and R. Chudeau, *Missions au Sahara*, vol. i: *Sahara algérien*, by Gautier, Paris, 1908, 8°; vol. ii: *Sahara soudanais*, by Chudeau, Paris, 1909, 8° . . . . . . CLXXXIb

H. Hubert, *Mission scientifique au Dahomey*, Paris, 1906, 8° . CLXXXII

H. Hubert, *Contribution à l'étude de la géographie physique du Dahomey*, Paris, 1908, 8° (Science thesis, Paris) . . CLXXXIIa

H. Hubert, *Mission scientifique au Soudan*, 1st fascicule (*Météorologie*), Paris, 1916, 8° . . . . CLXXXIIb

J. Meniaud, *Haut-Sénégal, Niger* (*Soudan français*). Séries d'études publiées sous la direction de M. le Gouverneur Clozel; 2nd series: *Géographie économique*, Paris, 1912, 2 vols., 8° CLXXXIII

G. Nachtigal, *Sahara und Soudan*, transl. by Gourdanet, Paris, 1883, 8° CLXXXIV

G. Schweinfurth, *Im Herzen von Afrika*. E.T., *The Heart of Africa*, 1873. In French: *Au cœur de l'Afrique*, transl. by Toreau, Paris, 1870, 2 vols., 8° CLXXXV

(*c*) Asia

L. Cahun, *Introduction a l'histoire de l'Asie*, Paris, 1896, 8° . CLXXXVI

Sven Hedin, *Durch Asiens Wüsten*, Leipzig, 1899, 2 vols., 8°. French trans.: *Trois ans de lutte au désert d'Asie*, Paris, 1889 CLXXXVII

Sven Hedin, *Im Herzen von Asien*, Leipzig, 1903, 2 vols., 8° . CLXXXVIIa

Sven Hedin, *Transhimalaya: Entdeckungen u. Abenteuer in Tibet*, Leipzig, 1909, 2 vols., 8° CLXXXVIII

Huc, *Souvenirs d'un voyage dans la Tartarie, le Thibet et la Chine pendant les annècs 1844, 1845, et 1846*, Paris, 1850, 2 vols., 8° CLXXXIX

P. Landon, *Lhassa* (French translation of *The Forbidden City*), Paris, 1906, 8° CXC

J. Legras, *En Sibérie*, Paris, 2nd edn., 1904, 16° CXCI

E. Lunet de la Jonquière, *Ethnographie du Tonkin septentrional*, Paris, 1906, 8° CXCII

Maître, *Les Jungles Moï*, Paris, 1912, 8° . . . . . CXCIIa

P. S. Pallas, *Voyages en differentes provinces de l'Empire de Russie et dans l'Asie septentionale*, translated from the *Reisen* by Gauthier de la Peyronie. New edn. revised by Lamarck and Lancles, Paris, vol. ii, 8°; 1 atlas, large 4° . CXCIII

E. and O. Reclus, *L'Empire du milieu: Le climat, le sol, les races, la richesse de la Chine*, Paris, 1902, 8° CXCIV

F. von Richtofen, *China*, vol. i: *Introduction*, Berlin, 1877, 4°; vol. ii: *Nördliche China*, 1882, 4°. *Atlas von China*, vol. i: *Nördliche China*, 1885, f°: vol. iii, *Südliche China*, Tiessen, 1912, 4°. *Atlas von China*, vol. ii: *Südliche China*, Groll, f°, n.d. (1912 ?) CXCV

J. Sion, "Le Tibet méridional" (*Ann. de Géogr.*, vol. xvi, 1907) **CXCVI**

P. Vidal de la Blache, "Le peuple de l'Inde d'après la série des recensements" (*Ann. de Géogr.*, vol. xv, 1906) . . . **CXCVII**

A. Woeikof, "Climat de la Sibérie orientale" (*Ann. de Géogr.*, vol. xii, 1898) . . . . **CXCVIII**

A. Woeikof, *Le Turkestan russe*, Paris, 1914, 8° . . . **CXCVIIIa**

(*d*) America

H. Beuchat, *Manuel d'archéologie américaine*, Paris, 1912, 8° . **CXCIX**

A. P. Brigham, *Geographic Influences in American History*, Boston, 1903, 16° . . . . **CC**

P. Le Cointe, "Le Bas-Amazone" (*Ann. de Géogr.*, vol. xii, 1903) . . . . **CCI**

P. Le Cointe, "La Forêt amazionienne" (*Bull. Soc. Géogr. commerc.*, Paris, vol. xxv, 1903) . . . . . . **CCIa**

L. Capitan and H. Lorin, *Le travail en Amérique avant et après Colomb*, Paris, 1914, 8° . . . . **CCII**

A. Métin, *Étude sur la colonisation du Canada, La Colombie britannique*, Paris, 1907, 8° . . . . **CCIII**

E. C. Semple, *American History and its Geographic Conditions*, Boston and New York, n.d. (1903), 8° . . . . . **CCIV**

(*e*) Oceania, Australia

J. Cook, *Voyages* (French transl. 1776–8, 4 vols, 4°) . . **CCV**

J. F. Fraser, *L'Australie : Comment se fait une nation*, adapted by Feuilloy, 6th edn., Paris, 1916, 8° . . . . . **CCVI**

G. Lespagnol, "Sur le caractère désertique de l'Australie intérieure" (*Ann. de Géogr.*, vol. vii, 1898) . . . . **CCVII**

P. Privat-Deschanel, "L'Australie pastorale" (*La Géographie*, vol. xviii, 1908) . . . . **CCVIII**

A. de Quatrefages, *Les Polynésiens et leurs migrations*, Paris, 1866, 4° . . . . **CCIX**

H. Russier, *Le partage de l'Océanie*, Paris, 1905, 8° . . . **CCX**

J. Sion, "Océanie et Indo-Chine: Notices bibliographiques" (*Rev. de géogr. ann.*, vol. i, 1906–7, Paris, 1907), 8° . . **CCXI**

B. Spencer and F. J. Gillen, *The Native Tribes of Central Australia*, London, 1899, 8° . . . . **CCXII**

B. Spencer and F. J. Gillen, *The Northern Tribes of Central Australia*, London, 1904, 8° . . . . **CCXIII**

(*f*) Polar Societies

A. Byhan, *Die Polarvölker* (vol. 63 in the collection "Wissenschaft und Bildung", Leipzig, 1909, 16°) . . . . **CCXIV**

M. Mauss and H. Beuchat, "Essai sur les variations saisonnières des sociétés eskimos : étude de morphologie sociale" (*Année sociol.*, vol. xi, 1904–5) . . . . . . **CCXV**

Nordenskjöld, *Le Monde polaire*, transl. by Parmentier and Zimmermann, Paris, 1913, 8° . . . . . . **CCXVI**

(*g*) Europe and France

R. Blanchard, *La Flandre*, Lille, 1906, 8° . . . . . . **CCXVII**

P. Boyé, *Les Hautes-Chaumes des Vosges*, Paris, 1903, 8° . . **CCXVIII**

F. Briot, *Etudes sur l'economie alpestre*, Paris and Nancy, 1896, 8° CCXIX

F. Briot, *Nouvelles études*, Paris, 1907, 8° CCXX

J. Brunhes, *Géographie humaine de la France*, 1st vol. (vol. i of G. Hanotaux, *Histoire de la nation française*), Paris, 1921, 4° CCXXI

P. Bureau, *Le paysan des fjords norvégiens*, Paris, 1906, 8° . CCXXII

J. Cuijic, *La Péninsule balkanique : géographie humaine*, Paris. 1918, 8° CCXXIII

A. Demangeon, *La Picardie et les régions voisines*, Paris, 1905, 8° CCXXIV

J. Levainville, *Le Morvan : étude de géographie humaine*, Paris, 1909, 8° CCXXV

P. Mantoux, *La révolution industrielle en Angleterre au XVIIIe siècle : essai sur les commencements de la grande industrie moderne en Angleterre*, Paris, 1906, 8° CCXXVI

P. Milioukov, *Essais sur l'histoire de la civilisation russe*, transl. by Dramas and Soskice, Paris, 1901, 8° CCXXVII

Ch. Rabot, *Aux fjords de Norvège et aux forêts de Suède*, Paris, 1906, 8° CCXXVIII

J. Sion, *Les paysans de la Normandie orientale : étude géographique*, Paris, 1909, 8° CCXXIX

M. Sorre, *Les pyrénées méditerranéennes : essai de géographie biologique*, Paris, 1913, 8° CCXXX

C. Vallaux, *La Basse-Bretagne* ; *étude de géographie humaine*, Paris, 1907, 8° CCXXXI

P. Vidal de la Blache, *Tableau de la géographie de la France* (vol. i, de Lavisse, *Histoire de France*), Paris, 3rd edn., 1908, 4° CCXXXII

(*h*) Maritime Expansion

P. Herre, *Der Kampf um die Herrschaft im Mittelmeer*, Leipzig, 1909, 8° CCXXXIII

A. T. Mahan, *The Influence of Sea Power upon History*. In French : *Influence de la puissance maritime dans l'histoire*, transl. by Boisse, Paris, n.d. (1899), 8° CCXXXIV

A. Philippson, *Das Mittelmeergebiet, seine geographische und kulturelle Eigenart*, 2nd edn., Leipzig, 1907, 8° . . . CCXXXV

G. Schott, *Geographie des Atlantischen Ozeans*, Hamburg, 1912, 4° CCXXXVI

C. Vallaux, *Géographie sociale : La mer*, Paris, 1908, 18° . . CCXXXVII

INDEX